*Urban and Rural Development
in Third World Countries*

William M. Alexander
California Polytechnic State University

Bakheit Adam Azrag
Central Washington University

Wayne G. Bragg
Washington University, St. Louis

L. T. Fansler
California State University,
Long Beach

Mamdouh Fayek
California State University,
Long Beach

Valentine U. James
University of Virginia

Hassan Omari Kaya
University of Dar es Salaam

M. T. Knipe
California State University,
Long Beach

Donald E. Mbosowo
University of Jos, Nigeria

Thomas M. Meenaghan
Loyola University of Chicago

Shah M. Mehrabi
Mary Washington College

Stanley W. Moore
Pepperdine University

Jonathan N. Nwomonoh
California State University,
Los Angeles

Mwatabu S. Okantah
Cleveland State University

Janet J. Palmer
Lehman College,
City University of New York

Godfrey Roberts
Rutgers University

Frank A. Salamone
Elizabeth Seton College,
Yonkers, New York

Eugene B. Shultz, Jr.
Washington University, St. Louis

Jean L. Shultz
Washington University, St. Louis

Bamijoko Smith
Howard University

Mark Speece
University of Alaska, Anchorage

Ramses B. Toma
California State University,
Long Beach

Lako Tongun
Pitzer College, Claremont, California

Dwayne Woods
University of California,
Santa Barbara

Joel Zimbelman
California State University, Chico

Urban and Rural Development in Third World Countries

Problems of Population in Developing Nations

Edited by
Valentine James

McFarland & Company, Inc., Publishers
Jefferson, North Carolina, and London

British Library Cataloguing-in-Publication data are available

Library of Congress Cataloguing-in-Publication Data

Urban and rural development in Third World countries : problems of
 population in developing nations / edited by Valentine James.
     p. cm.
   Includes bibliographical references and index.
   ISBN 0-89950-584-8 (lib. bdg. : 50# alk. paper) ∞
     1. Developing countries.   2. Agriculture—Economic aspects—
Developing countries.   3. Developing countries—Population.
4. Appropriate technology—Developing countries.   5. Technology
transfer—Developing countries.   6. Urbanization—Developing
countries.   7. Rural development—Developing countries.   I. James,
Valentine Udoh, 1952–   .
HC59.7.U73   1991
338.9'009172'4—dc20   90-53499
                                                          CIP

Manufactured in the United States of America

McFarland & Company, Inc., Publishers
 Box 611, Jefferson, North Carolina 28640

To my mother,
Mrs. Elizabeth James Inyang

Acknowledgments

This work began as a result of the encouragement given to me by my mentor, Dr. Christine Schonewald-Cox, during my tenure as a University of California President's Fellow (1986–1988). I am deeply appreciative of the confidence of the award and the friendship of all those who gave of their valuable time to contribute papers addressing the concerns of the developing countries.

My interest in the development aspects of Third World nations began as a result of the positive response that the seminars I conducted around the United States on the subject of natural resource depletion in Africa received. I met many scholars who had similar interests and wanted to discuss the subject at length.

Encouraged by Dr. Schonewald-Cox, I contacted the contributors and received tremendous responses. Hence, special thanks must go to each of the contributors. Dr. Dennis Ehrhardt deserves praise because he provided the atmosphere conducive to the continuation of my scholarly work in the Department of Geography/Urban and Regional Planning when I became a faculty member at USL. Particular gratitude to Sidney Fontenot, my graduate assistant.

Special thanks to Ms. Peggy Vincent for working very diligently and conscientiously in getting several drafts of the manuscript ready and for her proofreading. Mrs. JoAnn Byrd deserves praise for her assistance in typing part of this work.

My wife, Melanie, and my sons, Marshall and Jonathan, deserve the highest mention. Melanie, for her role in the initial phase of the work. She was particularly responsible for the hundreds of letters of communications with the contributors and for being very understanding and supportive during the editing of this work. Marshall and Jonathan, for their understanding when I was not available when they needed me.

As the editor of this work, I assume full responsibility for any errors.

Valentine Udoh James, Ph.D.
The University of Virginia
School of Architecture

Contents

Part I
Resource Policy: Population and Agriculture

Part II
Appropriate Technology and Technology Transfer

Part III
Sociological Implications of Urban and Rural Development

Part IV
Economic Issues of Development

List of Figures

List of Tables

Introduction
Urban-Rural Development:
A Search for Future Directions

Oostuizen (1987: 114), in exploring the degree to which Africa's social and cultural heritage has enhanced or decreased its development patterns, contends:

> Traditional Africa has a cyclical concept of time which overvalues the past and greatly devaluates the future. In traditional African thinking time moves, as it were, anti-clockwise—from the present to the past—and therefore these two dimensions of time predominate. This is because of the belief that man's being finds its orientation in the past—a fact that can easily be deduced from African myths, sayings, proverbs, rituals and so on. Time consists of events, and because the future is a non-event, it is not given any emphasis.
>
> Traditional man moves from the present, "the period of conscious living," to the mythical period, the centre of gravity of which is in the past. The life cycle, from birth until entry into the perpetuated tribe in the hereafter, is not a movement to the future but a movement in reverse. The end is actually in the past, and there is no emphasis on final fulfillment.
>
> In such a perspective there are no future goals to aim for, and therefore planning for the future is not a priority. And since the future does not imply more than a few months, it cannot be expected to usher in a golden era. This approach to time has resulted in Africa's most pressing contemporary problem: the inability to plan for the future, both in terms of needs and population growth. Because of the devaluation of the future dimension, planning does not feature in traditional Africa's cultural heritage. This, together with the fact that personal immortality is based on the creation of a large progeny, has contributed to Africa's biggest dilemma—a population explosion.

The increasing populations and the economic recessions in many developing countries are generating deep-seated political and sociocultural changes in these countries. Much of the existing literature on Third World development has been piecemeal treatment of isolated cases without a comprehensive investigation of the interrelationships of all the parameters or variables that affect the quality of life of the people.

In an attempt to overcome the limitation of narrowness in scope, the chapters in this book cover a wide range of topics that deal with 1) the

1

transformation of Third World nations' economies and demographies in the process of urbanization, 2) the changes in the political arena and development policy, with particular reference to urban and rural development, and 3) the issues of infrastructure needs and provisions. It is a genuine attempt to compile chapters that shed some light on the subject of urban and rural development in Third World countries. The majority of the work represents substantial statements on the present conditions and predicted conditions if current trends of development, development efforts, policies, and planning continue in the Third World countries.

It is the aim of this introductory chapter to highlight the reasons for grouping the contributors into several aspects of the urban-rural phenomena in the Third World and after accomplishing the grouping task, to critique and embellish the theses or major thrusts of some of the works from practical and theoretical viewpoints.

All Third World nations are confronted with the tasks of improving the quality of life of the inhabitants of both rural and urban communities. Thus, like the planning of the developed countries, the planning that is envisaged for the developing countries entails the four basic currents of planning, which deal with physical, social, economic, and policy issues.

In grouping the works of the contributors, the editor chose to include chapters that address similar topics under the same category. One such topic is resource policy: population and agriculture.

The alarming population increase in the Third World countries requires drastic, immediate, and long-range plans to address the problem of uncontrolled population growth. There is a direct correlation between the exponential increase in population and resource depletion. Thus, the task confronting Third World governments requires approaches that are systematic, comprehensive, and futuristic.

It should be emphasized that when developing countries specify the activities that their societies will engage in, allow or tolerate, and prohibit, they set standards that directly or indirectly impact the standard for development. Implementing and enforcing those standards are sometimes problematic. This argument is made in Roberts's chapter in Part I: "The true test of a policy is when it is implemented." He stresses the impact of birthrate on development. The uncontrolled population explosion in the Third World has led to several problems, as the reader of this book will discover. The way a Third World country organizes to deal with this problem of population explosion depends upon the culture, history, and institutional structure of that society. The difficulties of formulating public policies in relation to the human condition are made obvious by the chapters in Part I.

Public officials seem to have a resigned or unconcerned attitude toward a comprehensive development strategy for their countries. This type

Figure 1.1: Downtown Lagos, Nigeria, January 1988.

of attitude troubles leaders such as Chairman Rawlings of Ghana, who asserted in the January 18, 1988, issue of *West Africa* that this type of behavior (not caring) happens in the day-to-day lives of public officials and policymakers of his country.

Urbanization has transformed the world into many forms, as can be witnessed in many cities of the world. As far back as between 1750 and 1800, only about 3 percent of the world lived in cities. The number of urban inhabitants has increased tremendously since then, and it should be pointed out that the Third World countries have experienced the bulk of the increase in the population of urban dwellers.

Homelessness, which has increased globally, is now a major concern in many developing countries. This problem has increased in many Third World countries because people migrate to urban centers with the hope of improving their lives. Policies to curb urban squatters have failed in many countries. Figure 1.1 shows a homeless woman bathing one of her children in the central business district of a major city in Nigeria.

Another aspect of overpopulation is that depicted by traffic conges- tion. Cities such as Lagos and Ibadan, Nigeria, have suffered tremendously due to the lack of good transportation networks. In Lagos, the transporta- tion planners have devised policies that can help in alleviating some of the congestion problems. One such policy is to allow only certain cars with

Figure 1.2: Lagos: Taxicab in central business district.

particular licenses (alphabetical) to use the Lagos roads on certain days of the week. This policy has lessened the traffic problem in Lagos. Figure 1.2 shows the central business district of Lagos. Despite the attempts being made to resolve this problem, it is obvious that because of the growing population of the city of Lagos, more aggressive and bold efforts have to be taken by the transportation department in order to plan for the future.

In Part I, Smith offers a refreshing theoretical underpinning of resource management in Africa. His main thesis is centered on policy that can induce self-sufficiency and poverty alleviation. Policies concerning agricultural production should be viable and should sustain development efforts in developing nations. His assessment of the infrastructure situation in Africa, with particular reference to transportation problems, is accurate. The unavailability of good roads to link rural and urban areas poses great problems in many developing nations in Africa. This argument is amplified in Nwomonoh's chapters. Nwomonoh seems to agree with Smith that small-scale farmers should be encouraged through incentives such as government loans, fertilizers, and other local amenities that increase the farmers' productivity. An example of such a case where the government made tremendous strides toward enhancing the farmers' productivity has begun in Nigeria. Mr. Okon U. Nyah (personal conversation), the assistant executive officer for the Nigerian Agricultural and Co-operative Bank, contends that the efforts have had some success, but unfortunately some small-scale farmers do not use the loans for agricultural purposes when they obtain the loans.

The policies that deal with the issues of agricultural development in the Third World must address the corruption problems. It is not the view of this writer that this is the case in all developing nations, but past experiences in some developing nations seem to indicate that government programs have failed because of mismanagement or because the implementation of the policies was not handled properly or because of misdirected efforts.

Some private individuals are involved in monopolistic trade, which hampers distribution and production policies of the governments. It is impossible for government programs to work or succeed when the greed of private individuals works against the genuine efforts of the government to improve the quality of life of the public.

Nwomonoh's chapters elucidate the strategies that could be adopted to improve Africa's agricultural productivity. He emphasizes the role of small-scale farmers in these endeavors and concludes by stressing the importance of international cooperation, storage facility, improvement of Africa's infrastructure, marketing innovations, and the cooperation of the Nigerian private sector. It is encouraging to learn from my recent trip to Africa in 1988 that some of these strategies have already begun. Many countries of Africa can avert mass famines such as the ones that occurred in 1979 and the early 1980s. Increasing the food supply of developing nations has been one of the major tasks confronting the United Nations. Toma's chapters in Part I discuss the issue of food shortages and possible ways of increasing food production and food supply. Toma very expertly enunciates the reasons for the global shortage of food and for grain losses in developing nations. The strengths of the chapters are that they are systematically written and their recommendations are comprehensive. In providing possible solutions to the food shortages in developing nations, one has to investigate the domestic and international reasons for the problem, and like Nwomonoh's chapters, Toma's chapters, although brief individually, adequately address this issue in such a way that a student of Third World development can easily understand. Recent indications from Ethiopia show that the 1988 food aid requirements for that country were over 1.3 million tons, which surpasses the amount of food aid that was given during the 1984–1985 food aid. It has also been determined that in order for Ethiopia to avert widespread famine and destruction of lives, there has to be a sustained international assistance.

One of the omissions of the chapters in Part I is the politics involved in the delivery of aid to developing nations. For example, it is estimated that Ethiopia receives very little long-term development aid from the West or from the Soviet Union. There is a disproportionate treatment of poor nations that require aid. For instance, Ethiopia is said to receive $2 per head per year, compared with $20 in neighboring Sudan and $35 in Somalia. The influence of world politics on the development of emerging nations determines whether or not progress is being made (*African Business* 1988).

Part II of this book deals with the issue of transferring technology from developed countries to developing countries. The issue of appropriateness of the technologies that are transferred is discussed theoretically and practically by the authors: Palmer, Mehrabi, Bragg, E. Shultz, and J. Shultz.

Probably one of the most frustrating things for a Westerner who visits a developing country is how slowly things are done. A trip to a commercial bank for transactions will prove to be a major task that could take a great deal of time. Such delays are not present in developed countries because of the influence of automation. Palmer's chapter documents the benefits that developing nations can achieve by incorporating information technologies into their development plans. She notes: "The application of information technologies to development process can benefit less developed countries in many ways." An example of an African country (south of the Sahara) that has experienced a slight technological success is Nigeria. There has been some experimentation by foreign companies in Nigeria. Investing technologically in a developing country like Nigeria means taking a great risk. Volkswagen of Nigeria has had some success despite the fact that its assembly section has been closed due to the economic problems of the country. The sales of cars have dropped a great deal. However, the company has managed to function effectively and efficiently (see Figures 1.3, 1.4, and 1.5). Nigerians from all over the country have benefited from the education and training that are being provided by the company. Some Nigerians have been sent to West Germany for technical and managerial training, and Nigerians play vital roles in the policy-making phases of the company.

However, in order for the transfer of technology from a developed to a developing country to succeed, certain measures must be taken. A publication in *West Africa* magazine (January 1982: 221) suggests the following measures: (1) The technology transfer must be a full-time, fully funded, and directed effort on the part of the source of the technology. (2) Without active, informed, and enthusiastic technologists, the efforts will fail. (3) People trying to transfer technology must have access to a broadly based body of technical information and experience. (4) They must have the freedom and the motivation to see opportunities aggressively and to respond quickly to calls for assistance. (5) Person-to-person contact over a long period of time between initiators of concepts and practical engineers

Figure 1.3: Serviced cars.

Figure 1.4: Men at work.

Figure 1.5: An engineer at work.

is essential. (6) Merely providing information in the form of reports is usually ineffective. Additional work in tailoring the solution to the problem and training the engineer is often required. (7) The transfer is complete when the technology becomes generally accepted practice. (8) The transfer requires considerable liaison—the people who develop the ideas, their agents, and the people who originate the concepts. Sometimes they will need assistance from other sources of expertise.

One of Mehrabi's chapters discusses the economic effects of implementing sophisticated technology. His argument is that more jobs are created through the use of machines, and thus "progress" is achieved. On the other hand Shultz and Shultz's chapter on the case study of Bhopal, India, gives a warning about the type of accident that can result when adequate measures are not taken into consideration in the transfer of sophisticated technology to Third World countries.

The decline of the Nigerian economy and recent government policy, which reduced licenses for importing foreign products, have caused the established industries to experience economic crisis. Such crises have led to strikes in companies such as Peugeot Automobile of Nigeria (PAN) in Kaduna in October of 1985. Another unrest of workers was experienced in Volkswagen of Nigeria (VON) in Lagos in the month of December 1985 (Bangura 1987).

The transfer of technology to indigenous citizens, the improvement of the standard of living of local citizens, and the provision of the products at reasonable prices may not always be successful when sophisticated technologies are transferred to developing countries. As a matter of fact, Nigeria experienced some setbacks in the past with the establishment of assembly plants in that country.

It is only recently that assembly plants are making slight profits. Policymakers must take into consideration the costs, benefits, and risks involved in establishing sophisticated and advanced technologies in Third World nations. The planning of development must be seen as a gradual process that demands time and evaluation. Serious thought must be given to the transfer of hazardous technologies.

Part III deals with the ramifications of land use in both urban and rural environments. Human activities affect the environment positively and negatively. The history, culture, and civilizations of mankind have shaped human settings globally. Human activities require space in order for the established goals and objectives to be achieved. The environmental attributes such as topography and agriculture are shaped through human activities. In recent times, we have seen how human activities have exacerbated the climatic problems of the world. For example, the increase in deforestation has affected weather patterns, resulting in desertification.

Woods's chapter examines how the urban-rural crisis is linked to policy decisions of Third World countries. His emphasis is on a particular case study in the Ivory Coast. This chapter touches upon the problem of migration. People move from rural to urban areas for many reasons. The factors that influence such migration are economic, physical, and social. These factors can be classified as the *pull* factors. The other classification is the *push* factors, which include such aspects as lack of employment, poor social amenities and facilities, and severe climatic or physical factors.

The impacts of rural migration on the urban centers are many, but it should suffice to mention that such migration usually results in higher unemployment and increase in crime, and the development of squatter settlements. When the infrastructures of the urban areas cannot support the numbers of people migrating to the area, results such as shown in Figures 1.6, 1.7, and 1.8 predominate. Homes are constructed without proper planning on the outskirts of cities, streets are not paved, and during the rainy season, they are virtually inaccessible by car. In many parts of urban centers, open gutters are found next to houses. These gutters become breeding grounds for mosquitoes. Public health suffers as a result of such ineffective planning. Figure 1.9 shows an example of a well that is used by some inhabitants of Orile-Iganmu, Nigeria. This is a suburb of Lagos where efforts to provide tap water to this part of Lagos are under way. But the point that must be made here is that the city of Lagos has grown so much that it is difficult to provide services to surrounding communities.

Figure 1.6: Unpaved road, Orile-Iganmu, Nigeria, January 1988.

Figure 1.7: Open gutter with poor drainage, Orile-Iganmu, Nigeria, January 1988.

Figure 1.8: Poor drainage system poses health problems, Orile-Iganmu, Nigeria, January 1988.

Figure 1.9: Well water, Orile-Iganmu, Nigeria, January 1988.

There is certainly difficulty in allocating the resources, and many past government policies have neglected the dynamism of urban growth. Urban expansion in the developing countries has moved into the buffer zones that protected the natural areas from degradation. The net results of what is common in many developing countries are urban squatters, slums, shanty populations, health hazards, and indiscriminate land speculation.

Faced with the rural and urban problems, many developing countries are making drastic changes. As a response to the need for a change, the current Babangida administration in Nigeria has as the basic tenet of its 1988 budget the objective of pursuing growth linkages between rural and urban sectors and between food-related and other industries. The budget emphasizes an in-depth examination of the infrastructures and self-containment policies. Table 1.1 shows the Nigerian 1988 budget. A considerable amount (approximately $700 million) has been allocated to the maintenance of urban roads and highway systems. This goal, if accomplished, will alleviate many of the country's transportation problems.

TABLE 1.1: Nigeria Budget, 1988: Special Reflationary Fund

Ministry or other recipient	Purpose	Allocation (* million)	Allocation ($ million)
Transport	urban transport	700	175
Mines & Power	flat steel	350	87.50
States & local govts	school maintenance	325	81.25
Works & Housing	direct labour projects	250	62.50
Employment, Labour & Productivity	job creation	200	50
Finance & National Planning	interest payment	180	45
External Affairs	embassies	160	40
Police	armed-crime prevention	120	30
Education	computer courses & women's education	100	25
Health	rehabilitation of institutions	60	15
Social Development & Youth	child welfare	40	10
Cabinet office	inventory control	15	3.75
TOTAL		2,500	625.00

Source: 1988 budget speech.

*=Naira

Some of the chapters in this book stress the miserable conditions of the transportation system in developing countries and the lack of roads in rural areas. The bold effort by the Nigerian government is a step in the right direction.

The priorities of the country are well defined in the budget. For example, the significant role of industrialization in the development of the country is recognized; hence the allocation of $350 million for the purpose of developing flat steel. Urban and regional planning have a role to play in the systematic development of young nations. In this regard, efforts must be put into planning for the gradual development of all sectors of the society. Such development should take into account all the aspects mentioned in the Nigerian budget. Implementing programs listed in Table 1.1 could be difficult, but with strong leadership, developing countries can achieve their goals and objectives within the sphere of development.

Part IV addresses the economic issues of development in the Third World. The chapter by Alexander is worth separate mention because it examines the nature and the necessities of the intervention of the "First World" into Third World development. This theoretical essay discusses the American attitude and the issue of population threat to the economic stability of the Third World. If the reader is interested in a conceptual interpretation and explanation of how commodity and work must be treated, Alexander's chapter is certainly worth examining in great detail. Tongun's and Speece and Azrag's chapters are case studies of the Sudanese economic and marketing issues. These chapters offer unique opportunities for the reader to comprehend and appreciate the Sudanese planning dilemma. The last chapter in Part IV, by Moore examines the choices that Third World countries have in terms of their development strategies. Here, Moore discusses the constraints that Third World countries face in their development struggles.

The reader of this book is bound to appreciate the efforts of the governments of several countries in many parts of the developing world, and in particular the efforts of the contributors, to explain the causes of problems that developing nations are confronted with as they make sincere efforts to provide decent standards of living for their citizens. It must be emphasized that the central aim of this book is to restructure the major problems of the Third World countries and to shed some light on malnutrition, disease, illiteracy, unemployment, and squatters in urban as well as rural areas so that practitioners, scholars, policymakers, and planners can begin to suggest possible ways of resolving some of these issues and discover new ground for research.

Part I
Resource Policy:
Population and Agriculture

1

Population Policy in the Third World: The Need for a Conceptual Framework

Godfrey Roberts

Population policy is an area subject to both intense debate and frequent changes in priorities. The true test of a policy is when it is implemented as a program. National population policies implemented as programs have had mixed results. The success of population-influencing programs is affected by a variety of factors such as cultural and religious values and the desire of parents to determine their family size free of intervention by the state. The complexity of this relationship emphasizes the need for a framework for population policy that could be implemented as programs directed to achieve specific goals.

Definitions of Population Policy

A variety of definitions have been suggested in the literature for population policy. A review of some of these definitions reveals a range of perceptions from very general to clearly antinatalist.

The most general definition of population policy is that proposed by Stillman (1971), which states: "government actions which are designed to affect the demographic variables of fertility, mortality and migration or have an important unintentional effect on them" (p. 1). Bergmann (1974), with reference to the population influencing policies in the United States, proposes the following definition: "government actions towards objectives which involve the influencing of population policy as, legislative measures, administrative programs, and other government actions intended to alter or modify existing trends in the interest of national survival and welfare.... The major purpose is to control population size, but consideration may also be given to influencing its composition or geographic distribution" (p. 381). In his definition, Elridge (1968) introduces birthrate as the major concern in population policy.

Nortmann (1975) defines population policy as "direct measures of governments to reduce birth rates" (p. 10). Although this is perhaps the most antinatalist definition of population policy, it does reflect the policy in much of the Third World where more than 80 percent of the people live under governments which have policies to reduce birthrates. Driver (1972) believes that the Nortmann definition is too narrow and suggests that "direct measures of governments" be changed to "direct and indirect measures of governmental and non-governmental organizations." A definition that applies both to countries that have policies to reduce birthrates and to countries that have policies to increase their population size is proposed by Davis (1971): "A deliberate attempt through government or quasi-governmental measures, to change or maintain the rate of population growth" (p. 6). Davis's definition, which is broadly applicable, could be used as the working definition for population policy in the Third World.

Policies and Programs

Although the term *population policy* is used to refer to all national policies directed to influence population change, in practical terms population policy in Third World countries refers to fertility-influencing policies. This is very evident when we review population policy in Third World countries, especially those in Asia and Africa. The five-year plan of the government of India (1961) states, "...the objective of stabilizing the growth of population over a reasonable period of time must be at the center of planned development." Since that time, the Indian government has continued its national policy of recognizing the need to reduce birthrates. The implementation of these policies has had mixed results. Population growth was recognized as a problem in the early sixties, and population policy guidelines were established. In the early seventies, India, along with many other Third World countries, joined the bandwagon that development and not population control was the only humane and ethical way to reduce population growth rates.

In the late seventies, in a clear shift in population policy priorities, Prime Minister Indira Gandhi established the mandatory sterilization program. The program led to extensive human rights abuses by overzealous officials. This resulted in a backlash which led to the defeat of Prime Minister Gandhi and her party at the elections. In recent years, the Indian government has adopted an approach where family planning is widely available along with an emphasis on education and communication. Overall, the Indian government has integrated family planning, health, education, and communication programs in an ambitious attempt to reduce population growth rate by half in three years (United Nations Fund 1986).

China announced the one-child-family program in 1979, but since that time has made several changes in the implementation of the policy (Greenhalgh 1986). By 1982–1983, there was a national program for mandatory Intrauterine Device (IUD) use by women with one child, abortions for pregnancies not authorized by the government, and sterilization of couples with two or more children (Aird 1985). By 1984, the program known as the "one child glory certificate program" was introduced in which parents limiting their family to one child were given certificates with various social benefits in housing, education, etc. The experimental pill for men, "Gossipol," which was tested among 8,000 men, indicated the intensity of the effort (United Nations Social and Economic Commission 1985). Resulting from the strict one-child policy in China, there were reports of infanticide of female children. This was due to the preference for male children in the society. In response to these problems, by 1986, the government had relaxed the program and begun to make exceptions by allowing a second child, especially for rural families (Greenhalgh 1986). Studies by Greenhalgh (1986) and others indicate that China has increasingly begun to integrate socioeconomic development with the aggressive one-child-family program.

Although a developed country, Japan shares many of the values and traditions common to Third World countries in the Asian region. The rapid declines in fertility which began after the Second World War and remain below replacement today provide an interesting model for Third World population policymakers. The population situation in Japan is attributed to general socioeconomic development along with extensive use of voluntarily induced abortion and delayed marriage (*Family Planning Perspectives* 1987). Japan has achieved fertility declines like other Western industrialized nations, but unlike most of these countries has also experienced declines in out-of-wedlock pregnancies. Also, Japanese women are less likely to marry than their counterparts in other developed countries (*Family Planning Perspectives* 1987).

Bangladesh is a low-income country with a high level of illiteracy which contributes to a high population growth rate. Prime Minister Ershad has announced a renewed effort to reduce birthrates by family planning, socioeconomic development, and targets to reduce growth rates (United Nations 1987). In recognition of his efforts, he was given the Population Award by the United Nations in 1987. Singapore is the only country in the world to experiment with a selective population policy. Concerned over the future genetic quality of the population due to higher fertility among less educated women, Prime Minister Less introduced a variety of programs to increase birthrates among women with college degrees and to reduce birthrates among the less educated. In 1984, the government inroduced the "Graduate Mums Scheme" as an incentive for less educated women to get sterilized (Palen 1986). The program has been significantly modified over the last year due to opposition from both within the country and abroad. Pakistan, the tenth most populous country in the world, has set targets to reduce the growth rate and has a variety of socioeconomic development programs to reduce birthrates (United Nations 1987). Other Asian countries like Malaysia, Nepal, Thailand, and Indonesia have recognized the socioeconomic benefits of reducing population growth rates and have begun to implement programs to reduce family size.

The Second African Population Conference held in Tanzania in January 1984 endorsed a statement recognizing the need to curb rapid population growth on the continent (Popline 1984). This was a radical shift for a continent that was strongly pronatalist. The efforts among the African countries to control their population growth have been supported by the United Nations. Among fifty-three countries identified by the United Nations Fund for Population Activities for priority funding in 1984, thirty-three were in Africa (*Popline* 1984). In a development equally welcome to everyone concerned with world population trends, the Regional Conference of Arab Leaders held in Jordan in March 1984 called for an integrated population policy in the region where population planning would be included in all aspects of social and economic development (United Nations 1984).

Asia, with three-fifths of the population of the world, will undoubtedly be a major contributor to population growth in the future. However, most Asian countries have family planning and other more aggressive programs like the availability of abortion and sterilization and incentive programs for a small family integrated with socioeconomic development.

It has been suggested that many Third World countries are in a demographic trap (Brown 1987) and are not able to go beyond the second stage of the demographic transition where death rates have declined but birthrates have not declined fast enough to keep pace. Yet, if recognition of the problem and establishing policies and programs are the first step, the population giants in Asia are rapidly moving in the right direction and African countries have made a start.

The Need for a Conceptual Framework

There is little doubt that population policy in most Third World countries is intended to be fertility-influencing policy. Five-year plans and other government documents and statements made by national leaders are almost entirely limited to fertility policy. Thus a conceptual model for population policy has to be primarily a fertility-influencing policy. However, the experiences of countries like China, India, and Singapore indicate there is considerable uncertainty on how to establish the programs to implement the policies.

Berelson (1969) suggested several possibilities on how population policy could go beyond family planning. Several of these approaches such as mandatory sterilization, incentive programs and delayed marriage have been attempted in some countries. Coale (1973) and others have suggested that countries have to reach a certain level of development for the family size desired by the individual, and what is good for the community and society, to begin to converge. The *World Bank Development Report* (1984: 55) has developed the same concept:

> Individuals in isolation act to the detriment of each other unless they know that their fellows will act in a manner that serves the general well-being—and even individuals may not act in the public interest themselves. If parents had their way, many of them would wish to limit the fertility of others: if children had their way, many of them would wish to limit their own parents' fertility.

Hernandez (1985) has proposed the concept of the "individualistic approach" and the "international approach." The individualistic approach consists of policies directed to individuals and families as outlined in the models suggested by Hardin (1968) in "Tragedy of the Commons" and the proposal by Berelson (1969) for measures beyond family planning. The international approach concerns policies that nations might pursue as suggested in the "spaceship ethic" of Callahan (1971) or the "lifeboat ethic" suggested by Hardin (1974). These successes or failures of programs in countries provide the most valuable conceptual framework.

National and global politics have also been a problem in establishing a model for population policy that is humane and could be implemented without violating individual rights. For example, at the World Population Conference in Bucharest in 1974, most Third World countries, including China and India, supported the concept that development and nonaggressive population control programs are the only humane ways to influence birthrates in the Third World. Ten years later, in 1984, at the World Population Conference in Mexico City, the same Third World countries came out in favor of aggressive policies and programs to reduce birthrates in their countries. However, the United States did not support this position because of the administration's opposition to restrictive population control measures, especially abortion. Subsequently, the United States, charging the United Nations and other private agencies with supporting abortion, cut off funds to the United Nations Fund for Population Activities and Planned Parenthood International. This resulted in the reduction of programs in many countries.

In attempting to identify a conceptual framework, the lack of clarity in the relationship of population policy to programs is evident. In a study on population education programs as a component of population policy, Roberts (1977) has shown that educators in India and Sri Lanka perceive population education (which is teaching population concepts) as a program that would create the small family norm. The issue of how an educational program could create a small family norm is not clear and raises ethical questions of the role of an educational program in creating a set of desired values in the learner.

Ethical Issues

Various United Nations declarations support the right of parents to determine the size and spacing of their family. Several United Nations instruments, such as the 1948 Universal Declaration of Human Rights, The International Women's Year Plan of Action (1975), and Population Plan of Action (1974), support this right. At the World Population Conference in Mexico City in 1984, 149 countries reached the consensus that population change is an intrinsic part of the development process and supported the right to family planning information and services for adolescents and women.

Opinions on how we should respond to the issue of population growth range from the position taken by Hardin (1975), that population growth is a cancer, to that of Simon (1984), that population growth is desirable and essential for the future global economy. Commoner (1974) claims that poverty causes overpopulation, and Third World countries are not able to go beyond the second stage of the demographic transition due to "demographic parasitism," where the resources that should have been put back into the development of the Third World were taken away by the colonizers. Much of the recent literature supports the view that family planning and other aggressive fertility control programs must be implemented concurrently with developing programs such as improvements in income, health, and education.

Good things are happening in much of the Third World. Family planning is getting popular, general development programs are being implemented, and traditionally pronatalist societies are implementing programs to reduce birthrates. However, the rush to implement population control programs in countries like India and China has resulted in extensive human rights violations and negatively affected the programs.

2

The Impact of Structural Adjustment Policies on Agricultural Transformation and Poverty Alleviation in Africa

Bamijoko Smith

It is not too often that a consensus is reached on the severity of an international problem and the urgent need for its resolution. However, little comfort can be derived from the broad consensus which has emerged on the failure of agriculture and food production in Africa. The rapid deterioration in standards of living, increased rates of malnutrition and undernourishment, rising rates of poverty, falls in real disposable income, and the reappearance of diseases thought to have been eradicated ten or fifteen years ago are some of the visible manifestations of this failure. While these problems clearly show the serious cost of policy mistakes for which both international and domestic policymakers must share full responsibility, they have now made it evident that successful development policies cannot be assumed to be irreversible.

In spite of the bold statements of intent heralding a noticeable shift in the policy environment, it is my feeling that there is still a wide gap between rhetoric and reality. In spite of the growing affirmation of the primacy of food and agricultural production in Africa, it is my deep concern that these changes may not necessarily lead to a situation where agriculture can reach the critical threshold or turning point, thereby facilitating not only structural transformation in these economies but also meeting the most important condition for the achievement of self-sustained growth.

Views are now converging on the following major issues relating to the food and agricultural crisis in Africa: (1) It is now apparent that no enduring development strategy can be achieved without the transformation of agriculture, due to the important linkages between agriculture and development. Because a significant percentage of Africa's population depends on agriculture for income and employment generation, the

22

consequences of continued agricultural failure will be costly in human terms. (2) The success of agricultural transformation is now closely linked to the achievement of profound structural changes in the rural areas. The central role now being attributed to agriculture should now be based on small-scale agriculture. (3) With the increasing population growth rates in Africa, the achievement of technological breakthroughs in agriculture may be the only way out for most of the African nations.

While I am in total agreement with these three crucial points, it is important to stress that African nations face the daunting task of achieving agricultural transformation when their nascent industrial sectors are at the brink of collapse. The failure of Africa's nascent industries to make the transition toward the production of intermediate capital and producer goods makes it extremely difficult to achieve a technological breakthrough in agriculture. It is now clear that technology import dependence is not a sustainable option.

As the economic crisis worsens in Africa, the need to achieve expenditure reductions and switches makes it almost impossible to undertake the simultaneous development of the agricultural and industrial sectors. The development of a technologically dynamic agricultural sector is made possible by (1) the net transfer of resources to agriculture at an early stage of economic development, accompanied by (2) the development of a modern industrial sector to produce input requirements necessary for the transformation of agriculture. The generalized bias against agriculture in the last two decades is testimony enough that a net transfer of resources to agriculture has not occurred. What we did witness was a net transfer of surplus from the agricultural sector (Kihl & Bark 1980; Lee 1981; Mellor 1973). With the failure to achieve industrial transition, the collapse of agriculture has meant that the two dominant sectors need to be developed simultaneously. Where should the necessary resources be obtained?

With the ability to design and implement several policies simultaneously being limited, some development policies must now precede others, especially if maximum benefits are to be derived. Careful consideration should now be given to the appropriate timing and sequencing of public policies.

It is the purpose of this discussion to identify the changes in the policy environment and to concentrate on those policies aimed at increasing food production and achieving agricultural transformation. This discussion will identify the structural impediments confronting agricultural transformation and suggest possible ways for their elimination. The success of agricultural transformation will be linked to the success of industrialization and the profound changes in the rural areas, including a strategy of integrated rural development.

The Immensity of the Food and Agricultural Crisis in Africa

It is most appropriate to begin by adducing some of the relevant indicators:

1. The growth rate of food production has averaged 1.5 percent annually for the continent of Africa. This is well below the population growth rate, which has increased from a 1960–1970 average rate of 2.5 percent to a 1970–1980 average of 2.7 percent.

2. Between 1970 and 1982, the gross domestic product (GDP) grew at about 3 percent annually. This is roughly the same rate as the population growth. In effect, there was no improvement in per capita income for the entire continent. Since terms of trade have deteriorated during the same period, there has been a real decline in per capita income.

3. Africa's present population growth rate of 3.5 percent is the highest in the developing world. Children less than fifteen years of age now constitute 45 percent of the total population. Twenty percent of Africa's total population is now below the age of five years (World Bank 1986a).

4. In terms of GDP, per capita income, food and industrial production, levels of education, life expectancy, and infant mortality rate, twenty-two of the thirty-six poorest nations are in sub-Saharan Africa.

5. According to World Bank statistics, the number of people in poverty in sub–Saharan Africa may rise by nearly 70 percent over the 1970 level (World Bank 1986b, c).

6. In 1960, 11 percent of the population in sub-Saharan Africa lived in urban areas. By 1981, 21 percent of the population lived in the urban areas. In countries like Cameroon, 37 percent of the total population was living in urban areas by 1982.

7. The 1980 per capita food production was four-fifths of the 1970 level. The growth rate of agriculture and food production output has dropped from a 1960–1970 level of 2.7 percent to 1.3 percent during the 1970–1980 period. Per capita output in similar periods declined from 0.2 percent to −1.4 percent. For the same periods, food output declined from 2.6 percent to 1.6 percent (World Bank 1986).

8. According to United Nations statistics, 72 million Africans, one in five are suffering from malnutrition. This figure is expected to reach 110 million by the year 2000. It is estimated that in some countries, half of the children die before the age of five years. With natural disasters aside, extreme cases of malnutrition, starvation, and unemployment are common occurrences. In some countries, standards of living have deteriorated to levels below 1970, and for some, even below levels at the time of independence. Even in a country like Zimbabwe with adequate food production, it is estimated that 20 percent of Zimbabwean children under the age

of five have second- or third-degree malnutrition, and up to 30 percent are stunted in their growth (Tandon 1986).

In light of these alarming developments, some prevailing assumptions relating to the social and economic conditions in Africa should now be abandoned. For the author's immediate purpose, the following circumstances are identified:

1. The notion of the predominantly rural character of poverty and malnutrition should now be abandoned. High levels of poverty and malnutrition are now common occurrences in most urban areas. As the economic crisis worsens, high rates of unemployment, underemployment, and significant decline in real disposable incomes have exacerbated the urban crisis. The existing physical and institutional infrastructures in the urban areas are incapable of meeting the increased demands of the growing urban population. Utility services, whose consumptions have come to be accepted as being costless or inexpensive, are slowly disappearing. Supplies of water, electricity, and housing can no longer be adequately provided for the majority of the urban population. Medical services, including the availability of hospital beds and medicine, can no longer be adequately provided for the urban population. Where they are available, they are priced beyond the reach of most consumers.

When these developments are coupled with the prohibitive costs of basic staples, it is not surprising that malnutrition, poverty, high mortality rates, and the reappearance of diseases thought to have been eliminated now threaten a good portion of the African population. The situation has worsened to the point that some countries are now considering forced expulsion of some segments of the urban population. The government of Zambia has warned urban slum dwellers that unless they voluntarily leave the urban areas, the government will take action to remove them.

2. The illusion of peasant and rural self-sufficiency should now be abandoned. There is a prevailing theoretical orientation which seems to suggest that peasant (subsistence) agricultural production is a major impediment to increased agricultural production and transformation. The most notable advocate of this position is Goran Hyden. In his studies of peasants in Tanzania, Hyden argues that there is an "economy of affection"; the self-sufficiency of the African peasants, Hyden contends, is a major obstacle to policies aimed at national development. In such a situation, Hyden argues that the state should break the self-sufficiency of the peasants. This theoretical orientation has been translated into practical policies with some support from the World Bank and other international agencies. In light of the recent emphasis on small-scale farming, it is evident that the original policy of "breaking peasants' self-sufficiency" has been a disaster. No policy which has acted to marginalize the peasants can be considered successful.

3. A related assumption which should now be abandoned is that which sees poverty as a natural state in Africa and other parts of the Third World. When policies that were originally formulated to eliminate poverty act to further marginalize a majority of the population, it is difficult to view poverty as a "natural" condition.

4. The assumption that rural sectors are uninformed should also be abandoned. Commercial agriculture has significantly affected rural communities. Urban elites and civil servants have been attracted to commercial agriculture. Coupled with the rural elites, they are the main beneficiaries of credits and other services in the rural communities. A project-based approach has brought few benefits to the poor small farmers (Sanyal 1986).

Some Important Changes in the Development Policy Environment

As the social and economic crises intensify in Africa, we have witnessed some important changes in the direction of development policies. I will concentrate only on those that are centrally related to the objectives of this chapter.

At a more general level, stabilization and structural adjustment policies (SAP) designed by the World Bank and the International Monetary Fund (IMF) have dominated the debate over the changes in development policies. By definition, SAPs are designed to reduce pressures on the domestic economy, pressures which are likely to result in internal disequilibrium between supply and demand. These pressures are often manifested in the form of balance of payment problems, domestic inflation, chronic budget deficits, and adverse changes in domestic output. Policy instruments such as credit constraints, reduction in government deficits, reduction in public expenditures, currency devaluation, and price and market reforms are utilized to achieve these policies.

Nearly all forms of adjustments bring into focus two principal preoccupations of the African nations: the need to achieve permanent adjustments to structural problems which have impeded the effective implementation of any enduring development strategy and temporary adjustments to externally generated pressures. Problems relating to permanent adjustments include (1) the overwhelming dependence on foreign exchange earnings from the sale of commodities; (2) the limited possibilities of achieving domestic substitution; and (3) the failure to achieve any effective transition from commodity-based economic activities to industrial-based economic activities. By temporary adjustments, the author is referring, for instance, to the external shocks generated in the 1970s, such as oil price increases, declining commodity terms of trade, and the accompanying balance of payment problems. It can now be argued that these externally generated shocks are no longer temporary because they have now created permanent structural problems.

The most interesting questions relating to SAP in Africa are now the effectiveness and relevance of these policies and the resolution of the African crisis. With the renewed focus on public policy formulation and implementation in Africa, there are several concerns that should now be expressed: (1) What are the capacities of African economies to undertake SAP at least within the context of IMF-supported policies? (2) As presently constituted, how effective are SAPs in carrying out meaningful adjustments? (3) With the significant reduction in real disposable incomes accompanying the increased pressures on the states' resources, do current SAPs now threaten some of the positive achievements of the 1960s and 1970s?

The transitional cost of adjustments and the capacity to adjust are to a large extent dependent on the structural characteristics of the African economies. It is this sober realization that has generated renewed interests in bottlenecked economies. In the context of current debate over SAPs, opponents of the fund's policies argue that there are intractable problems (structural characteristics) which act to reduce the capacity of African nations to carry out meaningful adjustments. With these structural obstacles, contractionary adjustment policies end up exacerbating the already serious economic crisis (Crockett 1981; Diamond 1978).

SAPs stress the need for expenditure reductions and switches. Implicit in this recommendation is the need for resource reallocation, greater efficiency in resource use and economic management, increased supply capacities, and the elimination of distortions which have been accumulated over the years.

When consideration is given to the alarming trends that have been identified, expenditure reduction becomes a contentious policy recommendation, particularly if such reductions would act to worsen the climate of increased poverty, declining real disposable income, and declining food production. At a time when the legitimate demands on the states' dwindling resources are increasing, it is not surprising that attention is now being focused on the adverse effects of SAPs on the majority of the African population.

Expenditure switches or resource reallocations are now necessary in order to achieve effective economic management. In the context of the central relationship between the industrial and agricultural sectors, how can the resource requirements of both sectors be simultaneously met? What are the capacities of African nations to switch and provide adequate resources necessary for the transformation of the agricultural sector?

At a more specific level, we are now witnessing a growing affirmation of the primacy of food and agricultural production in any viable development strategy for Africa. It is my position that no successful stabilization policy can be achieved without adequate domestic food production; by implication, a significant change in agricultural policies.

Numerous institutions, including the Economic Commission for Africa (ECA), the World Bank, and the United States Agency for International Development, have declared their commitment toward improving food and agricultural production in Africa. These affirmations of support for agriculture should not be interpreted or welcomed as the emergence of a unified approach toward the resolution of Africa's food crisis. These declarations are laden with contradictions that are likely to prevent any meaningful transformation of Africa's agriculture and food production.

There still remains a major conflict between the management and technocratic aspects of food production on the one hand and the overall development strategy upon which the formulation and implementation of agricultural policies must be dependent. While incentives aimed at improving agricultural productivity, such as higher farm prices, low agricultural taxations, more flexible marketing arrangements, and more public expenditure in the rural areas are important, they do not necessarily lead to the transformation of the agricultural sector. While the emphasis on small-scale agricultural production and the shift from the project-dominated approach to rural development are welcomed changes, adequate consideration should now be given to the basic prerequisites or conditions for successful implementation of these policies.

The need for adequate coordinating capacities dictates that the administrative, management, and political obstacles to rural and agricultural transformation be eliminated. The translation of these bold statements of intent to reality will be dependent on the successful establishment of an enduring development strategy. Such a strategy should have multiple objectives, including increasing economic growth, expanding opportunities for productive employment, reducing poverty in both rural and urban areas, developing an integrated rural strategy, slowing down the rate of population growth, and establishing the necessary forward and backward linkages in order to facilitate economic transformation.

There is also a sense in which the changes in the development policy environment do not necessarily coalesce. This is most evident in the insistence on a free market approach to the allocation of resources and rural development. I question whether these objectives, which are now part of current stabilization policies, are compatible with those of rural development and small-scale farming. These concerns will be addressed in the next section. Before such an attempt is made, it is necessary to determine how the permanent food import dependence of Africa severely limits the effectiveness of stabilization policies.

Africa's Food Trap—the Permanent Import Food Dependence

The purpose of the discussion in this section is to account for the policies leading to and encouraging Africa's food import dependence. Why has this consumption become reinforcing?

Unlike the experience of Asia, we have witnessed significant changes in food consumption in Africa even before the transformation of agriculture (Lee 1971; Mellor 1973). Such changes are no longer restricted to the growing urban population in Africa. Two dominant factors have influenced the reinforcement of import dependent food consumption: food aid dependence and domestic agricultural policies. These have been largely influenced by domestic and international macroeconomic policies, such as foreign exchange regimes and terms of trade for agricultural and industrial products. This discussion will concentrate on the latter.

Foreign exchange regimes influenced by the volatility in international financial and monetary policies have significantly influenced agricultural policies and food import dependence in Africa. A case in point is Nigeria. During the peak of the oil boom, with the Nigerian naira being overvalued, Nigeria was importing food to the tune of approximately $5 billion annually.

The cost of domestic food production, changing tastes, and reduced demands for domestic food have made domestic food production almost irrational. Over the years, government policies including price controls have kept prices of imported food several times below the prices of locally produced food. Andrae and Beckman (1986) have shown that in just a decade Nigeria became dependent upon wheat imports from the United States. By 1983, this amounted to 25 percent of Nigeria's total import bill (Andrae and Beckman 1985).

The decline in oil revenue and the continued rise in food imports have created serious problems for policymakers. With the continued import dependence of the industrial sector for intermediate inputs and raw materials, the scarcity of foreign exchange earnings has complicated the already existing serious problems. The Manufacturers Association of Nigeria, in its latest periodic review of the Nigerian economy, reported that for the first half of 1987, capacity utilization in industry fell from 30 percent to 25 percent. This decline is well below the 55 percent capacity utilization objective that was set. The 66 percent devaluation of the Nigerian naira has resulted in a fourfold increase in the local value of imported raw materials, spare parts, and machinery.

In January 1987, the federal government of Nigeria imposed restrictions on the importation of wheat. By June 1987, there were acute shortages and soaring prices of wheat and bread. These shortages have severely affected flour mills, which were already operating at 20 percent of full capacity.

With the importation of wheat effectively banned, nearly 90 percent of flour used in Nigeria is smuggled in from neighboring countries. Following the ban on wheat imports, biscuit makers and bakeries experimented with the production of "composite flour," which is made of 75 percent wheat flour and 25 percent maize flour. The changing tastes of consumers meant that there was a poor market response to this substitute for imported flour. The limited possibilities of domestic substitution accompanied by the inadequate knowledge or research of consumers' preferences indicate that domestic producers are now in a desperate search for raw materials. The situation has been complicated by the fact that even when imported raw materials are available, the prices of most consumer goods are beyond the reach of most consumers (*African Business* 1987a, b, c).

Changing tastes and food consumption patterns are no longer restricted to the urban population. These developments, occurring before the transformation of agricultural production, now have profound consequences for domestic food and agricultural policies. For instance, in Somalia, a significant portion of the population has shifted their consumption from locally produced cereal such as maize and sorghum to imported grains such as rice, wheat, flour, and pasta. Preference is given to foreign grains even though rice and pasta are produced locally. It has been argued that preparation of locally produced grains is time and labor intensive since they are unprocessed. Since imported grains are easy to prepare, they have become attractive even to the rural population (*African Business* 1987d).

The policy implication of this shift in consumption is the increased foreign exchange requirements to meet the increases in food imports. The result is to worsen the balance of payment position of the food importing country. The increased demand for imported food acts to reduce demand for domestically produced grain. The result is further depression or reduction in the prices of domestically produced grain and, by implication, a disincentive to domestic production. The situation is further complicated by the fact that scarce resources are now being used to increase domestic food production.

Any policy aimed at banning food imports can be sustained only if domestic food policies lead to increased food production and an increase in the quality of domestic food. In relation to domestic grain production, steps should now be taken to increase processing capacities. At a more general level, domestic food consumption should be harmonized with domestic food production.

Changes in exchange rates alter the prices of home goods and affect the country's terms of trade. When exchange rate fluctuations are accompanied by price variation (instability) of imported products, they adversely affect the ability of the country to undertake domestic production. When African nations are forced to reduce imports due to foreign exchange scarcity and declining international reserves, they should be concerned about the cost of domestic inflation and slow growth. With a rise in the domestic prices of traded goods, there is a shift from traded to nontraded goods. This shift puts upward pressures on nontraded goods with a potential inflationary effect.

Deficit food supply may not lead to domestic inflation if the country has enough foreign exchange reserves to meet the increased or additional food requirements. When the unavailability of foreign exchange reserves is accompanied by the need to provide simultaneously for, the resource requirements of both the industrial and agricultural sectors, then there are increased pressures that are likely to lead to a recessive inflationary environment.

Price inflation need not arise from the price increase of one commodity. However, when there are limited substitutes or when the prices of other commodities increase, then domestic price inflation is inevitable. One now witnesses a situation where policies aimed at reducing domestic inflation are largely ineffective and recessive. The existence of structural bottlenecks means that pressures on prices can persist even when conventional indicators show no excess demand. When currency depreciation and exchange rate adjustments are implemented in such a climate, they create a recessive inflationary situation. The objective of achieving domestic economic stabilization is then made more difficult.

Attention has also been focused on the possibilities of achieving domestic substitution and export diversification. Even if one accepts that under free market conditions there will be a tendency for a production shift from low to high cash crop production, the recent precipitous declines in commodity prices have helped to worsen the terms of trade against agriculture. The ability of the African nations to induce substitutes in the short run following an exogenous shock is very limited.

While existing conditions of nonspecialization in most African nations inhibit their ability to diversify their trade sectors, the incorporation of new commodities into their export baskets is also restricted by cost competitiveness. When diversification leads to increased production of similar exports, there is a tendency for market prices to be depressed, thereby further aggravating the foreign exchange crisis. Quite often the limited possibilities for domestic substitution act to reduce the effectiveness of currency devaluation policies, with serious consequences for industrial output, domestic food production, income generation, and employment.

Obstacles to Agricultural Transformation in the Wake of the World Economic Crisis and the Changing Requirements of International Commercial Agriculture

In the wake of the world economic crisis and the subsequent structural transition in the world economy, we now witness some major tendencies which have acted to reinforce structural obstacles to agricultural and economic transformation. These tendencies have not only reinforced dualism within agriculture, but they have extended it to the entire economy. We are now witnessing three sets of contradictions, at the international level, the sectorial level and the social level (De Janvry 1973, 1975, 1981).

At the international level, the contradictions relate to the worsening balance of payment position, declining terms of trade, and the foreign exchange shortages. As I have attempted to show in the previous section, these developments have severely affected the performance of the agricultural and industrial sectors in the African economies. At a more general level, they have acted to increase the vulnerability and level of dependence on the world economy by the African nations. The latest manifestations of these developments are the precipitous decline in commodity prices and the worsening debt crisis.

At the sectorial level, serious problems associated with domestic agriculture and industrial stagnation have now emerged. The expansion or contraction of industrial production and capacities is now largely determined by external forces. For both the import substitution industrialization (ISI) and the export-led growth strategies (ELG), the "return to capital" determines the productive capacities of the industrial sector. In the ISI strategy, the "return to capital" is determined by the domestic demand. Declining domestic demand for industrial products acts to restrict the expansion of industrial capacity and the ability to import raw materials, producer goods, and intermediate inputs. In the context of the ELG strategy, the return to capital creates a derived demand or consumption of capital goods needed for the production of export products. The capacity to consume capital goods is therefore determined by the external demand for export products (De Janvry 1981).

The failure to achieve transition from the elementary or first stage of ISI to the critical stage of intermediate capital goods production has made economic transformation extremely difficult. The acute foreign exchange crisis now being experienced by the African nations makes economic transformation almost impossible. This situation holds true for the more advanced African industrial economies such as Zimbabwe, Kenya, and Nigeria, as well as for the rest of the African nations. Since little or no progress has been made in reducing their dependence on imports of capital and intermediate inputs for domestic production, low capacity utilization in the domestic industries makes domestic production almost irrational.

The increasing costs of productive inputs now result in most consumer goods being priced beyond the reach of most consumers. Furthermore, the crisis in balance of payment and foreign exchange earnings, now accompanied by the increased need for productive inputs, have acted to generate pressures for reduction in labor cost. The need to restrain the variable cost of production now results in a deepening structural dualism. These developments have serious implications for the agricultural sector.

The capital requirements for the industrial sector create internal price distortions with serious consequences for the agricultural sector. Since the impact of internal price distortions is greater on agriculture, there is a shift in agricultural production away from domestic foods, particularly those consumed by the majority of the population.

As the structural deficits and foreign exchange crises intensify, the need to increase the exports of agricultural products is accompanied by the increased export and import of food. The production and export of industrial raw materials and "luxury" food, such as coffee, fruits, and vegetables, are increased. Accompanying this development is a deterioration in the production of domestic staples. The disincentives for domestic food production and the adverse effects of internal price distortions caused by the import requirements of the industrial sector further discourage the production of domestic staples.

Within the agricultural sector, the development of commercial agriculture and the movement away from basic food production indicate that the subsistence agricultural sector becomes external to the commercial agricultural sector. The commerical sector, through its production and export of industrial raw materials and "luxury" food, is now integrated into the world economy. When the food sector is a component of the export sector, foreign exchange earnings can be used to import consumer goods. When the food sector is not a component of the export sector, then there is acute poverty due to limited domestic production and the inability to import food.

It is in this sense that I can speak of the "marginalization" of the mass of the population as both producer and consumer. The commercialization or mechanization of agriculture leads to some dynamic development of the agricultural sector but without any significant reduction in the tendency toward structural dualism within agriculture and the marginalization of the population.

Since the majority of the African population is involved in agriculture and is still residing in the rural areas, the development of a functional dualism within agriculture has serious social consequences for the African economies. When agricultural commercialization destroys the resource base of the rural population, the task of agricultural transformation becomes almost impossible. In effect, the extreme dualism within the rural structure becomes the major obstacle to rapid agricultural growth and transformation.

The impression should not be conveyed that the development of commercial agriculture is unnecessary. The dilemma still remains one of avoiding a situation where agricultural commercialization is not likely to create a sustainable food and agriculture strategy. The pressure to mechanize is now influenced by efficiency and increased productivity considerations. An additional factor is the need to gain international price competitiveness. To achieve these objectives, additional pressures are placed on the foreign exchange crisis due to the need to import input products, such as fertilizers and pesticides.

The reliance on cash crop production is now untenable in the wake of the changes in the international market. We are now witnessing the steepest decline in commodity prices since the Great Depression. Since 1984, and for the very first time in history, practically all commodity groups have experienced price declines. From mid–1984 to 1985, there was a 20 percent fall in real commodity prices, with an additional 15 percent decline for the first half of 1986. The irony of the situation is that the increased supplies or overexpansion of production was in large part a reaction to the encouraging prices in the late 1970s. While the supply of commodities increased by 8 percent between 1984 and 1985, commodity prices have declined by 27 percent in real terms from 1984 to mid-1986. The decline in commodity prices is occurring at a time when significant steps have been taken to increase domestic production. In the case of Côte d'Ivoire, the collapse in the prices of coffee and cocoa providing 60 percent of export earnings has put a severe strain on the country's economy. Coffee prices have dropped by 44 percent and cocoa prices by 20 percent. The crisis in Côte d'Ivoire (the world's largest producer of cocoa) was occurring at a time when that country was expecting a record crop for the third successive season (Blackburn 1987).

There are two related developments that are potentially threatening to the prospects for agricultural transformation. First, the threat posed by substitutions made possible by technical progress in the industrial nations:

The increased production of synthetic substitutes for natural products is indeed potentially threatening. Second, the increased production and subsidization of agricultural products in the industrialized nations will continue to create a major obstacle towards agricultural transformation. When these developments act to depress commodity prices, production substitution may be undertaken in the African nations in such a way that countries may end up investing and increasing their production of similar cash crops. This will result in a further depression of market prices and an accentuation of the already severe foreign exchange crisis. The objectives of agricultural commercialization should now be brought consonant with the objectives of national development and rural development.

Policy Implications

This analysis has been designed to examine some of the complex problems relating to the central task of establishing a viable and sustained development strategy in Africa. I have taken the position that a prerequisite for the successful implementation of any such strategy should be the transformation of agricultural production and the rural sectors. But it is now clearly evident that agriculture will not be able to reach the critical threshold without a major breakthrough in the industrial sector. Even with a dynamic industrial sector, the rapid rate of population growth will severely limit the assimilative capacity of the industrial sector. An additional difficulty is the need to satisfy, simultaneously, the resource requirements of both the agricultural and industrial sectors.

In light of this daunting agricultural and economic transformation, what are the consequences of continued failure to achieve increased agricultural production or food self-sufficiency? For the majority of the African nations, poor and short of foreign exchange, the consequences of agriculture and food production failures can be starvation, poverty, malnutrition, and food riots. These developments have become common occurrences.

Policymakers should now incorporate into their national development strategies the following:

1. Overall policy framework or development strategy should give adequate consideration to the objective of agricultural transformation and the elimination of structural dualism in the rural areas.

2. The objectives of agricultural modernization should now be made compatible with those of increasing small-scale agricultural production. The realization of this objective necessitates some fundamental changes in the formulation and implementation of agriculture production policies. The basic relationships within agriculture should now be harmonized, including those between (a) domestic food production and food imports and

(b) export-oriented agriculture and domestic food production. This task is now made extremely difficult by the changing tastes and preferences of consumers.

There are clear indications that small-scale farming with rapid population growth does not necessarily prevent the development of a highly productive agricultural sector. For historical purposes, the experiences of Japan and Taiwan indicate that they were able to achieve a widespread increase in productivity and income within the existing framework of small farm units.

In order to achieve these objectives, certain basic prerequisites must be met. A minimum infrastructure, including water supply, electricity, and roads, should be established. In the case of Japan and Taiwan, the establishment of these minimum conditions preceded the introduction of improved farm technology, seeds, chemicals, pesticides, and fertilizers. With the collapse of the physical and institutional infrastructures in most African nations and the prevailing administrative and managerial inefficiency, it is clear that these minimum conditions cannot be established unless steps are taken to rebuild the necessary infrastructure.

3. What should be the logical sequence for achieving rural transformation? The increasing involvement of elites in agriculture cannot be taken as a positive step toward agricultural and rural transformation. If agricultural subsidies geared for the rural cooperatives are largely controlled by rural and urban elites, there is a tendency for them to control rural cooperatives and the appropriation of surplus. Any notion that rural elites are any more willing or capable of bringing about reforms in the rural areas should now be abandoned. The idea that a single set of policies or institutions can effectively resolve organizational and distributional problems is also fatally flawed. To avoid some of these problems, there has been a tendency to adopt a technocratic approach toward complex agricultural and rural problems. Changes should now include a shift in emphasis from technique orientation. Since the potential beneficiaries of these policies are the rural population, they should now be actively involved in the formulation and implementation of policies aimed at improving the quality of their lives. Agricultural research, which in the past has had little or no impact on productivity and output at the farm level, should now be abandoned. High payoff and relatively inexpensive technology should be the focus of current research. Research should also be aimed at strengthening the linkages between extension and research services in the rural communities and the improvement of rural institutions.

4. The need to develop permanent intersectoral linkages between the agriculture and industrial sectors should now be given the highest priority. Some of the mystique surrounding the role of industrialization should now be abandoned. There is little evidence so far that the industrial sector has

played a decisive role in establishing the necessary conditions for self-sustained development. As Mamalakis (1985) has correctly observed, development should not be a process of transition from agriculture to industry and then to services, but it should be multisectorial. It should be viewed in the context of a transition from "embryonic" primary activities, including rural agriculture, services, and industries, to a more advanced combination of a highly productive rural and urban sector, including industry, agriculture, and services. What has been absent is the ability to make the transition from one stage to another.

No industrial strategy will be viable if it is dependent solely on the urban consumers. The availability of consumer goods in the rural areas does not translate into an effective integration of the rural population into the domestic market. What good is it if they cannot earn income to buy these goods? They must, therefore, be integrated both as consumers and producers. An important dynamic element in the industrialized economies is the integration of the central relationship between consumer and capital goods production. The incorporation of labor therefore becomes a necessary condition for the development of this relationship. In contrast to this growth requirement in the industrialized nations, there has been no such attempt to integrate the majority of the African population as both consumers and producers. The marginalization of the majority of African population has meant that policies aimed at capital and consumer goods production have had the negative effects in Africa and the Third World.

Questions relating to the timing and magnitude of intersectorial transfer and the related intersectorial conflicts can be resolved only at the political level. Those forces controlling the predominant patterns of resource allocation and access to reproductive capital will determine the intersectorial transfer of resources. The political prerequisites of the dominant forces in society will determine not only the requirements of the industrial but also the specific conditions under which policy shifts can occur. Where available resources are scarce, the organizational and distributional structures of the dominant forces could act to block intersectorial transfer of resources.

5. Finally, priority should now be given to the production of food and other agricultural products in the food deficit areas. As long as food production is still concentrated in the food surplus areas, it would be extremely difficult to break the cycle of food import dependence and all the related social and economic problems.

3

Agricultural Policy and Production in Sub-Saharan Africa: Problems and Prospects

Jonathan N. Nwomonoh

Introduction

Agriculture is the main component of the economic sector of the developing nations. In Africa, agriculture is at the heart of its economies, and it is in crisis. The crisis of food deficits has now become so perennial and so widespread that it can no longer be attributed to the outcome of a particular political or climatic occurrence such as war, ethnic strife, or drought (Lofchie and Cummins 1982).

The general pattern of agricultural performance in Africa south of the Sahara is rather bleak (Hinderink and Sterkenburg 1983). It has become evident from many publications that Africa's agricultural crisis has reached epochal proportions, manifested in declining per capita food and agricultural production, chronic malnutrition, rising food aid requirements, and growing reliance on food imports (FAO 1980). The root of this agrarian crisis can be traced to rising populations, economic and political crisis, environmental disasters, and a severe global recession. But the general characterization of food crisis does not sufficiently portray the region's internal differentiation. While a majority of the nations within the region are experiencing a decline in both their total agricultural and food output per capita, a few nations have shown a substantial increase in their total agricultural and food output per capita.

This chapter examines the trends in agricultural development since the 1960s and suggests a framework within which future agricultural policies may be considered. There is an urgent need for African governments to formulate policies and programs to reverse the widespread decline in agricultural output. The objective of this paper is therefore to highlight some of the themes that any successful production-focused rural development strategy must embrace.

Trends in Agricultural Development Since Independence

In summarizing the crisis in African agriculture, the *World Bank Report* (1981: 45) lists five trends which evolved over the past two decades: (1) The growth rate of agricultural production began to decline and, in the 1970s was less than the rate of population growth almost everywhere. (2) Agricultural exports stagnated, and African shares in world trade declined for many commodities. (3) Food production per capita was at best stagnant in the 1960s and fell in the 1970s. (4) Commercial imports of food grains grew more than three times as fast as population, and food aid increased substantially. (5) More of the population shifted its consumption to wheat and rice (as evidenced by the soaring imports of these food grains), which increased food dependency and created in many countries a mismatch between local production possibilities and consumer demand, since wheat and rice in these countries can only be grown at costs far above import parities.

Africa is endowed with many natural and human resources. The continent has been credited with 12 percent of the world's arable land and about 30 percent of the world's land surface classified as unused but potentially productive. In spite of the availability of land areas in Africa for cultivation, it is the only major region of the world where per capita food production is declining. While Africa's agricultural labor force represents about 14 percent of the world's economically active population in agriculture, its food production record is not all that spectacular.

During the first decade after independence, agricultural production grew in volume by 2.3 percent a year, or roughly at the same rate as population growth. In the 1970s, however, production dropped to about 1.3 percent a year, while population grew to about 2.7 percent (World Bank 1981). This drop in production is due to the fact that African governments are attempting to industrialize their countries and neglecting rural agriculture. Rural-urban migration and climatic problems exacerbate the drop in production.

In Africa, as elsewhere in the Third World, cereals supply two-thirds to four-fifths of caloric intake, making per capita grain production a basic indicator of both economic productivity and individual welfare. During the two decades following the Second World War, grain production per person in Africa either remained steady or increased slightly, peaking in 1967 at 180 kilograms. This level, roughly one pound of grain per day, is widely viewed as the subsistence threshold, below which malnutrition begins to erode human development and labor productivity. Since 1967 per capita grain production has been declining. In 1983 and 1984, years in which low rainfall depressed the harvest, per capita grain production was 118 and 120 kilograms, respectively, down more than a third from the peak (Figure 3.1).

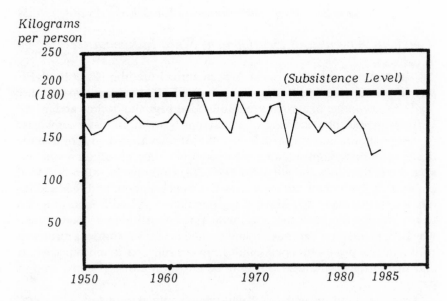

Figure 3.1: Per capita grain production in Africa, 1950–1984. *Source*: USDA, *Food Problems and Prospects in Sub-Saharan Africa*, Washington, D.C., 1985.

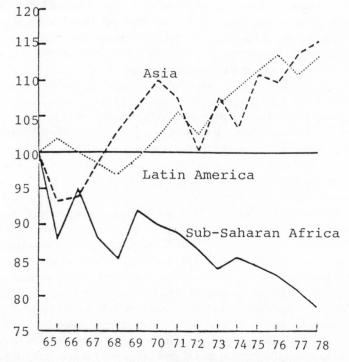

Figure 3.2: Index of food production per capita. *Source*: USDA, *Food Problems and Prospects in Sub-Saharan Africa*, Washington, D.C., 1981.

Per capita food production levels in Africa are therefore low, and they are declining rapidly as compared to Asia and Latin America (Figure 3.2). In the other major regions of the world, per capita food production has increased during the past two decades. But as the graph shows, in Africa, per capita food production has been falling so quickly that by the end of the seventies it was almost 25 percent below the 1961–1965 average. As per capita grain production has declined in this agrarian society, so has per capita income. At an April 1985 meeting of the Economic Commission for Africa, the African ministers of Economic Development drafted a memorandum to the United Nations Economic and Social Council. They observed that as a result of sluggish economic growth and a high rate of population growth, per capita income, which was growing at negligible rates during the seventies, has consistently declined since 1980 at an average annual rate of 4.1 percent, and average per capita income is now between 15 and 25 percent less than 15 years ago (Brown and Wolf 1985).

Export Production

Only three countries—Kenya, Malawi, and Swaziland—managed to increase their agricultural production by more than 4 percent a year in the 1970s. For many African countries, the real disaster was their failure to boost agricultural exports. As a consequence, African exporters lost market shares in all but three crops—coffee, tea, and cotton (Bernard 1985).

Food Production

Food production rose by about 2 percent a year in the 1960s or at approximately the same rate as rural population. In the 1970s, however, production increased only by an average of 1.5 percent a year. In fact, for Africa as a whole in the 1970s, growth in food production was not only well below the increase in total population but also well below the increase in rural population (World Bank 1981).

This trend continued in the 1980s. Per capita grain production trend for Africa suggests a deteriorating food situation since 1980 (Figure 3.3). The famine and near famine conditions in some 22 African nations in 1983–1985 attest to this deterioration (Brown 1985).

What is significant is that this decline occurred over a period when the various governments and external sources of finance focused more strongly on food production projects than ever before. Between 1973 and 1980, about $5 billion in aid flowed into agriculture, $2.4 billion of which was from the World Bank. These projects have so far failed to boost output or

Kilograms

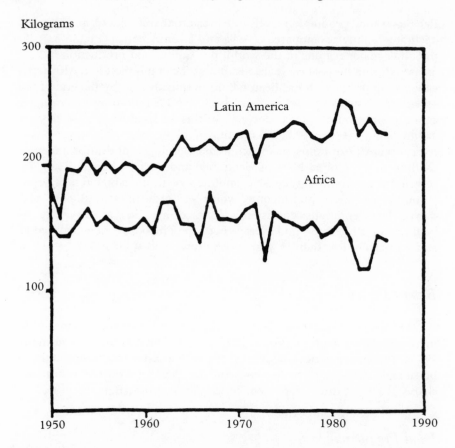

Figure 3.3: Per capita grain production in Africa and Latin America, 1950–1986. *Source*: USDA, *Food Problems and Prospects in Sub-Saharan Africa*, Washington D.C., 1985.

have been offset by declines in other parts of the food economy (World Bank 1981).

Foreign Debt

In addition to declining per capita food production and income, Africa's foreign debt is growing, partly because of rising food imports. Wheat and rice account for about 82 percent of gross cereals imports. While this is partly due to lagging growth of domestic food production, it is largely the result of the rapid rate of urbanization and of economic policies. Consumption patterns shifted from the traditional staples to wheat and rice, a practice exacerbated by overvalued exchange rates, which often make imported cereals the cheapest source of supply, argues the World Bank Project.

The region's cereal import bill climbed from $600 million in 1972 to $5.4 billion in 1983, a ninefold increase. By 1984 food imports claimed some 20 percent of total export earnings. Meanwhile, servicing the continent's debt, projected to reach $170 billion by the end of 1985, required an additional 22 percent of exporting earnings. In extreme cases, such as the Sudan, 80 percent of export earnings are required to service debt (Brown 1981).

Domestic Policy Reform

The immediate and continuing economic crisis in Africa is overwhelmingly a production crisis. It is a crisis which has arisen from the widespread adoption of structures for prices and incomes which have provided inappropriate production incentives. In particular, they have proven to be inadequte incentives to agricultural producers, and this has been aggravated by the development of costly and inefficient marketing systems for both inputs and outputs (World Bank 1983). Since the 1970s, several organizations have presented their agenda for action for addressing this production crisis. In 1978, the *Food and Agriculture Organization Regional Food Plan for Africa* was published. It postulates a growth rate for agricultural production of 3.9 percent a year for 1980–1985 and 4.2 percent for 1985–1990. This amounts to a tripling of the growth rate achieved in the 1970s. To reach this level, the plan calls for investments of $65 billion in 1975 prices, or $125 billion in 1981 prices, over a fifteen-year period (1975–1990). The plan further postulates rapid economic growth, greatly accelerated agricultural production, and a high degree of government and external support. It provides a useful macroeconomic framework and helps to indicate the outlines of an investment program in agriculture as well as possible financial constraints. In this report the emphasis is on the policy framework (World Bank 1981).

The Lagos Plan of Action was a statement of development strategy adopted by the African heads of state at the meeting of the Organization of Africa Unity held in 1980. The plan endorses objectives for the African states to achieve a more self-reliant, more economically integrated Africa by the year 2000. The Lagos Plan deals with short to medium-term responses to Africa's current economic difficulties. It focuses on how growth can be accelerated and how the resources to achieve the longer-term objectives set by the African governments can be generated, with the support of the international community. The plan further calls for investments of $22 billion in agriculture for 1980–1985, at least half coming from domestic sources (Browne and Cummins 1985).

The 1981 World Bank *Report—Accelerated Development in Sub-Saharan Africa: An Agenda for Action*—builds on the Lagos Plan of Action. The report discusses the factors that explain slow economic growth in Africa in the recent past, analyzes policy changes and program orientations needed to promote faster growth, and concludes with a set of recommendations for the donors. The report lists three areas of domestic policy inadequacies which have played a critical role in the development of Africa's agricultural crisis. They are (1) trade and exchange policy which has overprotected industry, held back agriculture, and absorbed much administrative capacity; (2) too little attention paid to administrative constraints in mobilizing and managing resources for development; and (3) a consistent bias against agriculture price, tax, and exchange rate policies. The World Bank *Report* (1981: 50) sees three policy areas badly in need of change:

> Support for smallholders. Most countries have gone for big, government-operated estates—and thus, usually, for disaster. By contrast, Kenya opted for the small man, who quickly took to growing tea, coffee, sugar cane and the other crops once thought to be the preserve of large estates. One Kenyan survey found that, on farms of less than half a hectare, output per hectare was 19 times greater and employment 30 times greater than on farms of eight hectares or more.
>
> Marketing. Through parastatal bodies, African governments generally control the marketing of export (and other) crops, as well as the supplies of fertilizers and seeds for farmers. And an expensive job they make of it: in Kenya (which is generally praised for its agricultural policies), parastatals charged farmers anywhere between 23 percent and 48 percent of the final price of their crops for marketing, storage and transport.
>
> Prices. Governments in most African countries fix both farmgate and consumer prices for basic foods. They also decide how much food to import. Almost invariably, farmers lose out: in the small free markets that exist, prices are often two to three times higher than official prices. Governments also tax export crops, a prime source of revenue. Again, farmers lose: export taxes have averaged 40–45 percent in Africa.

Strategies for Agricultural Development

Africa's development problems require attention to the following goals: accelerating the rate of output growth; expanding farm and nonfarm employment opportunities; reducing the most serious manifestations of poverty, particularly malnutrition and disease; and slowing rates of population growth. Over the next half century, small-farm development strategies involving labor-intensive, capital-saving technologies represent the most economical approach to achieving these goals.

The burden of this task falls on the shoulders of the large number of small peasant producers, 80 percent or more, who cultivate and raise the bulk of the region's crops and livestock (World Bank 1980). Stabilization of traditional agriculture is imperative to meet national and regional food needs and to resolve some of the problems of rapid urbanization and unemployment. Rural and national economic development efforts must go forward together. Traditional agriculture constitutes the underpinning of all the nations of Africa, the sector of the economy that involves the largest portion of the population. About 70 percent of the land and 60 percent of the labor expended in African agriculture are involved in traditional productions (Vermeer 1983). The peasant producers account for the bulk of agricultural output in most African countries. Focus on small peasant producers is a more cost-effective way to raise output than other alternatives.

The World Bank *Report* claims that during the 1960s and 1970s, many African countries directed a substantial proportion of their agricultural investment toward large-scale government-operated estates which involved heavy capital outlays for mechanization. Why did they follow such a course? First, there was the notion that only a rapid transition to mechanized, highly productive schemes, as practiced in the industrialized world, would overcome the stagnation linked with the traditional low-input methods. Also, it was considered a reasonable solution to labor shortages, where these existed. But most of these ventures did not fulfill expectations, and their contribution to growth was small when compared to their cost. They were beset with problems of management, overemployment of staff, underutilization of expensive machinery, and maintenance of equipment and infrastructure.

There are, however, many factors responsible for the lagging growth of domestic food production and export crops, and there have been marked variations in the performance of individual countries. Domestic disturbances and price policies that have turned the terms of trade against agriculture have been important in a number of countries. It also seems clear that unfavorable weather has been a more frequent problem since the late 1960s than in earlier years. Nevertheless, the decline in the average rate of increase in food production from 2.6 percent for the 1961–1970 decade to only 1.5 for the 1970–1980 could partly be attributed to the inability of the traditional farming systems to respond adequately to the problems and demands resulting from rapid population growth and the goal of accelerated development. There is a great need, therefore, for policy reform directed at research designed to introduce scientifically advanced methods of production.

Successes of Small-Farmer Development in Kenya and Zimbabwe

Kenya's experience of success illustrates the importance of some of the factors that condition rural development possibilities in sub–Saharan Africa.

Since its independence, it has achieved a record of consistent agricultural growth. The success that has been realized in promoting smallholder production of coffee, tea, grade cattle, and hybrid maize offers impressive evidence of the readiness of African farmers to innovate when feasible and profitable innovations are available. During the decade following independence in 1963, Kenya's agricultural sector grew at a buoyant rate of more than 4.5 percent per year, and it was able to achieve steady and substantial increases in the volume and the value of its agricultural exports. Earnings from these exports helped fund the development of a sizable manufacturing sector. Since the mid–1970s, Kenya's agricultural growth rate slowed slightly, but it continued to average about 3 percent per year during the past decade (Kenya 1983).

Many developmentally oriented aid organizations like the World Bank have expressed serious doubts that Kenya can continue its high rate of growth. In this judgment, Kenya's extraordinary, rapid pace of agricultural development from 1963 to 1973 was attained largely by implementing a set of agricultural policies that is sometimes referred to euphemistically as the "soft options." These included (1) the expansion of land under cultivation in reasonably fertile areas; (2) the removal of restrictions that prevented African farmers from growing export crops; and (3) the introduction of scientifically advanced methods of production (Lofchie 1986). Kenya continues to achieve a positive rate of growth in agriculture. Its success in implementing policies conducive to agricultural growth differentiates it fundamentally from most African countries.

At independence in 1980, Zimbabwe inherited a dual agrarian structure of roughly 5,000 large commercial farms and 700,000 smallholders. The fundamental problems in agriculture were the low productivity of smallholders, widespread poverty and malnutrition among commercial farm workers, a large landless population, and a rural infrastructure that had been battered by the guerrilla war. In 1981, the government identified the achievement and maintenance of food sufficiency and regional food security as an important national objective. One of the fundamental policy dilemmas that Mugabe's government has skillfully addressed is the redistribution of land and income to the urban and rural poor while maintaining the productive capacity of its commercial agricultural sector—a major earner of foreign exchange (Eicher 1986). Peasant farmers grew massive maize surpluses in 1986. Even before the 1986 bumper harvest, Zimbabwe's Grain Marketing Board was sitting on 1.4 million tons of maize, more than twice the suggested reserve against the worst-case drought scenario (Askin 1986).

Some reasons for such striking successes as noted in the *World Development Forum* (1985, 1985b) are: 1. The government has paid farmers good prices for their crops, thereby providing them an incentive to produce.

2. The pre-independence infrastructure—roads, railroads, extension services, marketing outlets—continued to be well maintained and was significantly expanded into the largely black rural communities. 3. The government made a concerted effort to assist the largely black areas. Agricultural extension services were shifted away from primarily white farmers to the needful small black landholders. 4. A political and social climate was maintained that encouraged many efficient white farmers and technicians to remain in the country and continue to produce.

In any consideration of the future prospects for the development of Africa, the development of the small-scale peasant sector and the role of the small producers in planning and decision making cannot be denied priority. Through this form of arrangement, fixed producer prices and marketing and other institutional arrangements designed to support the government and related interests could be declared on behalf of the poor peasant farmers. The preoccupation of some African governments with taxing agricultural export earnings in order to pay for national development, and the craze for foreign exchange earning, have resulted in many government decisions and actions that have retarded the development of the agricultural sector and the supply of food.

Without a drastic and revolutionary development of agriculture, Africa cannot hope to succeed in modernizing its economies. Moreover, there can be no lasting economic progress or takeoff until the level of agricultural productivity is substantially increased. Revolutionary changes in agricultural productivity are a prerequisite for successful economic and national development.

A country's level of food production is determined in part by its natural resource endowment—area of arable land, inherent soil fertility, rainfall, irrigation potential and growing season—and in part by how wisely it manages its resources. The natural resource base indicates agricultural potential; effective management is the key to realizing that potential (Brown 1982). In order to increase agricultural production and provide surplus for export, the organization and management of production have to be made more efficient in practically all the African countries.

Improved systems of farming and the application of modern technology to farming, which involves the assistance of industrialized nations in the education and training of rural farmers, will result in better levels of agricultural output and lead to better supplies of food, especially protein-rich food items, which are needed to improve the diet of the farming population. As better diet improves the health of the farmers, their level of productivity will improve, and much of the labor that is currently tied up in agriculture can be released for other forms of nonfarm employment. Thus, in the final analysis, agricultural progress in Africa will ultimately depend on the increase in productivity of the peasant farmers who form the majority of agricultural producers in the region. By improving their productivity and managerial skills, fewer peasant farmers, using improved technology and farming larger acreages, will be able to produce all the basic needs of their countries and provide surplus for export.

The location of factories in the rural areas to process agricultural raw materials and offer employment within the agricultural environment facilitates development in Africa. The economic development in Africa will be considerably accelerated when African nations cease to export agricultural raw materials and replace this trade with one in processed agricultural goods.

If Africa is to increase its agricultural production significantly in the next ten to fifteen years, there must be "a fundamental shift in Africa's research priorities" (Eicher 1986). Eicher ranges comprehensively over the history, problems, and needs of African agriculture, and concludes that "improved agricultural production technology is a sine qua non for expanding food production." Among the points made in his "research agenda": 1. Africa's "Human Capital" requirements should be investigated; a strong indigenous, scientific, managerial and academic community must be created. Training, whenever possible, should take place in Africa. 2. In general, Africa's agricultural development problems are long-term and should not have to be dealt with on an ad hoc, short-term basis. 3. Emphasis should be placed on researching promising new crops, including tree crops, animal nutrition, animal health and range management. 4. Sound crop and livestock production strategies should be prepared in Africa, not in Washington, Rome or Paris on the basis of secondary data and supervisory reports on projects that have failed.

Forming a green revolution must be the first order of business for sub-Saharan Africa, and this, according to Adebayo Adedeji, the United Nation's special representative on Africa's economic crisis, means "not so much large increases in government expenditures which have proved wanting by past experience, but appropriate policy changes." Such changes, Adedeji claims, should look to higher price incentives for agricultural output, greater security of land tenure, broader hospitality to private investment—in short, a "stimulative environment." Then the rest—advances in methods, research, extension services, land reclamation, transportation networks—would more readily follow (*World Development Forum* 1985c).

4

Population Growth and Food Supply in Africa

Jonathan N. Nwomonoh

The current population of Africa, estimated as 583 million, is around 10.9 percent of the world population. The continent contains 22.3 percent of the world's land area, giving it one of the lowest population densities in the world (United Nations 1982, 1983). Prior to the nineteenth-century up-surge of world population, the African continent contained a higher proportion of mankind, but it appears that while European, American, and Asian populations grew quickly, those of Africa remained largely stationary (Worldwatch 1987).

Wilcox (1940) surmised that the population of Africa remained more or less constant at about 100 million until the latter half of the nineteenth century; Carr-Saunders (1936) believed that the total declined from 100 million in 1650 to 90 million in 1800, when it started slowly to rise again; and Durand (1967) considers that the increase was more prolonged, although slow at first.

A host of reasons can be given for the relatively low population total of Africa, some of them environmental, some economic, and some social. About one-third of Africa may be categorized as desert, and another large area as semidesert. The major deserts are the Sahara, the Namib, the Kalahari, and parts of the Horn of Africa, none of which are conducive to dense populations. At the other extreme, the heat and humidity of the equatorial zone have encouraged luxuriant vegetation, poor soils, and a proliferation of diseases which have impeded mastery of the environment by man. The major pest of livestock farming in Africa has been the tsetse fly. The problem is widespread in the tropical zone and impedes the development of large forest area. The locust is another pest that has devastated large tracts of cropland in Africa.

Environmental difficulties are not the only cause of the sparseness of the population of Africa. Africa has been inhabited since the dawn of human history. With the exception of the Nile valley, much of the continent has not witnessed the evolution of peasant civilization based on irrigation as known to Asia. Before the colonial era, urban life was confined to a few widely scattered regions. Frequent intertribal conflicts caused high mortality. Population densities rose mainly as a result of external aggression.

Then there was the scourge of slavery, which according to some authorities meant the exodus of tens of millions of Africans to the New World and to Islamic countries. More recently colonialism caused considerable losses among the Africans. Another limiting factor has been the epidemic spread of veneral diseases, which have greatly reduced population fertility in many parts of Africa.

As Africa is particularly remarkable for its ethnic diversity and its political fragmentation, its population is very unevenly distributed. While there are large tracts of land that are uninhabited and sparsely populated, there are also pockets of dense concentration. The Mediterranean zone of the Maghreb, the Nile Delta, and much of its valleys in Egypt and Sudan, Ethiopian highlands, the environs of Lake Victoria, the highlands of Rwanda and Burundi, Northern Nigeria, the Guinea coastlands of West Africa, Coastal Natal, and southern Transvaal, and many islands around the African continent support very high densities of populations. Of the fifty-three African nations, only five (Ethiopia, Egypt, Nigeria, South Africa, and Zaïre) have populations over 30 million, and constitute about 47 percent of Africa's population.

Population Growth

Perhaps no other continent's destiny has been so shaped by population growth as has Africa's in the late twentieth century. African nations have the highest birthrates in the world, an average of 47 per 1,000, and the highest death rate, 18 per 1,000. As a result, Africa's average annual rate of population increase is about 3 percent. According to United Nations projections, Africa's 1980 population of just under 500 million will triple within a forty-five-year span, reaching 1.5 billion by 2025 (Goliber 1985).

Also, two demographers, J. Caldwell and P. Caldwell (1985:1) recently concluded that

> Sub-Saharan Africa may well differ from other regions of the world in the nature and timing of its demographic transition. No national population in tropical Africa displays any signs of fertility decline and population projections show Africa moving from about 10 percent of world's population at present time to close to 24 percent before global demographic transition is complete.

These figures do not account for such regional variations as those between Mauritania, Libya, and Botswana, which have densities of about

2 persons per square kilometer, and Rwanda, which has approximately 216 persons per square kilometer.

African nations with the lowest birthrates are Mauritius, 20.8; Seychelles, 25.8; Tunisia, 35.6; and Egypt, 36.9. These nations have effective family planning programs. These birthrates are so high that they are already retarding economic progress, thus frustrating national development aspirations and producing a demographic situation that could have serious social, economic, and perhaps political consequences. Virtually all African governments will have to contend with the population growth momentum built-in when populations are dominated by young people. In many African nations children under fifteen years constitute almost half the total population, a share far higher than in most countries. The first obvious problem is that a large number of people move into the reproductive span. Thus the age distribution of Africa's population carries a strong potential for continued rapid growth. Other factors encouraging high fertility include availability of basic health services and the eradication of diseases like yaws. A large family helps to assure economic survival. Neonatal and the general death rates were and are so high that it was essential to produce numerous children in order to be certain enough survived to enable the family to have an adequate productive and defense capability. This is an important survival strategy.

Food Supply

Food production in Africa has not kept pace with population growth; thus some African countries that were self-sufficient in food in the 1950s have become net importers of food in the 1980s. Various publications sketch a picture of decreasing output, food shortages, rising imports, soil erosion, famine and even mass starvation (FAO 1980). The annual rate of change of the total agricultural and food production for Africa compares unfavorably with the already disquieting figures for the developing world in general. The subject of food supply is important because an extremely serious situation exists today in Africa where the continent is experiencing a breakdown in the relationship between its people and their natural support systems. The central question that this paper addresses is: What can be done to drastically increase the growth rate of agricultural production from the current 2 percent to 4 percent annually?

Even though agrarian, Africa is losing the ability to feed itself. In 1984, 140 million of its population were fed entirely with grain from abroad. In 1985, the ranks of those fed from abroad will almost certainly increase. A mid-February assessment of Africa's food situation by the United Nations reported that some 10 million people had left their villages in search of food, many of them crowded into hastily erected relief camps. In late April, the Economic Commission for Africa reported that starvation death had passed the 1 million mark, reminding people everywhere that space-age technology and famine coexist.

In Africa, as elsewhere in the Third World, cereals supply two-thirds to four-fifths of caloric intake, making per capita grain production a basic indicator of both economic productivity and individual welfare. During the two decades following the Second World War, grain production per person in Africa either remained steady or increased slightly, peaking in 1967 at 180 kilograms. This level, roughly one pound of grain per day, is widely viewed as the subsistence threshold, below which malnutrition begins to erode human development and labor productivity. Since 1967 per capita grain production has been declining. In 1974 African grain production reached a low 116 kilograms per person. This was due, in part, to low rainfall and it could also be speculated that the impact of a lingering drought also contributed to this low production (Figure 4.1).

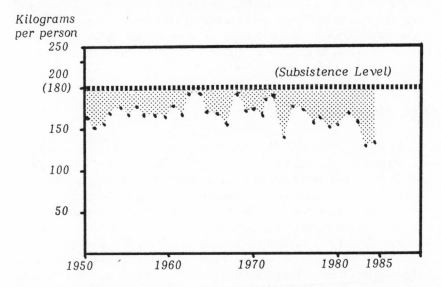

Figure 4.1: African grain production. *Source*: Adapted from USDA, *Food Problems and Prospects in Sub-Saharan Africa*, Washington, D.C., 1985.

In the sixties the per capita food production for Africa fluctuated between 92.0 and 98.5 kilograms (Figure 4.2). In the seventies, there was a drastic decline in per capita food production. Figure 4.2 indicates that the decline was down to 78 kilograms by 1978. When compared with Asia and South America, Africa seemed to have faired the worst in food production during the decades of the sixties and seventies.

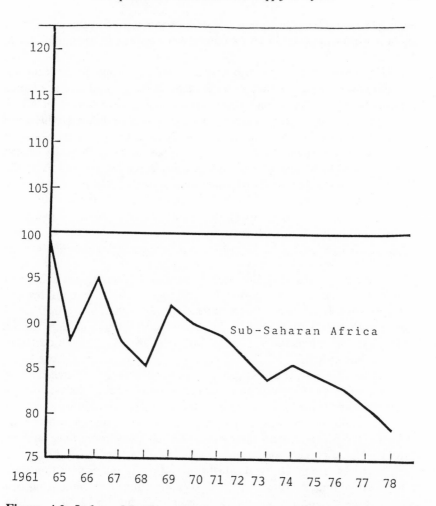

Figure 4.2: Index of food production per capita. *Source*: USDA, *Food Problems and Prospects in Sub-Saharan Africa,* Washington, D.C., 1985.

Foreign Debt

As per capita grain production has declined in Africa, so has per capita income. The African ministers responsible for economic development and planning are now painfully aware of this trend. At an April 1985 meeting of the Economic Commission for Africa (ECA), they drafted a memorandum to the United Nations Economic and Social Council, which was in effect a plea for help. They observed that "as a result of sluggish economic growth and a high rate of population growth, per capita income, which was growing at negligible rates during the seventies, has consistently declined since 1980 at an average annual rate of 4.1 percent, and average per capita income is now between 15 and 25 percent 5 less than 15 years ago" (ECA 1985).

The neglect of the agricultural sector of the economy by Africans and African governments resulted in large importation of food. A dependency on imported food can be seen across many major urban centers of Africa. It is estimated that cereal import in 1983 was $5.4 billion, which is a ninefold increase from the cost in 1972 of $600 million. The rising cost of imported food increases the continent's foreign debt. Many of the African countries are having great difficulty servicing their debts (ECA 1985). Some have had to discontinue development projects because foreign banks and foreign governments will not grant loans because of the inability of African countries to repay the loans.

Obstacles

The reasons for the poor and decreasing per capita production of foodstuffs in Africa are reasonably well understood, yet complex and difficult to resolve. The primary problem is poverty. Modern agriculture requires investments in technology, research, machinery, and training that many African nations cannot afford. But there are other factors curtailing African food output.

Among these are the weather and a lack of arable land. Three-quarters of Africa below the Sahara is too dry for farming without irrigation, and few countries have water management systems that enable them to use their meager supplies effectively. This makes sustained production extremely difficult for African farmers. Climate and drought conditions have not been kind to Africa in the past decade.

Beyond periodic climatic catastrophes, pricing policies on foodstuffs and selective migration from rural to urban settings are factors that bear significantly on the per capita food production in Africa. Storage and distribution are two other major obstacles. Foreign food shipments are limited because there is so little storage capacity in the recipient countries. Existing facilities are plainly inadequate, and they allow significant losses from insects. And with few paved roads in the outlying regions of some countries, it is virtually impossible to deliver food to some rural areas where the need is often greatest. Similarly, rural farmers often cannot deliver their harvest to city markets before it spoils.

A lack of foreign exchange limits the amount of food that many African nations can buy to satisfy their needs. In some nations, agriculture is not the highest priority. Resources are severely limited, and sometimes industry or public health gets more attention. In others, food problems are compounded by government corruption, warfare, revolution, or political strife. Some nations have opted for policies that subsidize food for urban consumers rather than stimulating stronger production by offering farmers better prices. These policies encourage reliance on imported food and aid rather than strengthen self-reliance. However, many African nations have given food production high priority. Another major obstacle is that the weakness of the state, and the position and role of peasantries are, according to some recent incisive studies, crucial factors contributing to the backwardness of agriculture in Africa (Hart 1982).

Political Leadership

Most of the agricultural decisions made by African leaders since independence regarding state farms and settlement schemes were partly a function of the ignorance and inexperience of political leaders and their foreign advisors.

A few African political leaders are having second thoughts about their decisions. In a recent interview with the editor of the *Third World Quarterly*, Julius Nyerere (1984:815), retired president of Tanzania, said:

> There are certain things I would not do if I were to start again. One of them is the abolition of local government and the other is the disbanding of the cooperatives. We were impatient and ignorant.

Strategies for Increasing Food Production

Food aid is at best a temporary solution to Africa's food crisis. However, it is the long and hard process of agricultural development that holds promise for Africa. Clearly, the slow rate of development of some African economies has been the outcome of the lack of understanding and cooperation between the different sectors of the economy with regard to the paths to be followed toward the achievement of development.

The immediate and primary development objective of the African countries is the provision of adequate supplies of food of acceptable quality for their populations. The burden of this task falls on the shoulders of the large number of small peasant producers, 80 percent or more, who cultivate and raise the bulk of the region's crops and livestock (World Bank 1980). Stabilization of traditional agriculture is imperative to meet national and regional food needs and in resolution of some of the problems of rapid urbanization and unemployment. Rural and national economic development efforts must go forward together. Traditional agriculture constitutes the underpinning of all the nations of Africa, the sector of the economy that involves the largest portion of the population. About 70 percent of the land and 60 percent of the labor expended in African agriculture are involved in traditional productions (Vermeer 1983).

5

Postharvest Grain Losses in Developing Countries

Ramses B. Toma

For those concerned about the world food supply, the primary focus has always been the two major dimensions: population and food production (Pimenthal 1978). Although per capita food production has increased moderately in recent years, per capita production remains low because of population increases (Vogel 1978). World food stocks declined from 170 metric tons in 1960 to only 100 metric tons in 1976, while the reserve, measured as days of world consumption, decreased from a one-time high of 103 days to 31 days (National Academy of Sciences 1978). In developing regions, the estimated percentage of population with a food intake below the critical minimum limit (1.2 times the basal metabolic rate) is 15–30 percent (Vogel 1978). An FAO study indicates that in the year 2000, a total of sixty-four countries will be unable to feed their populations in their own lands.

Cereals are the most important food source for the world population. Cereals provide over half of the total food energy supplies in the developing world (Vogel 1978). Compared to 1974–1976, the world production of cereal grains in the 1980s increased by less than 20 percent, from 1,397 to 1,639 million metric tons. The production of cereal grains in Africa dropped by 7 percent in 1983, from 70 to 63 million metric tons (FAO 1983). Imports of cereals in 1983 amounted to over 40 percent (26.0 million metric tons) of the total production in Africa and almost 20 percent (12.7 million metric tons) for South America (Table 5.1). The increasing dependence of developing countries for food supplies underlines the urgency for developing countries to boost their food production and minimize their food losses. Increasingly, experts are beginning to realize that we must look at alternatives for means of increasing the world food supply. One area which has become prominent in recent years is "the third dimension of food supply . . . food losses" (Bourne 1977). The world food supply can be increased by identifying and controlling food losses. The purpose of this paper is to identify the different categories of food losses (grain) and examine the role of sanitarians and health inspectors in solving problems in the light of impending technological implemenation (Krieberg 1970).

TABLE 5.1: World Grain Production[a]

	1976–1976[b]	1983	Import	Export	% Import of 1983 Prod.
World	397,476	1,638,847	219,174	224,398	
Africa	69,899	62,730	25,949	2,663	40
N. America	295,185	287,457	14,023	127,457	5
S. America	61,626	70,655	12,725	23,816	18
Asia	548,293	743,795	85,883	12,667	11
Europe	225,552	256,893	47,978	45,326	19
Oceania	17,955	31,829	483	10,192	1
USSR	178,965	185,488	32,132	2,277	17

[a] Measured in 1,000 metric tons (including wheat and flour in equivalences).
[b] Base year = 100.
Source: 1983 FAO *Production Yearbook*, Vol. 37, p. 155 (8); 1983 FAO *Production Trade Yearbook*, Vol. 84, p. 109.

Definition and Types of Postharvest Losses

Postharvest concerns the deliberate separation of food from the medium and site of immediate growth (FAO 1977a, b; Pimenthal 1978). Postharvest food losses occur in five major groups: 1. Durable (grains and legumes). 2. Fruits and vegetables, roots and tubers. 3. Animal products. 4. Fish, crustacea, and other marine products. 5. Miscellaneous commodities.

In this paper, we address primarily grain losses, even though many of the situations apply to other food products as well. Food losses may be expressed in quantifiable terms such as weight loss or momentary losses, or in nonquantifiable terms such as nutritional or energy loss (Abdussalam 1983; NAS 1978). All quantifiable losses are used for economical comparisons.

Food loss also deals with quality loss, i.e., deterioration of the product (but not to the extent of actual spoilage) and the discarding of food. This is very difficult to measure because standards of quality vary greatly from country to country (Abdussalam 1983; FAO 1983). Also, what is considered edible in one culture may be considered inedible in another. Therefore, while awareness of quality is important, it is not used often in published literature to express food loss. Today, most of the data on postharvest losses are expressed in terms of weight loss (tons, kilograms, etc.).

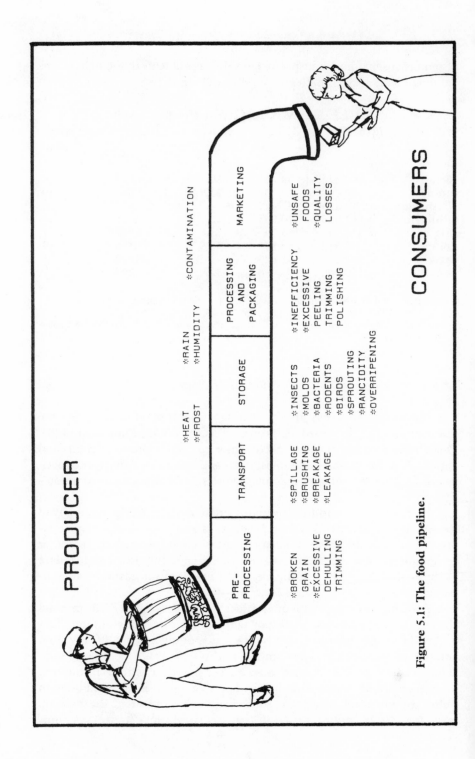

Figure 5.1: The food pipeline.

Estimated Postharvest Grain Losses

A major priority item on the agenda of the Seventh Special Session of the United Nations General Assembly in 1975 was the reduction in post-harvest food losses. A 50 percent reduction in losses was the target to be achieved by 1985. It was generally believed that such a reduction could greatly reduce or even eliminate the need for some developing countries to import large quantities of food. Based on conservative estimated minimum postharvest grain losses in developing countries, 42 million metric tons were lost in 1976 and 47 million metric tons in 1985 (NAS 1978). One can easily assume that if these losses were saved for consumption around the globe, it would feed the estimated 500 million malnourished and hungry people at a rate of 0.1 ton/person/year (close to average rate of consumption/person/year in most developing countries).

Causes of Food Losses

While food losses are locality-specific, they can be categorized into five major areas. Using the model that Malcolm C. Bourne of Cornell University has designed (Figure 5.1), none of these areas are mutually exclusive and they are, in fact, highly interrelated.

When we look at the typical causes of food losses, we note that the first is biological and microbial. Damage occurs by insects, mites, rodents, birds, large animals, and microbes such as molds and bacteria. The second type of food loss is due to chemical and biochemical reactions, i.e., fat oxidation, enzymatic reactions, and contamination with harmful substances.

A third type of food loss is mechanical, and may be due to spillages, abrasions, bruising, excessive polishing, pulling or trimming, and defective or damaged containers. The fourth type of food loss is physical and is intended to include excessive or insufficient heat and improper humidity control in storage. The fifth type is physiological, as occurs in the sprouting of grains and tubers, and in the deterioration of fruits and vegetables. Last, but not least, is food loss resulting from psychological or simply human aversion, for whatever reason (Bourne 1977; FAO 1969).

Role of Sanitarians

Methods to prevent postharvest losses are numerous, but it is extremely important to recognize and to consider sociocultural parameters and to work within these. Additionally, it is essential to find solutions which will accomplish the desired results at a price which the country can afford.

The storage environment is extremely important in preventing loss. Bins made of metal, rubberized cloth, baked bricks and cement mortar, reinforced cement, or paddy-straw mud structures can all be designed to control moisture and entry of pest rodents and birds (UNIDO 1979). Particular care must be given to the control of rodents, which not only consume the grain, but contaminate it with their excrement. Moisture control will reduce insect infestation and fungi growth. Temperature control, where possible, will reduce the multiplication rate of insects.

Recommendations

Sanitarians, public health inspectors, food inspectors, and environmentalists, if present, can all play a rewarding role in reducing grain losses. Most developing countries can indeed reduce or eliminate food losses if a real involvement of their sanitarians and health inspectors comes to fruition. It is not sufficient simply to erect storage areas of simple design utilizing local resources, and it is meaningless if there is no plan for continuous supervision and testing. Trained individuals should be utilized to monitor and evaluate operations to safeguard food safety and quality. Aside from frequent inspection by these individuals, educational efforts such as conducting sanitation and hygiene education workshops and seminars would go a long way toward helping people to consume safe food with minimal losses (Borgstrom 1973; UNIDO 1979).

Preventing postharvest food loss is vital in the battle against world hunger. It has been suggested that it should be termed Gross National Waste and be established as a debit item on the ledger, balanced against the Gross National Product (Borgstrom 1973). The United Nations Food Waste Program for developing countries was targeted for 1985, but the results of that program have not been published. It will be of interest to see what improvements and gains have taken place. One may find that we have only begun to reveal the tip of the iceberg.

6

World Food Shortage: The Third Dimension

Ramses B. Toma, L. T. Fansler, and M. T. Knipe

Introduction

The world food supply equation has two major dimensions: (1) increase in food production, and (2) solving the problem of population explosion, which is increasing at a faster rate than food production. There is a third dimension which is often neglected: the reduction of food losses.

As the world's poulation continues to increase, a similar increase in food availability is necessary merely to maintain the current world population. Much research has elaborated the effects of stabilizing population (especially in developing countries), increased food production, and increased knowledge and education levels to meet world food needs.

Postharvest food losses include cereal grain products, fruits, vegetables, dairy, animal, and marine products. Cereal, the most important food source of energy for the world population, always receives priority.

International recognition of the importance of postharvest losses in perishable foods came when a meeting of experts on the reduction of food losses from perishables of plant origin was convened jointly by F.A.O. and the United Nations Environmental Programme in 1980 (FAO/UNEP 1981). Fruits and vegetables are on the top of all food categories needed for prevention of the so-called malnutrition diseases of the developing world (i.e., beriberi, pellagra, scurvy, goiter, xerophthalmia, and others). The purpose of this discussion will be limited to fruit and vegetable postharvest food losses.

Causation of Postharvest Losses

Perishable produce differs in its physical and biochemical characteristics from durable goods, as summarized in Table 6.1. The mechanisms and causative factors of losses are thus quite different between the two groups and also different among the perishables. Durable commodity losses are limited to insects, rodents, and fungi, whereas perishable commodity losses are primarily due to microbial spoilage (Coursey 1983). Within the category of perishables, postharvest characteristics vary greatly from leafy green vegetables to soft-flesh fruits. However, like grains, perishable losses occur at all levels of the postharvest system (i.e., losses may occur during preparation, transportation, storage, processing and packaging, and marketing).

TABLE 6.1: Characteristics of Durable and Perishable Crop Products

Durables	*Perishables*
Low moisture content, usually 10% to 15% or less.	High moisture content, typically between 50% to 90%.
Small unit size, typically less than 1 gram.	Large unit size, typically 5 g to 5 kg., occasionally even larger.
With low respiration rate, with very small generation of heat.	High to very high respiration rate, heat production is therefore high.
Hard texture, not easily damaged.	Soft texture, easily damaged.
Stable, natural shelf life of several years.	Perishable, natural shelf life a few days to at best several months, according to type of produce.
Losses mainly caused by external agents, such as moulds, insects and rodents.	Losses caused partly by external agents, e.g., rotting by bacteria and fungi and partly by endogenous factors, respiration, senescence and sprouting.

Source: *Postharvest Losses in Perishable Food of the Developing Countries*, 1983, p. 491. (adapted from FAO/UNEP 1981).

Perishable fruits and vegetables have been found to be most susceptible to injury by chemical, enzymatic, and microbial reactions if improper handling occurs (Abdussalam 1983). For example, loss of tomato harvests in developing countries may be as high as 50 percent greater than loss of grain.

Technical and Nontechnical Losses

Coursey (1983) listed the factors that affect postharvest losses into technical and nontechnical losses. Technical factors are physical, physiological, and phytopathological.

Physical losses include the related injury resulting from faulty handling, packing, transportation, and improper storage conditions before reaching the market (Abdussalam 1983). Physical injury is considered the most damaging factor, due to the accelerated rate of decomposition after fruits and vegetables are injured.

Physiological losses can occur internally by a series of metabolic reactions, leading to chemical and biochemical changes which are irreversible. Thus, these changes affect the color, texture, and flavor of the produce, resulting in produce unfit for human consumption, and degrade the nutritive value.

Phytopathological losses are by far the major single cause of postharvest losses in fruits and vegetables due to microbial spoilage. When compared to phytopathological losses, bird, rodent, and insect infestation are minor concerns to farmers.

Nontechnical losses are of greater concern in developing countries than in developed countries because of the amount of capital investment allocated, poor communication in transferring knowledge and information to workers, absence of long-range planning, short-term policy and inadequate facilities for transportation, packaging, and faulty marketing techniques. It is of interest that each developing country has its own set of nontechnical problems, not uniquely approaching a solution in similar manners.

Definition of Losses

At the Seventh Special Session of the United Nations General Assembly in 1975, a resolution was passed calling for a 50 percent reduction of postharvest losses by 1985. However, few accurate figures are available for losses of perishables measured by a described methodology (Table 6.2).

Loss definitions have been classified into quantifiable (weight loss, economic loss) and nonquantifiable (nutritional loss, energy loss, and quality loss).

A manageable definition of postharvest food loss established by the Food and Agriculture Organization of the United Nations/United Nations Environmental Programme in 1980 is summarized in Coursey (1983: 485) as follows:

> "*Postharvest*" begins at the moment of separation of the commodity from the plant that produced it (mechanically or manually). Act with the intention of starting it on its way to the table. The postharvest period ends when the food comes into the possession of the final consumer.
> "*Food*" means weight of wholesome edible material that would normally be consumed by humans. Inedible portions such as skin, stalks,

TABLE 6.2: Nongrain Staples, Vegetables, and Fruits—Losses Reported by Commodity

Commodity	Estimated Loss (Percent)
ROOTS/TUBERS	
Potatoes	5–40
Sweet Potatoes	35–95
Yams	10–60
Cassava	10
VEGETABLES	
Onion	16–35
Tomatoes	20–50
Plantain	35–100
Cabbage	37
Cauliflower	49
Lettuce	62
FRUITS	
Banana	20–80
Papaya	40–100
Avocado	43
Peaches, apricots, & nectarines	28
Citrus	23–33
Raisins	20–95
Apples	14

Source: *Post Harvest Losses in Perishable Foods of the Developing Countries,* 1983 (adapted from NAS, 1978).

leaves, and seeds are not food. Potential foods are not foods; they do not become food until they are accepted and consumed by large populations. Feed (intended for consumption by animals) is not food.

"*Loss*" means any change in the availability, edibility, wholesomeness or quality of the food that prevents it from being consumed by people.

The 1978 National Academy of Science (NAS) series on postharvest losses concerning perishables established that losses in perishables are extremely difficult to quantify, in general due to variations in variety, texture, storage conditions, and crop duration, except in reference to a particular commodity at a specific location. Though the average minimum loss reported by the NAS in 1978 for fruits and vegetables averaged 21 percent, references not included indicated estimates of 40–50 percent. Table 6.2 presents Coursey's simplified form of the NAS 1978 report.

Reduction of Postharvest Losses

Universally applicable advice concerning how to reduce losses and increase the food availability is not practical because the reduction of food losses involves more than just technical issues (i.e., lack of long-term planning, budget deficits, lack of training for farmers, and poor marketing strategy). Reform programs must be sensitive to the cultural, socioeconomic, and political needs of a society.

In developing countries, the reduction of fruits and vegetables postharvest losses requires efficient step-by-step mechanisms to identify and eliminate weak links from preprocessing to marketing. Many experts agree that there are numerous economic and social reasons for giving preference in economic policy to strategies of increasing food supply through elimination of postharvest losses rather than through expansion of food production in developing countries by cultivating new lands which would be more costly in terms of land reclamation, irrigation, and fertilization. However, the final decision is up to developing countries to take a course of action.

Wos (1983: 8) listed the following points concerning reduction in postharvest loss:

> The strategy of decreasing losses is economical and less expensive because it requires less capital investment per unit of the final product than a strategy of increasing production extensively, especially in the short-term.
>
> The actions taken to decide on a strategy of loss elimination are usually accessible by using local resources and in most cases do not require expensive imports.
>
> Numerous benefits may result from changes and improvements in production management because the strategy of post-harvest loss reduces unemployment and increases production growth to feed millions of the poor and hungry.
>
> Limiting losses will free some resources, especially land, which may then be used for other purposes (i.e., industrial, housing, and mining).
>
> A strategy of decreasing losses boosts moral and educational values through self-sufficiency and achievement. Also, it teaches the results of human work and the rational use of goods that have been produced locally with less dependency on imports.

Comments and Recommendations

1. Food is a human necessity (main source of energy), and the acquisition of food is a science. Without food science, certain technology in preservation and transport of perishable items would *not* be feasible.

2. Vegetables, fruits, and tubers are among perishable items and are excellent sources of complex carbohydrates, vitamins, and minerals. It is unlikely that these essential nutrients (if high postharvest losses occurred) are provided in correct proportions through high percentages of calories consumed from grains in developing countries. Therefore, it is a priority item on the developing countries' agendas if they desire to combat malnutrition.

3. At any point, there is always a percentage loss which should be minimized.

4. Because of their soft texture, most vegetables and fruits can be easily damaged after harvest, making the product unsalable. Therefore, all perishable items should be handled efficiently and in a short time to reduce losses due to bruising, rotting, and/or improper storage conditions.

Since developing countries have no adequate means of artificial cooling and refrigeration to extend shelf life, more simple methods of food preservation are available in these areas. They are also easily learned by the people of that particular locality. Sun drying, pulp evaporation, and certain acids for pickling are good examples of such means of preserving perishables. Wooden boxes and burlap sacks can be used instead of dirt pits for storing foods, and they can also be reused. Also, proper storage could easily include rough sheds and open areas for good air ventilation and shielding from direct sunlight, which raises the temperature and accelerates decomposition.

It is essential for all of us to develop research methods for preserving fruits and vegetables by simple means that uniquely fit conditions in developing countries on an individual basis in order to produce products that are acceptable to their culture. It remains to be seen whether developing countries also implement these methods to improve the welfare and economy of their populations.

Part II
Appropriate Technology
and Technology Transfer

7

Applying Information Technology to the Development Process

Janet J. Palmer

Introduction

The information age is posing new challenges for all the world's countries but especially for LDCs (less-developed countries). While a few LDCs, e.g., South Korea and Brazil, appear to be benefiting from the infusion of information technology into their economies, most are not. After reviewing the literature, Dosa (1985) reported that most leaders of LDCs recognize that the future of their nations will be dependent upon a knowledge-based economy. However, many LDCs have yet to experience success with the requirements of the industrial age or even the agricultural age. Therefore, the suggestion that LDCs should bypass former ages and leap directly into the information age has provoked controversy.

This chapter explores how information technology is affecting LDCs and how it can be incorporated into the development process. The LDCs which have met with success from their participation in the information economy will be analyzed and discussed as potential models for other LDCs. Problems that have surfaced because of the exigencies of the information age will also be noted. Strategies and policies for LDCs desiring to enter into the information economy will be presented as possible solutions for problems associated with the information age. The importance and need for research concerning the information activities of LDCs will be discussed. Finally, after examination of all the evidence, the reader should be able to discern the strategic role that information technology is playing in shaping the future of LDCs.

Development and Information

Progress in LDCs has occurred through development—a process of planned change. For LDCs, change has been directed toward improvement in living standards and the quality of life. To effect such change, all manner of resources are employed—economic, technical, physical, human, and information, particularly scientific, technical, health, and commercial information. (Saracevic et al. 1984:192–193). Historically, LDCs have lacked necessary and/or adequate resources for development. Consequently, LDCs have received aid from a variety of development sources. Not until the 1980s, however, did development planners begin to consider information as a separate resource. In the information age, information is no longer a sideline of development but a legitimate development tool by itself (Dosa 1985:149).

Information as a Resource

Information was first classified as an economic resource in 1963 by the Wharton Graduate School of Business economist Adrian M. McDonough. Along with human resources, information could perhaps be considered the most important resource for development of future economies. Increasingly, for LDCs, the "economic development gap" has become a "knowledge and information gap" (Edfelt 1986:188). This idea has been well expressed by Galenter (1984:20), who said, "The trade wars of the past will become the information wars of the future." Where once nations struggled to acquire power by becoming land-rich, today they compete to become information-rich. In the information age, the ability to manipulate and manage information is equated not only with power and economic advantage but also with developed nation status. Rateau (1981:6) states, "It is a capacity to manage and handle ... information ... that makes a country developed. A constant of underdevelopment is a country's lack of ability to manage and apply ... information services." The requisite information services which increasingly differentiate developed nations from LDCs are embodied in the information technologies of computers and telecommunications.

Information as Technology Transfer

The information technologies of computers and telecommunications are one of the newest forms of technology transfer. Dosa (1985:147) lists the following ways in which information technology can be transferred:

1. Hardware—devices, equipment, parts, materials, entire systems;

2. Information—data, documentation, software, standards, specifications, licenses, service contracts, manuals, maintenance handbooks, guidelines;

3. Knowledge—understanding of the origins and potential impacts of technology or process; competence to plan, manage, and evaluate

applications; skills and know-how; relevant policy issues; ability to adapt and diffuse innovation.

Information technology transfer involves diverse and complex areas of development. Development planners who wish to use information technology as a development tool need to be knowledgeable concerning the many information systems available to LDCs. One source of such information is the *Directory of United Nations Information Systems* (United Nations 1980). This directory lists over two hundred information services, clearinghouses, information centers, and databanks. Such information systems need to become incorporated into the development process of LDCs with more frequency as systems become more cost-effective, user friendly, and more specifically directed toward development needs.

Benefits of Information Technologies

The application of information technologies to the development process can benefit LDCs in many ways. Haas and Ruggie (1982: 196–197) list the following benefits:

• Decision makers can gain access to information otherwise unavailable to them, thereby improving national and international policy-making.

• Poorer countries can acquire power and economic advantage from their information activities, thus compensating them for their lack of power base in other areas.

• Cognitive learning can be restructured and expanded as individuals learn to apply new sources of information acquired from electronic systems to problem solving.

According to Slamecka (1985:181), the cognitive development of individuals in LDCs has been inhibited by the lack of training in problem-solving skills, absence of libraries and reference materials, and large classes emphasizing rote learning. Consequently, Slamecka calls the potential impact of information technology upon the cognitive skills of the LDCs' population "unsurpassed." While conceding that overcoming this conceptual barrier would be difficult, Slamecka believes that information technology holds more promise to make this change than anything else.

Neelameghan and Tocatlian (1985:160) also discuss the benefits derived from the application of information technologies to development. These include the following:

• An increased volume of personalized information exchanges and communications; for example, by use of electronic mail.

• An enhanced capability for more frequent interpersonal and intergroup dialogues with the use of networking, electronic bulletin boards, and computer conferencing.

• An increased potential for personal and professional growth; for example, with the use of personal computers.

Slamecka (1985:181) rightfully cautions that technologies need to be delivered if they are to be of benefit to LDCs. He cites, for example, videotex as a technology with much potential for development because of its already widely available and highly accepted technological base — television. Videotex broadcasts information either one way or interactively between a database and a computer or a specially equipped television set. The use of such a familiar medium for information delivery would also be enhanced by the user-friendly format of videotex — menu-driven, frame-by-frame presentation.

Still more benefits of information technology have been cited by Edfelt (1986:191):

• More competitive positions for business, such as banks and airlines. Banks can access foriegn-exchange trading information on-line via satellite, and airlines can access international reservation networks.

• Databank services. Agriculturalists, for example, can access information from databases regarding climate, planting, harvests, prices, costs, and research.

• Library services. Public libraries can be electronically linked to video display terminals and other devices to provide users with the full text of documents, reports, and articles.

• Health services. National health care organizations can improve their services in tracking diseases, diagnoses, treatment, prevention, and the fostering of intra- and inter-country contact between medical professionals. Shortages of medical personnel can be alleviated. Urgent medical tests can be performed with electronic instruments by transmitting their signals over cable and microwave networks.

• Educational services. Education can be improved with the use of computer-based instruction and other interactive technologies. Shortages of education professionals could also be alleviated.

Slamecka (1985:182) stresses that the potential benefits of information technology applied to LDC development depend upon several factors: LDC policies, the adaptivity of the people involved, the methodology of the applications, the attention and assistance offered by the information industry and governments of the industrialized nations, and the approaches taken by the world decision-making groups toward information technology problems.

Are LDCs taking advantage of the benefits of information technologies? Are LDCs making progress into the information age? What social forces are helping or hindering the movement of LDCs into the information age? These questions can be answered by review of current global trends and their impact upon LDC development.

Trends Affecting Information Technology Transfer

LDCs, like other nations, are in various stages of development in their transition to the information age. Some are lagging behind. For example, even though LDCs represent approximately 70 percent of the world's population, they have only 7 percent of the world's telephones. The telephone, one of the oldest and most basic of communication technologies, is, practically speaking, not accessible to vast numbers of the world's population. The average industrialized nation has 50 telephones per 100 persons; Latin America has 5.2 telephones per 100 persons. Africa has 0.7 telephones per 100 persons with 30–40 percent estimated to be out of service at any one time. Asia has 2.8 telephones per 100 persons, but there are more telephones in the city of Tokyo than on the entire continent of Africa (*South* 1986:51).

Some LDCs, however, are advancing so rapidly into information economies that they stand in danger of losing their LDC status. These LDCs, referred to as NICs (near industrialized countries), include South Korea, Taiwan, India, Brazil, and Mexico. NICs are forging new frontiers in the international information economy and are forcing the industrialized world to take serious note of their advancements (Botelho 1987:38). NICs appear to be the realization of the statement of the noted scholar and communication consultant Wilson P. Dizard, Jr. (1982:90), who said, "There is no reason why they [LDCs] cannot begin to challenge the West in some areas of high technology." The reasons why some LDCs have been transformed into NICs can be understood from an examination of some trends currently affecting the global economy.

Production Sharing

Production sharing was first identified in 1977 by Peter Drucker, the renowned management scholar and consultant. Drucker predicted that production sharing would become a dominant form of industrialized organization in the world economy. Production sharing enables corporations in industrialized nations to obtain the benefits of the lower costs of labor and operating expenses in LDCs. The LDCs benefit from production sharing because of the introduction of new technologies and increased employment opportunities for their economies (Power 1983:30). Something of a turnaround has occurred lately, however, regarding the production-sharing trend. LDC governments and private enterprises are actively seeking foreign corporations to form manufacturing and marketing alliances. This LDC strategy has brought considerable success to India, South Korea, and several Caribbean nations.

India. In the city of Bangalore, India, government officials are busy promoting a new high-technology industrial park to make room for its fast-growing information technology industry. Just a little more than a decade ago, no computer industry existed, whereas by 1986 the city was home to dozens of domestic computer and electronics manufacturers as well as TNCs (transnational corporations). These manufacturers include some of the most successful companies in the information industry. Texas Instruments of the United States exports software manufactured in Bangalore. Hewlett-Packard Company, also of the United States, has a contract with a Bangalore company to manufacture its computers. Other companies awaiting government approval to locate in this Silicon Valley city of India include Data General Corporation of the United States, N. V. Philips of the Netherlands, L. M. Ericsson Telefon, A. B. of Sweden, and the Yokogawa Hokushin Electric Corporation of Japan.

All this activity in the information technology industry is working to benefit the local population of Bangalore. A computer systems analyst who formerly worked in Silicon Valley in California left his position there to return to Bangalore to found his own computer consulting business as well as one of India's first schools to teach computers at the primary level (Matt Miller 1986:34).

South Korea. In South Korea, as in Bangalore, government officials have adopted an aggressive attitude toward development of the information technology industry. Their long-term strategy has also been successful by the formation of alliances with foreign corporations for manufacture and distribution of their products. In this respect, South Korea's success has been phenomenal. Rising from a scarcely developed nation a mere decade ago, South Korea is now a pivotal force in the international microcomputer industry. The computer-related organizations with which South Korean organizations have linked are notable.

• Tri Gem Computer, Inc., landed a manufacturing contract with Computerland Corporation, the world's largest personal computer retailer.

• Daewoo became partners with Leading Edge Products of Massachusetts to manufacture its computers and to date has captured 6 percent of microcomputer sales. No other foreign company's machine can claim such a significant portion of the microcomputer market.

• Samsung Semiconductor & Telecom Company has linked with Novell, Inc., of Orem, Utah, as its American distributor for its manufactured goods.

• Hyundai has an alliance with Blue Chip Electronics, Inc., of Chandler, Arizona, to market its computers.

• Qnix Company has perhaps the most enviable alliance in its relationship since 1983 with the software industry giant, Microsoft Corporation of Redmond, Washington. This corporation is the manufacturer of MS-DOS (microsoft-disk operating system), the de facto industry standard DOS for IBM and IBM-compatible microcomputers. All South

Korean firms entering the IBM-compatible market must obtain their MS-DOS license from Qnix.

The local fallout of the South Korean microelectronics industry explosion has also worked to benefit the local population. The Qnix Company developed the first word processor in the Korean Hangul alphabet as well as a line of Hangul computer printers and terminals (M. W. Miller 1986:8).

Caribbean Nations. Small island nations with limited resources might tend to dismiss entry into the information technology industry as wishful thinking, but not so for several Caribbean nations. Jamaica, Barbados, and the Dominican Republic are profiting from the information technology industry too, but not in manufacturing. Instead, these island nations, as well as other LDCs (South Korea and Mexico), have entered the information services industry, specifically that of data entry. With the use of satellite communications, source documents, typically from the United States, are transmitted via facsimile equipment to so-called offshore offices where operators keyboard the data into computers. Then the digitized data are transmitted over phone lines, once again using satellite technology. As in production sharing, the chief benefit to users of offshore offices is the cost savings in labor. However, an additional benefit includes access to available clerical employees. Clerical office workers have become more difficult to recruit in the United States since the feminist movement encouraged many women to abandon clerical work for nontraditional careers.

The information services industry in the Caribbean nations has developed because of the production-sharing trend. TNCs and LDC private enterprises have worked together to produce a thriving new industry for the Caribbean nations. Promotional strategy by LDC governments has played an especially important role in the development of the information services industry. For example, Caribbean Data Services is an American Airlines subsidiary with offshore locations in Barbados and the Dominican Republic. In Jamaica, the government views the offshore data-entry industry as a priority sector for both immediate and long-term development and diversification of its productive base (*Skywritings* 1985:40).

However, not all development in the information technology industry has resulted from the production-sharing trend. In fact, one LDC has gained international attention for bucking this global trend.

Brazil. Brazil has chosen to follow a more independent route on its way to the information age. Such a position has made Brazil something of a maverick in the international economy. However, Brazil is also a prime example of an LDC which has successfully harnessed information technology for its development. Unlike India, South Korea, and the Caribbean nations where joint ventures and the export market are emphasized, Brazil's strategy is directed toward fostering a locally controlled computer industry. Brazil's information industry has targeted its own population as its sales market. As the West's eighth largest economy, Brazil has a sizable population on which to market its computer products. Before 1974, Brazil imported most of its computer-related products, but in the seventies began to develop a plan to reduce its dependence on foreign imports. This plan resulted in Brazil's National Informatics Law of 1984, which generally banned the import of anything with a microprocessor. In addition, the law required 70 percent ownership of Brazilian computer organizations with Brazilians controlling their management and technical decision making.

The Brazilian strategy currently appears to be working well. Between 1975 and 1986, the number of computers produced by Brazilian firms rose from 5 percent to over 75 percent. In 1986, more than 270 Brazilian firms accounted for 55 percent of the $2.7 billion domestic market for computer-related goods and services (Botelho 1987:36–45).

Should other LDCs follow a strategy similar to Brazil's? Generally, most LDCs do not have a sizable technically trained labor force to develop computer-related technologies or a mass sales market of computer-literate citizens. In addition, Brazil's isolationist trade policies regarding the information industry could backfire on her. Other nations perceive Brazil's policies as excessively "protectionist" and could instigate unfavorable economic policies toward Brazil which could work to undermine her growing success in the information industry. Consequently, other LDCs desiring to emulate Brazil's strategy need to be aware of possible pitfalls on her chosen path to success in the information industry.

Decentralization

Another current trend which has influenced organizations worldwide and information technology management is that of decentralization. In the past, a centralized approach for information technology transfer was necessary because of the high cost of technology and the scarcity of skilled technicians. Several organizations, such as the International Bureau of Informatics (IBI) and various programs of the United Nations Education, Scientific, and Cultural Organization (UNESCO) guided LDCs toward establishing centralized, national computation centers and agencies as well as centralized documentation and information dissemination services. Centralization as a favored form of information technology transfer, however, is now in decline.

The reasons for the increasing popularity of decentralization as a method of information technology transfer include the increasing affordability of information technology, the buildup of a skilled technical labor force, and a different perspective on managerial practices. For example, shifting budgetary decision making to lower organizational levels promotes decision making closer to the unit affected by the decision. Supposedly, such decision making is improved because participants are more familiar with the problems to be solved. For these reasons, decentralization has become popular as a method of organizational management and information technology transfer.

The trend toward decentralization in the information industry is known as distributed data systems (DDS). This approach allows information to be more accessible to users when dispersed throughout organizations. Convenient multiple access points tend to encourage more usage of the DDS. Distributed data systems can result in more flexible responsive information systems for the benefit of their users (Slamecka 1985:180).

Regional Cooperation

What could become a significant trend affecting the development of LDCs is that of regional cooperation. In the past, the flow of aid to LDCs has generally been north to south. In the so-called Buenos Aires Plan, a call was made for greater south-south dialogue. The objectives of this plan were to promote a more equitable information flow and technical cooperation among LDCs. Thus, LDCs could share their expertise and experience in solving their common problems. The plan resulted in a 1979 study of the feasibility of linking some sixty LDCs via satellite or terrestrially in a computer-operated south-south development network (DEVNET). Although the organization responsible for this network development, the Inter-Press Service (IPS) of Rome, mainly delivers news, their telecommunication setup could also be used for other messaging systems and for the transfer of scientific, technical, and development information among LDCs (Neelameghan & Tocatlian 1985:156).

Organizational Assistance

The trend toward organizational assistance in development is expected to play a most significant role in the future of LDCs. These organizations include nongovernment organizations (NGOs), such as international scientific and professional associations, and private voluntary organizations (PVOs). The NGOs place great emphasis upon the fostering of human resource networks. Such organizations can offer assistance to LDCs for collaborative research, consultation, training programs, newsletters, and computer conferencing. The PVOs emphasize small-scale, people-to-people projects and informal communication modes. Some PVOs have begun to provide training in information processing and microcomputers to aid local institutions (Dosa 1985:150). Slamecka (1985:181) states that the need for access to human assistance, such as that provided by the NGOs and PVOs is of far more importance to LDCs than access to raw data.

An example of organizational assistance is that offered by the National Association of the Partners of the Americas (NAPA), headquartered in Washington, D.C. One NAPA project in which this author participated involved the establishment of a postsecondary technical institute in Ecuador and included NAPA grants for the purchase of microcomputers, software, and computer training for an instructor.

As the current trends of production sharing, decentralization, regional cooperation, and organizational assistance continue to expand their influence, more LDCs can be expected to participate in the information economy. However, despite the availability of assistance from various development sources, transition to the information economy is not likely to be smooth. Many problems surround entrance into the information economy.

Information-Related Problems of LDCs

Although great diversity exists among the LDCs of the world— culturally, politically, economically, socially—all LDCs share problems common to developing nations (Saracevic et al. 1984:193). Some of these problems arise because of the requirements and nature of information technology transfer. Not coincidentally, these same problems also exist in developed nations making the transition to the information economy (Noor 1984:193). What effect information technology transfer has upon a society will depend upon its infrastructure.

Infrastructure refers to an internal framework of support, including all of society's systems (e.g., economic, sociocultural, technical, educational, political, and legal). Nations desiring to enter the information economy need to develop an infrastructure which incorporates information into its every system. According to some developmental specialists, LDCs are said to lack adequate information infrastructures (Lunin and Eres 1985:144; Neelameghan and Tocatlian 1985:157). The inadequacies of the information infrastructures run the gamut from lack of economic and human resources to a lack of the necessary management skills. An examination of the problems confronting LDCs regarding information technology transfer demonstrates the need for LDCs to strengthen their information infrastructures.

Economic Problems

The LDCs generally face staggering balance of payment problems coupled with inflationary economies. Consequently, government allocation of funds for acquisition and maintenance of information technology is severely limited. Although the costs of information technology are receding, they are still high for LDCs proportionally on a per capita basis. Also, in LDCs many pressing national needs such as sanitation and education compete for the scarce financial resources. Therefore, government authorities may be reluctant to divert funding to the collecting, processing, accessing, publishing, delivering, and often translating activities accompanying the use of information technologies (Neelameghan and Tocatlian 1985:161).

Another economic aspect of information technology transfer involves human resources. The labor force in LDCs generally consists of massive numbers of unskilled or minimally skilled workers. Because the chief economic advantage of LDCs has been their supply of cheap labor, LDCs fear that highly automated work environments might cause jobs to disappear and unemployment to rise. In addition, industry demands for workers who must be trained and retrained would tend to drive up the costs of labor. Consequently, automation could have a negative impact upon LDC economic activity. However, the transfer of information technology into LDC economies can stimulate new domestic information industries for hardware and software manufacture, component development, or the information service industry, thus producing new sources of employment (Slamecka 1985:179). Examples of such information industry offshoots were demonstrated in the previous discussions of India and South Korea.

Sociocultural Problems

The impact of information technology upon an LDC's sociocultural system can be viewed both positively and negatively. Previously, note was made of the potential of information technology to change the way people think and solve problems. Also, the role of electronic communication of information in helping to develop a more literate population was noted. News, for example, is now often delivered live via satellite. However, if that information has been distorted because of faulty transmission or errors, whether unintentional or deliberate, so that people are misinformed, the effect of such information would be negative (Neelameghan and Tocatlian 1985:161).

Currently, much debate exists in the international communication industry over such direct broadcast satellites (DBS). These DBS systems beam signals directly to a location despite the absence of a terrestrial communication network. At issue is the right of a nation to require prior consent before DBS signals are transmitted into a particular country. The United Nations General Assembly has adopted a resolution recommending that approval be required by the receiving country. Although not binding, the resolution is an example of the deep concern over the so-called sovereignty issue and could be precedent setting (Bortnick 1985:166).

Leaders of LDCs have a vital interest in the sovereignty issue; they want to insure that their nation's cultural heritage is preserved. Customs and traditions which fuse a society together can disintegrate when new ways take their place. Even basic symbols which distinguish one culture from another, such as dress and language, can be eradicated. Such changes can lead to a weakening of social cohesion and fragmentation of attitudes and motivations (Neelameghan and Tocatlian 1985:160). Extending these concerns to the effects of information technology on a society, O'Connor (1985:330) writes of skeptics who warn of the "hidden social costs of the 'computer revolution.'" Such critics claim that human creativity could be atrophied and customary forms of social interaction might possibly disappear without their replacement by new, equally robust forms. Actually, no one knows what the consequences of information technology will be on the sociocultural system. Only time will tell.

Because of these potentially damaging effects of foreign information technology, whether delivered in the form of an electronic database, foreign-made hardware, or satellite broadcast, all forms of information technology are viewed cautiously and critically by many LDC authorities. Problems of sovereignty as they pertain to information technology transfer will likely increase as nations move closer to Marshall McCluhan's vision of the world as a global village.

Technical Problems

The classic problem associated with any type of technology transfer is whether it is appropriate or inappropriate for a particular LDC. Information technology is no different in this respect from other technologies. Technology is a major determinant of the future, so care needs to be taken that the shape of that future is tailored for the needs of LDCs.

Menou (1984:87) claims that appropriate information technology to fit the particular economic and sociocultural conditions of LDCs has yet to be invented. Furthermore, Menou believes that information activities, products, and services have had little impact upon LDCs because they try to follow the model of industrialized nations. These models, in Menou's opinion, are inappropriate and unrealistic for LDCs.

Concern with the appropriateness of technology arose after years of attempts to apply inappropriate technology to LDCs. Following World War II, when development aid to LDCs began in earnest, technology was applied in the name of modernization, often with unsatisfactory results. Once a development project was completed, the local benefactors were often unable to continue the project because of lack of skill, knowledge, mechanical parts, or simple desire. Consequently, technology needs to be carefully assessed before transfer. If the technology is alien to local reality and experience, its introduction is likely to be met with resistance by its intended beneficiaries (Neelameghan and Tocatlian 1985:160).

A vast number of technical problems are associated with information technology transfer. The areas of communications and computers are exceedingly complex. Frequently, government officials in LDCs are not fully aware of the potential problems attached to information technologies. Rapid advancements in technology mean that even highly trained technicians must constantly update their knowledge and skills. Problems of international standards and compatibility, for example, which once concerned only a few individuals at centralized computer centers, have now become the problems of many more individuals as information technology follows the distributed data system pattern of organization.

Educational Problems

If information technology is to serve LDCs, the academic discipline of information systems needs to be taught in educational institutions. However, there is a shortage of adequate information systems faculty, facilities, and instructional materials in LDCs. Also in scarce supply in LDCs is a manpower base of information systems scientists, documentalists, informations officers, and other information systems specialists. Currently, some LDC information systems professionals receive their education abroad. While some students return to their homeland, others do not, thus contributing to the so-called brain drain. Whether this type of foreign-based education is "appropriate" for LDC students is debatable. However, LDCs generally lack comparable educational programs for the preparation of information systems professionals and technicians. Other LDC information systems specialists receive their education from home-based continuing education programs. The bulk of LDC information systems students, however, receive their education from the schools of library science in their homeland.

The direction and content of information systems education present a national dilemma for LDCs. The decision of where to house such programs within the educational infrastructure is at the heart of the issue. The orientation of library schools for information systems education is to benefit the masses. If information systems education is directed toward development goals, particularly industrialization and modernization, such a redirection could be labeled elitist. The "elitization" of information systems education means that more information would be available for fewer people. The LDCs need to consider both educational outcomes carefully in relation to their most desirable priorities (Saracevic et al. 1984:194–198).

Saracevic et al. (1984:198) question whether the information systems curriculum in LDCs needs a change of direction. They claim a need exists for better relations and more cooperation between the information science educational activities of developed countries and LDCs. Such linkages could lead to faculty exchanges, consortiums, seminars, conferences, and joint research projects. In addition, more public funding needs to be channeled into the basic public educational system to improve mass literacy in reading, writing, and arithmetic. New attention could be focused on computer literacy and computer-assisted instruction as well (Edfelt 1986:200).

Political-Legal Problems

Many political and legal problems surround the introduction of information technology into LDCs. For example, a citizen's right to privacy could be denied by a government's inappropriate use of the storage and retrieval capabilities of information systems (O'Connor 1985:329). Other problems involve copyright protection, contractual relationships, research ethics, and data security (Dosa 1985:149). However, the problem which has captured center stage in the political-legal arena concerns transborder data flow.

Transborder data flow (TBDF) involves the electronic transmission of digitized information across national borders for storage or processing by computer. The LDCs claim a right to decide what information crosses their national boundaries. The TBDF issue involves both tariff and nontariff barriers to the information flow. Some barriers are designed to prevent access of foreign information technology manufacturers to LDC markets. Other obstacles include discriminatory pricing schemes, domestic processing requirements, or adherence to standards inconsistent with a TNC's standards. Perhaps the barrier considered the most objectionable by TNCs is the placement of a so-called custom duty or value-added tax on corporate data processed in an LDC (Bortnick 1985:164–167).

TBDF has become an extremely controversial issue between nations pressing for the free flow of information versus nations demanding their right to sovereignty regarding whatever crosses their borders. Practically speaking, only Brazil has been visibly successful in upholding this sovereignty right through her enactment of the Informatics Law. The TBDF problem is expected to be a major topic of discussion in the next round of global trade talks.

The talks, known as the Uruguay Round, scheduled in 1988, sought to draft trading rules for four sectors which were not covered—agriculture, services, investment, patents, trademarks, and copyrights. The Uruguay Round included discussion of the GATT (General Agreement on Tariffs and Trade) to govern trade in information processing for the first time. The LDCs are expected to use these talks to continue their quest for a "new world information order." By pursuing this quest, LDCs hope to strike a more balanced distribution of power among nations in the global information economy. Whatever the outcome, the Uruguay Round talks are expected to lay the ground rules for a new era of trade relations between industrialized and developing nations (Pine 1986:27).

Management Problems

Information is a resource and, like other resources, needs to be managed. Both public and private enterprises are experiencing difficulties managing information resources in LDCs because the concept is not a common one. For example, while LDCs cite the high cost of obtaining electronic information, available information often goes underutilized. Officials, unaware of existing information services, often introduce new systems which can be counterproductive.

One of the major management problems concerns the sheer volume of data that needs to be processed. For example, at the national level, data need to be collected and managed for national accounts, the population census, natural resources, and the national bibliography. The task of systemizing, updating, and maintaining such a volume of data is very complex. This type of task is bound to become even more difficult as LDCs shift from centralized to decentralized computer centers (Slamecka 1985:180).

Part of the problem surrounding the management of vast quantities of data is that in the past, LDC officials concentrated on acquiring data. In the future, their acquisition of data needs to shift to a more qualitative approach. The LDCs are not alone in dealing with this particular problem. Difficulty in handling quantities of data is referred to as "information overload" and is a problem common to all nations. With so much data available, officials can easily become buried under mounds of computer printouts. At the other extreme, however, data users may locate pertinent information after a search but be unable to acquire the full text of the document because of the lack of document delivery service in LDCs. The use of facsimile equipment could provide a solution for this problem.

Other problems that users of electronic information frequently encounter include difficulties in reading foreign language documents or databases. Even if written in a user's native language, the accessed document may be written in highly technical language or at an extremely high intellectual level, adding yet another barrier to the successful use of information resources. These problems can be very stressful when combined with the often general inexperience of electronic information users (Neelameghan and Tocatlian 1985:160–161). Nevertheless, LDCs need to persist in their efforts to surmount the many problems that information technologies present and continue to incorporate information technologies into every system within their infrastructure.

Information Strategies for Development

Whether the application of information technologies to LDCs might lead to alternate development strategies is open to speculation. Doubt also exists whether such strategies would be appropriate or realistic for LDCs. If the fundamental problem facing LDCs is that of a poor standard of living caused by the low productivity in the economic sector, can information-based development strategies address this central issue? Is the suggestion that LDCs bypass the industrial age and leap directly into the information age utopian or feasible? The question can also be raised regarding the best sequence for applying information technology to development (development-technology or technology-development) (Slamecka 1985:182). An important determinant of how successful LDCs will be in applying information technology to development will be their ability to engage in strategic planning.

Strategic Planning

Information strategies should not be developed in isolation but in conjunction with the economic, sociocultural, technical, educational, political-legal, and management systems operating in any particular LDC. One strategy will not suffice, as LDCs are in various stages of development regarding information technology; for example, South Korea versus certain African nations.

In addition, information strategies for development need to be initiated by the LDCs. To wait for planning by external governments, agencies, and organizations would be bad strategy. While external sources can offer assistance, the information strategy needs to originate within the LDCs themselves. The strategy should not be limited in level but include all levels—international, national, regional, and local. All sectors need to be involved in information strategy development—government units, agencies, institutions, organizations, and public and private enterprises.

Information strategies should involve a phased implementation plan relevant to the needs of a particular LDC and adapted to its stage of information technology development. Each planning group should develop goals and objectives, adopt a budget, assess current conditions, generate options, assign priorities, establish targets, train required personnel, implement the plan, and regularly evaluate, update, and/or modify the plan. Accountability for performance needs to be integrated into each part of the overall strategy (Noor 1984:193–199). Along with information strategies, LDCs need to develop information policies. Planning will be to no avail if some guidelines are not developed.

Information Policies

Information policies need to be realistic, mindful of the goals and resources of the LDCs, and flexible because of the dynamic nature of information technology. For example, some LDCs, after assessment, might decide to enter the computer manufacturing industry, while other LDCs might decide to enter the information services industry. The point is, an LDC needs to determine for itself what its goals and objectives should be in regard to the application of information technology to its development process. The following is a list of policy objectives for LDCs suggested by Edfelt (1986:196); however, they may not be appropriate for all LDCs: 1. Maximize information resources. 2. Achieve national control over the production of information resources: 3. Enable society to have universal access to information resources. 4. Enhance the cultural/political environment, and strengthen national identity and sovereignty.

Although the importance of developing information strategies and policies cannot be denied, their successful implementation will depend upon the quality of information available to development planners. Planning needs to be based upon adequate, accurate, and timely information, yet this very basic resource may not always be available.

Research

Research in international information activity is extremely scarce due to the lack of a conceptual framework, information theories, and data (Dosa 1985:146; Menou 1985:169). The lack of data is a serious problem because of its relevance in carrying out activities in the information age. Existing data are deficient on many scores—inaccurate, incomplete, irregularly collected, and unstandardized—making comparisons of international information activity extremely difficult. The serious implication of this lack of research is well expressed by Menou (1985:175). He warns that comprehensive and continuous research is needed to enable nations to understand and control the information society before it inflicts damages as did the industrialized society.

Menou (1985:175) suggests several actions which need to be taken to generate information research: 1. An international effort needs to be established to define data categories and develop information indicators and indexes for use at local, national and international levels. 2. An international effort needs to be aimed at development of the systematic collection of data on a regular basis using a database involving relevant socio-economic indicators. 3. Standing committees need to be established for researchers to facilitate the development of compatible methodologies and cooperative endeavors.

In addition, foundations and other grant sources could make more funding available to encourage researchers to study international information activity. The results of such research could be used by LDCs in formulating their information strategies and policies.

8

The Transferability of Management Technology to Third World Countries

Shah M. Mehrabi

This chapter examines the transfer of a particular technology—the technology of getting results through organization; that is, management technology. The successful transfer of appropriate management technology can be important in improving the capacity of Third World managers to respond to the multitude of institutional demands which accompany the process of economic development.

The Growing Management Gap

In a great many instances, the inability of a less-developed country (LDC) to achieve expected goals is partly due to the fact that institutional demands have outpaced the capacity of civil servants and business managers to cope with them. The commodity in this case is "management capacity," the ability of managers to mobilize scarce resources to achieve organizational goals. The result is a growing management gap between demands and their fulfillment.

Management, according to Jedlicka (1982:11–15), is the major variable which affects the technology transfer process negatively or positively. Experience has shown that the failing dimension in technology transfer efforts has been the management of the process. That failure ranges from bad planning to improper training of middle-level people to a formal style of conduct between representatives and clients which too often results in rejection of any technology offered, regardless of suitability.

Transfer studies over the past three decades, Jedlicka reports, indicate failure often occurs because clients were not effectively involved in the transfer process. The primary reason for this lack of involvement concerns the philosophy of the transfer agency. If the agency assumes that clients do not have decision-making skills or cannot be provided skills to plan and implement a specific transfer strategy, then the result will likely be a self-fulfilling prophecy.

One factor influencing the growing management gap is the phenomenal growth in the number, size, and complexity of Third World institutions. In the public sector, growing institutional demands are caused not only by the fact that the population of many LDCs has been growing at rates exceeding those experienced by the industrialized nations during comparable periods of industrial expansion, but also by the fact that the scope of public sector activities has been rapidly expanding. These phenomena are exacerbated by the high degree of urbanization in LDCs.

Larger Organizational Units

According to Pratten (1971) and Bryce (1960), in many Third World countries, the public sector is not only responsible for traditional public sector activities in a Western capitalist sense but for an expanding range of commercial, financial, and manufacturing activities as well. Historically, production processes in these and other activities have tended to progress toward larger organizational units due to economies of scale and available technologies.

As a result of these factors, economic growth has been accompanied by organizations of increasing size, complexity, and an ever-expanding need on the part of management for greater control and coordination. In the public sector, development goals and programs must be prioritized and multitudes of sectorial inputs and outputs effectively balanced. In the private sector, functional goals must be coordinated and monitored in a timely manner.

While the situation certainly varies from country to country and within country from sector to sector, it does appear that complex organizations of greater size and responsibility are proliferating in the Third World and that they will play an increasingly larger role in the process of economic development. As a result, the expanding demands placed on Third World managers are sufficient to strain the capacity of even the most effective managers in the industrialized nations.

Lagging Management Development

Rapidly expanding institutional requirements, however, only represent the demand side of the equation. The supply side is dictated by the lagging of Third World management development and innovation. The rapid growth of institutional needs has simply outpaced the capacity of many

Third World managers to create, borrow, or adapt suitable organizational technology.

This lapping innovativeness in LDC management is no simple matter to analyze. Indeed, it appears to be the result of a confusing web of historical, economic, and cultural factors. For example, it has been argued by Weidner (1964) that in many LDCs the administrative systems left behind by European colonial powers were not especially geared to fostering rapid organizational change. In addition, many managers in LDCs are not adequately trained in the skills which might allow them to control and direct large complex organizations. In many instances, these managers are appointed for their functional skills (e.g., physicians, lawyers, and engineers) rather than for their management capabilities.

Similarly, where education for public and business administration is available, curricula tend to emphasize theory rather than techniques of problem solving. These problems are further compounded by bureaucratic methods which unduly emphasize formalistic approaches not responsive to organizational goals.

Finally, according to Phatak (1983), myriad cultural variables influence management innovativeness through the established set of civic values, methods of social interaction, and attitudes toward certain types of work.

The end result of these influences is the maintenance of administrative systems which fail to emphasize the processes of goal specification and attainment. As a result, the institutional rewards for innovation and problem solving are insufficient to warrant the required effort on the part of local managers. The management gap continues to grow, and critical needs go unmet.

Emphasis in the literature has been placed on the general notion that transfer of management techniques is necessary to bridge the "effectiveness gap" between industrialized and LDCs. Ghymn and Evans (1979: 123–129) concede that there may be some validity to such a generalization; however, as a practical matter, cross-cultural transferability from a developed country to an LDC should not be assumed.

Technology Accessibility

It can be reasonably argued that management techniques are capable of assisting Third World managers to utilize scarce institutional resources effectively, including themselves. The question is, how available and how accessible are these techniques? They are generally available but not always accessible.

Most process- and person-embodied techniques can be theoretically acquired simply by purchasing one or more management handbooks. The majority of such techniques are not governed by patents or royalty agreements. Ample literature is available regarding practical problems or implementation. In reality, however, their true accessibility is limited by the fact that they are difficult to implement without formal training and on-the-job experience.

Product-embodied technology, on the other hand, may be more accessible. The technology used to produce management-related devices is highly competitive and generally is governed by patents, royalties, and foreign supervision and control. However the use of this technology in its "finished product" form is actively encouraged by equipment manufacturers. According to Garland and Farmer (1986), accessibility is limited by financial resources.

Inadequate Communication of Innovations

The problem of technology accessibility is generally not a matter of the existence of appropriate management tools; rather, the problem is one of adequate communication. In industrialized nations, management innovations are communicated through a wide array of professional journals, conferences, commercial training programs, and promotional literature of one sort or another. Indeed, managers find themselves literally inundated by the constant flow of program announcements and publication lists.

This process of continually announced innovation does not exist, or exists only weakly, in most LDCs. The Third World manager generally has received little if any formal management training, and he does little if any managerial reading. His sense of professional identity is more likely to be tied to the agency or company in which he is employed than to the task he performs.

Where functional identity does exist, it is likely to be tied to the type of academic training received (e.g., agriculture, engineering, law, economics) rather than his current position. Membership in professional associations tends to be related to these disciplines rather than to specific business or public administration activities.

Where management-related associations do exist, their role in actively communicating management innovations is restricted by limited membership and even more limited financial resources. Where university programs in business and public administration play an active part in training and publication, these channels tend to emphasize theoretical issues over innovative adaptation of available technology to day-to-day problems. The one area where communication of management innovation appears strongest is in the area of product-embodied technology. In this instance, the desire to sell is the prime motivation. The degree of active promotion in this area depends in large part on the perceptions of potential markets by producers.

In a growing number of instances, promotion of management-related equipment in LDCs is being seen as an integral part of world markets by multinational firms. Japanese, European, and American computer salespeople are becoming a common sight in some Third World capitals. There is some recognition, however, that such modernization may result in acquisition of inappropriate gadgets using scarce funds. Nevertheless, vendors of management-related equipment can play an important role in introducing new solutions to traditional problems.

It would appear that modern management technology certainly is available but not necessarily accessible to many Third World managers. Now let us examine past and current attempts to improve this situation.

Transfer Agents and Programs

According to Sequeira (1979), the process of transferring management technology can be considered as either autonomous or induced. *Autonomous* technology transfer refers to those activities which occur as a natural result of international trade and foreign investment. The transfer agents involved in this process during the late 1950s through the mid–1960s were generally multinational companies. The most recent wave (which is still ongoing) consists of the attempt to transfer the technology of U.S. business management to specific Third World institutions.

Colonial Administrators

The transfer agents involved in the first wave were primarily colonial administrators. The transfer process they employed was less one of management development than bureaucratic transplantation. In spite of the darker side of colonial rule, the results of this first wave were rather remarkable. The major drawback was that the resulting systems were primarily designed to administer policies and programs created by the colonial authorities rather than to design and develop management capacity to respond to local needs. As a result, the colonial legacy generally was one of lagging management innovation.

Agencies and Institutions

The transfer agents involved in the second wave sought to overcome this legacy through formal education and training in modern public administration. Throughout the 1950s and 1960s, training in public administration was big business. During this period a number of agencies and institutions were involved in the effort.

The second wave of technology transfer began to fade in importance during the mid–1960s. The transition was nearly complete by the early 1970s. By this time, the annual rate of public assistance provided by the U.S. Agency for International Development was less than half the average for the period 1955–1963. The reason for this decline according to Siffin (1976: 27–42), was the growing conviction that the key to development was not so much the general improvement of public administration as the fostering of indigenous economic growth through effective domestic and international policies.

Business Management Models

The third and present wave of technology transfer involves many of the same agents involved in the second wave. The most noticeable in terms of expenditure appear to be the United States Aid for International Development (USAID) and the United Nations Development Program (UNDP). In both these cases, the emphasis has swung from national training and civil service reform to the implementation of business management models within specifically targeted institutions. This is not to say that assistance is not provided to national training institutes or civil service organizations, especially by the UNDP, but merely that the emphasis appears to have moved in another direction.

Another group of transfer agents consists of the World Bank and the various regional development banks. In this group, the emphasis is placed on management and organization reviews intended to assess the institutional viability of prospective borrowers. These reviews are generally performed by private consultants as a condition for loan approval. The World Bank encourages the employment of consulting firms of the borrower's nationality and generally leaves to the borrower the responsibility for selection, administration, and supervision of the consultant. In certain cases, these reviews may lead to follow-up efforts aimed at organizational improvement.

From this review of past efforts at induced management technology transfer, it can be seen that management tools and techniques have been actively exported to the Third World via international lending agencies, voluntary organizations, aid institutions, and providers of management-related services. Such technology transfers, however, are likely to be a poor substitute for the continuous flow of information regarding management innovation which takes place in industrialized nations via professional associations, conferences, and publications.

The induced export of management technology is primarily temporary project-specific action rather than an intrinsic and continuous process. In addition, the adaptation of technologies principally designed to meet the needs of industrialized nations is certainly not as satisfactory as the creation of management innovation and communication capabilities within LDCs themselves. Nevertheless, until such indigenous capability reaches maturity, induced technology transfers are likely to provide valuable assistance. Technology transfer activity, of course, is not synonymous with actual technology transfer. The potential transferability of management technology is a matter for dispute.

Problems of Transferability

Historically, it is clear that a great deal of transfer activity has taken place. It is less clear how much actual technology transfer has occurred. The results are mixed. In certain instances, success has been significant and of continuing impact. In others, the only constructive output appears to have been the provision of temporary employment (and a few interesting experiences) for a number of consultants, professors, and agency representatives.

Some of the more obvious problems of transferability can be grouped under the following headings: (a) conflicting value systems, (b) inappropriate transfer agents, (c) inappropriate use of transfer mechanisms, and (d) unrealistic expectations.

Conflicting Value Systems

Eager to spread their particular management philosophy, many technical assistance experts fail to be aware of the normative foundations of Western management technology. Even relatively value-free management techniques are not altogether value-free. Rather, many are biased toward such implicit values as rewarded achievement, wage motivation, individual accountability, and productive efficiency. To an unknown degree, Ronen (1986) concedes that these values may be responsible for the past success of Western management methods. The problem is that these values are not universally shared.

According to Riggs (1964), social prestige systems in LDCs often lean toward "ascriptive" rather than achievement-related variables. Where the former are predominant, managers are rewarded according to who they are rather than what they accomplish. In these cases family position, educational level, organizational rank, and personal contacts are more important than results. Much of a manager's energy is expended in building systems of friends and supporters—often via the judicious distribution of organizational rewards. In certain instances, the manager may also be called upon to favor those with ascriptive characteristics similar to his own. These may be members of the manager's family, tribe, or religious affiliation. Deihl (1981:12–16) asserts that employment and promotion based on ascriptive characteristics may be considered not only acceptable but morally commendable.

Similarly, the Western belief in wage motivation may run counter to local economic realities. The most obvious difficulty is the scarcity of available funds due to low productivity or due to government attempts to hold the lid on wage-push inflation. In these cases, however, incremental wage and bonus schemes can still be effective. The more intractable cases occur when wages represent only part of the individual's income. Professional-level positions in government and business are often seen as respectable occupations by members of the elite class whose main income flow is derived elsewhere. In still other instances, public sector and private sector employees hold multiple jobs in an effort to increase earnings. Where the second job provides the main source of income, wage policies in the first location of employment tend to be less effective.

Robinson (1984) asserts that the American business model's preoccupation with accountability has also been found to run counter to certain values regarding appropriate modes of decision making. An example is the consultation decision-making process of *ringi-sei* practiced in Japan. This decision-making process acts to diffuse rather than pinpoint responsibility. By the time a decision is reached, not one man but all those who took part in the process have become responsible for the decision. According to Stifel, Coleman, and Black (1977), responsibility has been diffused, and all are committed to success. In this environment, Schnitzer, Liebrenz, and Kubi (1985) concede that strict accountability in the traditional model of business organization is not considered desirable by business and public executives.

A final example of conflicting values concerns the Western ideal of efficiency. This is generally construed to mean maximum output per unit of labor. It has been argued by Weber (1958) that this value is a direct descendant of the Protestant work ethic. In certain instances this work ethic may conflict with the local leisure ethic. To some extent, the local preference for leisure may be influenced by poor wages, undesirable working conditions, and dietary and other health disorders. However, even controlling for these effects, it appears that the value of nonwork time is more highly regarded in certain cultures than is generally assumed by Western models.

What is important with regard to each of these value systems is that transfer agents must be aware of them as well as the cultural and economic biases inherent in their solutions to management problems. Only in this manner can management technologies truly be tailored to local conditions. Where recognition and adaptation do not take place, transfer agents are likely to develop elaborate programs which fall into disuse once the technical assistance team has departed.

Inappropriate Transfer Agents

In spite of the sincere efforts by international and domestic organizations in selecting transfer agents, the best are not always selected. Whenever much must be done in little time under great uncertainty, mistakes are inevitably made. Consulting firms and universities are asked to perform tasks which are marginally within their scope of expertise. Many find it difficult to decline. In addition, the choice of individual members of the technical assistance teams themselves has a major impact on the potential for the successful transfer of management technology. Finding qualified individuals is no easy matter. The exigencies of getting the job done do not always allow for getting it done with the right staff. A Latin American observer (Weidner 1964), for example, characterized the staff of one UN effort as "including about 20 percent who were successful, 40 percent 'so-so,' 20 percent poor and 20 percent terrible."

Weidner (1964), reviewing an American university program in the Far East, commented that there should be a higher average quality in the group. There are a few outstanding persons, but there are also a few ringers. It takes only a few of the latter to flavor the prevailing opinion about the entire group. It would be better to leave them home and have a vacancy in the organization chart.

As a result of errors of this sort, international and domestic organizations are becoming more careful in selecting transfer institutions and the specific members proposed for each project. However, as long as environments and individuals remain largely unpredictable, problems of this sort will continue to be part of the transfer process.

Inappropriate Use of Transfer Mechanisms

The successful transfer of management technology has also been hindered by the use of inappropriate transfer mechanisms. By these we mean the institutional arrangements designed to convey information and knowledge. Some of the more common problems according to Globerson (1978:48–62) include inadequate executive support, inappropriate selection or use of counterparts, overemphasis on formal training, and inadequate provision for follow-through.

What has often not been recognized is that the real work begins after the reports and recommendations have been completed. Successful implementation is the acid test of management technology transfer, not the existence of impressive feasibility studies or well-designed recommendations, no matter how detailed. The problem, however, is that studies and recommendations can be prepared within a reasonably short time frame, usually one year or less. Implementation, on the other hand, is open-ended. Depending upon the type of activity involved, successful implementation may take one to five years, sometimes longer.

Unrealistic Expectations

A final factor which can be said to contribute to the poor performance of previous attempts at transferring management technology is the existence of unrealistic expectations. The first of these is excessive time optimism. This tends to place an undue burden on the task team and counterparts, and reduce the potential for lasting change.

Secondly, there is an unrealistic tendency to view host-institution executives as enlightened and benevolent leaders of economic development. Merely because an executive is eager to receive technical assistance does not necessarily mean she is eager to introduce change.

Thirdly, technical assistance teams tend to believe what they are told by host-institution representatives. In many cases, however, what they are told does not reflect reality. This is not to imply that host-institution representatives are misrepresenting the facts. Rather, technical assistance teams, according to Thurber and Graham (1973), are often unfamiliar with the degree of formalism found in Third World institutions. Hardiman and Midgely (1978:32–41) state that this problem may be characterized as one in which formal goals, policies, and procedures are not put into practice. Although this problem occurs in industrialized nations as well, the extent of such formalism is not as germane.

The problem for technology transfer occurs when institutional formalism is overlooked. In such cases, the technical assistance team may spend a good deal of time revising current procedures (which were never followed) and preparing detailed programs which (like their predecessors') will be reviewed by executive committees, issued over the signature of the top executive, and never implemented.

When considering the various obstacles to successful transfer of management technology, it is not surprising that success has often been limited. Rather, it is remarkable that it takes place at all. The problems involved in selecting appropriate transfer agents, overcoming inherent biases and conflicting value systems, avoiding mistakes in the use of transfer mechanisms and in readjusting unrealistic expectations may appear insurmountable. Luckily, these problems do not all pertain to each project (although some observers might dispute this). Management technology is indeed transferable, but the difficulty of the task must not be underestimated.

Is Modern Management Technology Appropriate?

Thus far we have argued that a management gap exists in much of the Third World, that management techniques are available which are able to improve the effectiveness of Third World managers, and that much of this technology is transferable—albeit with difficulty. The question we now turn to is whether the use of modern technology is an appropriate method of dealing with Third World institutional problems.

In recent years, there has been growing concern regarding the second generation effects of technology transfer. These include dualism, urban unemployment, and technological dependency. While much of the current literature directly concerns methods of physical production, the arguments can be extended to management technology as well.

Effect on Employment

According to Stewart (1979), advanced technologies are often detrimental to developing countries due to their inherent bias toward capital-intensive methods of production. Stewart argues that modern technologies were designed in response to high income demand and the relative factor endowments (land, labor, and capital) of the industrialized nations. Their transfer to LDCs, which do not share these same relative endowments, necessarily leads to distortions in local factor utilization. Among the results of these distortions is widespread unemployment.

The problem is that modern technologies are often superior to traditional methods insofar as they are able to generate a given level of output using less labor and less capital. Since these technologies are used to produce goods for a given level of demand, the degree of employment generated is less than would have occurred had simpler or more traditional methods been used. While superior technologies are necessarily the most appropriate given the shortage of capital resources in most LDCs, Stewart argues that the products produced by this technology may have superfluous characteristics which exceed the needs of LDCs. The LDCs may be paying for these superfluous characteristics by unnecessarily high unemployment. The proposed solutions to these problems are the redesign of product characteristics to make them fit local needs and the reduction of scales of production so that more labor-intensive techniques are once again advantageous.

When extended to management technology, this argument suggests that the methods of management which result from the adoption of modern management technology may exceed what local conditions require and that the capital (financial and human) invested in this technology might better be used to promote more widespread use of basic management tools such as simple accounting manuals for cooperatives. In addition, there is a presumption that modern management technology is designed to complement organization and production systems which are themselves inappropriate to the needs of LDCs. These systems should be changed rather than propped up by modern management technology.

Finally, Stewart suggests that the adoption of inappropriate production processes and accompanying organizational structures may have unnecessarily created the existing management gap. She implies that the use of more appropriate organizational structures would reduce the need for managerial and entrepreneurial talent and thereby reduce the need for imported managers and management technology.

Labor Saving versus Resource Saving

The critical question in this debate is whether or not modern management techniques are principally labor saving or resource saving in their impact. To the degree that they are labor saving, adoption of these techniques may contribute to the unemployment problem. On the other hand, to the degree they are resource saving—i.e., capable of maximizing the productivity of land, capital, and perhaps even scarce management skills—they will improve overall factor utilization and increase national welfare.

Although there has been no empirical study of the labor impact of modern management technology in less-developed countries, there is reason to believe that the resource-saving emphasis is likely to be greater than the labor-saving emphasis. In the majority of technology transfer engagements, it can be argued, increases in management productivity have allowed the existing number of managers to control organizational resources better. More importantly, this additional control could not have been obtained simply by increasing the number of managers or subordinates. The introduction of modern management technology, therefore, may not result in higher unemployment but in increased managerial effectiveness.

Relevance of Organization Size

There is an additional aspect of the Stewart argument which merits consideration. This is the accusation that modern management techniques are necessarily tied to large-scale organizations which in themselves are inappropriate to Third World needs. This is an important point, for it must certainly be admitted that many management tools are designed to solve problems of large-scale organizations. In response to this criticism, would one agree that in certain instances the size of public and private institutions is inappropriate and that a move toward intermediate-size institutions is desirable? Johnson and Mellor (1961:44–52) argue that this certainly appears to be the case in relation to agricultural credit and extension services.

However, not all Third World needs are best served by intermediate-size institutions. It is difficult to conceive of efficient small-scale telecommunication networks, hydroelectric programs, or public water and sanitation systems. Even where operational units might be of intermediate dimensions, the problems of central coordination and allocation will inevitably dictate the need for large-scale approaches to comprehensive planning and budgeting. What must be acknowledged by adherents of the small-is-beautiful approach is that LDCs do not face the problems encountered by the industrialized nations at the turn of the century. The current size of Third World populations and the extent of public service and production are vast in comparison. Telephone companies do not serve hundreds but hundreds of thousands. Public utility customers do not number in the thousands but millions. If the need of these organizations cannot be met through efficient decomposition, they then are logical candidates for techniques designed to serve the needs of bigness.

In general, the instances in which modern management technology is distorting appear to be the exception rather than the rule. However, this is based on the assumption that appropriate techniques will be applied to appropriate needs. There is always a danger when introducing modern technology that certain techniques will be adopted because of their modernness rather than their effective contribution. In these cases, the funds could best be applied elsewhere.

9

Implementation of High Technology and Its Effect on Third World Countries

Shah M. Mehrabi

Introduction

Slowly emerging throughout industrialized societies is something akin to another Industrial Revolution. A technological development came about in the early 1960s that has had and will continue to have a greater effect on wages and structural employment of labor in the future. This development was the result of research involving the use of mechanical arms. The success of this has led to research in other areas of robotics and finally the use of robots in some industrial environments. They are now employed in several different types of production processes. The extent of wage and employment effects is still not known, although a study by Engleberger (1980) indicates that facts are beginning to trickle in.

At present, there are approximately 15,000 robots and 20 million laborers employed in manufacturing in the United States. Entrepreneurs in the United States are slow to invest in robots because of the perceived accompanying risk, i.e., breakdowns and the attitudes of the unions. Nevertheless, they have at their fingertips the technology to reduce some of these risks.

Further increases in technological knowledge will inevitably increase the robot population throughout the world, including Canada, and Mexico and other Third World countries. Currently, most of the robot population is found in Japan. The Japanese are experimenting with robots to save human lives, create a higher standard of living, and more importantly provide profits to the entrepreneur. In the United States, John Deere is experimenting with robots for materials handling and enjoying considerable success in this endeavor.

The structural unemployment and concomitant sociological problems that may follow the implementation of high technology such as robotics need to be considered. This paper explores some of the answers to these disturbing questions. From a purely economic point of view, robots are substituted for labor for the attendant savings that accrue to a firm. This is the positive economic approach, but human issues are sought in the justification of robots, which involves normative economics.

The aim of industrialized societies must be carried out with some degree of prudence while coinciding with economic growth and profits. While reducing structural unemployment through programs to retrain their human resources, industrialized societies can maintain with some difficulty a semblance of economic stability in their countries.

Positive Economic Approach

If a firm is faced with a decision on what resources will be used to produce some output, the cheaper resources are chosen as long as they can be used in the desired production. When the resource price ratio is changed, the process is repeated. This is referred to as *substitution*. The goal is to maximize savings to the firm as a result of this substitution. Indeed, profits are a motivating factor to business, and the success of robots in some types of employment has led to their substitution for labor. This substitution has been brought about in part by the loss of productivity in subhuman work required in some types of employment. Some examples are work involving excessive heat, shock, vibration, noise, liquid sprays, and gases.

The viability of robots for industrial use depends upon their cost and productivity relative to labor. Indeed, economics is the preponderant motive in robotics. When a business invests in robots, it will consider a number of things. Among the more important ones are the payback period, the rate of return on investment, productivity, and performance. The following are brief examples and discussions, and can be expanded, but not within the purview of this chapter.

Payback Period

Why the implementation of high technology such as robots? A look at Table 9.1 will help to answer this question. A robot's lifespan may be estimated to be about seven to nine years; therefore, one can assume that the average life of a robot is eight years, and this value is used for calculations concerning depreciation. Following Example 1 (Table 9.1), the payoff period is 2.26 years. By doubling the shift time, the payoff period is reduced to 1.13 years. The shorter the payoff time, the more desirable the high technology, and the company accountants are pleased. The importance of this example can be seen in the total annual labor savings through the substitution of a robot. Employing the robot for two shifts gives an approximate payback period of 1.13 years, which leaves 6.87 years clear for the robot to contribute to profits with no capital outlay other than maintenance and repair.

TABLE 9.1: Examples Justifying the Use of High Technology

Typical Inputs:

I = $48,000
L =$12.00 per hour
E = $ 1.40 per hour
    Assume 250 working days a year, robot replaces one human operator

Annual depreciation,	Return on	$= \dfrac{S \times 100}{I}$
eight years	investment (ROI)	
straight line =$6,000		
Annual savings		
resulting from robot =$S		

P = Payback period in years
I = Total investment of robot and accessories
L = Total annual labor savings
E = Annual expense of robot upkeep

Typical examples of payback period of robot installments:

    Formula: $P = \dfrac{I}{L-E}$

Example 1: One Shift $\dfrac{48,000}{12(250 \times 8) - 1.4(250 \times 8)}$ =2.26

Example 2: Two Shift $\dfrac{48,000}{12(250 \times 16) - 1.4(250 \times 16)}$ =1.13

Return on Investment Example:

	8 hours per day operation	16 hours per day operation
A. Robot costs		
Annual depreciation	$ 6,000	$ 6,000
Annual upkeep	2,800	5,600
Total annual robot costs	$ 8,800	$11,600
B. Corresponding labor costs		
Wages, including fringes, at:		
$10 per hour	$20,000	$40,000
$12 per hour	24,000	48,000
C. Annual cost savings and ROI		
$10 per hour	$11,200	$28,400
	ROI=23.3%	ROI=59.7%
$12 per hour	$15,200	$36,400
	ROI=31.7%	ROI=75.8%

Rate of Return on Investment

Robots may cost from $10,000 to $150,000, depending upon the level of sophistication. Using the same figures from the payoff period in Table 9.1 (investment in robot and accessories is $48,000, and depreciation is straight line over 8 years), the rate of return on investment is shown for an eight- and sixteen-hour day in Table 9.1.

The figures show that the rate of return on investment is quite high from substitution. Consider labor costs of $10 and $12 per hour, which include fringe benefits. A single shift results in a rate of return of 23.3 percent and 31.7 percent, respectively. Sixteen hours yields a rate of return of 59.7 percent and a hefty 75.8 percent through cost savings by the substitution of a robot for labor. There are some firms such as Chrysler and Du-Well Products that utilize robots for triple shifts and appreciable cost savings.

Productivity

Labor is not so vociferous when robots are implemented where conditions are not conducive to continued safe human utilization. One area of production that qualifies with this condition is taken to demonstrate increases in productivity from the substitution of robots for labor. This is in die casting, where hazardous working conditions make the substitution more palatable to labor. Weisel (1981:134) notes that in die casting, robots are substituted for labor, revealing an approximate increase in production of 30 percent. Translated into monetary terms, this may eliminate the need to buy an additional robot and may allow a cutback on overtime or additional shifts for labor. In some plants, robots continue to work on extra shifts without human intervention.

Performance/Quality

Sophisticated quality control methods are being used in the manufacture of automobiles worldwide. Robots do not experience human lassitudes with regard to production. For example, the latter has several breaks during the workday as well as experiencing monotony and diminishing returns, while there are no such problems with the former.

A *Newsweek* (1983:18–19) study shows that robots can be more accurate than labor; e.g., robots knit the seams on a rear axle support into virtual seamlessness to within an alignment of less than 3/100 inch on BMW automobiles.

It is apparent that for both quality and performance, the robot outstrips the human. Contrary to popular belief, the robot in general is *not* faster than the human. The robot's strong suit is repeatability, under regular or adverse conditions, and its inexorability—i.e., the fact that it keeps on doing the same thing through coffee breaks and vacations. The final result is that the number of *good* units of output is usually larger with robots than with humans, other conditions being equal. So far there are certain advantages to robot substitution: 1. Increased production; 2. Reduced scrap and better quality (particularly in die casting); 3. Safety; 4. Payback period; 5. Return on investment; 6. Higher profits; 7. Better performance.

Normative Economic Approach

Probably one of the most important questions to be answered is how the substitution of robots will affect employment. The answer to this question becomes even more difficult when one considers that there is no history of sociological cost due to the substitution of robots for labor.

Looking at the explicit side of this study, it may be concluded that gains in productivity are good. There can be a net employment impact because the robotics industry employs labor as well as labor working as suppliers to this relatively new industry. Indeed there will be costs, but the benefits will outweigh those costs.

An equally important question to answer is: Will current technology support population growth, say, for the United States? The answer is emphatically no. Weisel (1981:134) estimated that we are experiencing an annual growth rate of robot implementation of 35 percent. This translates to an increase in population by some forty thousand robots per year by 1990. Forty thousand robots entering the work force per year represents about .06 of the blue collar workers per year, and this figure is not a disruptive one. Robots will enter the work force gradually. There will be no massive substitution that would be socially unacceptable.

It is in the area of human justification of robots that managers have the most difficulty. In the end, of course, all of human justification eventually comes back to the "bottom line"—the dollar. There is no doubt that robots will displace human workers. Exactly how many is a matter of conjecture. If a worker is displaced by a robot, what will happen to her? Some possibilities:

• The worker can actually be displaced; i.e., fired or laid off. If the worker takes a different job, there must have been an opening that someone was trying to fill. If so, was the original layoff of the worker a detriment to the economy?

• Suppose the worker gets a better job, one that requires a higher level of training or aptitude. The worker has had his employment upgraded, and the economy is better off than before, as is the worker. Training brought him up to a new skill level.

• It may also be true that the employee's company feels a responsibility to retain the employee within the company.
• Someone had to build the robot that replaced the worker. In addition, the building of the newly sold robot brings with it increased business for those companies that build the parts used to construct the robot.

As noted elsewhere in this chapter, the total number of people displaced by robots will be relatively small. When these numbers are discounted by the number of people hired for the robot industry's newly found prosperity, plus supporting company's new employees, new marketing representatives and so on, it is doubtful that the final number of people employed in the industry will be any smaller, and it is most likely that it will be larger.

Relevance of Robots in Developing Countries: General Observations

The issues raised in this paper have only scratched the surface of those that must be addressed on a global basis. In this paper, there is some discussion of the type of automation that is currently available in the United States and other industrialized manufacturers. Some simple and generally accepted measures to compare one small part of automation—the robot—to human workers doing the same job are also discussed. In general, they showed that the robot was very cost-effective as far as the economic comparisons are concerned. There are, however, other concerns.

We believe that the aims of developing countries must be carried out with some degree of prudence. For long-run survival of the economy, businesses must make a profit. Even in socialistic societies, there must be a "surplus" for the betterment of the populace. In order to take advantage of the technology available, this surplus in the form of economic growth must be balanced by a reduction of unemployment with programs to retain the human resources while maintaining some semblance of economic stability—a difficult task indeed. Perhaps one can look at Japan and consider its experience with an aging work force, a large-scale substitution of machines for labor, a forced march to keep innovation progressing fast enough to keep the economy expanding rapidly, and a breakdown of "traditional" values to keep ahead of structural unemployment.

Even with a lack of more definitive data, we believe we should continue with an air of optimism. The building of the newly sold automated equipment brings with it increased business for those companies that make the parts used to construct the machines and also increases the number of people hired for the robot industry's newly found prosperity.

More importantly, new industries in developing countries must compete with the products of developed nations, and implementation of robots offers substantial dynamic benefits that are important for changing the traditional structure of the developing economy.

10

Rootfuel: A New Strategic Approach to the Fuelwood Scarcity Problem in Third World Drylands

Wayne G. Bragg and Eugene B. Shultz, Jr.

Introduction

The fuelwood crisis in Third World drylands is serious and widely discussed, but only two solutions, reforestation and high-efficiency cookstoves, receive much attention. Neither has been very successful as a strategy for dealing with the fuelwood problem. Trees are hard to establish in arid lands, and reforestation is generally expensive, so rates of planting lag far behind rates of consumption in the major dry regions of the Third World. Efficient cookstoves often cost more than most people can afford, so rates of adoption are low.

We suggest that the solution to the fuelwood scarcity problem is not necessarily to grow more wood or to burn it more efficiently. Other materials can be grown and used as fuel; many will outproduce wood. Our own search for a practical alternative fuel crop has turned to dried non-woody roots of fast-growing annual plants of the family *Cucurbitaceae* (squash, gourds, pumpkins) found in all continents. In hot, dry lands, many species of this family will rapidly develop large taproots for the storage of water. We have discovered that the roots of one such dryland cucurbit, *Cucurbita foetidissima* HBK (called *calabacilla loca* in Mexico), are produced in abundance. The roots can be harvested easily by hand, cut easily when fresh, then sun-dried to give a hard combustible that we call *rootfuel*.

A test of this innovation has recently been carried out in rural Mexico with encouraging results. Rootfuel burns more slowly than wood, corn-stalks, and animal dung, and produces more coals. We found that these superior combustion characteristics were readily noted and appreciated. Our greatest concern, that the rootfuel smoke would impart an unacceptable flavor to food, did not materialize as a problem. Although more field studies must be carried out before rootfuel can be identified as a successful alternative to woodfuel, it appears that significant initial technical hurdles have been overcome. It is important now to examine the strategic aspects of application of rootfuel in Third World drylands, the subject of this chapter.

The Fuelwood Scarcity Problem in Third World Aridlands

The rate of desertification is increasing with the destruction of the natural tree cover, due to many factors, not the least of which is the pressure of population, which puts heavy strains on ecosystems. The greatest single demand for wood in aridlands is probably for fuel for the traditional three-stone fireplaces still predominant for cooking in the poorer regions of the world. Peasants do not cut trees out of malice but out of necessity; their food must be cooked to be digestible. They do not have the money to buy the petroleum-based fuels and stoves available in the metropolitan centers. Firewood supplies about 90 percent of fuel needs, and its consumption is about eight times greater than replacement rates (Blackburn 1987).

The heavy use of firewood by rural populations, while not the only contributing factor, is one of the major causes of adverse ecological changes in semiarid regions; social disruption of communities and migrating families; harsh conditions of life for those remaining on the land, especially the women; and the degradation of life-sustaining conditions.

The destruction of tree cover is particularly critical in drylands because of adverse effects on the rainfall cycle, since trees act as pumps, bringing water from the subsoil into the atmosphere. Deforestation leads to less rainfall. Further, erosion accelerates as desertification increases. We have observed this process in Mexico where whole denuded regions are washing away, despite government efforts to reforest and terrace. Sunkel (1981:102) reports that 72 percent of the soils of Mexico suffer high-level erosion. The dryland soils have lost their ability to retain the few rains that come, often with great force, and there is insufficient vegetation to soften their impact.

Projections of desertification, if it continues at current rates, call for 30 million acres (about the size of Saudi Arabia) to turn into dry barren land by the turn of the century. Desertification to a much smaller extent in central Africa since 1980 has had a devastating effect: 35 million people in jeopardy of starvation, of which 1 million have died to this date (Coates 1987).

In dry deforested regions, the life situation of the dwellers becomes increasingly difficult, and much of the stress is placed upon the women.

Women must now walk hours to find fuel, often bringing it home on their backs. They supplement when they can with such materials as cornstalks, other crop residues, and animal-dung cakes. The extra burden on women is physically demanding and carries with it a high opportunity cost that takes away time from family responsibilities and opportunities to generate income. Thus, family and village life is adversely affected.

The fuelwood shortage is of special concern in dryland regions where native trees typically grow slowly and tend to be thin, thorny, crooked, and tough. Biomass yields are low. Harvesting without good tools is difficult. New trees cannot be established easily in drylands. Therefore, there is a need for low-cost, accessible, easily managed, and ecologically sound fuelwood substitutes. An alternative fuel must require the use of only rudimentary tools, and it must grow readily in marginal soils and on erodible slopes without competing for relatively more fertile cropland or for limited irrigation water.

The Potential of the Rootfuel Approach

Solutions to the alternative fuel problem must be sought vigorously. It should not be assumed that all potential solutions will require long, expensive, and sophisticated research efforts in university laboratories, followed by long and costly implementation processes. Some innovations, like the one described here, can be implemented quickly and inexpensively with the help of local people, involving them as colleagues in the process.

Certain members of the ubiquitous *Cucurbitaceae* meet the technical requirements for a satisfactory woodfuel replacement and constitute an important partial solution to the many problems discussed above. Of special interest is *Cucurbita foetidissima*, a wild gourd plant that is indigenous to the drylands of northern and central Mexico, and the southwestern United States. Closely related plants of the same family are also of interest. The evidence of the botanical literature on the roots of the *Cucurbitaceae*, although not extensive or even sufficient, suggests that *Cucurbita foetidissima* is typical of many species of this large family dispersed widely in the drylands of the world.

Calabacilla loca (one of the many common linguistic group names of *Cucurbita foetidissima* in Mexico) is a fast-growing plant that produces an abundance of roots, even without irrigation, and it grows in all of the aridland types of soils that are known. Sufficient research (some 100 scientific papers, most from the Unviersity of Arizona) has been carried out on this plant to establish its potential as an economic crop. An interpretive review of this literature has been carried out.

The carrot-shaped taproots can be cut with a knife when fresh. The root pieces can then be sun-dried and used as rootfuel, an alternative to woodfuel (Shultz and Evans 1986; Bragg and Shultz 1987; Bragg, Duke, and Shultz 1987). The heating value of rootfuel is essentially the same as that of wood, but the combustion properties are different, falling between those of wood and charcoal (Bragg, Duke, and Shultz 1987).

We recently organized a test of the cultural acceptability of *Calabacilla loca* as a rootfuel, with the assistance of a Mazahua woman in rural Mexico, Claudia Gonzalez de Moreno, who cooked a typical meal, substituting only for the fuel (Bragg and Shultz 1987). The rootfuel was readily accepted for use in a three-stone fireplace. Ms. de Moreno promptly adjusted her technique to the combustion properties of the rootfuel. She stated that the rootfuel was superior to wood, cornstalks, maguey, or animal-dung cakes, all of which burn rapidly and produce few coals. Coals from relatively slow-burning fuel are desirable for cooking foods like rice and beans that need long simmering.

Ms. de Moreno volunteered throughout the test that there was no objectionable odor from the rootfuel, that there was less smoke than from her usual fuels, that the rootfuel smoke was less irritating, and that no objectionable flavor was imparted to the rice, tortillas, and eggs that she cooked. She and her husband and children all ate the food with gusto, and all indicated that it was excellent. Her small son, probably too young to be anything but frank in his expression of approval or disapproval, ate all of his food with obvious satisfaction.

Calabacilla loca's characteristics are those of an appropriate bioresource technology: (1) simple, (2) available locally, (3) labor-intensive rather than capital-intensive, (4) decentralized, (5) ecologically compatible, (6) self-reliant, (7) sustainable, and (8) culturally adaptable (Bragg 1987).

Calabacilla is adapted to the ecosystem, producing almost twice as much biomass in a summer as mesquite does annually on the same area of land, resistant to many plant pests, proliferative, and accessible to all. There are no exogenous techniques required for cultivating it as a rootfuel, nor does it require costly or imported fertilizers. It is simple and inexpensive to start a field of this plant. Growing on marginal soil, it can fit into a variegated cropping system without displacing any food or money crops. In addition, its dense growth and preference for well-drained soils mean that it can also serve as an erosion-control planting for sloping fields, terraces, and road banks.

In summary, utilization of *Calabacilla loca* and similar members of the same plant family for rootfuel promises benefits such as 1. A low-cost, accessible, easily managed, and culturally acceptable woodfuel substitute. 2. A fuel of higher quality than most of those presently used (more sanitary than dung cakes, slower burning than wood, more coals). 3. An ecologically sound fuel that will relieve pressure on the remaining tree cover. 4. Release of agricultural residues and animal dung for more useful service as fertilizers and soil conditioners, rather than fuel. 5. A method for stabilizing highly erodible soils, especially on slopes, because *calabacilla* produces multitudes of roots from the nodes of the many vines. The many taproots and the extensive development of secondary roots hold the soil, and the abundant leaf structure prevents forceful contact of rain with soil. 6. Relief of women from the heavy physical burden and the high social cost of gathering wood at a distance. 7. Deterrence of the desertification process. 8. Deterrence of the destabilization of rural life.

Strategies for Development and Dissemination of Rootfuel in Third World Drylands

Deployment sites must be chosen in areas where there is a serious firewood shortage and where people are open to trying new ideas. Pressure on the land must not be too great; there must be land available for planting the root crop, but the land can be of marginal value, such as slopes and road and path borders.

To a great extent, acceptance of new methods by local people depends on the degree of their involvement in problem identification and solving, and planning. Therefore, it is wise to minimize the demonstration activities carried out solely by development workers and to look for legitimate ways for local people to participate at every level. There are many such legitimate ways.

For example, local people can be given opportunities to work with development workers in using this novel fuel, with requests for their opinions and suggestions. The taste acceptability of foods cooked on unconventional fuels is always very important, and only local women, men, and children can make that judgment. In addition, women can work with their own fireplaces, cooking utensils, and the rootfuel to adapt their techniques as did Claudia de Moreno. Then they can explain their findings to their neighbors, probably more effectively than development workers can transfer techniques.

The widespread availability of cucurbits means that no one can monopolize rootfuel, an important feature in societies that have been traditionally cooperative rather than competitive. For example, there is still a deep sense of cooperation and sharing among the Mexican people, despite the individualism and competition brought by the Spanish conquistadors. The concept of the "limited good" described by Foster (1967) in his study of Tzintzuntzan in Michoacan State indicates a deep-seated desire to avoid profiting individually at the expense of others of the community. This concept is a theory of zero-sum growth (a limited economic pie): If one member prospers above others, it is considered evil if others are thereby necessarily impoverished.

Therefore, *Calabacilla loca* as an alternative fuel lends itself to the commonwealth; if planted in a communal plot, it could furnish cooking energy for a whole village. If the community is not organized collectively, it can be cultivated by each household for its own use, but since each neighbor could do the same, there would be no monopoly to create social distinction or new elites.

Many technological interventions fail to account for gender roles in traditional peasant societies. For this reason programs that introduced efficient cookstoves in Africa failed when they taught men, not women, to construct the stoves (Tongue 1987). In rural Mexico, like so much of the Third World, while men are in charge of the cultivation of crops, women do help, especially at planting and harvesting time, leading the bullocks, planting seeds, and helping with the collection. But women primarily take care of the children and cooking, including the fuel gathering. Similar patterns are seen in other traditional societies around the world.

Since women generally bear the burden of seeking fuel, they would have the motivation and the facility to encourage the use of alternatives to fuelwood. *Calabacilla* can grow in numerous presently unused places around the villages, and women can see to its propagation *in lieu of* the time now used in walking long distances for firewood. The economy of time and energy would be great not only in the cultivation (nothing needed after planting until digging) but also in the processing of the roots. A simple kitchen knife or machete cuts the root, and the sun dries it. Clearly, women will be more important than men in the utilization of rootfuel, so strategies for development and dissemination must take this into account.

This does not mean that only women will be involved in rootfuel development. In traditional societies it is important that consent and full support be obtained from the men. Further, it is likely that men will participate with women in the determination of the best techniques of growing rootfuel plants. Men would be only peripherally involved in determining the best techniques for burning the roots.

The following and similar activities would be useful in furthering the development and dissemination of the rootfuel concept and would be in consonance with the above-mentioned strategic considerations. (1) Surveys of appropriate sites for cultivation of *calabacilla loca* or alternative species of *Cucurbitaceae* that might be equally or more beneficial. (2) Involvement of local people in nonformal education on rootfuel from *calabacilla loca* and related *Cucurbitaceae*. (3) Development of pilot grassroots community projects in selected locations. (4) Development of small-scale demonstration plots managed by local people to show several methods of growing root-fuel cucurbits. (5) Marketing and economic studies on fresh roots, root-fuel, and seeds, since it is likely that all three will enter local marketing channels.

11

The Bhopal Disaster: Its Impact on Strategies for Future Transfers of Hazardous Technology

Jean L. Shultz and Eugene B. Shultz, Jr.

Introduction

Will we learn from Bhopal? Perhaps not, if we fail to look deeply at the forces and attitudes that presently control the way we transfer hazardous technology from the industrialized world to the Third World. Much has been written on the world's worst industrial disaster since it occurred in December 1984, but most of the literature deals only with the immediate level, the level of faulty equipment and process design, improper plant siting, management failings, operator error, poorly trained and disgruntled workers, and the like.

Not enough attention has been given to the larger issue of transfer of hazardous modern technologies that the Bhopal tragedy requires us to ponder if we would learn lasting lessons from that unfortunate experience. Bhopal must force us to reexamine our basic motivation for hazardous technology transfer, as well as our technology transfer strategies. Bhopal must bring about important institutional changes in corporate policy and practice as well as in governmental policies, laws, and regulations.

Our main point is that the lessons of Bhopal must be learned now rather than later, and this is not likely to happen if attention continues to be narrowly focused on technical factors and human errors, to the virtual exclusion of the larger issues of transfer of inherently hazardous industrial technologies. The ugly consequences of the accident must not be forgotten, so that difficult and more basic issues surrounding technology transfer and economic development may get proper attention.

A Preview of This Chapter

First, we will review some of the technical and managerial failings and human errors that were part of this tragedy. There were three major institutions involved: the parent corporation, Union Carbide (UC); its subsidiary, Union Carbide of India, Limited (UCIL); and the Indian government. Their differing views will be summarized, as well as those of some important Indian critics whose voices have not been widely heard.

But we must push ourselves to look behind proximate causes if we want to increase the likelihood of deep learning from this unfortunate experience. Accidents such as Bhopal must not be regarded as acceptable. Simple solutions—replacement of incompetent managers and faulty equipment or enforcement of neglected safety regulations—are necessary but only a bare beginning. Alone, they will not prevent future catastrophes. Technology transfer is not easy, and the transfer of hazardous technology is especially troubled with challenging problems.

We will explore some vital issues that those involved in hazardous technology transfer and Third World development must consider seriously. We will search for institutional and other changes that may help avoid putting large numbers of people at risk unnecessarily and irresponsibly. Questions will be raised about current beliefs in the field of economic development, so that better development strategies might result. Before concluding, we will talk about some useful and useless ways to think about the Bhopal disaster, because our beliefs about such events will affect our future actions or inactions. More than anything else, Bhopal is the outcome of how we think about development, technology transfer, and risk taking.

Was Bhopal an Isolated Curiosity?

The historic record of hazardous chemical technology confirms that Bhopal cannot be characterized as an isolated incident. In 1921 a chemical plant explosion in Oppau, Germany, killed 561 people. A 1947 fertilizer ship explosion took 562 lives at Texas City in the United States. There were 1,100 lives lost in a 1956 dynamite truck explosion at Cali, Colombia. Due to an explosion at a chemical plant in Flixborough, England, in 1974, there were 28 fatalities and 3,000 evacuated. The 1976 chemical leak at Seveso, Italy, caused 700 people to be evacuated; there were 200 skin disease cases and hundreds of animals killed. In 1979, there were 300 fatalities in the Novosibirsk, USSR, biochemical warfare plant accident. The 1984 gas explosion in Mexico City took 452 lives; 31,000 were evacuated, and 4,258 were injured (Bowonder, Kasperson, and Kasperson 1985: 8; Natkin 1985: 63).

At Bhopal, during the night of December 2–3, 1984, tons of methyl isocyanate (MIC) poured into the atmosphere of the heavily populated area around the plant owned by UCIL. This compound, one of the most poisonous of all industrial chemicals, is an intermediate in one pathway for the synthesis of the pesticide Sevin. This accidental release of MIC caused the deaths of at least 2,000 people. Some estimates indicate thousands of additional deaths. Perhaps 200,000 individuals were injured, of whom 30,000 to 40,000 were seriously injured (Mokhiber 1987: 6). However, the full extent of the tragedy cannot be known, as the aftereffects on health and lives are still taking their toll and accurate records were not kept.

The Bhopal experience was only one of a long chain of similar events shared by the industrialized world and the Third World. This fact underscores the urgency of dealing with the roots of man-made disasters rather than just coping with superficially immediate causes again and again. This is not to say that we can ignore immediate problems. They must be remedied and also carefully examined because they help us understand the nature of root causes.

Immediate Causes: Technical Factors and Administrative Failure

Background

The population of Bhopal increased rapidly from 1969 as industries were established and began to employ in the area. Carbide found an opportunity to participate in the development of the town. Manufacture of the pesticide Sevin was to enhance India's goal of growing all of its own food. But UCIL did not employ many people or produce as much Sevin as anticipated.

Government loans incurred by farmers due to the drought of 1977 became due in 1980. Also, farmers began to buy less expensive pyrethroid pesticides. At the same time, the Indian government provided subsidies to encourage small pesticide plants, permitting them to sell pesticides at half the UCIL price. The business of UCIL was poor, and after 1981, the company began to lose money. In 1984, only one-fifth of the expected production occurred. The inevitable began to take place: Sale of the plant was contemplated; early retirement was encouraged by incentives; and jobs were sought elsewhere by many skilled workers (Bowonder, Kasperson, and Kasperson 1985:7–8).

Instead of closing the Bhopal plant, a money-loser, its life was continued but with less qualified people and poor maintenance (Bowonder, Kasperson, and Kasperson 1985:8). Concern for the short-term economic health of the plant apparently prevailed over concern for safety; risks were taken so that money could be saved.

Technical Failures

Explanations of the technical causes of the accident vary. The literature speaks of the following: the refrigeration system designed to prevent runaway chemical reactions was not operating at the time, or for the five months prior to the disaster. Consequently, the temperature of the MIC in the storage tank was warmer than permitted by the operating manual for the plant (Mokhiber 1987:6). Varma (1986:142) stated that the refrigeration was turned off to reduce operation costs.

For many years, apparently, the instruments designed to measure temperature and pressure in the storage unit had been giving inaccurate readings. The scrubber system that would neutralize gas in case of a leak also had been out of order for several weeks. Not only had the neglected lines to the flare been corroded, but for ten days the flare, important for burning off excess MIC gas, had been closed down (Mokhiber 1987:6). But we submit that the foregoing technical details, as important as they are, are not as significant as larger issues of development strategy and transfer of hazardous technology.

Human Failures

Methyl isocyanate was held in storage for three months or more prior to the accident, a dangerous practice because the entrance of even a small amount of contaminant during that time can start a heat-producing chemical reaction in the tank (Bowonder, Kasperson, and Kasperson 1985:8).

Further, in the early 1970s, UCIL management had apparently argued for small storage containers and small amounts of MIC to be stored, as in Great Britain and West Germany, which allow drums no larger than 213 kg in capacity (Varma 1986:142). But UC insisted that large amounts of MIC be stored in large containers, just as at their Institute, West Virginia, plant (Mokhiber 1987:7). The Bhopal storage tanks held 15,000 gallons (Bowonder, Kasperson, and Kasperson 1985:8). Although UC has argued against in digenization of its overseas subsidiaries on the basis that host-country engineers and managers lack sufficient experience, in this case UCIL knew better.

Additional plant problems of this type include plant underdesign, inadequate training of workers, operator errors, lax maintenance, high turnover of staff, nonimplemented recommendations of a UC inspection team (Mokhiber 1987:7–8), and the nonreturn of an audit team to see if implementation took place (Ember 1985:61).

The fact that an inspection team from UC visited Bhopal, found major safety concerns, and rendered a May 1982 report describing a "serious potential for sizable releases of toxic materials" (Mokhiber 1987:8) is very significant. The team made many technical recommendations for correcting the deficiencies, but it is not clear why UC management did not force its Indian subsidiary to comply. Whether UC management intentionally or unintentionally ignored the report of its own engineers or gave permission to UCIL to ignore the recommendations has not yet been revealed.

Union Carbide, the parent company and majority shareholder of UCIL, has been criticized for failing to give warnings about such major safety concerns as runaway chemical reactions in storage tanks. Rote memorization by workers was characteristic of the UCIL training rather than understanding reasons for specific steps in plant operation. A safety audit team worried about the high turnover of personnel and the essential need for training and understanding of safety procedures. It was likely that training was insufficient (Ember 1985:62).

The Proximity of Squatter Homes

This was another serious aspect of administrative failure. Industrial facilities attract people in search of work. Squatter huts for thousands of people seeking jobs is a common phenomenon (Pearson 1985:58) and is generally the case in India's manufacturing areas. Thus, there were many people living near the UCIL fences at Bhopal. However, Varma (1986:140) makes clear that there were at least fifty bungalows around the site when UCIL applied for a license to build the plant in 1969. Also, there were a government housing project there and a busy commercial, trading, and residential area around the railroad station only three kilometers from the site at the time it was proposed by UCIL.

Further, population grew in Bhopal from 1961 to 1981 by 75 percent. Not only did the Madhya Pradesh state government allow such growth around the plant, but the squatters were granted legal status in April so that they could vote in December 1984 (Bowonder, Kasperson, and Kasperson 1985:13). How unfortunate that politics played such a key role in institutionalizing the risk for the squatters.

Perhaps we have yet to learn about our negative obligation to refrain from harming or risking harm, which takes precedence over our positive duty to give aid, as ethicist Barbara MacKinnon (1986:32–36), points out. The new chemical plant at Bhopal brought aid in the form of jobs, but workers and neighbors were placed at risk due to improper plant siting, laxity in safety enforcement, and failure to disseminate information.

Major Differences in Perspective on the Bhopal Disaster

Union Carbide (UC)

Union Carbide has claimed that Indian workers at the Bhopal plant seriously violated safety rules. Unlike the Indian government, UC insisted at first on sabotage as the explanation for the accident (Anon. 1985) and later concluded that it was a deliberate act of a disgruntled employee (England 1986:42).

This theme was "central to Union Carbide's defense in the Indian government's $3 billion suit on behalf of those injured and the families of those killed" (England 1986:42).

Union Carbide asserted that workers altered the facts in the company reports of the accident. They claim that the police did also and that the Central Bureau of Investigations of New Delhi and the Ministry of Industry and Company Affairs continued to aid in suppression of the facts. Therefore, UC took the position that it should not be held accountable but that UCIL and the government of India must shoulder the responsibility (England 1986:43–44). According to Varma (1986:141), UC regards safety as a responsibility of UCIL and blames the disaster on the inability of the Indian worker to handle high technology.

In an official statement, UC's chairman, Warren Anderson, focused on technical problems and UCIL management failures (*New York Times* 1985), indicating that "a unique series of events caused the tragedy" and that the Bhopal plant was operated with "total disregard for procedures." Union Carbide officials asserted that "lines of communication with Bhopal had broken down long before December 3, 1984," and Anderson acknowledged that "the appropriate people" at UC "should have known" about Bhopal's "severe contravention of safety procedures."

Indian Government

An Indian confidential report said that UC and its subsidiary UCIL were at fault due to design flaws, managerial error, operator mistakes, and faulty instruments. They took the position that cost cutting, not sabotage, was a major cause. The Indian government report also pointed out technical explanations: failure of certain equipment to operate, procedures inadequate to prevent such a large release of MIC, and unreliable gauges, as well as errors in judgment (Anon. 1985).

Further, the government report noted the lack of an alarm system, lack of an evacuation system, and no method to protect local inhabitants. The only warning system to alert the workers was human: odor detection, breathing difficulty, and irritated eyes! Also, local administration and the central government were not thoroughly informed of the hazards of manufacturing and storing MIC. Moreover, in the years of operation of the Bhopal plant, MIC had never been tested for its "basic characteristics, its potential neutralization or its antidote" (Anon. 1985).

Michael Ciresi, the Minnesota lawyer retained by the Indian government, accused "Union Carbide of subjecting Indian justice to a double standard: 'First they say that Indian courts are perfectly adequate, then they demand the right to question any decision there.'" Ciresi confirmed that coming to the United States first to file suit did relate to financial considerations.

"The legal efforts ... lay the groundwork for attaching U.S. assets of Union Carbide to pay for any future damage award" (England 1986:42). The Indian government argues that water was introduced into the storage tank accidentally during routine washing, in contrast to UC's position that the accident was caused by intentional introduction of water (England 1986:43).

Union Carbide of India, Limited (UCIL)

It appears that UCIL's hands were tied. The Indian government allowed the squatters to live near the plant (England 1986:44). Further, the Bhopal plant management need not accept responsibility for the fact that large amounts of MIC were stored at the plant. This was done at UC's request and by UC's design over UCIL's objections. Union Carbide of India, Limited can point out that after Bhopal, UC redesigned certain equipment in the parent plant in Institute, West Virginia (Varma 1986:140), suggesting that the technology transferred to India was recognized by UC as flawed.

Union Carbide of India, Limited could blame the Indian government and UC for the fact that UCIL's well-trained scientists and technicians were overqualified, underemployed, and uninformed due to the *turnkey* basis of technology transfer (Vaidyanathan 1985:9). Briefly, this term signifies the handing over of a completed factory to managers and engineers who never participated in its conception and design. Further, UCIL could criticize the government inspection system because there were only two inspectors. They were both mechanical engineers who knew almost nothing of the hazards of chemistry and lacked appropriate equipment to do their work (Varma 1986:140).

Indian Critics

It would be well if UC, UCIL, and the Indian government were to pay attention to the public outrage, to the victims of the tragedy, and to the Indian critics who continue to research and write about Bhopal.

Bhopal must not be forgotten, but as Shiv Visvanathan (1986:150) describes it, the Indian government is paying Bhopal's victims to forget. "Many have risen to the bait." He goes on to comment that not everyone wishes to forget but that man-made disasters are not easily retained. He continues (p. 150):

> A flood of an earthquake is absorbed in the calendrical cycle; the language of myth and religion is easily available to conceptualize it. Man-made catastrophe, on the other hand, is unmetaphorical and prosaically secular. It is subjected to quick erasure, to a kind of amnesia that denies to the victim even the right to remember.

Varma (1986:140) asserted that the Indian government sold out to UC, neglecting its duty to see that the safety and needs of the local people and workers had high priority. It approved the construction of a plant obviously defective from the safety design aspect, a plant believed to be rejected by Canada for that reason, according to Varma. It must accept responsibility for permitting a plant to be built for the use of such extremely dangerous chemicals near family housing.

The state government of Madhya Pradesh must also share the blame, according to Indian critics. It should be understood that governments and corporations have an absolute responsibility to their people to see first to their welfare. This, however, was not the case. The trusting local people expected such, as this telling remark of one survivor indicates: "I did not feel concerned. If the government permitted the factory they must have made sure of it" (Vaidyanathan 1985: 10). This helps to explain the growing anger of the local people (Vaidyanathan 1985:9–10; Varma 1986:140).

The state government was aware of serious problems for a long time, as revealed by the following: "The administrator of Bhopal Municipal Corporation issued a notice in 1975 to move Union Carbide's factory outside the city, because of its proximity to the city's population, and he was transferred" (Vaidyanathan 1985:10). In 1982 also, there was an appeal in the state legislature to move the plant. The government reply was that "there was no danger to Bhopal, nor would there ever be," according to Varma (1986:141).

Although the state government knew of three previous UCIL accidents in 1982 and 1983, its chief secretary stated that none was an indicator of such a tragic future occurrence (Vaidyanathan 1985:10). In a state of 45 million people and 442,841 square miles, there were only about twenty-four inspectors. There were a director of industrial health and safety based at Indore and two deputies, one at Indore and one at Bhopal. Thus, "authorities [were] ill-equipped to make proper inspections" (Vaidyanathan 1985:10–11).

In May 1982, three UC experts from the United States prepared a report pointing out serious flaws in the Bhopal operation. The clarity of the report was without question. In September 1982, the report and recommendations were sent to the UCIL management at Bhopal. How many of the recommendations were implemented is not well known. The state government did not enforce the recommendations, even after the death of Ashraf Khan, a worker involved in one of the accidents, according to Vaidyanathan (1985:10).

Among the many other offenses for which UCIL may be deemed guilty, according to Indian critics, are these: use of low-grade steels instead of stainless, over two years' use of equipment that required replacement in six months, lax maintenance, denial of gloves to the workers so that their working speed would not be decreased, shortage of breathing masks, and lack of devices for detecting gas leaks at Bhopal. The latter was the case at Institute, West Virginia, as well, asserted Varma (1986:141).

All of these shortcomings bear a direct relationship to efforts to economize, as do the various aspects of poor training of staff. Study manuals could not be taken home during training; notes could not be taken without special permission; the inexperienced and inadequately trained operated critical equipment since retrenchment and early retirement of the experienced were in full force. Without the ability to grasp necessary operational information due to lack of meticulous training, plant security was forfeited (Varma 1986:141).

The indiscretions of UCIL do not excuse UC. At the time of renewing the agreement to manufacture MIC in 1983, UC made a promise which it did not keep, according to Indian critics. It was to transfer all know-how of safety measures and equipment to handle "any sudden release of gas" (Varma 1986:142). Although UC disclosed none of these, the Environmental Protection Agency (EPA) reported from UC's own records at Institute, West Virginia, 61 MIC leaks, 107 phosgene gas leaks, and 22 MIC/phosgene leaks between 1981 and 1984. Up to the time of Varma's writing there were five additional incidents of leaks of toxic chemicals in UC's plants in the United States (Varma 1986:142).

In the context of the Bhopal disaster, "the network of relationships that exist among the power multinationals, Indian capitalists and the state and central government in India should ... be examined" (Vaidyanathan 1985:9). Such a study is certainly needed and may clarify what makes these groups do what they do and help us gain insights into needed institutional changes. Vaidyanathan further asserts that the few wealthy families of India are interested in buying large Western technology, not in developing indigenous technology with the assistance of Indian scientists. They invest with foreign corporations in any manufacturing endeavors where large profits can be realized, stressing no particular type of industry.

Repeated desperate warning in the fall of 1982 and the summer of 1984 by an Indian journalist, Rajkumar Keswani, went unheeded. At least five other journalists shared the duty of keeping the prospect of disaster of Bhopal before the public, unfortunately to no avail (Visvanathan 1986:154).

However, Visvanathan (1986:154) felt that the journalists' writings lacked the:

> crystal seed of a metaphor, one iconic image around which the conflicting imaginations could be brought to play. Bhopal is still a catastrophe in search of a metaphor, a vision that is more and less than Bhopal. An event like Bhopal should have created a sense of concern for the little Bhopals

in our lives and yet remained fluid enough to sensitize us to the destructive aspects of science and industrialism. . . . There is need for poets here.

Press Perspectives: United States vs. India

There was a substantial and obvious difference in press reports from the United States and India. In brief, Indian accounts dwelled on the enormity and shock of the disaster, the great loss of life, the plight of the injured, and the inadequacies, even venality, of UCIL, UC, and the government. Reports in the U.S. press were much less vivid in detail and often expressed grave concern for the future of the parent company, Union Carbide, a U.S. corporation.

An extreme example, a long article by Dobrzynski et al. in *Business Week* of December 24, 1984, entitled "Union Carbide Fights for Its Life," dealt with the possibility that UC would be driven into bankruptcy by lawsuits. The article gave the concerned reader some excerpts from UC's balance sheet, information on the plunge in its stock price, a report that UC had received sympathy calls from other companies, and the distressing news that Bhopal's closing might mean a $32.5 million write-off for UC in 1985.

By contrast, news in the Indian *Economic and Political Weekly* (e.g., Rameseshan 1984; ISG 1985; Das 1985a, 1985b; Prakash 1985; Banaji 1985; Jagdish and Vijay 1985) was filled with details: the plight of the injured; inadequacies of medical care; the cyanide antidote controversy; indifference of UC, UCIL, and the Indian government; disinformation given out by UCIL and the government; inadequate rehabilitation planning; neglect of women's health issues, and other overwhelming challenges.

We found, unfortunately, that much information in the Indian press appeared not to find its way into the U.S. press. But this is not to say that all U.S. accounts were like the aforementioned piece in *Business Week*. Excellent reporting and evenhanded analyses appeared in *Chemical and Engineering News*, a newsmagazine published by the American Chemical Society, especially in articles by Wil Lepkowski (1985a, 1985b, 1985c, 1985d, 1985e) and Lois Ember (1985).

Some Practical Problems in the Transfer of Hazardous Technology

Some problems that limit the effectiveness of hazardous technology transfer will be discussed: indigenization, remoteness, religious and other cultural factors, Multinational Corporations MNC managerial attitudes, and attitudes of host-nation government officials. This is not an exhaustive list. There are many other reasons why transfer of hazardous technology is fraught with difficulties, raising serious questions about its advisability.

First, indigenization means that the host country sees its goal as building up its own production ability. Consequently, not enough of the following are brought into the country: materials, equipment, and spare parts as well as experienced foreign personnel from the West (Lepkowski 1985c:10).

The second problem, remoteness, also means lack of spare parts and problems in maintaining safety standards and overseeing security practices. It may be difficult to interchange key personnel between the parent plant in the industrialized world and its copy in a remote location in the Third World.

The third concern, religious and other cultural considerations, may intensify the alien nature of new technologies. Cultural barriers can deter the acceptance of new technologies. Fatalistic religious beliefs, especially in the case of the less well-educated workers, may limit receptivity to the need for precautionary steps necessary when working with the hazardous materials. All this, together with the language barrier and insufficient experience with complex technologies, may mean lack of appreciation of dangerous industrial processes rather than a perverse determination to take risks.

The fourth issue, MNC managerial attitudes, includes the motive of short-term profit maximization, which may become all-absorbing. When short-term profit is the primary motive of an MNC, workers from another culture may be exploited. Poor working conditions and inadequate pay may be the result. This issue has to do with whether MNCs have a responsibility to their host-nation workers, a controversy that has not yet been adequately addressed.

The fifth issue deals with the attitudes of host-nation government officials. They may think in terms of profit maximization and modernization, to the exclusion of developing the human resources of their nation. Typical elitist attitudes of many government officials, including disdain for working people, may mean that social well-being, adequate working conditions, and pay may be ignored in the struggle to catch up with the developed world. Host-nation officials, overly eager to invite in hazardous technologies, may become involved in corruption. They may not concern themselves about safety parity; they may find reasons why a lesser standard of safety is satisfactory for the technology that is being transferred into their nation.

What Must Be Different? Some Changes to Consider

Increased Corporate Responsibility

There are systematic problems of technology transfer that have been neglected and that are still to be resolved. Patrick P. McCurdy, editor in chief of *Chemical Week*, has indicated some recognition of this (1985a: 3). He talks of the chemical industry's good record which it has maintained, outshining other industries over the years. However, he emphasizes that Bhopal has been the impetus for improving that fine record by further tightening of restrictions, procedures, and regulations as well as insuring that community and plant evacuation strategies are developed (1985a:3).

Plant safety improvement has been encouraged by organizations outside of the chemical industry also. Project Aftermath, funded by the U.S. Agency for International Development (USAID), utilizes industry volunteers who go to developing countries to help put emergency response plans in place. So far, twenty-three plants have volunteered to serve. "But why only 23," of the three hundred top companies in the chemical process industries? McCurdy queries (1985b:3). The need is overseas. We cannot afford blinders that allow narrow "me-first" attitudes to prevail (McCurdy 1985b:3).

Moreover, the "right to know" about what goes on in chemical plants is attracting much attention in the United States, and this issue should become just as important in the Third World. It is vital that local communities be fully informed about activities within the plant that may affect them. This will have to take precedence over the concern that sharing so-called classified information will give an advantage to the competition. McCurdy agrees: "We think such fears are exaggerated, if not groundless" (1985a:3).

The corporations that transfer hazardous technology to the Third World may have to assume a special obligation much like that of a parent. This may be an offensive concept to the host country. Nevertheless, a special relationship is necessary to guide and train the recipients when introducing inherently hazardous technologies alien to their previous experience. A viable alternative for the prospective host nation is to find ways to circumvent the need for products manufactured by hazardous technology.

As Pearson (1985:60) so aptly puts it, "The great technical and financial resources of multinational corporations confer on them a special responsibility to their workers, joint venture partners, subcontractors, and the communities in which they operate." John F. Ahearne (1986:204), of the U.S. Nuclear Regulatory Commission, gives blunt advice to the MNCs:

For overseas operations, these corporations should recognize the technological gaps between their knowledge and that of the countries in which they plan to operate. They should not take advantage of those gaps to reduce or dispense with any of the steps that they would take in the United States. Instead, they have a greater responsibility: where the technological base is weak, transnationals should insist on controlling design, construction, and operation. If they cannot, then the transnational corporation should not go into that country.

We endorse much of Ahearne's position, but we would point out that it obviously assumes that the transnational has all the requisite knowledge. This is an unwarranted generalization; in the case of Bhopal, clearly, this was not the case. Also, we perceive the need to include host-nation engineers and managers in the early stages of design and planning so that they are more knowledgeable than if they simply accepted a turnkey plant. Ahearne does not speak of this.

Although one might expect that MNCs involved in hazardous industry in Third World nations would work with host governments to set up workplace safety and environmental regulations, this was not done at Bhopal. Although it might confidently be expected that unprofitable businesses would be closed rather than sacrifice safe operating practices, this was not the case at Bhopal. Before we can assume that these problematic business practices were peculiar to UC and UCIL, studies are needed to find out to what extent they might be endemic.

The dissemination of clear information to all local residents, presenting carefully and simply the key aspects of the manufacturing enterprise with a thorough discussion of its hazardous characteristics and warnings about possible accidents, is also a reasonable expectation. This would include exactly what steps to take in case of evacuation, even to such details as the use of a wet washcloth through which to breathe. This might have saved many lives in the Bhopal disaster, as indicated by Bowonder, Kasperson, and Kasperson (1985:9). Of utmost importance would be instructions on how employees and local people would be informed of the occurrence of an accident.

All of this information would have to come to the people in various ways and repeatedly through the media, the use of posters, distribution of illustrated brochures using simple words in multiple languages, education in the schools, community organizations, and training courses given by the plant in cooperation with the local government.

Lepkowski (1985c:12) discusses the minimization of hazardous chemical inventories, as is the case in Europe where many chemical plants are located in heavily populated areas. Small inventories would limit the number of lives lost. We must insist that MNCs behave, as in Europe, through government regulation or international law. It appears that industry self-governance and marketplace regulation are unreliable and especially should not be trusted when industry is hazardous, complex, and difficult for the average person to comprehend.

Governments and MNCs must not allow facilities to be underdesigned or to be built to produce dangerous chemicals under unsafe conditions. If relatively safe technology is available in the industrialized world, then it is that technology which must be transferred, not anything less safe. According to Lepkowski (1985c:10), Charles Weiss, Jr., science and technology policy specialist at the World Bank, says that the United States should help other countries set up their own safety agencies, like the Environmental Protection Agency (EPA) and the Occupational Safety and Health Administration (OSHA).

A lesson that must be learned from Bhopal is that the turnkey approach is unacceptable. Indigenous engineers must be involved in the planning and design work before the hazardous technology is transferred, and MNC engineers and managers must be in charge of the new plant in the host nation until indigenous engineers and managers are brought to the same level of familiarity with the new chemical process.

Lepkowski (1985c:11–14) analyzes the World Bank's guidelines program to avert future disasters and discusses the possibility that private banks can assist in environmental protection as an aspect of their lending programs. We hope that bankers will consider the wisdom of doing this and take advantage of the strength of their positions as moneylenders. There is no reason that banker pressure should be limited to environmental protection; it can be used to force improvement in workplace safety as well. Large banks can hire the necessary technical talent to provide the internal capability to monitor MNC and host-government performance.

Increased Host-Government Responsibility

Can Third World nations, so eager to attract hazardous industry, also behave responsibly by providing the infrastructure, laws and regulations, quality fire departments, and other elements necessary to protect workers and citizens of their industrial communities? Can MNCs from the West encourage such actions in host countries and be dependable enough to postpone plant construction until good infrastructure can be assured?

Disasters such as Bhopal must inevitably lead to increases in the size of host-nation government and the extent of corporate regulation that governments will carry out. For example, when there is a record of inadequacy in the use of hazardous technology, corporate regulations cannot be regarded as sufficient. Legislation and regulations will be needed to test professional and nonprofessional workers to ensure that they are correctly trained. Regulations must be developed for the protection of the health and safety of workers and nearby residents. Regulations are also essential for proper siting of plants.

Further, there must be strict enforcement of these and other laws and regulations concerning hazardous industry, which means that adequate budgets for enforcement must be provided, not just at the outset but through each successive political administration during the life of the plant, which may be some twenty or thirty years. It may not be possible to ensure this; some administrations, those opposed to corporate regulation, will defeat safety legislation by the simple tactics of underfunding enforcement and appointing officials who are opposed to the legislation they are to uphold. Therefore, how can one be assured that reasonable regulations on hazardous technology will be enforced by the host nation?

Enforcement should be just as important to the MNC as it is to host-nation workers. Can MNCs recognize this and see that their corporate well-being is in jeopardy if they transfer hazardous technology into an unregulated environment? Enforcement of safety legislation and regulations is only one example of difficult systemic problems related to hazardous technology transfer. The safety problems may be less severe in host nations where there are long traditions of guarding the public safety and there is a large percentage of enlightened, educated, and politically active citizens who will make demands on a responsive and concerned government. Clearly, it is not easy to find many such host nations.

It would appear that if parent corporations, their subsidiaries, and host governments did assume their respective obligations and if every able citizen accepted the responsibility to be concerned and well informed, reduction in large-scale accidents might be expected. However, this may require democratic processes—freedom of the press, freedom of speech— and a high literacy rate and increasing mass education.

Conversely, such industrial disasters may be nearly inevitable where political circumstances do not allow an enlightened citizenry to express its concerns openly and when government fails to concern itself sufficiently with public safety. Therefore, the wisdom of transferring hazardous technology to host nations is questionable if these desirable characteristics are not in evidence. This aspect of investment analysis is not quantitative and is not part of classical economics. Nevertheless, we submit that it is crucially important for MNC management to consider.

Is it possible for MNCs and host-nation governments to rethink their frequent justification of various forms of bribery as essential to the conduct of international business? All the earnest culturally based arguments for bribery we have heard from mouths of Western businessmen have not convinced us that bribery is not a significant way that "oppressive" safety regulations are and will continue to be circumvented. This is especially serious if the transferred industry is inherently hazardous.

Perhaps the bribery issue should not be addressed on the basis of vague distinctions of cultural norms in various nations. Instead, maybe it should be analyzed on a pragmatic basis. Is it or is it not a significant way to get around safety regulations? If so, isn't bribery likely to increase the probability of accident and therefore catastrophic accident? If so, then measures must be taken to stop it, and MNCs and host-nation governments alike should find it good business to uphold those measures. It is bad business to take the risk of catastrophe. Neither the MNC nor the host government can afford a catastrophe.

A fundamental adjustment of attitudes and priorities is necessary. The long-term well-being of employees and local people must take precedence over short-term profit maximization, modernization as a development strategy, catching up with the West, various forms of trickle-down development strategy, etc. Humanitarian considerations must have highest priority, and the future prosperity of the MNC is linked to those considerations. One need only ponder the prospective fate of Union Carbide to be convinced of this.

Improved Postdisaster Litigation Procedures

Another essential institutional change deals with prevention of delaying tactics and the sale of assets during litigation. As Robert Hager, an attorney for twenty religious and public interest groups argues,

> Carbide and its powerful Wall Street owners stood to lose probably $5 billion or more if the Bhopal case reached an American jury. Carbide had to settle the case cheap, hide its assets, or get the case out of the U.S. courts to avoid or at least postpone potential bankruptcy. (Mokhiber 1987:8)

Hager's words were in response to the year-long delay of federal Judge John F. Keenan, who finally ruled that the case belonged in India. In the year of delay, Keenan was unable to bring about a settlement, by his own admission. Hager avowed that the delay prejudiced the case against the victims of the accident. Hager pointed out, according to Mokhiber (1987:8), that the year of delay provided time for UC to "liquidate substantial assets and make extraordinary payouts to its shareholders reducing its equity available to pay for any judgment awarded the Bhopal victims." Clearly, adjustments in litigation law to prohibit such delaying tactics appear essential, as do regulations to tie up assets during litigation.

Avoidance of Sudden Introduction

Union Carbide of India, Limited and other UC plants in India were built on a turnkey basis, as beforementioned. Consequently, well-educated Indian engineers and technical professionals became overqualified operators who were not properly aware of the materials at the plants, their chemical properties, etc. (Vaidyanathan 1985:9). This might explain why laborers may not be informed of likely dangers, why repair of faulty equipment and instruments is not expedited, and why evacuation strategies are not in place.

Leapfrogging over the gradual progression from simple to complex technology may be partly to blame. Were a more gradual step-by-step method of development the process for technical advance, perhaps industry and central and local governments would have time to recognize what regulatory measures must be established as momentum increases. Safety regulations appropriate to specific industries might be more apparent.

Development of International Law

The problem of inadequate international laws to govern the transfer of hazardous technology to developing countries must no longer be ignored. It appears that this overarching umbrella is essential since governments often allow careless practices to slip by and management frequently does a poor job of self-governance. The implementation of such laws needs strong support by the nations of the world.

Better Strategies for Development

Before better strategies can be formulated, old ones need to be examined and their weaknesses exposed. The old strategies gave us Bhopal. Varma (1985:144) expressed it eloquently:

> The roots of the Bhopal disaster go much deeper into such layers as indiscriminate industrialization, obsession with economic growth, fascination for spectacular science and technology—in short, into the whole paradigm of technology-based development at a rapid pace.

Bhopal should provide MNCs, host-nation governments, and investors the impetus to review their cherished notions about Third World development. First, basic questions should be asked about meanings and perceptions of "development." What does this word imply to the industrialist, the investor, the host-nation government official? Is economic development alone an adequate surrogate for development? Why has so much economic development been exploitative and destabilizing? What is lacking in the current concept and practice of economic development?

What are the other significant dimensions to development, not necessarily supplied through economic development? Is a tradıtional economic development project likely to be good for the MNC transferring the technology and at the same time good for a large percentage of the people of the host nation? Will it benefit only the elites of the host nation? If so, is this good for the long-term stability of the business climate of the host nation? What indicators of success, in addition to return on investment and other purely economic measures, would assist MNC management in making better Third World investment decisions?

Details of technology transfer strategy need to be discussed by all concerned. Should there be safety parity between the original chemical plant and the "copy" that is transferred to the host nation? When is a transfer complete? Ever? Should there be ongoing programs of interchange of key personnel between the original plant and the copy—safety engineers, chemical engineers, managers, even key foremen? Is safety parity enough? Or is the original in need of upgrading? If the original is upgraded, why shouldn't the copy be upgraded? If a parent corporation will not sacrifice safety to improve its balance sheet, is it permissible for its Third World subsidiary to do so? What are the continuing responsibilities of the parent MNC after the physical transfer of a plant to a host nation?

Why Hazardous Technology?

Questions need to be raised about the wisdom of purchased big technology, development styles that are handed down from the West, and the place of hazardous technology in the developing world without careful guidance from those with experience. Indeed, we must ask the basic question: Why hazardous chemical technology in the first place, anywhere? Safety alternatives can usually be found, as is the case in agricultural pest control.

Even if no highly toxic intermediate such as MIC was involved, accidents would still occur occasionally, but with much less serious consequences. Perrow (1984) points out that plant accidents of a certain type ("system accidents") will be an inadvertent part of the plant design if the process is "complexly interactive and tightly coupled." It seems likely that UC's currently preferred process for manufacture of Sevin fits that technical description. According to Perrow, system accidents should not come as a great surprise; their likelihood is built into the design of plants that are complexly interactive and tightly coupled. He cites many examples.

The point is that when system accidents happen, the presence of a highly toxic material greatly increases the chances of catastrophe. Therefore, we suggest that an alternative synthetic pathway that involves no intermediates such as MIC is strategically far more preferable to UC's present pathway for making Sevin, even though it may mean higher unit costs of production. We would hope that the chemical industry would take this into consideration in the future rather than choosing processes on narrow economic grounds.

In brief, the cheapest way to make a certain chemical product may involve taking a significant chance on catastrophe, a chance that is not present in a more expensive process for making the same product. Choosing the cheaper way rather than the process that avoids highly toxic intermediates will maximize short-term profit. But is this a responsible business strategy if it places at significant risk the lives of workers and neighbors and the investment of the stockholders in the company? The chances of a small accident becoming a catastrophe must be assessed, along with the usual estimations of investment return, before an intelligent investment decision can be made.

In the case of the pesticide Sevin, UC used another synthetic pathway for its manufacture for years before switching to the more economic current process; no MIC was involved in the older process. Also, it is feasible to make MIC as an intermediate but to consume it as it is made, so that the amount to be stored is small or negligible (Varma 1986:138). In both cases, Sevin can be manufactured with less chance of catastrophe when "system accidents" occur.

Such accidents should not be unanticipated. Perrow (1984:10) explains from the perspective of industrial organizational theory and from his personal observations of the shortcomings of typical everyday plant practice:

> Time and time again warnings are ignored, unnecessary risks taken, sloppy work done, deception and downright lying practiced. As an organizational theorist I am reasonably unshaken by this; it occurs in all organizations, and it is a part of the human condition. But when it comes to systems with radioactive, toxic, or explosive materials, . . . these routine sins of organizations have very nonroutine consequences.

Useful and Useless Ways to Think About Bhopal

The question of how people think about Bhopal and similar industrial disasters is obviously important. Our thoughts and beliefs, tend to control our actions. The tragedy can be perceived in many ways, some helpful, others unhelpful and even dangerous.

For example, if life is viewed through the lens of religious fatalism, one may believe that a man-made accident is an act of God, referring to a concept of a deity that perpetrates or at least permits such horrors, perhaps with an obscure purpose to be revealed later. Some may even welcome such tragedies as a form of cleansing, to rid their lands of Western technology and values. And anywhere in the world some may see a disaster as the harbinger of a new celestial order that will benefit a chosen religious few. Religious fatalists are unlikely to help find better development strategies; they may even hinder the effort.

Perhaps the commonly expressed Western perspective that risk is normal and that disasters are to be expected in an industrial society is another type of fatalism, but without the overt involvement of any concept of a deity. This view seems to say that one should not bother to give disasters much attention because nothing much can be done about them anyway. Such an attitude may be a reflection of popular notions that technology cannot be understood by any but the technological elites, so technology is essentially beyond one's domain of personal concern.

On the other hand, one finds this same notion embedded in Western technological industry, espoused by the technically trained and often coupled with the viewpoint that one must accept industrial accidents if one wishes to enjoy the many products and other benefits of modern industry. We have been and continue to be influenced to be comfortable in living with high-risk technologies. We tend to think of elevated risk as the normal condition and may not be aware that in many cases it can be ameliorated.

Then there are the positive thinkers and the optimists who prefer not to dwell on unhappy news, who would rather think only about all the good things that industry brings to us. These attitudes are often anti-intellectual and clearly not conducive to development of intelligent new strategies for technology transfer that will deal with root causes of man-made disaster.

Another view often expressed is that bad managers and poorly trained workers are just people problems that can be solved simply by changing people. This short-term solution might be the end of the search for long-term solutions to underlying problems. Similarly, if the position is that the technology is inadequate or faulty equipment is simply to be replaced, the quest may stop at that point. Short-term steps must be taken, of course, but we must continue the vigorous search for solutions to the basic flaws in the way we transfer technology.

Some think of the transfer of hazardous technology as justifiable on the basis that Third World nations need to take risks so that they can catch up with the West. Others believe that Third World people have a lower regard for life than is found in the industrialized world and use this as justification for transfer. These are exploitative diversionary beliefs that justify transfer to the Third World of dangerous technologies that are sometimes illegal or unwanted in the First World. Exploitation of the Third World is also apparent when lower safety standards are dictated or permitted for manufacturing in a developing nation compared to the First World.

Those interested in Third World development and concerned about the transfer of hazardous technology must be willing to ask questions such as these: What is wrong with the present system of economic development? What is wrong with prevalent modes of transfer of technology? Are there basic flaws? Are the flaws correctable? How, specifically, can the system be corrected?

To think usefully about Bhopal, we must be at least willing to entertain the possibility that the major problems are in the system called economic development and that such system problems can be ameliorated and perhaps even corrected. The major problems are not the incompetent employees and the faulty equipment, although there are plenty of both and they both cause plenty of trouble. The major problems are systemic. They are embedded in the way that Third World development is conducted, including the way we are transferring technologies. Recognition of this is the first step toward improvement.

Part III
Sociological Implications of Urban and Rural Development

12

A Regional Response to an Urban-Rural Crisis: The Case of the Ivory Coast

Dwayne Woods

> The emergence of superimposed urban structures on traditional societies in tropical Africa represents the focus of polarized development associated with extractive colonialism, whose main function was to gain the benefit of the vast store of raw materials present, with minimal interests in constructive periphery development.
>
> —William J. Davies

The rapid growth of urban centers in developing African states has become a serious policy problem. With scarce resources, these states are confronted with a constant influx of migrants from rural areas into the cities. The problem is compounded by the fact that usually the capital, the main economic, political, and cultural center in most Third World nations, attracts the overwhelming majority of those leaving the countryside. Over the last two decades, the number of urban residents in Africa has more than doubled. Although Goran Hyden (1985:188) is correct that "despite the fact that Africa had the world's highest rural-urban migration rate between 1960 and 1980, it remains today the least urbanized of all continents," several African countries—Zaïre, Cameroon, Ivory Coast, and Zambia— are reaching the point where over half of their populations live in cities, with the vast majority of these urban dwellers concentrated in the capital (Liebenow 1986:182–183). In light of African governments' inability to meet the exponential demand for housing and other social services, "bindovilles" have grown up around African capitals like wild mushrooms. They are a stark manifestation of the inability of African governments to control rural exodus to urban centers. Migrants, even with all of the problems they face when they arrive in the city, still believe that things are better there than in the poorer and economically stagnant countryside (Lipton 1977).

Urbanization, however, bodes ill for a continent which remains unindustrialized with an agricultural sector unable to meet the demands of its burgeoning urban population. Moreover, with one of the fastest-growing populations in the world at 2.7 percent—compared to 1.7 percent elsewhere—Africa's ecological and environmental carrying capacity is already under severe strain (UN 1982:37–39). The most dramatic examples of environmental and ecological strain are the rapid deforestation of the tropical rain forest in West Africa and periodic famines due, in part, to soil erosion.

As a consequence of migration of cities, African governments are faced with a twofold crisis. First, as the population in the city swells beyond the carrying capacity of the administration and the environment, the quality of life deteriorates dramatically for everyone. Traffic congestion, uncollected trash, the spread of infectious disease, and rampant crime are common occurrences in all African cities (Liebenow 1986:184). Second, as rural areas lose their populations, especially the young, agricultural output stagnates, thus threatening African countries' ability to feed themselves (Hyden 1985).

Explanations for rural migration to urban centers in Africa vary. One view (Amin 1974) is that economic factors are the primary reason for migration. Samir Amin (1974:94) notes that African economies were integrated into the international economic system in such a way that certain regions were developed while others were allowed to stagnate, eventually pushing Africans from poorer regions to seek out economic opportunities in richer ones. Another explanation is that psychological factors play a determinant role. Many migrants leave the countryside hoping to find a degree of liberty and status in the city which they are unable to achieve in traditional rural settings (Liebenow 1986:188). This writer tends to agree with Amin's assessment to the extent that it suggests that specific economic interests, whether local or international, and strategic policy actions determine how resources are distributed between social groups and regions, which in turn influence the pattern of migration within developing states. Therefore, to understand the urban-rural crises in Africa, it is necessary to conceptualize the problem within a political economic framework which views policy decisions and development strategies as a general reflection of certain socioeconomic and political interests. This is not to suggest that class interests determine government actions, only that policy actions in developing states are shaped by both national and international actors whose interests are reflected in development orientations (Sandbrook 1982:81).

This chapter examines the relationship between policy decisions concerning economic development and rural migration, in particular from the Northern region in the Ivory Coast to Abidjan. The author begins by showing how the uneven development between regions in the Ivory Coast is rooted in specific colonial and postcolonial policies which favored the development of the plantation economy in the South, especially in the Southeast. Then, after a discussion of the consequences of the government's development policies, the decision to shift from a concentrated form of development to a more diffuse, regionally based development strategy in the mid–1970s is explained in the context of the growing urban-rural crises facing the country. A short description of the major development program for the North, the construction of several sugar complexes, is analyzed as it relates to the state's attempt to curtail rural migration. Finally, the outcome of the regional development strategy is considered in terms of its usefulness to other Third World states facing the same dilemma of how to control urban growth and rural exodus.

Uneven Regional Development

Colonial Policy

After the First World War, the French embarked on a new economic policy for their colonies in Africa. Henceforth, the focus would be on developing the economic potential of the overseas territories (Sarrault 1923). The traditional commercial activity between French trading houses and Africans no longer sufficed in the eyes of the colonial administration. A more substantive exploitation was needed so that the colonies could bear the cost of colonial rule themselves (Zolberg 1964:23) and so that France could sell more of its manufactured goods to them (Suret-Canale 1971). In the Ivory Coast, the new colonial policy focused on the formation of a plantation economy in the Southeast; in particular, the production of coffee, cocoa, and bananas. Europeans were encouraged by the colonial government to settle in the Ivory Coast and produce these crops for export. Africans were drawn into the production of cash crops through a combination of personal economic motives and pressure by the colonial regime. The revenue generated by the selling of cocoa and coffee was enough to attract enterprising Africans to cultivate small plots to Ivorians from other regions than the Southeast who were willing to work the land, often in disregard of local customs. The head tax imposed on each African male was another factor that led many Ivorians to produce cash crops along with their traditional foodstuffs. Generally, the colonial government relied on "...two methods of direct coercion—taxation and forced labor" (Stryker 1971:128). These were the tools used by the French to carry out their new economic policy of *"Mise en valeur"* in the Ivory Coast. To facilitate the development of the plantation economy, the government invested heavily in the construction of roads, ports, and other infrastructure needed to move the crops to the market. These investments, however, were in the Southeast near Abidjan where coffee and cocoa production was located. Other regions, notably the savanna North, were ignored in the colonial government's investment programs. Richard Stryker (1971:128) stated:

> French colonial rule decisively reversed the traditional advantages of the savanna peoples in favor of those in the forest zone, especially in the southeastern area. This shift was due to longer and more intensive colonization in the south, to a far greater effort of mission and government education in coastal areas, to the introduction of cash crops suited to the forest zone, and to the creation of transport and communications facilities between the plantation areas of the forest and the coast, whence the cash crops were exported.

Much of the traditional trade that had taken place in the North had come to an end by the mid-1930s (Aubertin 1983a:35), leaving the northern region dominated by a subsistence economy, whereas in the Southeast, both coffee and cocoa production had increased substantially, providing African planters an important source of income.

This does not mean that the northern region was left unaffected by developments in the South. Colonial administrators turned to the northern region, including Upper Volta which had been attached to the Ivory Coast in 1933, as a source of cheap labor. While forced labor rules applied to every region, the use of Northern labor on Southern plantations did little for the economic development of the North. In general, African laborers had to work on European plantations at extremely low wages or with no remuneration at all. Forced labor rules, in essence, provided European planters with a virtual monopoly of the labor force. Much of the political and economic tension between African and European planters arose over this issue (Zolberg 1964). Without the favoritism of the colonial regime, European planters would not have been able to compete with African planters in the Southeast who offered better wages and living arrangements to those coming from the North (Aubertin 1983b:33). In 1946, when the forced labor laws were suppressed, the pattern of migration to the South that had begun as a result of involuntary migration evolved into a pattern of voluntary migration. Northerners continued to come to the South, either as traders, notably the Moslem traders, or as laborers (Person 1981:20).

African planters in the South soon surpassed the French plantations in output. By 1955, they were producing 95 percent of the cocoa and 85 percent of the coffee. With an unfettered labor market and rise in commodity prices following the Second World War, the economy of the Ivory Coast grew at a rapid pace, eventually making it the richest French West African territory. The surplus derived from the export of cash crops, however, was not rechannelled back into the rural sector, but to the urban sector—namely to Abidjan.

Abidjan emerged as the focal point of the country during the 1930s. In 1934, the colonial government moved the capital to Abidjan from Bingerville. With the location of the colonial administration in Abidjan, the city became the center of political and economic activity in the colony. Most of the European population resided in Abidjan. The African population in Abidjan increased from 50,000 in 1932 to 330,000 in 1955, but there were still strict limits on migration to the capital. Also, European neighbors were off-limits to Africans who were concentrated in areas designated for them by the colonial government (Cohen 1984:59). Due to the strict rules limiting urban-rural migration, the colonial government never had to face the consequences of its policy of neglect of upcountry areas. Although with the economic boom following the war some limits were eased, the general policy of restraining rural migration to the city remained. However, the major investment projects taking place at the time concerned the city. In the 1950s, storage facilities were enlarged and a deepwater port was constructed in Abidjan to increase the level of exports from the colony. Relying on zoning laws, taxation, and other special provisions, the colonial regime established an urban center capable of supporting economic development that depended heavily on productive agricultural exports (Cohen 1984:62). Accordingly, French colonialism structured in a decisive way the manner in which regions were integrated into the national and international economy. With the growth of the Abidjan subregions as the country's primary economic center and the subsequent neglect of other areas, a "center-periphery" relationship arose, "typically characterized by the emergence of a dominant city which forms the focus of polarized development, while the periphery hinterland remains relatively backward" (Davies 1975:36).

Interestingly, the first independent political activity in the Ivory Coast occurred in the rural areas. The Syndicate Agricole Africain (SAA), created in 1944, sought to organize the African producers in the Southeast. Although not in a formal sense a political organization, the SAA, led by Felix Houphouët-Boigny, prepared the way for the formation of the country's first political party in 1946, the Parti Democratique Africain (PDCI). Despite the fact that organizers of the SAA and PDCI were planters themselves, they focused their energies on the capital. As Michael Cohen (1984:60) states, "The links that were established between the rural and urban political groups at that time provided an important basis for understanding subsequent policy affecting urban settlements, and Abidjan in particular." Even more importantly, the "links" help explain why the biased economic development strategy instituted by the colonial regime continued after the Ivory Coast acquired independence in 1960. The urban and rural elite in the Ivory Coast had a common interest in maintaining the export economy in the Southeast. The overlapping of interest can be explained by the fact that the largest producers in the country were often prominent civil servants and top party officials (Gastellau and Yapi 1982: Chap. 5; Bakary 1984:45). With this in mind, it is easier to understand why the economic policies adopted in the postcolonial period reflected two dominant concerns—the development of Abidjan as a modern industrial city and the expansion of the export economy in the South.

Postindependence: A Concentrated Form of Development Is Adopted

The political elite who took over the reigns of power after independence pursued an economic policy similar to that of their former colonial rulers. The president, Felix Houphouët-Boigny, put emphasis on the expansion of cash crops in the Southeast and to the attraction of foreign capital and technology into the country. To achieve this, he thought it necessary to concentrate resources in the Abidjan subregion. The assumption was that European investors and skilled technicians would be more likely to invest and live in a modern city. To this end, ". . . urban development investments were subsidized by public revenue in order to facilitate exports and to encourage continued foreign investment" (Cohen 1984:62); however, little attention was given to the development of other regions and urban centers. Unlike their colonial counterparts, however, the government could not adopt this politically unacceptable policy of restricting rural migration to Abidjan. In any case, this was not seen as a problem in the early 1960s.

Political officials in the Ivory Coast saw concentrated development in the Abidjan subregion as the best development process for a new nation with limited economic resources (Stryker 1971:137–138). As one official put it, "The Ivory Coast rejects 'ineffective egalitarianism' in favour of the concentration of economic growth around carefully controlled 'poles of development'" (Cohen 1973:239). In supporting critical sectors in the economy within a specific area, Ivorian planners believed that scarce resources could be used more efficiently. Following the theories of certain Western economists who argued that it was wiser to concentrate limited economic resources instead of spreading them widely, the government invested heavily in state agencies which sought to develop the agricultural potential of the Southeast and import-substitution industries in Abidjan (Frelastre 1980:39–40). As one Western economist, W. Arthur Lewis (1967:35), argued, "The redistribution of limited resources to poorer regions would only 'nip development in the bud.'" Freidmann and Weaver (1979:126) noted that for these economists "the basic idea was that urban industrial growth could be diffused to the backward regions of a developing country by concentrating infrastructure and directing productive investments at selected points (or subregions) which had potential for economic expansion." Throughout the 1960s and part of the 1970s, this strategy of concentrated development seemed to work well for the Ivory Coast. With an annual growth rate of 7 percent over two decades, Abidjan was transformed from a small colonial city into a major metropolitan center with one of Africa's largest industrial sectors (Mytelka 1984).

In theory, the concentrated pattern of development should have eventually created linkages with the more underdeveloped regions (Hirschman 1958:183–185). In many ways, this did occur, but not in a way necessarily beneficial to the country. The type of linkages which evolved were those of dependency. Poorer areas depended entirely on Abidjan to meet their needs. Any development which occurred in upcountry areas was sporadic and depended on the political interests of government officials. According to Cohen (1973:239), "The government maintains its options by allocating 'development' according to political necessity." Since economic and political power were concentrated in Abidjan, political necessity tended to turn the government's attention to the capital. The option for those seeking to escape the stagnant situation outside of the Abidjan subregion was to migrate south. Therefore, the most dramatic linkage to develop was the intensive migration to the capital from the poorer regions, especially the North, in the country as well as from the surrounding West African states. With over 60 percent of all the jobs in the modern sector concentrated in Abidjan and a substantial part of the state's investment budget going to the city (INADES 1986), it is not surprising that Northerners saw migrating to Abidjan as a solution to the problem of economic underdevelopment in their region.

Northern Migration: The Exodus of the Young

Northern migration in the postcolonial period was a phenomenon among the young. Intrarural migration appealed mainly to young adults whose decisions were motivated by disparities in income, job opportunities, and access to money incomes (Plan 1975–1980). Unlike in the colonial period when Northern traders and laborers went south seeking economic opportunities in the rural sector, the vast majority of those descending south in the 1960s headed for Abidjan. The dominant belief among young Northerners was that Abidjan was where the action was. Northern cities like Odienee, Korhogo, and Frekessedougo had little pull on those leaving their small rural communities.

The government underestimated the attractiveness of the capital to those in poorer regions of the country. Cohen (1974:62) stated that "the dynamism of Abidjan was consistently underestimated by demographers who projected that the city would reach 400,000 by 1980; a threshold that was attained by 1967. The city grew at a roughly 10 percent growth compounded annually for 5 years." During the 1960s and 1970s, rural communities were losing their population in increasing numbers. In 1965, for example, there were 4.5 million people in the country, with nearly 4 million of them living in rural areas. By 1983, out of 9 million, nearly 4 million resided in cities (INADES 1986:8). By 1985, Abidjan had at least 20 percent of the country's population of 10 million.

Along with the concentration of educational and administrative services in Abidjan, the system promoted an urban image of progress and modernity in the schools. Therefore, the educational system played an important role in the urban-rural migration. Thus, as G. Christopher (1970: 46–47) noted:

> The education process presents the rural child with what could be called the "good things" of life, that is, consumer objects which are associated with the 20th century. Some of these objects are the television, a bicycle, spacious and modern houses. However, these objects are not generally available in the rural areas; it is much easier to obtain these things in the city. The style of life reflected in the educational system is European and this style of life is led by all of the country's political leaders.

The perception that things were better in the city was shared by parents as well, who believed that if their children remained on the land, they would be poor like them. This perception among Northerners was even more acute than in the South where coffee and cocoa production had produced some tangible material benefits for the rural population (Christopher 1970:47).

Increasing migration to the city only exacerbated a growing unemployment and underemployment problem. The modern sector could not expand fast enough to absorb the young who arrived in the city seeking jobs (INADES 1986:18). Many skilled Ivorians competed not only between themselves but with the large expatriate French community that came to the country to run the industries. A similar problem existed for unskilled Ivorians who found themselves competing with Africans from surrounding West African states for poorly paid jobs, or jobs in the informal sector. Ironically, the surplus labor in Abidjan contrasted with the labor shortages which began to appear in the countryside in the 1970s (Christopher 1970:11). With the loss of the young to the city, rural communities were becoming increasingly the sites of the old and the very young (Kanon 1978). In this respect, the urban crisis was directly linked to a growing rural crisis.

In a drive to diversify export crops in the South, the Ivorian government neglected the development of subsistence agriculture. The production of food crops was left to traditional methods at the very time that urban growth increased demand for food products. State investments went to the mechanization and expansion of large plantations generally. Increased mechanization and the spread of large-scale plantations reduced the available land to small-scale producers in the South, increasing the demand among the young for urban jobs (Frelastre 1980). In the North, the loss of the young hampered the expansion of the production of food products for export to the South. As with many Third World nations, the Ivory Coast saw its importation of basic food commodities increase while local production stagnated (Frelastre 1980). Thus, by 1975, the country's agricultural sector faced two major setbacks diminishing cultivable land in the South and labor shortages for food crop production in the North (Kanon 1978: 20–25).

Clearly, then, the type of development decisions made by the government in the 1960s had a major impact on how resources were distributed between regions and which sectors were developed. In concentrating on attracting foreign investment for industrialization and expanding cash crop production in the South, the government opted for a concentrated form of development within the Abidjan subregion, believing that wider economic benefits would eventually spread to the poorer regions. The cumulative effect, however, has been the sharpening of economic and social differences between the Abidjan subregion and the mostly rural upcountry communities.

In turn, regional inequality engendered an exodus from poor rural areas to the city. The most dramatic effect of this migration had been the spread of "bindovilles" around the periphery of Abidjan and a stagnating rural economy. Only in 1969, however, when the eruption of protests among students and the unemployed became too widespread to ignore, did the government realize the seriousness of the crisis (Cohen 1974). Added to these protests was growing pressure from Northerners to do something about the backwardness of their region and the loss of their young to Abidjan (Den Tuinder 1978:148).

A New Policy Framework and Development

Regional Development: A Diffused Pattern of Economic Growth

In a response to the growing social crisis in the country, Houphouet-Boigny held a series of "dialogues" with different socioeconomic categories and regional groups in 1969–1970. What became strikingly clear to the president and his ministers was that a different economic strategy was needed to correct the inequalities between regions. Mohammed Diawara

(1970:134), minister of planning, pointed out at the PDIC's congress in 1970 that "it was up to the country's public powers to put into place corrective actions in order to avoid an aggravation of regional disparities which could undermine the nation's social fabric and block further economic growth." Within this context, the president decided to jettison the policy of concentrated development around Abidjan for an economic strategy based on regional development. Instead of localizing resources in one subregion and emphasizing a sectorial approach to agricultural expansion, more resources would be allocated to several regional poles scattered throughout the country and a multisectorial approach to agriculture would be implemented. Plans were drawn up for every region with the intention of fostering regionally based economic growth by improving local infrastructure.

Several state agencies were created specifically for this purpose (Dubresson 1980:80). The Authority for the Development of the Bandama Valley (ABV) and the Southwestern Regional Authority (SORA) were established in 1969. In 1971, the Fund for Regional Development (FRD) was created. Each of these agencies was responsible for the construction of large infrastructural projects as a prelude to more localized programs for rural producers. Only in the North, however, did the government come up with a more ambitious program whose primary objective was to mitigate rural migration from upcountry communities to Abidjan by developing the entire region.

The president had promised a more balanced form of growth and the economic integration of peripheral regions in the past. During a trip to the North in 1965, Houphouët-Boigny promised that the "north would have its revenge and each peasant will attain equality with his brother in the south in five years," but little actually came from the visit. In fact, the gap between North and South widened considerably over the next five years. Therefore, the political pressure on the president to do something was mounting.

Also, as previously indicated, there was a realization that the regional imbalances were undermining further economic growth in the South. Migrants sought employment in the city, not in the countryside where they were needed. The economy depended on the export of cash crops. Without this revenue it was impossible to maintain a modern industrial sector in Abidjan. Despite the presence of foreign investors, much of the industrial activity in the Abidjan subregion had been financed by the state from the earnings of coffee and cocoa exports (Mytelka 1984:168). In the new economy strategy, the goal was to encourage a new type of industry based on large units of production oriented principally toward foreign markets. The North was chosen as the regional location for the government's new industrialization scheme.

The North and Sugar Production

A decision had already been made to construct one sugar plant in the northern city of Frekesseduogo. Production from this plant would basically meet local demand for sugar. As was mentioned in the preceding section, due to political pressure and a growing urban-rural crisis, the president felt that something more ambitious was needed for the North. Thus, Houphouët-Boigny announced during a tour across the North that ten sugar complexes would be built in the region, creating about thirty thousand jobs. The president also stressed the significance of exporting the surplus (Aubertin 1983a:9). He stated:

> The reason why the Government decided to take a number of drastic and energetic steps to reduce disparities between the various regions of the country was that it realized, all other distortions set aside, just how extreme and thoroughly abnormal those disparities were. A gulf was opening up between a forest-clad and heavily urbanized Ivory Coast...: it was a gulf that could have endangered our national unity and harmonious relations with each other.

The sugar initiative was born with the problem of national unity in mind. The details of how to implement and finance the sugar project were left to the ministers of agriculture and planning; however, Houphouët-Boigny made clear his principal objective.

> The sugar program would constitute one of the government's most decisive development efforts. Anxious to respond to the satisfaction of domestic needs as well as the possibility of exporting sugar, the sugar project will reflect our will to diversify our agricultural production and to ensure for ourselves the riches of our natural resources.... The program also has the ambition, which appears to me the most important aspect of it, to benefit regions previously ignored in the development process. (Aubertin 1983a:9)

At the time of the speech, sugar prices had reached a record high, leading government and private officials to view the commodity as a potential source of income. The decision to build all of the complexes in the North reflected a policy interest in promoting economic growth outside of the Abidjan subregion and slowing rural flight by the young. In many respects, the goal was to modernize a backward region as quickly as possible. As mentioned, ten sugar complexes were envisioned; however, the number was eventually reduced to six because of costs.

The Society for the Development of Sugar (SodeSucre) was created in 1975 to implement the government's regional development program. According to the minister of agriculture (Sawadogo 1977:156), an objective of SodeSucre was to provide jobs outside of the Abidjan subregion and stimulate local agricultural production. It was believed that the income generated by the plants and adjacent plantations would function as a mobilizing factor for local economies. The theory of linkages discussed earlier regarding the development of the Abidjan subregion was projected onto the Northern region. The complexes would transform local economies by introducing a constant source of revenue into a predominantly subsistence economic environment. As a result of this monetary income, Northern peasants would find a market for their agricultural products. Young Ivorians attracted to Abidjan would find the small urban centers near to the sugar complexes more appealing than the "bindovilles" around Abidjan. Thus, as Christopher (1970:56) observed, "The philosophy of Ivorian planners was that with the development of secondary semi-urban centers rural migration would be slowed."

Economic Effects of the Sugar Program

Without going into the complicated details about the cost and construction of the sugar plants in the North, it is important to point out that they proved to be much more costly than expected. Before the program was completed, the price of sugar had dropped considerably, thus undermining any hopes on the part of Ivorian officials to rely on exports to pay for the program (Bessis 1980:58). To a certain extent, however, the complexes achieved part of the objective set for them. An important source of revenue was introduced into the region, and the employment opportunities created helped to reduce migration. Indeed, a new phenomenon arose with the completion of the sugar complexes in the north in 1979–1981. For the first time, "a process of reverse migration [took place] away from Abidjan in the south towards the north" (Aubertin 1983a:126). Particularly, young Ivorians with some education but little chance of finding employment in Abidjan migrated north to work in administrative positions in the plants.

Ultimately, though, the project failed to achieve its objective for the simple reason that it became too expensive for the state to maintain its ambitious goal of creating semiurban units in a rural environment. SodeSucre was given a mandate to manage the complexes as business enterprises; that is, to make a profit as well as carry out a social program of creating jobs, providing new houses, and constructing roads in the North. With the double agenda, SodeSucre was limited from the start. The array of social programs hampered its ability to be profitable. The ensuing economic problems of SodeSucre must be understood in the context of the social role that it was required to play (Aubertin 1983a:126).

The social role that SodeSucre was required to play stemmed from the political and social exigencies which promoted the regional development program. Pressed by the growing urban crisis in Abidjan and a corresponding rural crisis with the young leaving the land in increasing numbers, the government attempted to recreate an urban environment within a predominantly rural milieu. Cities were planned around the sugar plants. Schools, clinics, and entertainment facilities were promised to those working at the sugar mills. The objective was to foster the growth of "medium-sized towns (10,000 to 50,000 inhabitants)," which would be seen "to offer advantages of urban life without the drawbacks of the big city (pollution, congestion, shanty towns, delinquency, unemployment) and to do so in the context of a specifically African lifestyle" (Plan 1975–1980:44). Most of these promises, however, remained unfulfilled when the sugar program ran into acute financial difficulties in 1980. The demand for sugar abroad did not grow as the government hoped, and the process continued to decline; thus, the state has inherited a large financial burden. Since the level of investment in the Ivorian complexes was relatively high, it was impossible to sell the sugar at competitive prices without major subsidies.

13

Ethnicity and the Urban Setting in Africa

Hassan Omari Kaya

Introduction

This paper is based on the argument that despite ethnic consciousness not being a monopoly of African states, it has become a salient feature of the political economy of Africa and is essentially an urban problem. It begins with a discussion of concepts such as race, ethnic group, and tribe, in order to tackle the problem of definition and then examines the relationship between the weak material base of the African economies and the intensification of ethnic consciousness. It later examines the reasons why ethnicity is concentrated in the urban environment.

Problematic Concepts

As a result of theoretical controversies, both in common parlance and academic discourse, it is essential that certain concepts should be initially defined and differentiated. These include: *race, ethnic group,* and *tribe* and its derivative *tribalism*. It will be shown later that most of these concepts are subjective categories.

Most social scientists do not refer the concept of race to a biologically specific subspecies of Homo sapiens. Instead, they mean a group of people which is socially defined as physically distinct, whether or not such physical differences exist. This makes the concept of race very "subjective," because the existence of a "race" is not dependent on certain empirically observable characteristics but on whether the members of a given society think that such groups exist. For instance, an Afro-American will be a "Negro" or "black" in America and could be categorized as "colored" in South Africa. The relationship between these subjectively perceived physical criteria and objective correlates of race is of central sociological interest.

An ethnic group, on the other hand, is socially defined in terms of cultural uniformities within it, like common customs, religion or language, and cultural differences between itself and other groups. However, two ethnic groups may be culturally identical, yet regard themselves as quite different. An example would be the Afrikaans-speaking whites and coloreds in South Africa.

The term *tribe* has quite different meanings. Often it means an ethnic group, but with the additional invidious connotation of primitivism. For instance, social scientists would refer to the Yourba as a tribe, but not the Turks or Danes. In this analysis, the term *tribe* will be taken to mean an indigenous African ethnic group that speaks a common language and has a feeling of solidarity. An ethnically based solidarity, especially of a political nature, is commonly termed *tribalism*. The latter is also subjective in the sense that what in Europe or Asia has been called nationalism, i.e., political movement for unification, autonomy, or independence on the basis of common ethnicity, would be referred as tribalism in Africa. Even among African intellectuals and political leaders, any divisive, particularistic type of nationalism which they do not approve is termed tribalism.

Both race and ethnicity, as already discussed, have become the basis of unjust distinctions between people in much of the world, including Africa. These invidious differences are expressed through prejudiced attitudes called *racism* or *racialism* if the basis of differentiation is held to be physical and *ethnocentrism* if the difference is cultural. Racism and ethnicity are types of beliefs, ideologies, or attitudes. However, students of race and ethnic relations are also concerned with actual behavior. This is because in terms of direct practical consequences, behavior is frequently more important than attitudes, i.e., how people of different ethnic or racial groups behave towards each other, and the effects these patterns of behavior have on their lives. Most of the intergroup behavior falls under the label of *discrimination*. One can discriminate in favor of or against certain groups. This works on the basis of stereotypes, i.e., a special kind of prejudiced attitudes, specific in content and dealing with alleged properties or qualities of certain groups. Thus in East Africa, to describe all Indians as greedy and dishonest or Chagga people as thieves would be to express stereotypes.

This chapter concentrates on the problem of ethnicity in Africa, and the following section analyzes how this phenomenon has become one of the salient features of social relations in Africa.

Ethnicity and the Political Economy of Africa

As already pointed out, ethnic consciousness is not a monopoly of African states, but it has become an important aspect of the social relations in the African countries because of the underdeveloped material conditions of those countries. In plural societies like those of Africa, characterized by meager socioeconomic surplus and unequal distribution of this social product, fear of being confined to the bottom of the receiving ladder forces the individual to seek the security provided by ethnic solidarity. This fear of insecurity is reinforced by social relations and attitudes which accept and sanction inequality as inevitable. Ethnic consciousness did not begin with colonialism, as it is sometimes argued. The latter intensified it. The Arab and European demand for slaves drove African communities into warfare with each other in order to obtain captives. Slave raids bred insecurity and forced some groups to submit to the protection of more powerful and dominant tribes. The new relations bred attitudes of superiority and inferiority among the ethnic groups.

Colonialism was more interested in exploiting the colonies for their resources than to develop them. Moreover, the colonialists saw that resistance to exploitation would be less effective if the colonized were kept divided. Even French colonialism, which did not apply the policy of "indirect rule," tended to choose administrative units which coincided with tribal divisions. Hence, when electoral politics were later introduced, the tribal divisions became the electoral constituencies. As long as political units coincided with tribal groups, campaigns for political support entailed the stirring of ethnic consciousness. Ethnic identification was further enhanced by competition among the adminstrative units for socioeconomic amenities. The colonizers built socioeconomic infrastructure such as roads, railways, and schools. in areas where it served their exploitative purposes. Ultimately, colonialism left a legacy of imbalances in which one ethnic group was far better provided with socioeconomic facilities than others. These disparities deepened attitudes of superiority and inferiority among the ethnic groups of African countries. Socioeconomic imbalances forced people to migrate to areas where colonial economic activities were concentrated, such as urban areas, plantations, and mines, in order to take advantage of the new goods and services. This was further encouraged by the colonial policy of taxation which had to be paid in cash. Another factor which currently forces people to move to the urban places is the increasing poverty in the rural areas. For almost two decades, food production in most parts of Africa has failed to keep up with the growth of population. Cash crops are often blamed for Africa's food crisis, but studies have shown that there is no wide evidence of cash crops thriving at the expense of food crops; indeed, the overall acreage of cash crops fell, and yields and per capita production of most cash crops fell even more steeply than food crops in recent times. It is argued that peasants who make up seven out of ten black Africans saw their cash income fall at the same time as food production per person declined.

Harrison (1987) rightly stated that poverty is the main growth sector in Africa. During the 1985 famine in Niger, 400,000 nomads are reported to have moved into the urban areas. In Ethiopia, husbands and sons set off from the countryside into towns in search of work or assistance. However, most of these towns or places of employment are far from the homes of the migrants. In most cases, employment opportunities are limited due to the low level of industrialization in most African countries, and when wage labor is available, the working and living conditions are quite appalling. This creates a situation of insecurity and lack of confidence among the migrants in the urban settng. Since the very limited modern socioeconomic opportunities exist only in the few urban areas, it is mainly in these areas that contacts between members of different ethnic groups take place on an extensive scale. This is reflected by the ethnic composition of the following African cities. In 1950–1960, there were representatives of 50 ethnic groups in Kampala; 60 in Brazzaville; 62 in Nairobi. In 1965, the population of Abidjan included 7 percent of the native ethnics, 11 percent of groups in the immediate vicinity, 36 percent from other groups in the country, and 46 percent from foreign countries. In 1948, the original ethnic group in Bamako accounted for 47 percent of the city's population, while in 1977, this ethnic group accounted for only 20 percent (Williams 1980). The following section discusses ethnic consciousness in the urban environment.

Ethnicity and the Urban Setting

The data presented in the preceding section on the composition of the African cities implies that the ethnic problem of African politics is first and foremost an urban one. Any significant interethnic contact at the village level is confined to those villages located near the periphery of the ethnic group and those close to the urban areas. Otherwise, interethnic experiences of the rural populations in Africa is obtained indirectly from stories of the urban dwellers who return occasionally to their native villages for a visit. Skinner (1966) has also observed this in respect to Indonesia and argues that ethnicity is essentially associated with urban centers and villages near ethnically heterogeneous cities. As already stated, urban life offers very little socioeconomic security. There is no guarantee for employment, no provision for care of the old; compensation for sickness or accident is low or nonexistent, and the few pension programs are quite meager. It is under these conditions of social insecurity that contact between members of the same ethnic group takes place on an extensive scale. It is quite common for them to help each other in difficulties like sickness, debt, employment, etc. By creating the "village" or "tribal community" in the town, the ethnic associations demonstrate and reinforce ethnic consciousness.

Literature on various African cities—for instance, Nairobi, Lagos, Abidjan, and Dar es Salaam—has shown how even with cultural assimilation, increased education, income, and urban experience, individuals in these cities tend to have friendship networks and ethnic political indentifications that are just as strong as those for persons who have not experienced these cultural changes. It should be pointed out that the base from which they select their friendship grows larger. Migrants first arriving in big cities enter immediately into an ethnically based friendship network rather than having to develop new ties on arrival. Studies in Nairobi and Dar es Salaam have shown that the majority of the people interviewed indicated that they stayed with either a relative or fellow tribesman when they first came to the city (Irvine 1975). This contradicts the integrationist theory, which sees ethnicity as a factor of diminishing importance in African urban areas as a result of changes in educational patterns, increased economic assimilation, or sheer passage of time and intergroup contact. This view is represented by authors such as Apter (1955) and Coleman (1964). The theory uses different behaviors as dependent variables. It defines ethnicity as a manifestation of certain cultural forms, such as mode of dress, religion, ritual practices, special foods, or languages. According to this view, the immigrant, and to a greater extent his offspring, often abandons and usually modifies his behavior the longer he stays in the city and the more he is exposed to outside influences and pressures. Therefore, it argues that it is in the urban environment that cultural assimilation and detribalization take place.

The basis of the argument is the erroneous assumption that contact and awareness breed understanding and cooperation. It does not take into account the fact that there are times when intergroup contact and familiarity could lead to contempt and hatred. This is more true when these groups meet in situations of great resource scarcity, and in the job market of an African urban environment. Furthermore, the representatives of this theory fail to distinguish between decline in loyalty to the tribal government or chief and to the tribal community. Often what they mean by detribalization is simply a decline in loyalty to "village authority." However, it does not necessarily follow that an individual who is no longer loyal to his village chief has also rejected the tribe as a community from which he expects a certain security in the hostile environment. Mitchell (1976) states that people in the rural areas are apt to take their tribe for granted, but when they come to town, their tribal membership assumes new importance.

Given the capitalist structures and values of the colonial legacy, competition for socioeconomic amenities is the most dominant feature of the urban setting. In the face of extreme scarcity, it could hardly be otherwise. Wagley (1975) emphasizes that it is important to identify the object of competition. This is because the more valuable the resource over which there is competition, the more intense the ethnic conflict. The net effect of this intense socioeconomic competition is individual insecurity. Therefore, ethnic group affiliation and identity can be understood as a mechanism to overcome this pervasive insecurity of the African urban setting. The limit imposed on the individual by his physiology and the pressure of other competitors impel him to seek allies in order to attain some of his goals. The unit chosen for alignment at any time and place varies with the nature of the one in competition. Within the extended family, the nuclear family alignment prevails; in the clan, the extended family; in the village, the clan; and in the city or urban area, the ethnic group. Therefore, for national politics, the ethnic group is the most relevant and significant form of alignment, and this is usually dominant in the urban areas.

The Future of Ethnicity in African Societies

It is common among the ruling factions in the African states to condemn ethnicity and proclaim the necessity of a national unity. Nobody takes these proclamations seriously because the very people who denounce ethnic identification are the ones who are institutionalizing it. They make it the basis for political and economic participation. Ethnic consciousness works in the interests of the ruling classes in Africa because it is the major antidote against the development of class consciousness among the working masses. Moreover, the ruling class in Africa, or bourgeoisie, is fragmented and ridden with contradictions. This has its origin in the colonial economic policies and was reinforced by the political line the colonizers adopted to maintain their power and curb African nationalism.

The colonial governments tried to check the march to independence by sponsoring reactionary parties. This strategy could work only if a political base for the party of reaction could be created. Therefore, the sponsoring of these parties was associated with the policy of making some regions or political constituencies autonomous and limiting the access of politicians to other regions. The colonialists also encouraged the fear of ethnic domination by exploiting the regional socioeconomic imbalances which they had created. All this meant the regionalization of the African ruling class within a particular country. Some authors have differentiated between "traditional," "modern," and "bureaucratic" bourgeoisie in Africa (Ake 1967; Shivji 1973). In respect to political integration, these distinctions are less important than regionalism. This is because the regions, as in Nigeria, were so isolated that it did not make much sense for the bourgeoisie to form political alignments on the basis of these analytical differences. Furthermore, the economy is so disjointed and the political system as inherited from colonialism so complex that alliances between the "traditional" or "bureaucratic" bourgeoisie from different parts of the country were hardly rewarding. Their economic interests did not necessarily coincide.

Moreover, if the ruling class had made these distinctions within itself the basis of its political differences, the resulting political parties would find it difficult to make their differences intelligible to the masses they intended to mobilize. Ethnicity is ideal to use for creating a political base because of the following reasons: (1) ethnic consciousness was already well-developed before independence; (2) its loyalty was something that made sense to a lot of people, and its utility was already demonstrated in the urban areas; (3) the appeal to ethnicity was likely to be successful in a plural society with little industrialization and rudimentary development of secondary associations based on job or professional affiliations; (4) the regions and political units tend to be homogeneous in ethnicity. Thus, to win an ethnic group was to win a political constituency, the result of which is that political candidates are not chosen for their commitment to the nation but because they can promise certain socioeconomic rewards to their ethnic constituents. There have been a number of theories on how ethnic consciousness in Africa will decrease. Morrison (1975) argues that ethnic consciousness will decline with modernization—schooling, urbanization, communication. As already pointed out, these aspects are said to bring people together. But experience has shown that ethnic loyalty in African countries increases despite modernization (Zolberg 1964; van den Berghe 1975).

14

Urban Growth and Criminal Behavior: The Study of Onitsha City in Anambra State, Nigeria, 1970–1981

Donald E. Mbosowo

Introduction

The growth of cities throughout Nigeria is the important phenomenon of the twentieth century. The growth is based on population and population movement. Ever since 1963, the population of Nigeria has been based on estimates projected from the census figures of that year. The true population of Nigeria still remains a matter of controversy since the decision by the Supreme Military Council in 1975 to annul the disputed census figures announced a year earlier. The United Nations estimate for mid–1974 was 61.25 million, with an estimated growth rate of 2.7 percent per annum. A 1976 estimate was 64.62 million. Current estimates put it at 100 million. Since demographic profiles are subject to regular changes depending on differential mortality and natality parameters which are often reflective of environmental differences in different ecological zones, it is obvious that inherent errors in these projections have been transferred into the developmental planning strategies of the nation for different sections of Nigeria with obvious distortions of the true situation.

It is usually assumed that up to 80 percent of Nigeria's population lives in the rural areas of the country. The density of population depends on the physical and spatial arrangement. The population density is greatest in the South, averaging 120 persons per square kilometer over the areas, and diminishing on approaching the Middle Belt where densities range from 11 persons per square kilometer in Adamawa Province to 36 in Plateau Province. Next follows a belt of relatively higher density north of the Middle Belt, reaching as many as 15 persons in Bornu in the extreme Northwest. In Eastern Nigeria, densities remain at 161 persons per square kilometer. The most populated divisions are Orlu, Uyo, Abak, Okigwe, where density of population ranges from 598 to 443 persons per square kilometer.

The major cities of developing countries, including Nigeria, consist primarily of migrants from the rural areas or villages (Breese 1969). Although this city growth is generally attributed to an economic "push" from an overpopulated agricultural area, one must not underestimate the great significance of the "pull" factor of cities, where more diverse occupational opportunities are available, wages are often higher, and better employment and educational opportunities are offered (Banton 1957: 214).

Industrialization and the concomitant development of a money economy often necessitate movement to the city for economic objectives. Young men leave their families to tend their land while they try to secure work in the city, thus creating a large pool of unmarried males whose main goal is to accumulate money (Elkan 1960). For example, the Igbo people leave their rural villages in large numbers because there is not enough land for all to farm and build homes. The Igbo people are known for their business skills, and since there are no avenues for business in the villages because of lack of infrastructure, most of them leave their rural areas for business enterprises in the cities. Also, since social status is built on wealth and not academic achievement, most university graduates have abandoned their office work and gone into business that brings in more money. The idea of gaining recognition from one's wealth, no matter by what means, has forced people into illegitimate means of economic success. The cities seem to be the places where the migration centers are.

Urban growth in Nigeria has brought about a lot of problems, including criminal activities. The statistical data for several cities in Nigeria have shown that crime is related to industrial development and urban growth. For example, a study of fifty prison inmates in Jos for the year 1984 revealed that 60 percent of them migrated to the city of Jos for jobs, and because jobs were not available, they turned to crime as a means of survival (Mbosowo 1984). Plateau State Police annual crime reports have shown a higher crime rate in the cities than in the rural areas. For example, in 1984, the state capital, Jos, recorded 5,253 crime cases as compared to its surrounding rural divisions, such as Keffi (737), Akwanga (350), Shendam (719), Barkin-Ladi (388), Lafia (671), and Mangu (828).

This evidence shows that cities absorb many people, including those who are there for burglary and petty robbery. Most people go to the cities to engage in robbery because no one may know them, as opposed to the villages where people know one another. Cities become hideouts for those who have not found jobs, but decide to make a living through criminal activities. Cities also offer far greater opportunities for criminal activities, as opposed to the villages where there is often little to steal except agricultural products, chickens, and goats. Robbery in villages is easily detected since people know one another, while it is easy to steal from strangers in the cities with minimum detection.

In Nigeria, certain cities have shown rapid population growth in the past years. For example, in the northern part of Nigeria, the city of Kano, with a population of 295,000 in 1963, had grown by 49.5 percent in 1979 and has continued to grow at the average annual rate of 2.5 percent, to 499,000 in 1984. Its growth emerged as a result of economic and political factors, and its initial contacts with the empires of Songhai and Kanem Bornu. Commerce and craft industries dominated their economic life in the precolonial period, and has remained a major industrial center. (*Economic and Social Statistics Bulletin* 1985).

In the southern part of the country, Ibadan, with a population of 627,000 in 1963, had grown by 49.3 percent in 1979 and has grown at the average annual rate of 2.5 percent to 1,060,000 in 1984, while Abeokuta, with 187,000 in 1963, which had grown by 49.2 percent in 1979, has continued to grow at the average annual rate of 3.1 percent, to 324,000 in 1984. In the Southeast, the city of Calabar, with 76,000 in 1963, had grown by 50 percent in 1979 and has continued to grow at the average annual rate of 2.5 percent, to 126,000 in 1984. In the eastern part of the country, the city of Enugu, with 158,000 in 1963, had grown by 17.1 percent in 1979 but has shown a high average annual growth rate of 4.8 percent, to 234,000 in 1984. And in the Middle Belt, the city of Jos, with 90,000 in 1963, had grown by 50 percent in 1979 and has continued to grow at the average annual rate of 2.5 percent, to 153,000 in 1984. The fact that Jos has a mild climate has made it an attraction for migrants (*Economic and Social Statistics Bulletin* 1985).

The growth of Lagos as an urban center started in 1861 following the British annexation of Lagos as a colony. Lagos became the colonial administrative center where trade and commerce gained administrative prominence. Lagos, with a population of 665,000 in 1963, had grown by 49.2 percent in 1979 and has also grown at the average annual rate of 2.6 percent, to 1,125,000 in 1984. Now the annual growth rate for Lagos, according to the National Population Bureau (1985) is 4 percent (*Economic and Social Statistics Bulletin* 1985).

Lagos has managed to remain a great center of attraction because of growth in economic activities, its importance as a political administrative center, increased industrialization, improved social amenities, infrastructure, and a good communication system. It is a melting pot, and most Nigerians would like to work in Lagos. In the process, it has become a den for criminals.

An important aspect of demographic change in Nigeria is the tempo by which cities have rapidly grown. Nigeria is generally believed to be a predominantly rural nation, but the rate of urban growth is one of the highest in the world. If the trend of the country's rate of urban growth continues unabated, the nation's urban population will double in fourteen years (*Guardian* 1984). The reason for such rapid urban growth is lack of rural development, and everyone wants to enjoy certain amenities in the towns.

The data in Table 14.1 show that Nigerian urban population has been growing at the rate of 2.5 percent per annum, with the exception of Lagos, which grew at the annual rate of 4 percent. People migrate from rural areas to cities and towns to work, enjoy amenities, belong to political organizations and professional associations. The urban population statistics also show that over 80 million people live in rural areas. Peil (1977) notes that cities are known to be centers of power and technology which are believed to contribute greatly to the rapid growth and development of urban centers. The cities are believed to hold the keys to the future of the society, thus making it necessary for sociologists to analyze carefully the nature of urban societies along with implications of their growth for the society.

TABLE 14.1: The Growth of Urban Population in Nigeria, 1980–1985

Year	Total Population (Millions)	Urban Growth
1980	84,445,728	13,608,785
1981	86,583,482	13,953,293
1982	88,775,353	14,306,522
1983	91,022,712	14,668,694
1984	93,326,962	15,040,033
1985	95,689,546	15,420,774

Source: *Economic and Social Statistics Bulletin,* January 1985.

Implications of urban growth include problems of all kinds, and one of the major problems is the crime rate, caused by the explosion of urban population. Crime and delinquency are social problems that should be investigated in great detail.

Research findings indicate the links between the growth of cities and increasing crime rates. So crime and delinquency have become urban phenomena.

This study attempts to identify some of the problems created by urban growth, with particular emphasis on the crime rate associated with it, in the city of Onitsha.

Definition of Concepts

Urbanization

Tisdale (1970) defines *urbanization* as a process of population concentration. It proceeds in two ways: the multiplication of point of concentration and the increase in size of individual concentration.

It is clear that no simple definition of *urbanization* exists. Generally, people have differed in their definitions of the concept. *Urbanization* is frequently used to refer to living in towns or cities as against living in rural areas or villages. For an area to be designated *urban*, the population must be relatively dense within a relatively confined area; e.g. 10,000 inhabitants or more.

Peil (1977) defines *urbanization* as a population living in urban areas, the process upon which the urban places grow or the spread of a manner of life and values which have come to be associated with such places. The "values" here act as a determining factor for individual concentration in the urban areas. When the concentration is multiplied in numerical strength, the growth of urban centers becomes a reality, and as a result, the population living in the urban areas increases.

Although urban population is widely understood to include the population resident in cities, the definition of *urban* is nevertheless a complex matter. The definition of *urban* often refers to administrative, political, and historical as well as demographic criteria. Wirth (1933) accepted the definition of *city* as a point of population concentration of large size, high density, and heterogeneity of inhabitants. He argues that high population density produces frequent physical contacts, high-pace living, the functional segregation of urban subareas, and the segregation of people in residential areas in which people with similar backgrounds and needs consciously select, drift, or are forced by circumstances into the same section of the society or city. Wirth concluded that the greater heterogeneity of the new cities produced a distinctive series of effects. Without a common background, Wirth felt, diverse people tended to place emphasis on visual recognition and symbolism.

The crisis that created the expansion of urbanization becomes more focused and translated into practical problems. Some of the general worldwide problems associated with urbanization are especially those of uncontrolled and unpleasant growth. This in turn leads to overcrowding, unemployment, substandard living and hardship, and criminality as a means of economic success.

Urbanization here is defined as the concentration of gradually increasing population in urban centers through the movement of people from villages or other less-developed areas. It is the process of creating groups of new individuals through environmental influences that change people's social, economic, and cultural behaviors.

Urban Growth

Urban growth here is defined as a continuous response of people to the elements of attraction in the urban center. These elements of attraction, or what could be called "pull" factors, include administrative, industrial, commercial, and educational opportunities. The term also encompasses infrastructure (light, pipe-borne water, improved communication system, transportation, etc.), socioeconomic opportunities, new experience, greater opportunities for self-employed jobs, and opportunities to make money illegally. The response to these elements is called *migration*. This migration turns into the physical reality of individual concentration in the urban centers. The interval and continuous responses to the elements of attraction or pull factors result in urban growth. Also urban growth is related to the movement of people from rural areas to the urban centers because of individual motivation, which could be called the push factor.

Apart from economic achievement, the push factor includes political persecution, killings through witchcraft, and land problems. Migration in response to pull and push factors in other areas, especially urban centers which attract people in search of better socioeconomic opportunity, new experience, or escape from persecution, results in urban growth. Peterson (1958) defines *free migration* as movement motivated by the individual's willingness to risk the unknown of a new home and breaking from a familiar social universe for the sake of adventure, achievement of ideals, or to escape a social system from which he has become alienated.

The concentration of population and the growth of the cities create conditions which contribute to criminal activities among those individuals whose economic goals have not become reality. Criminal activities become alternative means of surviving in the urban environment.

Criminal Behavior

Criminal behavior is a human act that violates the criminal law. This means that crime involves human behavior and the concept of law. In other words, criminal law identifies behavior that is criminal. According to the law, a number of specific criteria must normally be met for an act to be considered a crime and the perpetrator a criminal. For instance, there must be an act; the act must be injurious to the people or state; the act must be prohibited by the law; the act must be performed voluntarily or intentionally, expressed in the concept of *mens rea* (guilty mind); and when the harm is casually related to the act, the act is punished by law. Among those who favor this definition are Michael and Alder (1933), who assert that the legislative definition is the only possible definition of crime. In their view, the definition is precise and unambiguous, and identifies the heart of the subject, namely, its relation to the law. Other critics have pointed out that the notion of social harm is often invoked in delineating acts that are the proper concern of criminal law. In his discussion of criminal law, Hall (1960) observes that the notion of social harm is central to a legal conception of crime. It is Reckless (1950:8) who suggests that we should limit our attention to those illegal acts that have been reported to the police:

> To question: What constitutes crime? The modern criminologist must know that crime exists when a violation of the criminal code is reported. Otherwise, the phenomenon is a non-reported violation, and we are not sure philosophically whether a non-reported violation is a phenomenon at all. A star might fall in the heavens, but if no one saw it and reported it and got confirmation from others who saw it, then the star did not fall in fact. So the fact of crime is the reporting of a violation of a criminal code. Anything else is not a crime in fact.

This shows that crime relates to those acts for which an offender has been caught, tried, and punished (Korn and McCorkle 1957). In other words, the significance of crime as a legal phenomenon lies not so much in the idea that an act happens to violate the law but in the quality the act takes on when the machinery of law acts upon it. This study has been in line with Reckless's suggestion that attention should be limited to the criminal or illegal acts reported to the police.

Methodological Problems of Urbanization and Crime Waves in Nigeria

It is important to note that there are several limiting factors in the past studies militating against future progress in research into urban growth and crime rate in Nigeria. Such limitations include unreliability of population and crime statistics. There is a general agreement among Nigerian social scientists that there is not much useful information on the growth of Nigerian cities or on urbanization and its associated social problems from past censuses; those of 1952, 1953, and 1963 included no direct question on urbanization and urban growth.

The Rural Demographic Sample Survey of 1965–1966 was an attempt at a nationwide survey, specifically designed to yield data on rural-urban migration, but because of the lack of sophistication in the questionnaire design, the migration and urbanization information derived from the survey is very limited.

The conclusions and inferences in this study are based on the official data collected from police records. It is well known that crime statistics are gathered by different agencies for different purposes. The police department wants to know the number of arrests made, the number of true and false cases, and the number of cases successfully prosecuted in the courts according to due process of law. But some cases are usually not reported by the police in the process of investigation. This may be done through ignorance, inexperience, lack of adequate training and expertise in the science of crime investigation and detection, inadequate and inappropriate equipment, funding and interference from higher quarters especially as it happened during the Shagari Administration (1979–1983) and the brief period of Buhari and Idiagbon's repressive regime. During this period, the offenses which Idiagbon's alternative police force (the War Against Indiscipline Brigade) prosecuted were not mentioned in the police documents and cannot be accounted for by the police. These are parts of the cases which are not known to the police. Also, some people do not like to report crimes to the police for fear of being implicated in the course of eliciting information. This happens because quite a few officers have little competence to investigate a criminal activity on their own. Instead of applying their own skills of investigation (which they do not have in the first place), they usually try to get the reporter involved in order to supply certain specific information which may help the officer to present the case in court more effectively. He may even get the reporter to explain how the criminal activity happened, thus making her the chief prosecuting witness. This type of inefficiency has discouraged citizens from going to the police to lodge the first report (Mbosowo 1984:77).

Other problems in the police crime statistics:

• Police statistics are manually gathered, recorded, and crudely stored. This indicates that they are liable to manipulation, cancellation, erasure of figures, or other forms of destructive action.

• Some divisional police officers, in a bid to tone down the height of crime rate in their areas of jurisdiction, usually cause some cases to be unrecorded.

• Indiscriminate promulgation and abrogation of an ignorance on the part of police who may still hold people criminally responsible for offenses under such abrogated laws, which may cause such police statistics to be unreliable.

• Some cases reported, such as arson, have been caused accidentally, but some police stations record these cases as crimes, thereby causing a swell in the crime rate.

• In a densely populated town, police officers are not equipped with vehicles to make patrols to detect criminal activities. Those sent into the town perform their duties on foot, resulting in unproductivity and poor job performance. Hence, most criminal activities are not detected, and therefore there is no record because the police officers are unable to enter most parts of the city for a period of at least six months. Most citizens have no telephone to call the police when crimes occur in their neighborhoods. The few with telephones may call, but three-quarters of the time, the police will not go because either the only vehicle for that station is being used at that particular moment or it has broken down.

   • Reported and recorded criminal cases in the police stations, especially in a developing country like Nigeria, should not be taken seriously. This is because the records include the names of citizens who have been wrongfully accused. Sometimes the intention is to damage their reputation. A city in Nigeria is occupied by migrants from different ethnic groups. Tribalism is a major factor that is likely to lead to false criminal cases. The concept of *indegene* has become another powerful factor that produces migrant's maladjustments and subsequent crime in urban areas. Indegenes claim to be the owners of the city, and they make sure that the migrants who are regarded as "nonindegenes" face severe difficulties in gaining employment and economic success, and this contributes to the marked increase in urban crimes. The serious problem of indegene and nonindegene label is likely to result in poor relationship between the indegenes and migrants, in which the migrants may be falsely accused of criminal offenses, and most of the time, it is their criminal cases that are recorded.

   Despite the problems with police crime records, the police statistics are still regarded as better than statistics from the courts because the police have the firsthand experience with arrests. The number of convicted criminals in the courts is not reliable since it is hard to know when the judges are biased and when not. Most criminal cases by the people at the top level in the society are not dealt with by judges, because of their position in the society. Some convicted criminals at the lower courts are known to have been set free by the upper courts, so that the information thus gathered from the lower courts is useless and unreliable.

   Another problem is that there are few or no recorded studies of the urban centers in Nigeria with their associated crime rates. For these reasons, secondary data sources from the police were used in this study.

The Research Settings: Onitsha

   The town of Onitsha is situated on the west bank of the river Niger in Anambra State. It has a natural boundary with Asaba in Bendel State. The towns of Asaba and Onitsha are separated from each other by the river

Niger. The indegenes of Onitsha are said to have migrated from Bini and settled on the west bank of the river. The date of this settlement is not known by historians. The population was relatively very small until the arrival of the Royal Niger Company and the establishment of missionary schools, which attracted economic activities and hence an increase in population. Its status as the headquarters of the then Onitsha Province, coupled with increased attention by the government, made Onitsha an important administrative and commercial center.

The 1952–1953 census put the population of Onitsha at 23,456, and this increased to 38,403 by 1963. A very conservative estimate of the population of Onitsha for the year 1973, according to Okoye (1977), was 55,000. This was a growth rate of over 4 percent in a ten-year period. Over the last two decades, and especially since 1970, Onitsha has become a major center for both internal migrants in Nigeria and international business movement into the country. Onitsha has been referred to as having the largest market in West Africa. The new population estimate of Onitsha for 1978 was 72,481 (Okoye 1977). Today, Onitsha is the headquarters of the Onitsha Local Government Area in Anambra State. Onitsha has since this time enjoyed the amenities that benefit most urban centers. Such amenities include commercial-educational facilities as well as other social institutional amenities like schools, hospitals, and hotels of international standards. It has a mild climate with adequate rainfall.

All these favorable conditions, according to Adepoju (1974), have a strong pull on traders, small-scale industrialists, contractors, bankers, civil servants, businessmen, and foreign immigrants. Adepoju describes this as the pull for city-ward migration. Moreover, the strategic location of Onitsha has enabled Onitsha to assume a relatively high order of functionality in the national urban system at the level of interstate or subregional setting, particularly in labor mobility.

The intrastructural investments in Onitsha mark the beginning of the phase of rural-urban imbalance. It is within this background that we see Onitsha growing at a very rapid rate. The growth results largely from the influx of immigrants both from the surrounding villages and distant places within and outside Nigeria. This flow continues because Onitsha is the second largest importing port in Nigeria. This has drawn people from all walks of life into Onitsha to search for economic success.

Urban Growth and Crime: History and Pattern of Onitsha's Case

Historically, criminal and delinquent activities in Onitsha cannot be traced to a particular time or year. It is a well-known fact that even in the early sixties, the city had been associated with crimes of all sorts, hence the popular saying that Onitsha is the melting point of all criminal activities.

The Nigerian Civil War between 1967 and 1970 became a determining factor for urban growth and criminal activities in Onitsha. During the war, the Igbos, who are the indegenes of Onitsha, suffered great losses. At the end of the war, people from the surrounding areas started to migrate to Onitsha, and the business activities were dominated by the Yoruba and Bendel migrants. The Igbos at this time had no money to set up businesses, and there were no employment opportunities since most of the corporations and even the federal and state ministries destroyed by war were yet to be renovated. There was a concentration of both skilled and unskilled people who were basically unemployed but still had to survive.

At this time, there was no effective public control by either the army or the police. The social norms were not respected, and there was no regard for the law. What was foremost was "survival"; hence, a lot of people resorted to all kinds of criminal acts. Those who suffered from the effects of the war had to survive from the people who migrated to set up businesses in the city of Onitsha. People were killed or beaten up and their property taken away from them. Forcible rape and forgery were rampant. That is, people who decided to work for others for survival forged records and stole money, and those who had no money to pay for prostitution resorted to rape. People could hardly sleep at night, as there were always shootings at night. It is pertinent to mention here that the war actually toughened the Igbos, coupled with the need to survive in the light of acute unemployment, which then made the violation of the societal laws inevitable. Migration from local areas to the city of Onitsha after the Civil War became necessary in order to search for employment. Guns and rifles used during the war, together with the military training received by the Igbos, made it almost impossible for either the army or the police to control criminal activities. This period brought about mostly violent crimes like armed robbery.

Those who could not engage in violent crimes were involved in petty stealing and other sorts of petty crimes. Thus, the acute unemployment, breakdown of social norms, availability of guns and rifles, lack of effective public control on the part of the military and police, together with the fact that the war made an average Igbo man desperate and fearless, were responsible for the serious criminal activities in Onitsha after the war.

This situation continued until about 1973 when employment opportunities improved and more people were able to establish their own business. Gun control measures were instituted by the federal government, and the number of policemen was increased to control events in the city. More industries were established by the state and federal governments as well as individual enterprises. Federal, state, and local ministries were renovated, and employment opportunities increased. The Onitsha main market with the reputation of being the largest in West Africa was renovated by the government. The roads linking the city with other neighboring towns and states were put in order. These then had the effect of attracting a population explosion. In the shortest time, supply of labor became more than the demand, and this created a lot of social problems. The population explosion has brought about the existence of slum areas in the city of Onitsha, with all the social ills associated with it. The slum areas had been forgotten about by the government, and lack of government attention and lack of basic infrastructures and amenities, together with the psychological implications of such negligence made the poor parents in those areas lack interest in the welfare of their children, thereby allowing them to become delinquents. A police bulletin in 1976 showed that more than 40 percent of the crimes committed in Onitsha within the same period were committed by inhabitants of slum areas. It is estimated that after adding all the crimes committed within the city of Onitsha in 1976, the highest percentage was committed by residents of slum areas.

It was between the late 1970s and the early 1980s that the city of Onitsha became sophisticated, and many people have made a lot of money through all means available and have been able to afford higher standards of living. Greater emphasis was therefore shifted to materialism. Status and societal recognition was based on one's material accumulation.

Now the legitimate means of attaining economic success are limited, and only a few can get to the position of economic achievement. Since so many people could not find employment, they resorted to alternative illegal means of making a living. This to a greater extent is responsible for the ever-increasing incidents of armed robbery, burglary, stealing, and assaults. Also, the introduction of austerity measures by the federal government and the subsequent placement of a ban on the importation of certain items into the country put most young men who based their living on smuggling into trouble with the customs officials and the police. Those who lost their goods to customs joined or formed criminal gangs that operated day and night. Lives were no longer safe, and properties were vandalized. Thus, in Onitsha at the moment, robbery, burglary, forgery, duping, pickpocketing, impersonation, and rape have become the order of the day.

Urban Growth and Crime Rates

The rising crime rate in Onitsha is commonly thought of as resulting from a number of factors, including urban growth in particular. In short, this has been a social change, which started from the time of the Civil War to a deteriorating stage, and from the deteriorating condition to innovation and industrial development, which pulled migrants from the surrounding areas and from other states all over the country, including international immigrants. This shows that crime is related to the complexity of development associated with the worldwide process of industrialization and consequent urban growth.

This study uses the 1963 census data in analyzing the crimes committed between 1970 and 1972, 1973 census data for crimes between 1974 and 1976, 1978 census data for crimes between 1978 and 1980, while crimes committed between 1980 and 1981 will use census data of 1981. The crime rates have been calculated on a 100,000 population.

Table 14.2 shows that the population of Onitsha has been on the increase since 1953. In ten years, the population increased by 63.7 percent, at 6.4 percent per year. In 1973, after ten years, the population increased by 43.2 percent, at a yearly rate of 4.3 percent. In 1978, in a five-year period, the population increased by 31.8 percent at a yearly rate of 6.4 percent. In 1981, the population increased to 80,000 after three years at a yearly rate of 3.5 percent. The data revealed that the yearly population increase between 1963 and 1973 had dropped by 2.1 percent. This happened because during the Civil War between 1967 and 1970, many Igbo people who own Onitsha had moved into villages and other neighboring villages, especially the southeastern part of the country, for safety, since the war was concentrated in Onitsha and other parts of Igboland. Between 1973 and 1978, the yearly population increase had increased to 6.4 percent after the war because during this period, development had taken place in the city of Onitsha and most people migrated to the urban center of Onitsha for economic reasons.

TABLE 14.2: Population of Onitsha, 1953–1981

Year	Population[a]
1953	23,456
1963	38,403
1973	55,000
1978	72,481
1981	80,000

Source: Anambra State Department of Statistics.

[a]1963 data are derived from the census taken at that date. Subsequent years' figures are projections by the National Population Bureau. The calculations are partly taken at 10-year periods, while a 5-year period is taken for 1978, and a 3-year period for 1981. This is done because of the type of changes that took place within those intervals and the reflection in the crime rates.

Because of the commercial and industrial development in Onitsha, many people have migrated to the city. The "push" of hardship in rural areas and the "pull" of urban possibilities (jobs, schools, etc.) combined to bring them to the city. Perhaps they already had relatives or fellow villagers there. But there is little or no employment, not because economic development is lacking but because most of them lack the skills, and sometimes even other necessary qualifications to compete in the city. This condition leads to the involvement in crime.

Table 14.3 shows the aggregate of crimes that occurred in Onitsha between 1970 and 1981 and were reported to the police. In sexual crimes, prostitution seems to rank the highest. Prostitution is rampant in Onitsha because of a high "bride price" which prevents young women from getting married. Unmarried, young, and unskilled women migrate to the city, and because they are unemployed, they turn to prostitution. Those who have no hope of getting married involve themselves in sexual intercourse in order to have children of their own. The parents of such women take to court the

TABLE 14.3: Aggregate of Crimes Reported to the Police, Onitsha, 1970–1981

Crime	Year						
	1970	1972	1974	1976	1978	1980	1981
Sexual Crime[a]	668	324	535	816	1,255	256	51
Political Crime[b]	40	25	31	39	50	11	30
Occupational Crime[c]	495	335	472	558	625	149	399
Property Crime[d]	1,500	1,211	1,415	1,765	2,153	300	700
Public Crime[e]	356	189	230	286	391	31	85
Organized Crime[f]	1,122	1,100	1,335	1,634	2,325	405	703
Personal Crime[g]	108	61	6	79	74	55	59
Total	4,289	3,245	4,024	5,177	6,873	1,207	2,027

Source: Anambra State Police Annual Crime Reports.

[a]Sexual Crimes include forcible rape, extra-marital sex, carnal sex, and prostitution.
[b]Political Crimes: treason, sabotage, war collaboration, election rigging, radicalism—official records are only available on radicalism and corruption.
[c]Occupational Crimes: embezzlement, fraudulent sales, false advertising, price fixing, bribery, and products adulterations.
[d]Property Crimes: burglary, robbery, shoplifting, forgery, vandalism, gangs' theft, pickpocketing, and arson.
[e]Public Crimes: drunkenness, vagrancy, disorderly conduct, traffic violation, and corruption.
[f]Organized Crimes: armed robbery, gambling, racketeering, drug trafficking, and prostitution.
[g]Personal Crimes: homicide, murder, manslaughter, assault, and rape.

men who put the women or their daughters in the "family way," and the bastard children are always returned to the women's parents, according to the traditional norms of the Igbo people.

The most common and serious offense among the political crimes is corruption. This is one of the most pervasive problems in the area, but it is the least reported. Such offenses as bribes, payoffs, or embezzlement, which occur in every branch of government are very common. The data in Table 14.3 show that political crimes are the least reported. This is so because it is the crime of the powerful and is not reported because of the corruption in political links between the police and the intelligence organizations.

As Table 14.3 indicates, property and organized crimes are the leading offenses in Onitsha. The rate at which these offenses have been perpetuated seems to have been greatly influenced by socioeconomic factors. Chief amongst them, are scarcity of various foods, the relatively high value attached to owning ostentatious goods like television sets, stereos, and other household electronic equipments owned by those who could not afford them but have forced themselves to have them by all means. The crime the poor committed in an effort to live like the wealthy is the crime most recorded by the police. A crowding of thousands of poor with their cumulative disadvantage into the urban areas not only offers the easy chance for criminal acts but causes crime. The utter wretchedness of the city slums, crammed with poverty, idleness, vice, and crime of the whole metropolis, slowly drains compassion from human spirit and breeds crime.

The data in Table 14.4 compare crimes reported to the police between 1970 and 1972. The total number of reported crimes in 1970 was 4,289 or a

TABLE 14.4: Crimes Reported to the Police: Type by Rate per 100,000 Population, Onitsha, 1970–1972

Crime	1970			Crime	1972		
	No.	% of Total Crime	Population Rate[a]		No.	% of Total Crime	Population Rate[a]
Sexual	668	15.6	1,739	Sexual	324	10.0	844
Political	40	0.9	104	Political	25	0.8	65
Occupational	495	11.5	1,289	Occupational	335	10.3	872
Property	1,500	35.0	3,906	Property	1,211	37.3	3,153
Public Order	356	8.3	927	Public Order	189	5.8	492
Organized	1,122	26.2	2,922	Organized	1,100	33.9	2,864
Personal	108	2.5	281	Personal	61	1.9	159
Total	4,289	100.0	11,168		3,245	100.0	8,449

[a]Rates are based on the 1963 census: Population 38,403.

rate of 11,168 per 100,000 inhabitants, and has dropped to a crime total of 3,245 or a rate of 8,449 in 1972. The explanations for the 24.3 percent or rate of 2,719 drop in 1972 are discussed below.

The crimes by rate per 100,000 in 1970 were 11,168 and decreased to 8,449 in 1972. The data in Table 14.4 indicate that the rates for all types of crimes reported decreased. The percentage categories of crime between 1970 and 1972 seem to have followed the same trend except probably property and organized crimes. For instance, in 1972, sexual crime dropped by 5.6 percent, political crime 0.1 percent, occupational crime 1.2 percent, public crime, 2.2 percent and personal crime 0.6 percent, but property crime increased by 2.3 percent, while organized crime increased by 7.7 percent. The data reveal that organized crime increased almost 80 percent more than property crime.

The cause of this is clear. Immediately after the Civil War, in 1970, a lot of people rushed to the urban center with little or nothing to keep life going. Job opportunities were not available to absorb these people, and the law enforcement agencies were not adequate to control the daily activities of the urban dwellers, especially when they were exposed to hardship during the war, which lasted for three years. Moreover, most of the young men who fought in the Civil "Biafran" War still had some dangerous weapons with them, and this made committing crimes an easy job.

But in 1972, more factories were established in the place of old ones destroyed during the war; thus many people were able to gain employment. Both federal and state ministries started to employ people, and efforts were made by the federal government to reduce the number of arms used during the war, which were still in the possession of some "ex–Biafran" soldiers. More law enforcement agents were sent to the town to keep law and order. All these measures helped to reduce crime rate in 1972. It is important to note that although there was a decline in crime rate in 1972, the population of the city of Onitsha continued to grow.

The data in Table 14.5 compare crimes reported to the police in 1974 to crimes in 1976. The total number of reported crimes in 1974 was 4,087 which increased to 5,237 in 1976. Within the same period, the crime rate per 100,000 inhabitants was 7,430 in 1974 and increased to 9,414 in 1976. The data show that property, organized, and sexual crimes ranked highest, took over 80 percent of the total crimes reported to the police in 1974, and also totalled 81.4 percent in 1976. The data also reveal that property crimes had the increased crime rate of 636 per 100,000 inhabitants in 1976, followed by organized crimes with 544 and sexual crimes with 511. The percentage categories of the crime reports show that other crimes were declining. For example, political crimes dropped by 0.1 percent, occupational crimes 0.7 percent, public order crimes 0.1 percent, and personal crimes 0.2 percent. The data show that the crime decrease is insignificant as compared to the increase of crimes between 1974 and 1976. This shows a relationship between population increase and crime increase between 1974 and 1976.

**TABLE 14.5: Crimes Reported to the Police:
Type by Rate per 100,000 Population, Onitsha, 1974–1976**

Crime		1974		Crime		1976	
	No.	% of Total Crime	Population Rate[a]		No.	% of Total Crime	Population Rate[a]
Sexual	535	13.1	973	Sexual	816	15.8	1,484
Political	31	0.8	56	Political	99	0.7	71
Occupational	472	11.5	858	Occupational	558	10.8	1,015
Property	1,415	34.6	2,573	Property	1,765	34.1	3,209
Public Order	230	5.6	418	Public Order	286	5.5	520
Organized	1,335	32.7	2,427	Organized	1,634	31.6	2,971
Personal	69	1.7	125	Personal	79	1.5	144
Total	4,087	100.0	7,430	Total	5,237	100.0	9,414

[a]Rates are based on the 1973 population projections (55,000, National Population Bureau).

The data in Table 14.6 show a rapid change in the crime rates between 1978 and 1980. In 1978, the total number of reported crimes was 6,863, and it dropped to 1,207 in 1980. This is a drastic drop by 82.4 percent in two years. As the data show, the crime rate per 100,000 inhabitants was 9,509 in 1978, and dropped drastically to 1,666 in 1980. The data reveal the decline in the reported crimes as well as crime population rate between 1978 and 1980. The decline in 1980 reported crimes was attributed to the Operation Wipe-out Criminals which was carried out by the residents of Onitsha and its environment in the middle of 1979. This is an informal method of crime control where the citizens arrested and punished the criminals without the knowledge of the law enforcement agents. The severity of crimes made property and lives unsafe. The residents therefore decided to take the law into their hands and resorted to lynching, burning, and killing of all the suspected and apprehended criminals. Even those known criminals who ran away to the neighboring towns were traced and killed. The number was estimated to be 668 criminals. This exercise became a common practice, to the effect that the moment one committed any crime, no matter the nature, he or she was instantly killed or burned alive. Thus, people were afraid to steal, knowing full well that they would stand the risk of being lynched or burned to death if caught. This public reaction to criminal suspects and criminals helped to reduce the rate of crimes committed within this period.

TABLE 14.6: Crimes Reported to the Police: Type by Rate per 100,000 Population, Onitsha, 1978–1980

		1978				1980	
Crime	No.	% of Total Crime	Popu-lation Rate[a]	Crime	No.	% of Total Crime	Popu-lation Rate[a]
Sexual	1,225	18.2	1,731	Sexual	256	21.2	353
Political	50	0.7	69	Political	11	0.9	15
Occupational	625	9.1	862	Occupational	149	12.3	206
Property	2,153	31.2	2,970	Property	300	24.8	414
Public Order	391	5.7	539	Public Order	31	2.5	43
Organized	2,325	33.7	3,208	Organized	405	33.6	559
Personal	94	1.4	130	Personal	55	4.6	76
Total	6,863	99.9	9,509	Total	1,207	99.9	1,666

[a]Rates are based on 1978 population projections (72,481, National Population Bureau).

It is difficult to relate population growth to the crime rate between 1978 and 1980 because of the informal method used by the residents to reduce the rate of crimes in the city of Onitsha.

As the data in Table 14.7 show, the total number of crimes reported to the police in 1980 was 1,207, and within one year, the figure increased to 2,427. This shows an increase of over 100 percent in a one-year period. Also the crime rate per 100,000 inhabitants was at 1,509 in 1980, and increased to 3,035 in 1981. The data show that political, occupational, property, and public crimes were on the increase, while organized, sexual, and personal crimes were declining.

TABLE 14.7: Crimes Reported to the Police: Type by Rate per 100,000 Population, Onitsha, 1980–1981

		1980				1981	
Crime	No.	% of Total Crime	Popu-lation Rate[a]	Crime	No.	% of Total Crime	Popu-lation Rate[a]
Sexual	256	21.2	320	Sexual	451	18.6	564
Political	11	0.9	14	Political	30	1.2	38
Occupational	149	12.3	186	Occupational	399	16.4	499
Property	300	24.8	375	Property	700	28.8	875
Public Order	31	2.6	39	Public Order	85	3.5	106
Organized	405	33.6	506	Organized	703	29.0	879
Personal	55	4.6	69	Personal	59	2.4	74
Total	1,207	100.0	1,509	Total	2,427	99.9	3,035

[a]Rates are based on 1981 population projections (80,000, National Population Bureau).

It is important to note the relationship between population growth and crimes between 1980 and 1981. The data reveal that the rate per 100,000 population had increased in all the crimes. As the data show, the crime rate increase is as follows: sexual crimes + 244, political crimes + 24, occupational crimes + 313, property crimes + 500, public crimes + 67, organized crimes + 373, and personal crimes + 5. The data show that property crime (+ 500) ranked highest in its relation to the population, followed by organized crime (+ 373) and occupational crime (+ 313).

The increase in all crimes relates to changes in population and in human experiences and conduct. The population of Onitsha grew from 72,481 in 1978 to 80,000 in 1981 and had with it an increase in crime waves from a total of 1,207 in 1980 to 2,427 in 1981. From this we could say that an increase in urban population carries with it an increase in crime rate.

15

Possible Formulations for Family Policy in Third World Countries

Thomas M. Meenaghan

One of the major similarities of Third World countries and developed countries is the not fully resolved issue of whether there should be systemic family policy, and if so, what normative principles would guide it. Developed countries typically have proceeded in delineating all areas of social policy using one or more of the following perspectives: (1) policy as the logical extension of evolving individualistic definitions of legal rights; (2) policy as tied to the social good, which is the responsibility of the government; and (3) policy as requiring the implementative activities of local groups and communities. In analyzing the issue of family policy for Third World countries, it is the view of this writer that unlike the developed countries, the Third World countries should heavily stress the second and third perspectives in their formulation of social policy.

Of course, it is with considerable trepidation that anyone sitting in any given world sector approaches the topic of what should occur in another world sector. Nonetheless, this writer will do that, but on the provision that this chapter will review phenomena in developed countries so that policymakers in the Third World may make informed choices in their own developing countries. In the discussion, it will be suggested that both Third World and developed countries need to make choices in the areas of local structures within the society, possible governmental relations within society, normative principles to guide family policy, and the manner in which benefits might be delivered relative to the political questions of who (population) gets what (benefit) and how (program strategy).

Structural Units in Developed Societies

In developed countries, conventional discussion of family welfare, by both liberals and conservatives, has often stressed the individual along a quasi continuum of rights and duties. Implicitly, both political perspectives agree that the individual is an essential unit of the society. As noble as this focus has been, other units—most notably the family and the local community—have often not been adequately considered. Because of this, conservatives and liberals will have to think about how a more complex set of units can relate to each other if the goal of family welfare is to be achieved.

For too many conservatives, individuals stand prior to and in a sense beyond the society. For many liberals, individual rights in the area of welfare are a necessary component of a linear evolutionary process characterized by the extension of the legal prerogatives of individuals. Because of these varying basic perspectives, derived policy and political questions have often been divergent for the two political groups. For some conservatives, the primary concern has often been protection of the individual and her property from the abuses of government (Laquer and Rubin 1979). For the liberal, the concern has often been how to achieve more material supports from government, knowing that provision of such support will involve transfer of resources, income, and assets from some to others (Kahn and Kamerman 1977).

Such thematic concerns of conservatives and liberals in developed countries, however, have not developed in a vacuum. Issues of a social and philosophical nature have been complicated and have contributed to the prevailing concerns. Classical economic liberals, an important constituent of conservative thought though not the only current in the conservative stream, have tended to assume that individuals comprise the basic unit of life and that such a unit is not essentially good but in fact is rather depraved. Despite the corruption of the individual, each individual is seen through the competitive promotion of self-interests as instrumental in producing society, in producing a natural order of social cohesion (Neale 1976; Rae 1934; Chaudhuri 1967).

More collectivist thought, and certainly that of a utopian orientation, has typically stressed the rational and developmental potential of people. Social supports and other government strategies have been viewed as intimately intertwined with the process of growth and economic development for the society (Mencher 1970). In certain and limited respects, within both classical and economic liberal and collectivist perspectives, the individual, in a variety of ways, is seen as juxtaposed to the government and the economy in terms of interests and needs.

Somewhat in between the two perspectives of classical economic liberalism and collectivism, is the view of Wesley and others that stresses the interactive processes between person and social environment (Mencher 1970). Such a view has often led to an appreciation that positive approaches from the environment to the individual must be accompanied by some degree of change from within the person—moral and/or clinical.

As divergent as these social philosophical positions are, they all tend to minimize the central role of the family. Implicitly, they seem to suggest that the family, while it may be very functional for religious and socialization purposes, is not itself a central structure of the society. In a sense, families might be perceived as the arithmetic sum of individuals or even more narrowly construed as a domicile context in which disparate individuals live. In developed countries, even when advocates stress the role of family as a refuge for individuals and a means of group support for individuals, such advocates tend to suggest that the family merely serves as a supplement to the basic entities of the individual and governmental-economic institutions (Hess 1984).

The net result of the interplay of the political as well as the social-philosophical viewpoints discussed above has been the production of a threefold set of results affecting family welfare in devloped countries: (1) an excessive preoccupation with the debate over the rights and responsibilities of individuals and governmental structural units; (2) a lack of appreciation of what actual welfare policy and benefits do to families *qua* families (Moroney 1976); and (3) an omission within public policy of a focus upon the structure of the family itself, ranging from supporting it to helping it become stronger to preventing predictable sources of stresses from debilitating the family structure. Inherent in all three statements is the observation that the family must be seen not only as a central unit of society but also as socially desired and valued as an end in itself—not merely as an instrumental means. In a very real sense, this last observation is the most basic unresolved issue for both conservatives and liberals in developed countries; it is potentially the place where some evolving conceptions of liberal and conservative thought can seek common ground. It is a place where Third World countries may choose to make a value commitment which would shape subsequent family policy.

As one considers the family as a key social unit, one is led into a series of related considerations. First, that families live in real physical and social worlds, namely communities, and that such worlds differ with respect to each other in terms of amounts, rates, and types of family structure and stressors found therein. Second, that communities also differ with respect to each other in terms of resource profiles of ethnic, religious, and other voluntary organizations. These variable resources can and do interact with families and can or cannot be relevant to the family structure and its functioning.

While many people in developed countries value the family unit, they are also leery of government intrusion, especially intrusion into matters which might impact upon the domain of the family. Further, conservatives, especially those in the United States, often allow the viewpoints of "free market" conservatives to overshadow their strong concern for the family. More economically oriented conservatives, from Smith to Friedman, have tended to delineate a very specific and limited set of roles for government (Neale 1976; Friedman 1975). Typically, these roles have involved protecting exchanges in a market economy and adjudicating conflicting demands of competing interests.

However, one would be remiss in assuming, at least initially, that these defined roles did not originate independent of the social environment and the needs and striving of certain interests within it. At first, the use of mercantile, then capitalist, and finally industrial economic organization in many developed countries produced imperatives for both the mode of economic organization and the emerging capitalist class. Specifically, trade and banking functions required the cloak of governmental protection, and industrialism and industrialists required a degree of freedom and political expression to replace the abuses and control associated with monarchical forms of government. In short, a considerable amount of economic conservatism has been created not only in response to environmental phenomena but in direct relation to the interests and values of certain types of groups within the society. In related fashion, if today's environment is changing and if the stressors upon and risks for families are central to today's environment, a reassessment of the relation between government and the environment becomes necessary. This may be most applicable in the case of Third World countries.

When one moves beyond the economic wing of conservatism, one sees a possible set of desirable relations between government and family structures in Third World countries. One conservative tradition, which is found in Thomas Aquinas, Burke, and Jefferson, has been that a proper role of government is to do what is necessary when other societal units cannot fulfill a particular function (Mencher 1970). A second tradition of certain conservatives, dating to Aquinas, is to define a legitimate role of government as the pursuer and instrument for the natural "good," the moral instrument for the achievement of a better social order in keeping with the very essence of the human experience (Lippman 1955).

Perhaps the key question for Third World countries, given the possible valuing of the family unit, might be: How can government avoid or minimize the assaults upon the nuclear and extended family structures? Are not the imperatives of the family at least equal to the imperatives of the diverse interests, economic and other, that may already have been recognized in society?

For Talcot Parsons, the family structure is the very embodiment of the culture and norms of any society (Parsons 1967). Government, because it is an institution that is derived from and dependent upon the culture in which it operates, cannot choose to avoid dealing with that social unit which is the basic embodiment and beginning of the culture. A central role for government should thus be to devise public policy to protect the family structure and promote family interests.

Evolution of this key role for government in the area of family policy would be quite compatible with the traditions concerning legitimate governmental activities which have already been institutionalized in the twentieth century. These would include such diverse activities as providing flood relief, forecasting weather, patrolling the seas, paving roads, educating children, and so on. Such activities appear to be derived from, as well as consistent with, the principle of government doing for people what they cannot do for themselves, of government addressing an area for which there is little or no incentive for private parties within the free market.

Evolution of the role of government in family policy is also in keeping with the second-mentioned principle of government, accepting by many that government can and should help achieve the social good. To the degree that any society sees the family as a constitutive element in the social good, then government involvement in the area of family policy is quite compatible with the teleological (social good) conception of the state. Such a teleological conception has been reflected in developed countries in the abolition of slavery, insuring the voting rights of women, and various other protections for categories of people.

Rein (1970) has suggested that social policy, which impliedly could cover policy directed specifically toward families, can reflect four possible purposes. Policy could reflect the purpose of serving "necessary ends," such as providing and maintaining what is necessary for valued groups (Anderson 1979). Examples of this would be attempts to provide for and protect those who cannot take care of themselves. Policy can also be directed at social stability ends, whereby the larger society sees that cohesion and predictable behavior within the society are functional and as a result develops policies which help achieve social stability, or at least which attempt to minimize the degree of disruption. Efforts in the area of financial assistance, and even community medical care, could be seen as compatible with this specific purpose of policy. In a sense, behind both of these policy purposes—provision of the necessary or the basic to valued individuals and the achievement of cohesion—lies the concept of the government being responsible for the rights-entitlements of the individual and of the broader community.

However, policy can be and often is generated from an investment, or as Rein categorizes it, as a handmaiden perspective. Policy here serves multiple ends and is instrumental on a variety of levels. Generating policy to provide food for poor people does not just provide a good for the hungry but also serves a variety of interests ranging from farmers to food processors to grocery store merchants. Finally, policy can be viewed as serving as two or more valued ends. In this instance, a policy of full employment could be pursued because of positive effects for families, as well as for the economy. In these latter two categories of policy purposes, there is an obvious element of discretion and judgment on the part of the larger society concerning the "common good" of humanity.

If we reflect on the range of policy purposes reviewed in the above and keep in mind that there really are two basic kinds—(1) rights-oriented and (2) ends- or teleology-oriented—two conclusions appear relevant. First, it would appear that the area of family policy in the Third World should reflect both kinds of purposes and that it should reflect clear focus upon family units and not just upon discrete individuals. Second, it would appear that any projected family policy in the Third World, as in the developed countries, needs to confront the political and tactical questions of which families, located where, will have to be served with what program strategies. These tactical questions are crucial, given the relatively fixed nature of resources that will be available, at least for the near future, for social welfare in the Third World.

Family Groups, Policy Purposes, and Program Strategies

Central to affirming the desirability and utility of families in any society is the critical question of *who*, whom to address through family policy in Third World countries (Genovese 1984). Previous remarks clearly suggest that a possible option is the family unit itself. But beyond that, the answers are less clear: Should all families be covered? Should families be covered equally? Clearly, there are families currently reflecting needs which appear to be beyond the ability of the family unit to address adequately. In addition to these families, there are families with certain characteristics, such as number of parents, size, income level, which are at risk. Risk suggests that families which share certain characteristics stand more chance of actually becoming needy at some later point. Finally, there are families which seem fairly well removed from current need and for which current risks are not likely to overcome them in the immediate future. In short, these are families which appear to be "making it." It would appear that this latter family group, as well as the first two, deserves to be included within the scope of family policy. For while the first family group clearly reflects the rights perspective of "necessary" welfare and the second a mixture of rights and investment perspectives, the third group may most clearly reflect the teleologically oriented perspective discussed previously, i.e., promotion of the social good and the family itself.

Now, all three family groups—the needy, those at risk, and those that are making it—exist in space and physical space. That is, they will live in communities that have distinct geographical delineations as well as distinctive social characteristics in terms of such things as income, years of education, racial and ethnic composition, tribal affiliation.

It would appear that appreciation of the fact that different groups of families tend to distribute themselves within different types of communities is central to the issue of intervention. It should also encourage policymakers in the Third World to begin to see not only family as contrasted to individuals, but to see family in spatial terms (Meenaghan, and Washington 1982). Such a spatial consideration may afford a unique opportunity to policymakers to have a micro leverage point for family-related programs. It may also promote a functional nexus between expanding social relations among people and an important structure unit within the society, namely, the local community.

As the issue of whom to cover becomes identifiable via types of families within geographical and social communities, one can begin to detect the actual policy and program configurations. Communities that are characterized by a predominant pattern of families in need obviously will have to receive benefits which fulfill the "necessary" obligations of society. However, communities such as those in transitional areas, where risk clearly dominates over current need, may need preventative and supportive programs which take precedence over mere maintenance strategies. Finally, assistance to communities that seem to reflect little need and low to moderate amounts of risk would probably be characterized by developmental and preventive approaches. That is, the thrust of family policy to this last group should be to strengthen what works and to anticipate that some of these family units are prone to external social risks.

In summary, the strategy depicted above suggests there are four specific changes suggested for consideration by Third World countries in the area of social welfare (1) focusing on families; (2) understanding that there are different types of families relative to need and risk; (3) appreciating the critical contextual aspect of local communities for need, risk, and family functioning; and (4) programming differentially, from remediation to development to prevention in the different types of communities.

The local community should not be viewed as merely the repository of need and families at risk. Such a posture encourages future passivity and diminution of the role of communities, and probably reflects the sum of previous therapeutic efforts directed at individuals. Communities are also places where family members interact in countless social exchanges within the context of local associational and organizational life (Litwak and Szelenyi 1969). The specifics of such a context can include churches, ethnic groups, and civic and voluntary groups.

If family policy can reflect an appreciation of different kinds of communities by virtue of different kinds of family profiles, it might very wisely also consider that local communities offer a range of resources such as motivation, membership, and numbers to local families. Such resources could be directed toward remediation services to the current needy or toward prevention and developmental approaches to families in social areas where current need is not excessively high.

As one begins to appreciate the possible as well as actual exchanges between families and community resources, the two-edged issue of responsibility and provision presents itself to Third World countries as well as developed countries (Meenaghan and Washington 1980). It would be unwise and unfair to assume that local community resources can adequately address all the stressor situations facing families. This statement could be made with respect to communities reflecting any of the three types of family profiles. While local communities and their resources are critically relevant to families, it cannot be assumed that local communities on their own can provide the financial and other supports necessary to address the situations facing families. On the other hand, it would be unwise to turn over all family programming to the national government, since this would contribute to weakening the local community. What is suggested is a hybrid, whereby government assumes a major responsibility to and for families, but such responsibility is conceptually and operationally separated from the delivery of benefits to families within communities. Such an approach would acknowledge the role of government as both a rights-oriented and teleologically oriented institution. But it would not do so at the expense of the local community, its resources, and its traditions. It could be argued that by separating the principles of responsibility and actual provision, one could contribute to efficient, variable, and probably more relevant local program strategies to assist families.

When provision and responsibility concerns are distinguished, a corresponding topic is sugested: What should families and communities receive? Typically, in developed countries, the answer to this type of question has been that individuals should receive material, financial, medical, and therapeutic assistance from professionals to help individuals become more self-sufficient. As commendable as these benefits may be relative to Third World countries, the benefits appear to be narrowly defined, outstripped by the combination of actual need and risk, and likely to be excessively dominated by bureaucrats and professionals rather than by communities and families (Meenaghan and Washington 1980).

Benefits must include financial aids as well as some counseling and training. But relying exclusively on such types of benefits can promote a posture of responding only to demonstrated actual needs. Such benefits also, in real political terms, suggest that welfare will be perceived as being only in certain areas for certain people. If families and their different profiles are the central concerns, and the uniqueness of resources in different communities is also valued, then benefits should include a range of operations: financial assistance to families; vouchers to families for securing relevant educational and job training programs; efforts to make key government structures such as schools work in a more effective and relevant manner; responses by local resources for supportive and sustaining programs to families (Gilbert and Sprecht 1974). For this range of benefits to materialize, one would have to assume that the conventional strategy of developed countries to fund public agencies to define need and to devise relatively narrow and professionally controlled program strategies is not necessarily appropriate in Third World countries. Rather, benefits could be distributed directly to families and to local community resources defined broadly (e.g. community, religious groups) on behalf of families (Meenaghan and Mescari 1971).

When the thinking behind the delivery of benefits as well as type and range of benefits becomes modified, the thinking on evaluation of family welfare can also become modified. Traditionally, many welfare programs to individuals in developed countries have not worked—that is, they have not achieved what they defined as goals. Worse yet, in many areas, goals were not even articulated, perhaps not even seriously considered. Murray's recent analysis zeroes in on these severe limitations of current welfare programming in the United States (Murray 1984). However, one would be mistaken to conclude that due to the weaknesses in overall welfare policy and programming, there should not be an assertive family policy and family-focused benefits.

A more defensible posture for Third World countries to adopt is one which appreciates the need for family policy to be very effect-oriented, that is, characterized by well-articulated goals for different communities and for different types of families. The goals should be relevant to the dominant society and to the local community. This suggests a key role for the local community in defining and then negotiating with the larger society's funding and allocation bodies. Further, it suggests that besides effect-oriented evaluation, there should be a conscious attempt to promote community satisfaction measures of what is offered and how it is offered by professionals and others, whether they be local or translocal. Finally, the evaluation of programming differently for different families with a range of resources should proceed on the basis that there is a little compelling knowledge anywhere in the world on what works well with particular kinds of family and community profiles. In short, a tone of questioning, trying, and experimenting with innovative family programming could lead to progress.

Possible Principles to Guide Family Policy

In the previous sections of this chapter, there has been an attempt to spell out the functional relationships among government communities and families. It would appear that it might be useful to codify some of the normative principles that could guide a Third World country in operationalizing family policy. These are offered as reflections upon the previous sections but also as devices to assist Third World countries in thinking through their own normative choices given their local situations.

First, there should be an explicit emphasis upon the family as key unit of attention—not merely on individuals who happen to live in families. Recent developments in the United States suggest that a germane issue is the definition of *family*, if family is to be the focus. At least initially, *family* could be defined in the traditional, legal fashion, i.e., any two or more members related by blood or by law.

Second, any policy developed relative to the family should recognize the possible pluralistic and diverse quality of the country's people and its families. Policy in the area of family should be developed which would recognize that different cultural and ethnic groups bring differing perspectives and resources to the family experience. Such perspectives and backgrounds should be recognized, even utilized, in any attempt to support families. This principle would affirm the role of decentralization and local community variations.

Third, any developed policy should attempt to affirm, even maximize, choice at the family and individual level. This principle would suggest that there should not be central governmental imposition of a single strategy of support, but rather a variety of possible supports available from which families could avail themselves of assistance. Possible supports could and should include, in keeping with the second principle, supports within the local sector. This principle of family choice would affirm that government responsibility does not require government's direct provision of benefits to families.

Fourth, given the critical role of families in society, policy should be comprehensive and active, not merely residual and restricted to a few. As a result of this, two specific concerns should be reflected in any developed policy. There should be a focus upon ensuring an adequate or floor-level standard for families. This principle would initially require determining what a family needs to ensure. Once this was stated, even in tentative and preliminary terms, then subsequent efforts could be directed at explicating possible ways to meet the needs, again keeping in mind the prior principles.

In a related but distinct fashion family policy should also stress prevention. If families are indeed valued, then families that function well should be assisted to ensure that they continue to function well. This should be especially true for those well-functioning families that are subject to great stressors and risk within the society. Here the related principles of fairness and fiscal as well as social efficiency are suggested.

Fifth, policy that is developed in and for other sectors of our society should reflect a working sense of reciprocity relative to the family. This would suggest that concerns and possible effects upon families should be explicitly considered in the development and deliberative stages of "other" public policy. If this were done, then the value of family would be a criterion element in all public decision making in all policy areas.

The principle of reciprocity requires approaching family within a system perspective. This would suggest that changes in other institutional sectors can and will have consequences for the family. Some of the consequences may be negative, while the changes in the other institutional sectors may be positive. Further, this principle would question the assumption that it is acceptable for public policy to be generated in these other institutional sectors—e.g., the economy, transportation—but inappropriate for the public policy to be generated toward the family. Consistency, balance, and fairness in public policy suggest a proactive policy approach for families, especially since families often have to compensate for the breakdowns as well as the developments in other policy-supported institutional sectors.

Sixth, any public policy developed in the area of the family should affirm the quality of innovation and experimentation. Since few countries have done much to influence family life, there is little empirical evidence to justify any particular approach or strategy with respect to fast-changing conditions and pressures affecting families. This being the case, public policy can and should be developed and once in existence, should be carefully monitored to see that it is appropriate and used well. Relative to this principle, purposeful and variable use of local resources, private and public, to achieve relevant evolving family goals would be strongly suggested.

It is against the backdrop of these principles and the importance of focusing upon families and community groupings that the next section attempts to make even more precise the approach and choices that may be relevant for Third World countries.

Speculating on Family Programming in Different Communities

Previously it has been suggested that families can be characterized relative to need, risk, and current success in functioning. In keeping with the spirit of these terms, consideration of the use of the concept of *triage* might be useful (Coulton 1980). This concept basically requires answers concerning which parties or subjects will receive priorities in the allocation of scarce resources. To this concept, the spirit of the demographic technique of Shevky-Bell, social area analysis, could be incorporated. Together, triage and social area analyses could assist policy decision makers in the thorny questions related to allocation of resources for families and communities.

Initially, only those areas which scored high on family would be considered as a target. Next, each of these target areas could then be scored and examined relative to need and local resources, as well as by risk and local measures. Each examination could be set up in a two-by-two contingency table, with cells alphabetically assigned:

TABLE 15.1: Need–Resources

		Need	
		Low	High
Community	Low	A	B
Resources	High	C	D

TABLE 15.2: Risk–Resources

		Risk	
		Low	High
Community	Low	A	B
Resources	High	C	D

Focusing on "need" first, Cell D would suggest an area where current need is high but for which the local organization resource life is also strong. This cell location suggests the need for a strategy of maintaining and strengthening organizations that in turn would be instrumental in delivering benefits to families.

Cells C and B, in the Need–Resources table (Table 15.1), pose decisions for the society. Cell B shows an area where need is high but local resources are low. Cell C shows the reverse—good organizational supports relative to actual need. Conventional programming has often led to supporting individuals within the area depicted in Cell B, without adequately considering funding the community area in Cell C, so as to strengthen it and keep it functioning.

When family policy and benefits are directed toward the communities in Cell B, benefits would be probably directed toward rights and needs of families and social stability expectations of the larger community. Intervention could also proceed on a somewhat different basis, namely, organization and local resource building as constitutive elements in programming in families.

Correspondingly, a case could be made that an equal or nearly equal emphasis could be given to promoting policy and benefits for communities within Cell C as compared to Cell B. Here the positive current functioning of families and communities is recognized, and the goal of maintaining such functioning is consciously promoted. Here the teleological function of government policy would be stressed over the rights and benefits perspective. Concrete expression for this approach could be found in educational and developmental strategies directed at maintaining the life and quality of these communities and their resources.

Communities in Cell A would obviously have some families in need, but unless these communities scored high on risk, a case might be made that they should receive less policy attention than the communities that fall in other cells.

The same basic process of "sorting" communities can be done with risk relative to community resources and organizational life (Table 15.2). Communities that score high on risk and low on actual need could be examined as a separate group. Within that separate group, those communities that had a rich organizational life might be of special interest, maybe even receive the highest priority in terms of any subsequent intervention.

16

An Approach to Effective Family Planning in Rural Egypt

Mamdouh Fayek

The Problem

Periodic censuses show that the Egyptian population is growing at an alarming average rate of 100,000 people a month (Kerr 1981). The highest rates of population growth are in the rural part of the country.

Much research has been done on this subject, and many scholars have contributed in assessing the main sources of the problem. The findings and results of their statistical analysis indicated several factors which influence the problem.

Factors Contributing to the Problem

Early Marriage

The average age for marriage in rural Egypt used to be fifteen for girls and eighteen for boys. Lately, however, because of a severe housing shortage and economic difficulties, the average age of marriage has gradually increased to eighteen and twenty-three, respectively.

Children as Producer Durables

Although ostensibly stereotyped as irrational and fatalistic, rural Egyptians are in general rational in their decision making (Kelly, Khalifa, and El-Khorazati 1982). They see having children to be particularly profitable because children can earn money at a very young age, especially during cotton-picking periods.

Children also contribute by helping their parents with other chores, such as market activities of distributing farm products and so forth. They have proven to be producer durables in a low-income agricultural

188

setting where the household expenditure is rather minimal (Khalifa, Sayed, El-Khorazati, and Way 1982).

Attitude Toward Birth Spacing

The latest Egypt Contraceptive Prevalence Survey (ECPS) showed that the mean interval between marriage and the first birth is 17 months, while the mean interval between subsequent births is 28.6 months.

Children as Insurance and Security

Among the factors involved is the need for each mother in rural Egypt to feel secure. She worries about how she will be taken care of in her old age, knowing that she will probably survive her husband. Children give her this security, and the more there are, the more secure she will be. Having a good and caring son is a very imporant goal in a rural woman's life. Two or three sons are better, to ensure that at least one will grow up to be a good and reliable provider. Studies also show that among other reasons, fathers desire to have sons for security in old age.

Son Preference in Rural Egypt

The most recent data illustrate that most women in rural Egypt have a preference for sons. The 1980 published data give (a) 45 percent wish to have more sons than daughters, compared to (b) 26 percent who prefer to have daughters and (c) 29 percent who wish for an equal number of both sexes. The desire for male offspring can be so great that some couples in rural Egypt keep having children until a son is born.

Children as Status

Studies by a number of scholars showed the possible effect of family and kinship systems on family growth. In his book, Saad Gadalla (1978) relates religious values and cultural patterns, which assert the family cohesion that motivates marriage and reproduction resulting in a high birthrate. Indeed, studies show that families with high income in rural Egypt have a higher fertility rate. In their belief, an abundance of family members will emphasize the strength of the family.

Desired Family Size

Current data indicate that only one out of every three married women in rural Egypt believes that she has more children than she considers ideal

(Kelly, Khalifa, and El-Khorazati 1982). Evidently, the other two-thirds are unaware or simply do not care.

Infant Mortality

The most recent data showed that 130 of every 1,000 babies born in rural Egypt die within the first year. This ratio, however high it may be, constitutes an improvement over earlier estimates which were showing a level of over 150 infant deaths per 1,000 live births for the 1971–1973 period. Data also indicated that young mothers, because they are less able and/or less experienced in child care, lose infants more frequently.

Improvement of Health Care

According to one survey (Gadalla 1978), when asked about the reasons why infant mortality has declined, 70 percent of the responding villagers indicated agreement to reasons like the improvement of medical facilities, the availability of medicine and medical personnel, vaccination, and the control of epidemic diseases.

In those interviews, villagers indicated their acceptance and use of professional medical treatment and hospitalization, and acknowledged the poor quality of medical services available in their village through midwives and/or barbers. They also expressed their wishes to seek better medical treatment from outside, which they usually seek only when they are seriously ill.

Knowledge of Family Planning and Contraceptive Methods

In a sample survey fielded in 1972 (Gadalla 1978), less than one-third of the surveyed women in rural Egypt approved of the use of family-planning methods at that time. Surveys conducted through 1980 indicated acceptance to be at an 80 percent level. Approval is lowest among the youngest and oldest women. The ECPS results show that 91 percent of all married women know at least one family-planning method. This situation is likely going to remain the same in the next two decades.

Education

In his analysis of the survey data from rural Egypt regarding education, Atef Khalifa (1976) discussed the important influence of education on the women's fertility behavior. His analysis showed clearly that the increase of educational level of the wife, on the average, resulted in fewer pregnancies, less pregnancy loss (miscarriage), and less childhood mortality.

The Up-to-God Factor

In her study "Attitudes of a Group of Egyptian Medical Students Towards Family Planning," Theresa El-Meheiry (1984) found that 25 percent of the surveyed students believed that family planning should be left in God's hands and concentration should be on raising the standard of living and expanding the habitable land beyond the present meager 3.5 percent of the entire countryside. These are the would-be doctors whose responsibilities may include helping family planning in different parts of the Egyptian countryside.

The State of Family Planning in Rural Egypt

The major effort on the part of the Egyptian government regarding family planning was the initiation of the Population and Development Project (PDP) in 1977. This is a community-based program providing improvements in family planning "delivery systems." The program stresses particular points which should create favorable situations conducive to attaining constructive population activities in rural areas. The PDP was introduced to handle the family-planning project on a socioeconomic and programming level. Every mother village and four satellite villages has an advisory committee PDPAC composed of "elected officials and recognized opinion leaders from among women, youth, and elders" (Khalifa, Sayed, El-Khorazati, and Way 1980).

Recruited volunteer female workers, called Raiyda Riyfia, from targeted villages would make visits to women villagers to offer information, answer questions, correct misunderstandings, supply contraceptives, and collect data needed for evaluations. These personnel would report to the head of the program council.

Results of the 1980 Egypt Contraceptive Prevalence Survey (ECPS) showed that only 15 percent of all women in Upper Egypt and 12 percent in Lower Egypt were aware of the Raiyda's presence. Of those women, only 60 percent obtained information on family planning and only 20 percent received contraceptives. Similarly, results of those surveys with regard to fertility behavior show that the impact of the PDP is not substantial.

Concerning the attitudes of the villagers toward their future use of family-planning methods, results show that 59 percent of currently married nonusers intend to use a contraceptive method in the future. When those women were asked about when they intend to use it, only 50 percent knew when they might start using contraceptive methods; 20 percent would use it within two years, and 17 percent would use it after two years. While 53 percent said they would use the pill, only 9 percent said they would use an

Intrauterine Device (IUD). It is possible to discern that major shortcomings are hampering the potential of meaningful gains from this program. It would also appear unreasonable to anticipate any significant changes in the situation without modifications in the procedure of the program's implementation (N. Amin 1985).

A Proposal for a Population-Oriented Model

In his book *Is There Hope*, Saad Gadalla (1978) proposed to change the family-planning model to a population-oriented model. He talked about proponents from highly industrialized countries who believe in the theory of solving population growth problems of developing countries through establishing sociopolitical systems committed to overall development and improvements of the lifestyles of all the people. Convinced by this theory, the Egyptian authorities adopted a new policy in 1973 to reflect it. However, serious plans for effective implementation have so far not materialized.

Unless the effort is widened to incorporate a spectrum of areas concerning socioeconomic and cultural issues as a whole, significant birthrate decline may remain hard to achieve. Research findings have indicated that most villagers are highly incognizant of national and local problems pertaining to population growth and of contraceptive methods and their use. Therefore, remedies will have to include strengthening communication, education, and information. Effective means of informing will have to be used. These include mass media literacy education programs, as well as involvement of local leaders and preachers.

A 1984 report of the PDP meeting of the executive leaders (N. Amin 1985), indicated that lack of motivation on the part of the villagers has always been a major problem. Harsh conditions and poverty breed apathy. Therefore, it is only logical to start at the root of the problem and create ideas conducive to persuading and motivating the villagers to get involved in family-planning programs.

This approach has been examined in a pilot project initiated by the Social Research Center of the American University of Cairo in collaboration with the Ministry of Social Affairs and the Egyptian Family Planning Association in January 1976. The pilot project was meant to reactivate the functions of a neglected Rural Social Unit in a village called Shanawan (Gadalla 1978), about thirty miles north of Cairo. A limited budget of £E2,000 ($) was allotted to this pilot project. Volunteer laborers from the community were recruited to repair, remodel, and paint the building. All the work was accomplished in two months. Community leaders contributed in successfully activating the nursery, the women's club, and the literacy classes for adult men and women, all of which have since been growing in attendance and use. Experience has shown us throughout the years that the entire national Egyptian population can rally behind their popular leaders if indeed there is a national crisis. If minimal private donations can be collected from all working citizens, it can add up to a substantial amount, which can be matched by benevolent international agencies to replicate a comprehensive family-planning center throughout rural Egypt.

The Proposed Family-Planning Center

Based on the Shanawan experiment, it seems possible that a center can be built to fit the needs and objectives of family planning in rural Egypt. The elements of the center would include a reception office, an administrative office, a clinic, a nursery, media rooms, literacy classrooms, the social workers' (Raiyda Riyfia) meeting room, bathrooms, and a kitchen and banquet facility (Figure 16.1). Outside of the building, there should be ample space for a stable and parking area. The design should be amenable to future expansion (Figures 16.2 and 16.3).

The center should preferably be built by volunteer labor in order to save cost, and more importantly to elicit badly needed involvement by the villagers themselves, which would give them the distinct feeling that the center is indeed their own and for their well-being and the betterment of their future. The collaborative effort between the designer, the authorities, and the villagers has to be well coordinated.

The method of construction should be as simple as possible and should not call for the use of expensive modern equipment. An excellent example of such a simple method was accomplished by the renowned Egyptian architect Hassan Fathy (1973) in his design of the experimental village Qurna near Luxor in Upper Egypt. Fathy dug in deeply to revive vernacular crafts of using the earth to build, an idea which lends itself well to the nature of the situation regarding convenience, climate, and practicality of cost and techniques. In his work, he developed an "aided-self-help" system for peasants and villagers to build their own homes. Quoting the results of experiments on adobe brick mixture, which were previously carried out by Colonel Debes and Mustapha Yehia. Fathy (1973) concluded that although the experiments indicate that the material is durable and withstands rainstorms, additional experiments should be done continually for perfecting the mixture characteristics.

For foundation, the most cumbersome problem is the settling of the mud buildings, which causes cracks. These cracks can be easily patched up and eventually will blend. Cracking should stop after the building compacts the soil beneath it. Care should be observed in waterproofing the

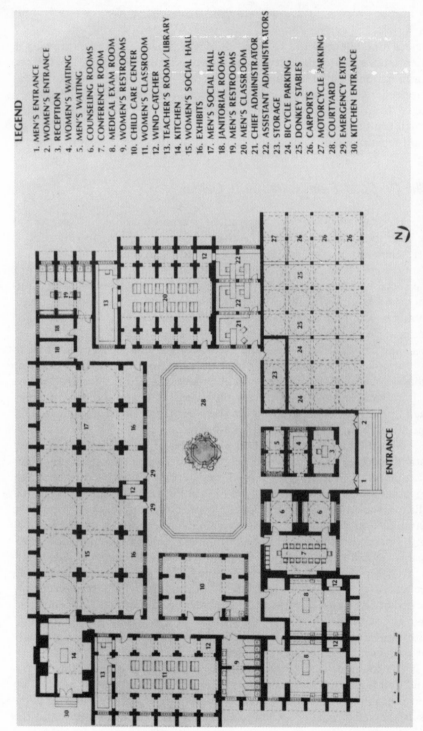

LEGEND

1. MEN'S ENTRANCE
2. WOMEN'S ENTRANCE
3. RECEPTION
4. WOMEN'S WAITING
5. MEN'S WAITING
6. COUNSELING ROOMS
7. CONFERENCE ROOM
8. MEDICAL EXAM ROOM
9. WOMEN'S RESTROOMS
10. CHILD CARE CENTER
11. WOMEN'S CLASSROOM
12. WIND-CATCHER
13. TEACHER'S ROOM/LIBRARY
14. KITCHEN
15. WOMEN'S SOCIAL HALL
16. EXHIBITS
17. MEN'S SOCIAL HALL
18. JANITORIAL ROOMS
19. MEN'S RESTROOMS
20. MEN'S CLASSROOM
21. CHIEF ADMINISTRATOR
22. ASSISTANT ADMINISTRATORS
23. STORAGE
24. BICYCLE PARKING
25. DONKEY STABLES
26. CARPORTS
27. MOTORCYCLE PARKING
28. COURTYARD
29. EMERGENCY EXITS
30. KITCHEN ENTRANCE

Figure 16.1: Proposed plan for a family-planning center in rural Egypt.

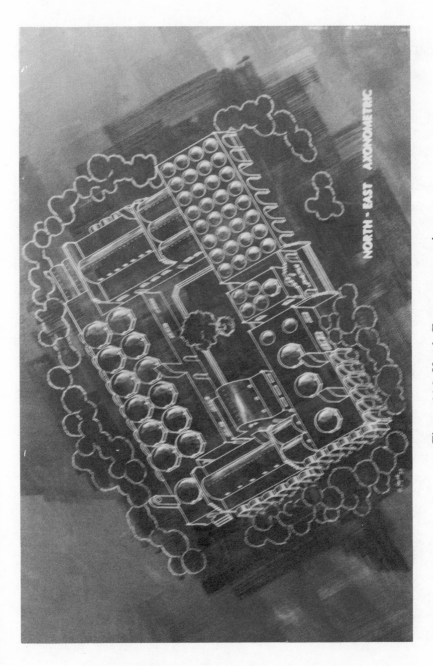

Figure 16.2: North–East axonometric.

Figure 16.3: South–West axonometric.

foundation to minimize the settling problems (Fathy 1973). Fortunately, sun-dried earth brick is an extremely poor conductor of heat, and it retains the heat for a long time, which makes the mud brick house cool during a hot day but warm during the night. Also, the Malkaf (wind catch) device has proven effective for many centuries in Arabic architecture. It may be set up precisely at the right angle to catch the wind and let the hot air escape at the top. For heating, Fathy devised an oven with a system of inside partitioning directing gases of combustion backward and forward to "allow more time for the heat to radiate into the room before it escapes" (Fathy 1973). When the fuel dies down, the doors of both the fire and chimney can be closed to allow an all-night radiation of warmth into the room.

Indigenous crafts such as Mushrabya (claustra), Sabra (wood door making), and furniture building should be allowed to flourish in building the center. Local methods and designs may be improved upon by the introduction of supplementary educational means of adding durability and quality. Within design guidelines, local artists should be allowed to express themselves in decorating the building to enhance the feeling of belonging.

The Proposed Design

Identifying the Client of the Project

The client of this project would be a committee composed of representatives from the following three groups:

1. The users, who are the inhabitants of a mother village and possibly as many as four satellite villages. Of those villagers, volunteers would be recruited to donate their labor, which would be critically needed to accomplish the project. Two leaders would be elected to represent the villagers on the committee.

2. The consultants who represent the sponsoring international organizations which would have donated funds to the project and would be interested in following up on the proper use of their funds.

3. Representatives from pertinent Egyptian government agencies; namely, the National Populations Council and the Population and Family Planning Board.

Two individuals from each of these three groups along with the designer would form a committee of seven.

Goals of the Project

1. To educate the villagers about the negative effect of overpopulation and the positive effects of family planning.

2. To educate the villagers on the proper use of contraceptive methods.

3. To follow up on the consistency of usage of these contraceptives by the villagers and bring needed information and data to the center for evaluative research.

4. To alleviate the illiteracy problem affecting family-planning awareness.

5. To counsel both men and women villagers on their social and medical problems pertaining to the family-planning methods.

6. To create a collaborative and cooperative social atmosphere in the community conducive to generating feelings of concern about the well-being of that community and the entire country.

7. Since an Egyptian village may contain anywhere between 3,000 and 30,000 inhabitants, a proposed center should either be situated in one large village or conveniently located to serve more than one village. The total inhabitants to be served would be up to approximately 30,000.

8. By tradition, there is a distinct social demarcation between men and women in the use of physical space. Interaction between the men villagers would be during meetings, classes, and ceremonies. Women would similarly interact with other women. Mothers would be able to leave their little children in the nursery to be cared for during counseling time or doctors' visits.

9. Statistics show that crime in Egyptian villages is uncommon. This would mean that security measures for the center can be normal.

10. Selection of a center site should consider centrality as well as accessibility. A characteristic green belt surrounding the center with palm trees and other trees would help create a special attractiveness to the center, projecting an image of hope to the villagers.

11. The center should be oriented to utilize the wind and shade in helping to ventilate the interiors.

12. The quality of building would not be as refined as if it were built by professionals. It would be as expected to result from the self-help method of adobe brick building and the volunteer workmanship of the villagers. Hopefully, among the volunteer villagers, a few would be local practicing artisans. These would be called upon to help train the volunteer villagers and check their workmanship.

13. It is apparent that both material and labor cost of the building would be minimal. The operating and maintenance cost would have to be borne by the agencies involved for sometime until the villagers can afford to pay for the services received at the center. Since most of the materials used do not easily wear out, it is expected that the building would last for a long time.

14. While adaptive reuse should be only a possibility in the far future,

plans of expansion should still be considered. Flexibility of the site's size should be available to accommodate varying population size.

15. Design of the interior space would greatly depend on the understanding of the users' needs, cultural patterns, and psychological inclinations.

16. It would be essential to treat the entire interior space as public space regarding maintenance and cleanliness.

17. Since the majority of rural Egyptians are illiterate, appropriate signage would have to be provided for different parts of the center.

Facts about the Project

Manpower and Workloads

Based on the population size to be served, and in relation to the service needs and the allocated operating cost, the employees should be determined as follows: a receptionist, a senior administrator, five social workers, two teachers, two babysitters, and two janitors.

The Area Perimeter

It has been indicated that the Egyptian government would approve the allocation of a maximum of an acre of land as a site on which to establish a pilot center. The site should be selected by the committee either out of state-owned or private-owned land.

User Characteristics

The projected facilities would be used by villagers, most of whom are illiterate, impoverished, and truly simple in nature. Aside from the local basic traditions and customs, they are mostly incognizant of many universally human and civil practices. Yet, judging from findings of scholars and researchers who lived and studied in that environment, the Egyptian villagers can learn and adapt to what they are taught. Therefore, it would be reasonable to assess that learning, and getting accustomed to the facilities would not be a cumbersome task for them, especially if the center is built as a refined version of their own architecture instead of an alien architecture.

Community Characteristics

The average density of population in Egyptian villages is about 700 persons per square kilometer (1,800 per square mile). Most villagers are very religious. They also adhere to such unwritten but conventional and cultural codes as family unity, respect and compassion for the elder, and strictness in raising children. Especially in raising girls, no such thing as dating is allowed; marriage is in most cases arranged by the parents.

Roads

Except for the major intercity roads, most of the roads in Egyptian villages are silt, suitable only for farm animals, carts, bicycles, and motorcycles. A little rain makes this type of road almost impassable. A better road is the compacted-silt type, which is found only on a limited basis in any village in rural Egypt. These are somewhat less vulnerable to rain and are appropriate for automobiles. The main artery is the paved road that joins towns and cities.

Behavioral Patterns

Generally, Egyptian villagers are not fast-paced people and are not keen on exactness of time either. Many wear no wristwatches and judge time by sunset and sunrise. An average villager wakes up at dawn and usually retires just after sunset. However, with the advent of electricity and television in rural Egypt, these patterns are not as consistent as they were in the past. Rural Egyptians have rare access to phones for confirming or canceling an appointment with the center or to keep in touch with it. Consequently, proximity of the center to most villagers is an important factor.

Climate

Since the problem of overpopulation has proven to be worst in Upper Egypt, it would be logical to build the pilot center in that area. Most of Upper Egypt's climate is characteristic of a hot, arid environment with a great difference in temperature between day and night. By day, the ground is hard hit by massive solar radiation due to an almost cloudless sky. During the night, however, the ground radiates back a great amount of its stored heat and becomes cool. From April to June, sporadic depressions from the Sahara traverse the country toward the Nile Delta, bringing excessively dry winds and often creating dust and sandstorms (*khamasin*) which can persist for three or four days at a time. Summer and winter are the principal and longest seasons (May–September and November–March).

Soil Characteristics

The Nile alluvium when freshly deposited is very soft, plastic, and sticky, but on losing moisture, it hardens into a tough soil. The land in rural

Egypt is mainly formed of such silt. Its main components are silica and other insoluble matter (60 percent), and ferric oxide and alumina (22 percent).

Code Survey

Building codes in the Egyptian countryside are virtually nonexistent. Artisans, and in many cases villagers by themselves, have built homes of different quality, using local methods thousands of years old without any government inspection or permits. Deeds have to be recorded, however, for the ownership of land and the dwelling built on it.

Surroundings

Aesthetically, the site environment can be characterized as mountainless and forestless. The topography is very flat and uninterrupted. Local architecture in rural Egypt is generally very poor in both design and construction and can be divided into two main categories:

1. The majority of dwellings are one-story and built of mud brick with roofs made of long stalks and straw-reinforced mud holding them together, along with straw mats and thatch.

2. In another category, a few dwellings belong to well-to-do landowners and families. These are made of stone foundations, plastered red-brick walls, tiber roofing, and plank or terrazzo floors.

Psychological Implications

Based on findings from countless interviews conducted with villagers by different scholars, there can be a major psychological influence on the villagers' attitude toward the goals of the center. If the center staff and community leaders succeed in getting the people involved, and if they enthusiastically convey ideas and perform services, the center can become a major uplift to the villagers' spirits and hopes for a better future.

Cost per Square Foot

Using the criteria that Hassan Fathy used in establishing the cost per square meter in 1950 at £E3.8($) and deducting the proportionate amount he established for labor, since in this case labor would be donated, the cost per square meter would be £E1.98($). If this amount is converted to cost per square foot, it must have been £E.22($) back in 1950. Converting this into dollars, it comes to approximately 22 cents at the Egyptian official rate. Data show that inflation in Egypt during the past thirty-six years may be considered to average 7 percent per year. This makes the cost per square foot in 1987 about $2.50. That figure was also checked against present material cost and was found to be reasonable.

Table 16.1 shows the itemized budget for the requisition of site construction of the center, while Table 16.2 is the work schedule.

TABLE 16.1: Maximum Budget

A.	Building costs: approx.	25,000 sq ft. at 2.50	$ 62,500
B.	Fixed equipment	25% of A	15,500
C.	Site development	15% of A	9,500
D.	Total construction	A+B+C	87,500
E.	Site acquisition		10,000
F.	Moveable equipment (furniture, etc.)	20% of A	12,000
G.	Professional fees	6% of A	4,000
H.	Administrative cost	1% of D	870
I.	Contingencies	15% of D	13,000
Total:			$214,870

TABLE 16.2: Schedule of Work

Week	2	4	6	8	10	12	14	16	18	20	22	24

Site [¦¦¦¦]

Foundations [¦¦¦¦¦¦¦¦¦]

Walls [¦¦¦¦¦¦¦¦¦¦¦¦¦]

Domes [¦¦¦]

Plumbing and sewerage [¦¦]

Power [¦¦]

Claustra [¦¦]

Plastering [¦¦]

Interior walls [¦¦]

Floors [¦¦]

Interior fixtures [¦¦¦]

Furniture [¦¦]

Landscaping [¦¦¦]

Signage [¦¦]

Decoration [¦¦]

Concepts of the Project

Service Grouping

The center should include facilities for the following services: administration, social counseling, medical asistance, literacy education, child care, and social activity.

People Grouping

The social demarcation between men and women would have to be addressed in relation to entries and public spaces. This segregation cannot be enforced as strictly in cases of social counseling, administration, or reception.

Activity Grouping

The logical way to group the different spaces would be to combine the functioning spaces for women closer together; namely, child-care center, women's literacy classroom, women's social hall, and women's rest rooms. On the other hand, the men's spaces would include men's literacy classroom, men's social hall, and men's rest rooms.

Sequential Flow

Most important to the success of the center is the logical and sequential flow of the space use, bearing in mind the grouping that was mentioned in the preceding item. Various planning attempts would have to be made toward the most workable solutions.

Climate Control

The heat-retaining characteristic of adobe brick, plus the thick walls necessary when building with this material, results in an efficient means of climate control. The dome concept, with the windows across the sides letting the warm air out and replacing it with cool air, is especially effective. In addition, the Malkaf concept, which was mentioned in this study, and the use of claustra work for sun breaking and allowing breezes in shaded areas are effective ways to combat the climate.

Character

In developing the center, the main factors involved would be
1. Budgetary constraints.

2. Practicality and functionality.

3. Indigenous architecture and crafts, enhanced by technical refinement.

4. Total avoidance of contrivance and pretentiousness in using form with substance.

When these factors are carefully addressed, a special character for the center commensurate with its goals will indeed materialize.

Concurrent Scheduling

Following the training of volunteer villagers to work on the construction of the center, coordinating schedules for different participating trades to work concurrently would be most important for best efficiency and timely completion of the project.

Space Needs of the Project

Based on the facts and the concepts of this study, it seems that the space required for the center would be well within the acre that the Egyptian government would allocate. Some details of space requirements are discussed in the following items.

Parking Requirements

In allocating parking spaces, several factors should be carefully considered:

1. Estimating the capacity of parking should be based on the busiest time of using the center; namely, the festivities time.

2. An average villager does not own a motorcycle or a bicycle and usually prefers to walk fairly long distances than to tire his animal (donkey) by riding it. He would rather save it for important tasks such as transporting farm products.

3. Women villagers can only ride animals or walk. They do not ride bicycles or motorcycles, even if their family owns one.

4. Most employees would have local residences, so that by either walking or riding bicycles, motorcycles, or animals, they would not waste much time in transport to and from the center.

5. Privileged personnel who have motorcars would drive up to a certain point before dirt roads take over, then walk or ride bicycles or donkeys the rest of the way. It would be reasonable to assume that the two doctors would be in this category.

6. Inspectors or auditors from the main city would visit the center on occasion, using either automobiles or passenger-carrying motorcycles.

With the above-mentioned requirements in mind, the following parking areas would be considered adequate: (1) 25 spaces for animals (donkeys) at 32 square feet each equals 800 square feet; (2) 25 bicycle spaces at 20 square feet each equals 500 square feet; (3) 5 motorcycle spaces at 40 square feet each equals 200 square feet; (4) 3 automobile spaces at 150 square feet each equals 450 square feet. This would total 1,950 square feet of needed parking area. With the addition of 30 to 50 percent maneuvering space within the parking facility, the total needed area would come to 2,700 square feet.

Interior Space Needs

The Receptionist The receptionist's duties include keeping appointment records for the doctors, the counselors, the administrators, the classes, the child-care center, and the social hall. About 175 square feet of space would be needed for a desk with a return and a few built-in cabinets for this function (Figure 16.4).

Waiting Space Two waiting spaces would be needed for men and women. These spaces would accommodate a maximum of twelve to fourteen people on settees. A total of 300 square feet will be needed for this function (Figure 16.5).

The Administrators Each center should have a supervisor and two administrative assistants. The supervisor would assign duties and promote the center. He would coordinate the activities of the social workers and the doctors along with the literacy classes and the social hall functions, and most of all, he would schedule and promote family-planning awareness presentations, exhibits, and speeches by visiting community leaders. He might delegate authority but would not delegate responsibility. The administrative assistants would keep the activities records and help the supervisor carry out his responsibilities.

The administrative office would need three desks with returns, filing cabinets, and storage cabinets. There would be additional seating for three visitors. The total office space is estimated at 600 square feet.

The Social Workers Most of the working hours of the social workers are spent in the field on house calls. They still spend some of their time at the center for coordination and review with each other. They report to the supervisor on a regular basis. Their activities log and records would be kept at the administrator's office. Social workers schedule meetings with women villagers and leaders regularly and on occasion.

A six-person meeting table and built-in cabinets would be needed for this function. The needed space is estimated at 425 square feet (Figure 16.6).

Figure 16.4: Reception area.

Counseling Rooms In case of the need to counsel two families or two members of one family at the same time, two rooms would be needed. Such a room of about 275 square feet would have seating for three (Figure 16.7).

The Medical Office Two doctors and two nurses would be needed. Two examination rooms would be needed, each requiring a sink cabinet with storage, an examination table, and a guest chair (a male villager would usually accompany his wife while she is being examined by a doctor

Figure 16.5: Waiting space.

or nurse). Supply cabinets would be needed for keeping contraceptives and medicine. Also, refrigeration would be necessary for some medication, along with a small incubator for sterilizing tools. A total of 885 square feet is estimated for the medical facility (Figure 16.8).

Classrooms Two literacy classes would be required, one for men and another for women. Each would accommodate twenty-five villagers. Desks would be designed for adults with minimal space for desk storage. Projection for some audiovisual lessons would be accommodated. Natural as well

Figure 16.6: Conference room.

Figure 16.7: Counseling room.

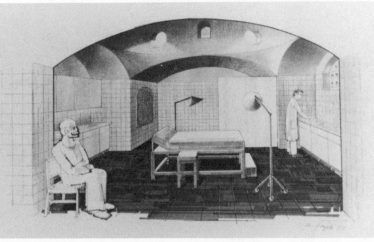

Figure 16.8: A medical examination room.

Figure 16.9: A classroom.

Figure 16.10: Women's social hall.

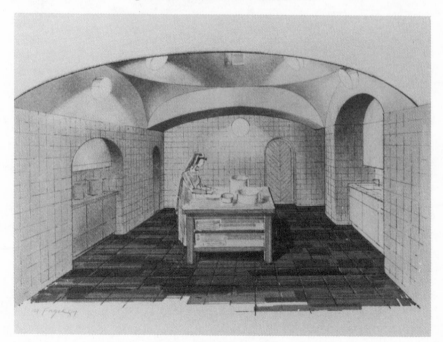

Figure 16.11: Kitchen.

Figure 16.12: Child-care center.

as artificial light would have to be generously provided. A total of 2,350 square feet would be needed for classrooms (Figure 16.9).

Teachers' Rooms A male teacher and a female teacher would have separate rooms for their preparation and evaluating the progress of the adult pupils. Each room would be about 275 square feet and would contain a desk, two chairs, and built-in cabinets.

Social Halls Two separate social halls, each about 2,900 square feet in area, for accommodating one hundred persons would be needed. Those halls would be for multipurpose use during wedding parties, circumcision parties, exhibits and shows, speech or lecture presentations, funerary receptions, and other group functions (Figure 16.10). These halls would be served by a kitchen space of about 700 square feet equipped to cook for two hundred people. Whoever would reserve the space would provide the food, drink, and utensils, but would use the facilities and would have to leave it clean (Figure 16.11).

Child-care Center This would be a space for children ranging from babies to toddlers and small children left temporarily by their mothers during counseling or a doctor's appointment. Two babysitters would be needed. The space would need soft flooring and furniture. It would also need cabinets to store toys and a private bathroom. An abundance of light would be needed for this space of about 1,000 square feet (Figure 16.12).

Figure 16.13: Men's rest room.

Rest rooms In establishing the capacity of the rest-room facilities, ac-·commodation would have to be made for the maximum capacity of the social halls of two hundred people. This would be divided between the men's and the women's rest rooms. Eight stalls for women, six for men plus two urinal basins, would be sufficient, in addition to the four sinks for each rest-room area. The total rest-room area would be about 800 square feet (Figure 16.13).

Janitorial Room About 200 square feet of space would have to be provided for two janitors whose responsibility it is to keep the center in clean and sanitary condition at all times. This room would contain a basin and ample storage space for cleaning equipment and supplies.

Storage A minimal storage space of approximately 300 square feet would be needed for the center. This would be for possible needs of supply spaces for different functional areas, such as the classrooms, the medical examination rooms, the social halls, child-care center, the kitchen, and the rest rooms.

Courtyard A courtyard is an indispensable part of such a facility in the hot climate. It is necessary for ventilation, illumination, and providing a delightful feeling of airiness. In addition, it creates more room in the case of need for gathering. An area of about 4,000 square feet would be needed for the courtyard.

17

Capturing Yauri's Peasantry

Frank A. Salamone

Introduction

Certain development problems in the Third World are logical consequences of deliberate colonial policies. Hyden (1980) has centered attention on one colonial policy that has had major implications for postcolonial development; namely, the capturing of the African peasantry. By "the capturing of the peasantry," Hyden simply means that the central government takes measures which render all independent economic, political, and sociocultural achievements impossible for the peasantry. It destroys all sources which aid their separate existence, in effect, rendering them dependent upon the central government for their very existence.

Significantly, the colonial government was able to effect the destruction of the peasantry only in greater or less degree, through the cooperation of indigenous rulers. Under the British system, these "native authorities" often discovered that their own interests coincided with those of their colonial "protectors." After all, they knew their areas better than did the British administrators assigned to them. Therefore, they were often able to structure the "reality" these officials saw in such a manner as to structure their interpretations and behaviors in ways quite favorable to their personal interests.

In the *Yauri Day Book*, we have a document that enlightens our understanding of the processes involved in the cooperation between colonial and native authorities in the capturing of the peasantry. The *Day Book* also presents a textbook example of the costs and limits of a mutually constructed colonial reality.

Basically, the *Day Book* is a diary between Abdullahi, the emir of Yauri (*Sarkin Yauri*), and P. G. Harris, the district officer at Yauri. It consists of a series of entries in Hausa of appointments, government lists, policies, and numerous other day-to-day details involved in the actual running of an emirate in Northern Nigeria in the period May 17, 1828–September 2, 1831. However, what is truly fascinating about the book is the insight the scribbled questions and answers allow into the development of the relationship between a "native authority" and a political officer at a period in the history of indirect rule when it had become firmly established and had not yet come under vigorous and concentrated attack. It is revealed in the *Day Book* in its pure and unadulterated form, with no apologies deemed necessary.

It is therefore able to offer an unclouded version of the process through which Yauri and probably similar emirates extended the power and control of the central government over previously independent rural areas. It did so essentially through attending to the minutes of everyday life. By effecting control over these minute aspects of sociocultural reality, Yauri was able to erode the power and privilege of local groups.

Yauri offers an ideal case study of the content and process of indirect rule and the manner in which it extended centralization because British administrators often used it as the very model of a progressive emirate flourishing under indirect rule (Smith 1970:74).

Yauri does, in fact, exhibit the general characteristics of indirect rule which Dorward (1974) and Crowder (1970), among others, have noted. There was, for example, a "working misunderstanding" between the colonial administrator and native authority that eased the control of the central authority over those outside political administration. The prevailing colonial ideology was at work, and it placed the Hausa higher on the cultural evolutionary ladder, as "Hamites," than their "subject" peoples. Moreover, the British recognized that they required the cooperation of the Hausa and Hausa-Fulani rulers in order to rule the vast tract of land they conquered in 1903. Therefore, they were cooperative in removing and overlooking any legal niceties that might hinder effective control over the hinterlands. As Crowder (1970:xi) phrases it, "These same chiefs had removed for them by the colonial regime many of the limitations to their authority from below."

Setting

Yauri is located in the northwest corner of Sokoto State, Nigeria. It is the smallest of the fourteen Hausa emirates and their westernmost outpost along the Niger River. Its frontier status is implicit within its ranking as one of the *Hausa banza* (bastard Hausa states). Although it paid tribute to the Fulani sultan at Sokoto, it was never a Fulani state, and its rulers have been careful to stress their Hausa identity.

Befitting a frontier state that had also become a refuge area for those seeking to escape slave raids, Yauri had long been an ethnically heterogeneous area. By 1800, its Hausaized rulers and indigenous peoples (Kamberi, Shangawa, Reshe [Gungawa], Hune [Dukawa], and Lopawa) had worked out basic patterns of political and economic relationships. Basic patterns of ethnic interactions and political stances led to the emergence of ethnic identities. Changes in political, economic, and occupational positions have led to changes in such identities. Over time, other groups have entered the area, providing specialized goods and services. The Fulani have provided dairy products, meat, and fertilizer. The Serkawa, an occupational if not yet an ethnic category, are professional fishermen. Each indigenous group has a specialty which identifies it with its proper ecological niche and therefore its position within society.

Abdullahi and P. G. Harris

Abdullahi and Harris demonstrated a professionalism that contrasted with the clumsy amateurism of their predecessors J. D. C. Clarke and Aliyu (Crowder 1973; Salamone 1975). Aliyu and Clarke had dismembered Yauri, almost destroying its independence through merging it with a neighboring emirate. They had also brought about their own downfall through angering the Reshe, or Gungawa, Yauri's "most industrious people."

Although Abdullahi and Harris differed in competence and style from their predecessors, they did not differ that much in their aims. They continued to seed the consolidation of central authority over rural peoples.

Unlike Aliyu, however, Abdullahi in seeking to effect the centralization of authority endeavored to advance structural not idiosyncratic interests. Abdullahi was the legitimate heir of the Jerabawa dynasty, Yauri's ruling family. Aliyu had been a Fulani usurper whom Clarke had illegitimately placed on Yauri's throne. Unlike Aliyu, then, Abdullahi knew Yauri was at ease in meticulously observing its traditional forms and earnestly sought the cooperation of the "common people" (*talakawa*) in his endeavors. Yauri's interests and his were inextricably intertwined, for he depended not only on the British but also on the goodwill of the Yauri people.

Harris also presented a sharp contrast with his predecessor. He had attended public school, studied law, had a distinguished military record (including Nigerian service), and had risen rapidly through the ranks of the postwar Nigerian administrative service. As befitted an "enlightened" political officer, he studied anthropology, receiving a diploma in 1933, and published ethnological articles in prestigious journals. All in all, he was the very model of a gentleman-scholar, one who appreciated Hausa-Fulani culture and identified the success of British goals with those of the emirs.

Quite clearly, in aiding Abdullahi strengthen his control over the peasantry, Harris furthered British interests. He was also changing traditional power relationships in Yauri while claiming to preserve them. The stability resulting from the imposition of British rule significantly frustrated resistance to Hausa rule (cf. Smith 1970:21; and especially Crowder 1970: XIV, XXIII). That stability altered traditional patterns of migration into Yauri, and the Hausa population grew. Additionally, there was an increase in the number of people who changed ethnic identity from Reshe to Yaurawa to Hausa. It was a change Harris favored and aided, for Hausa-Reshe solidarity facilitated achievement of British economic goals.

Capturing the Peasantry

The *Yauri Day Book* clearly proves that Abdullahi, in a very brief time, began to manipulate Harris in very subtle ways. He had earned Harris's respect and had begun to press for the implementation of policies important to Yauri. Abdullahi obviously knew that the closer he could depict those policies as furthering British interests, the better chance they had of being implemented.

Both powers agreed that the pacification of the peasantry was essential. Groups outside governmental domination posed a threat to the stability of commerce and indeed to the very legitimacy of the government itself. Thus, they decided to make an example of the Hune (Dukawa) as the most blatantly rebellious of Yauri's groups. To do so, they had to subdue them and subject them to the regular and peaceful collection of taxes. Further, the Hune had to petition for their return to Yauri, reversing their actions under the previous regime that had governed Yauri.

The *Day Book* is filled with the language of power. Even a simple tabulation of topics from any period, such as May 17 to December 31, 1928, reveals that fact; 44 percent of all discussions concerned economic matters, while education accounted for but 5 percent, and health for 1 percent. The first three pages of the *Day Book* are concerned with laws regulating farming and commodity marketing. Not only does Abdullahi exhort farmers to be more industrious, but he also encourages them to sell their produce only on Yelwa's market day. Yelwa is the capital of Yauri. Abdullahi was not only looking out for the economic well-being of his emirate; in so encouraging the farmers, he was also extending his power through being better able to regulate trade and tax it. Indeed, Abdullahi and Harris were fascinated with taxes and collected all sorts of information that enabled them to get a better grasp of the economic potential of Yauri. In so doing, they began to understand and seek to control every aspect of Yauri's life. Abdullahi's influence extended into such modern areas as immigration and emigration.

Logically, Abdullahi began to attack the ancient privileges of district and village heads, emphasizing his independence from their feudal ideals

and practices. Coincidentally, he was also able to assert his political independence in so doing. Harris provided Abdullahi with an ideal "human
rights" issue. The chief of Gabbas had been using forced labor on his personal lands. He appears to have promised payment in some cases. In the
process of investigating and correcting the abuses, Abdullahi and Harris
impressed upon headmen the fact that laborers must be paid and that com-
moners must be left alone to farm their lands (YDB:48). The incident
underscored Abdullahi's commitment to encourage commodity production and to exert his right to regulate it. Not only did he tighten his hold
over the local market, but he also used a bean lorry to monopolize all grain
trade with the South. The lorry was still in use in the 1970s.

The *Day Book* clearly demonstrates Abdullahi's ability in using
colonial reality as a means for extending his power. The best example is
the manner in which he handled the threatened migration of the Shanga
Hune. To lose this last remnant of the Hune would have mocked his asser-
tion of rights over those living in Montagora. Abdullahi learned that the
promise of lower taxes was luring the Hune to Kontagora to join their
relatives. Since taxes in the area were to be uniform, he rightly suspected
foul play. An unscrupulous tax collector was charging lower taxes, under-
reporting the returns, and embezzling money. Abdullahi appealed to the
colonial power to enforce its laws and help him to keep "his" Hune in Yauri
(YDB:80–81).

Of course, Abdullahi had to act out his role. No slackening in his effort
to return the "lost" Hune to Yauri could be allowed. No attempted tamper-
ing with Yauri's unity escaped his notice. An excerpt from the *Day Book*
(134–135) suffices to illustrate his concern:

> Will you please inform the Chief of Bussa to stop getting into my affairs
> and the people of my Emirate? He is always sending C.I.D.'s [police
> detectives] to the people of Ngaski and those of Kwanji town. I have never
> sent a person to his town without his notice. I was annoyed with what he
> did the day before yesterday. I heard that he sent a boat to Yelwa secretly
> to take somebody called Azaru who comes from Yelwa. He sent Mallam
> Mayahi and Isa; they were his messengers. Isa then said he can't go any-
> where without a prison approval from me. He then came and told me of
> what the chief of Bussa asked them to do. I asked them to inform the
> other man, Mayahi, to go back to Bussa, and he, Isa, not to return.

Few emirs could match Abdullahi in playing the colonial game, for he
carefully worked at shaping the perception of British administrators. He
conscientiously consolidated his reputation for honesty by refusing to
tamper in the internal affairs of other emirates. Thus, when two con-
spirators appealed for his aid in overthrowing village heads in Kontagora
in return for their aid in supporting his territorial claims, he speedily arrested

the leader of the plot and informed Harris (YDB:225–226), thereby assuring himself of British support for his own emirate's integrity.

Additionally, Abdullahi clearly understood the value of using symbols to promote his position as a "progressive emir." For example, he used Western tailors, drove a Ford automobile, used a checkbook, attended movies, purchased Yoruba music to play on his Victrola, knew how to type and owned his own typewriter, purchased cigarettes by the packet, bought articles on the installment plan, wore Western shoes, slept on a mattress, and enjoyed other Western status symbols. This familiarity with Western gadgets put Harris and other Westerners at ease in their dealings with Abdullahi, a relaxation Abdullahi was able to use to his own advantage.

It is obvious that Harris began to rely increasingly on Abdullahi's advice and his interpretation of Yauri's local life, history, and traditions. Abdullahi used Harris's interest in anthropology as a prime opportunity to press his perception of Yauri's historical and sociocultural reality in his interpretation of traditional relationships. (See, for instance, YDB: 64–66, 68–70, 112–113, 163ff., for some idea of the range of topics covered.)

The manner in which Harris and Abdullahi worked together to master the "cattle Fulani" (*Filanin daji*) is a prototype for the manner in which Abdullahi shaped Harris's perceptions and extended the meaning of "traditional" within the colonial context. The fact that it furthered the achievement of British interests makes it an especially instructive case. First, it is important to note that a careful reading of the *Day Book* supports Adamu's (1968) contention that the government of Yauri had not regulated the movements of the *Filanin daji* for quite some time. Indeed, the *Day Book* documents a very careful campaign to establish Yauri's right to levy a cattle tax (*jangali*), command escape routes, compel rinderpest prevention, collect tax receipts, direct the return of stolen cattle and other matters clearly related to controlling cattle people. Toward accomplishing that goal, Abdullahi had lists of cattle kept up-to-date so that he knew what cattle were in which town or village. He also had receipts checked and cross-checked with neighboring areas.

A complaint he levied on September 5, 1928, displays the use he made of British help in extending his domination. He charged the Fulani with hiding their cattle and lying about their number. Harris sent police with receipt books and the power to countermand the orders of village heads. Moreover, fines against those who were found to have lied were to be levied at twice the usual rate per cattle; namely $4 instead of $2. So thoroughly did these colonial measures work that by 1931, Abdullahi was found to be confidently correcting Harris's temporary replacement regarding the appropriate measures to tax the Fulani, putting these forward as of longstanding and traditional usage rather than of scarcely three years' duration.

Such actions support Smith's (1970) contention that a strong emir generally dominated a new officer.

An integral part of Abdullahi's plan to consolidate his power was the strengthening of the Reshe-Hausa alliance. The British had made it absolutely clear that they admired the commercial Reshe and deemed them to be the most industrious of Yauri's peoples. Abdullahi's understanding of that reality was but another proof of his legitimacy, for the Jerabawa dynasty had cemented their power through a recruitment of Reshe into the Hausa ethnic group (Salamone 1974a:283). Since the Hausa had replaced Reshe rulers, this link served many purposes. It aided in legitimizing his reign, provided allies, and maintained British favor. Therefore, he quite clearly advised Harris that any increase in Reshe taxation would lead to their emigration from the emirate. The mere threat of such an emigration had led to their predecessors' downfall (YDB:208–209). Harris followed Abdullahi's advice.

Abdullahi's very success, however, led to some failures, for his role as an emir, even a "progressive" one, precluded certain behaviors and beliefs, at least in the British mind. Abdullahi's efforts to secure quality education in Yauri unfortunately fell into that category. Indeed, Abdullahi had a genuine commitment to learning. His early instruction at the provincial school at Kano had instilled a lifelong love for Western ideas and their developmental values. Teaching at Birnin Kebbi had only served to increase his convictions. Abdullahi knew that modern schooling was the path to success in the colonial and postcolonial world. In fact, he understood that it was the combination of modern training and a valid claim to traditional legitimacy that had led to his own success, and he perceived that lack of that education was the single most important reason for the differential development of North and South in Nigeria.

The inherent logic of indirect rule, unfortunately, militated against the attainment of his dream. That logic held that there must be local financial support for all local governmental functions, including education. Additionally, that logic presumed an innate hatred between missionaries and Muslim emirs, precluding mission education (Graham 1966:167–168). The consequences for Yauri were inexorable: On the brink of independence, an emirate noted for its progressive leadership found itself with only 4 schools, 15 classrooms, and 450 students, less than 1 percent of the school-age population. Most of its teachers, moveover, were Igbo or Yoruba, a situation embarrassing to Abdullahi, a former teacher.

18

Third World Development: The Contribution of Latin American Liberation Theology

Joel Zimbelman

Introduction

The term *liberation theology* denotes a movement among predominantly Roman Catholic Christians in Latin America (but in other developing nations as well) that seeks to provide, through the development of a comprehensive vision of history and society, a theological justification for the economic, political, and spiritual transformation of the continent. It is a movement firmly committed to improving the existence of the people of Latin America and their chances for a full and prosperous future. Taking as its impetus the general Catholic social teachings developed at the Second Vatican Council (1962–1965) (Abbott 1966: 199–308), Latin American theologians and bishops forged a surprisingly unified vision of what the Christian faith implied for the development of their continent. In 1968, the Second General Conference of Latin American Bishops, meeting in Medellin, Colombia, issued a document that outlined the theological, social, and political dimensions of a position that would eventually become known as liberation theology. By the early 1970s, several works of liberation theology had been written that advanced the methodological foundations and biblical warrants for the new theology. It was during these years that North Americans and Europeans became aware of the movement through the writings of Gustavo Gutierrez, Juan Luis Segundo, Rubem Alves, José Miguez-Bonino, and others.

Liberation theology employs theological, political, and economic concepts to formulate its vision. It advocated economic development, the just distribution of wealth, the establishment of universal literacy and educational opportunities, and the creation of participatory democracies. Though a politically radical and leftist movement within the more established traditional Roman Catholic churches, its commitment to the elimination of poverty, oppression, and injustice has permitted its theologians, lay supporters, and other committed persons outside the church to galvanize their movement around a number of concrete goals based on shared moral imperatives. In summary, liberation theology attempts to relate Christian belief to concrete beneficent action for the poor and dispossessed of society. It aims for the optimistic and hopeful in life, while recognizing that there are nearly insurmountable obstacles to the establishment of the Kingdom of God in history.

Since the early 1960s, liberation theology has grown in intellectual depth, creativity, and strength. Its theology is consistently denounced by the Roman Catholic Curia and Magesterium, but its ethical and economic program appears to have strong support from many individuals who share their social program and moral vision while either opposing or remaining neutral to their theological formulations. Liberation theology shows little sign of losing its vigor, its controversial approach to theological reflection and social analysis, or its strong following among both North American and Latin American liberal Catholics and Protestants.

In this article, I provide an overview of the theological, political, and economic elements present in liberation theology and discuss the movement's relation to the general economic and social development concerns of Latin America. First, I describe the Christian and Marxist components of the movement, discussing how liberation theology holds these often incommensurable elements together. Second, I discuss liberation theology's critique of the "developmentalist" paradigm that presently informs the economic and social development of the continent. This is followed by a discussion of the economic paradigm of "radical liberation from dependence" that is introduced by liberation theology as an alternative to the developmentalist paradigm. I describe what such liberation demands with respect to restructuring the economics of development, politics, and the social fabric of Latin American society. Finally, I offer some criticisms of liberation theology's reflections on the issues of development and indicate some deficiencies in its theological vision and economic and social proposals. Here, I am concerned as well to indicate necessary areas of further work and research.

Christianity and Marxism in Liberation Theology

Christian Theology

Liberation theology initiates its theological reflection in its experiences of poverty, oppression, injustice, and the "cries of suffering humanity for deliverance" (Wolterstorff 1983:43) that define Latin America's contemporary social order. It is a theology grounded in phenomenological concerns—the concerns of the lived situation—rather than one that aims for precise metaphysical, doctrinal, or ethical clarity. For the liberation theologian, all legitimate reflection about the meaning of life, theology, politics, and ethics must originate with reflection on the lived situation of poverty, exploitation, and hopelessness that defines the reality of most of the population of Latin America. Looking at reality through the "optic of the poor" in this way means, correspondingly, that all reflection and action must possess a commitment to and a "preferential option for the poor" (Segundo 1976:81–95). This preferential option demands a commitment to advance the interests of those persons who live on the "margins" of society and who are unable to participate fully or meaningfully in the social community. Indeed, for liberation theology, the only authentic theology is one that directly relates the message of salvation in Jesus Christ to the physical, psychological, and spiritual liberation of humanity (Gutierrez 1973:36–37). As Hellwig notes, "The life of prayer and faith are not seen as side by side with social concerns, but coincident with them. Theology is not found alongside the concern with the causes of suffering, but arises out of that concern" (1977:143). Gustavo Gutierrez, a leading Peruvian liberation theologian, expresses well the logical relationship between living the Christian life and ministry to the needs of the poor when he notes, "First comes the commitment to charity service. Theology comes 'later'—it is second. The Church's pastoral action is not arrived at as a conclusion from theological premises. Theology does not lead to pastoral activity, but is rather a reflection of it" (Gutierrez 1970:244–245; see also Segundo 1976:75–81).

This methodological position—one that advances a commitment to liberation as the necessary first step in determining a theological agenda—provides liberation theology with the foundation from which to advance a program of development. The Gospel is interpreted as speaking unequivocally to the normativeness of the struggle for liberation (Miranda 1974; Cassidy 1978). Liberation theology attempts to delineate the intimate relationship that exists between the Christian evangelical imperative— sharing the "Good News"—and the requirement to do justice. As Camilo Torres notes:

> I discovered Christianity as a life centered totally on love of neighbor.... It was later that I understood that in Colombia, you can't bring about this love simply by beneficence. There was needed, a whole change of political, economic, and social structures. These changes demanded a revolution. That love was intimately bound up with revolution. (Berryman 1973:357)

For the liberation theologian, the imperative to "do justice" shapes the doctrinal understanding of the evangelical imperative. *Orthopraxis* (commitment to and engagement in a process of action that will advance liberation) is logically prior to and takes precedence over *orthodoxy* (right belief). For liberation theology, it is the former that is the criterion for measuring the correctness of usefulness of any theological formula, rather than, as in the traditional Catholic church, the reverse (Kirk 1979:144).

From this understanding of the fundamental demand of the Christian message, liberation theology advances several important claims concerning the nature and task of theology. In opposition to the traditional Roman Catholic and Protestant formulations of the scope and task of theology (which is understood as a tool that assists the church, through the provision of wisdom in the exercise of rational knowledge, to reflect on correct doctrine), liberation theology suggests that authentic theological reflection is that which engages in the political interpretation of the Gospel (McCann 1981:157). The Gospel message of salvation in Christ is political in nature and is only fully embodied when it informs the way in which humanity develops its communities. As Hellwig notes, this thesis of the political nature of the Christian message "is a protest against a common assumption in Christian theology: That the history of the world, with its political structures and economic and social dispositions, is irrelevant to the Redemption" (Hellwig 1977:141). Liberation theologians devote considerable effort to justifying an interpretation of the Christian message that advocates worldly political involvement (Gutierrez 1973:220–232). They have supported this position by suggesting that the two important theological doctrines of creation and redemption are intimately and dialectically related. Traditional Catholic theology has emphasized the importance of establishing a doctrine of salvation, predicated on the death and resurrection of Jesus Christ, that then serves as the litmus test for an authentic profession of faith for those that wish to join the community of believers (the Church). The created order (the world and its structures) is not itself the object of redemption, but rather serves simply as the reality in which the Church creates and defines itself. Liberation theology formulates instead a doctrine of "salvation history" that extends the saving work of Christ to all humanity (both Christian and non–Christian), to all social structures, and to all of God's creation. All of history is under God's providential guidance, and redemption is universal. "For the liberation theologian, the only valid use of the term 'salvation history' is that which equates it, not with the history of salvation, seen as the subverting by the power of the gospel of all those structures which are obstacles to the full human and spiritual development of the human community" (Hellwig 1977:141).

While there are a number of logical and theological problems with this formulation (Wolterstorff 1983:47–53), it has the advantage of shifting the traditional emphasis of Christianity from one of bringing bodies into the Church (as a means of assuring their salvation) to a formulation that visualizes an active partnership between God and humanity in social construction and political involvement. The result of this shift is that liberation theology ceases to draw the strong distinction between Church and World that is the hallmark of traditional Roman Catholic and Protestant thought. Collaboration between Christians and non–Christians on programs of political and social justice is not only possible but necessary to the redemption of creation. Christians and non–Christians possess common goals and strategies, though they may not share an ultimate justification for these formulations. The role of the Catholic priest and liberation theologian Ernesto Cardenal as minister of culture in the Sandinista government of Nicaragua is a trenchant expression of this prescription for Church-World interaction. Not only must Christian and non-Christian work together to solve the problems of the world, but the Church and her members must listen to the questions and suggestions of the World concerning the nature and scope of their efforts (Segundo 1973:72–74, 83).

Marxist Critical Theory and Social Analysis

In addition to restructuring traditional theological doctrines in support of its position, liberation theology also appropriates a number of elements from traditional and revisionist Marxist thought (including the ideas of Marx himself and the synthesis of his philosophy in the works of members of the Frankfurt School). First, Marxism offers a framework for social analysis. Second, it provides a formal structure and gives coherence to the process of critical thinking that liberation theology employs. Third, it provides a range of substantive political, social, and economic goals that inform the development agenda acceptable to many liberation theologians. Critics of liberation theology (Costas 1974:255–258; Sacred Congregation for the Doctrine of the Faith 1984; Kirk 1979:143–203) have argued that these Marxist elements may be fundamentally incompatible with essential orthodox Christian doctrine. The analysis of this criticism would take us beyond the scope of this paper. For our purposes, it may be most instructive to indicate the Marxist ideas that are important to the process of reasoning and justification in liberation theology and that support the moral imperative for liberation and development.

A number of individuals (Robb 1978; Miguez-Bonino 1975:21–38) suggest that Marxism provides a range of relevant and effective tools for social analysis. They, and others, argue that Marxist social analysis is most successful at uncovering the nature and causes of social alienation, oppression, class differences, dependency, and poverty on the continent (Segundo 1973:100–102, 1976:9, 56–57). Employing Marxism's "scientific" analysis encourages constructive theological reflection on the lived reality of Latin America. Such a process should provide strategies for overcoming the intractable problems of the continent, and thus permit the Church to fulfill the demands of love and justice that are a requirement of the Gospel. Marxist social analysis, then, in conjunction with theological reflection on the lived situation, offers the most tangible, relevant, and beneficial way of overcoming the crisis of Latin American society.

Tools for successful social analysis are not the only resources provided by Marxism. There are a range of epistemological and methodological presuppositions central to Marxist thought that are appropriated by liberation theology. Liberation theology's understanding of the status, scope, and function of the Christian community, the nature of theology, ways of using Scripture to support specific moral postures, and its understanding of humanity's goals are all profoundly informed—and transformed—by Marxist categories. These ideas inform the phenomenological and praxiological method of theological reflection advanced by liberation theology and provide normative recommendations for how to effect liberation and development.

First, borrowing from Marxist value theory, liberation theology argues that all action must be partisan; what counts as moral and therefore required action by the authentic Christian will be a function of the lived reality and the needs of the group whose interests one wishes to advance. Descriptively speaking, there can be no such thing as value-neutral reflection or action. Morally speaking, one's task must be to determine which partisan position one will take (that is, who will be the object or beneficiary of one's action and what the goal or purpose of one's action will be). According to liberation theology, the Christian must be aligned with the oppressed, the marginalized, and the poor in opposition to the oppressors, the holders of power, and those that control the means of production in a society. The moral acceptability of a specific program of development is a function of whether or not such a program advances the liberation of the Latin American people.

It is not liberation theology's support of the poor and oppressed specifically that is Marxist. In this regard, the movement follows in a long and vigorous tradition of Christian biblical interpretation (both Catholic and Protestant) that locates in the Scriptures a justification for criticism against wealth and the exploitation and avoidance of the needs of the poor. Many nonliberationist biblical scholars recognize that numerous Old and New Testament passages clearly support the doctrine of a "preferential option for the poor" and "solidarity" with the victims of injustice. What I am suggesting, however, is that the moral absolutism and sufficiency of aligning oneself with the poor is a distinctively Marxist contribution to this theological formulation. For the liberation theologian, the only action that counts as moral action is that which is undertaken with respect to the poor. And as long as one engages in this sort of action, one is fulfilling fully the mandates of the Gospel. In fact, the Marxist doctrine of privileged access is at work in this formulation as well, for the liberation theologian claims that unless one is "doing the truth" on behalf of the poor and exploited, one cannot really know the true meaning of the Gospel, and one cannot claim to embody a truly Christian existence and lifestyle. Such a formulation has the effect of making absolute and exclusive the biblical mandates to a degree not normally seen in the Christian tradition. Such formulations diverge radically from traditional Catholic thinking on ethical and moral issues, which has claimed that (1) the natural law informs the structure of morality in the same for all persons regardless of their situation, circumstances, needs, or aspirations and (2) the moral imperatives of the Christian life call believers to a range of actions and aspirations, not all of them associated with beneficent and just actions toward the poor.

Liberation theology is informed by Marxism's materialism, which encourages a focus on this-worldly rather than other-worldly concerns. While liberation theology clearly possesses an appreciation for the transcendent and spiritual, particularly in its doctrines of the person and work of Jesus Christ and the Kingdom of God (Sobrino 1978), its Marxist voice has urged liberation theologians to focus their attention on issues of physical and concrete well-being.

Third, liberation theology replaces the traditional Christian understanding of history as a progression from the promise of salvation to its fulfillment in the incarnation of Christ with a Marxist understanding of the dialectical and conflictual nature of history. Liberation theology suggests that while we can talk of progress, such progress will only be attained through a process of class struggle. In fact, liberation theology's commitment to a theology that is partisan or partial to the poor and dispossessed grows out of this understanding of conflict in history and society. One is forced to take sides in all struggles. Not to do so is to support passively the agents that retard true liberation and humanization.

Fourth, Marxism's optimistic conception of human nature has infused liberation theology with a belief that wanting may be the most important element in getting. That is, while other social traditions in the Christian church (including St. Paul, St. Augustine, Luther, and most recently in the United States, Reinhold Neibuhr) have emphasized the facts of human sin and the way in which the contingencies of human existence can subvert ideals and goals (thus forcing compromises), the liberation theologians have avoided discussion of this issue. Rather, liberation theology appears to hold to the assumption that pure motives, intentions, and dispositions, linked with a commitment to liberation, are the important elements required for attaining the desired goal of liberation.

Fifth, liberation theology posits the importance of *cota catechesis* (teaching) and conscientization (consciousness raising and the development of a critical attitude toward all structures) as ways to encourage proxis and bring about liberation and transformation (de Lima Vaz 1968:578–581; McCann 1981:164–172; Segundo 1976:108–110, 179). This commitment to conscientization is a specifically Marxist contribution to methodology. In order to encourage this process, liberation theology has encouraged the organization of "base communities" (grass-roots and locally organized groups of peasants and workers) in which the mandates of the Gospel are to be enacted and critically reflected on. This shift away from Catholicism's traditional locating of theological reflection in intellectual communities and the magisterium (the teaching office of the Roman Catholic church) to the communities in which the poor, exploited, and alienated can assume responsibility for their own critical education (with the help, of course, of enlightened lay leaders or priests) is perhaps liberation theology's most important contribution to the development of an indigenous theology.

The importance of this shift in theological authority to the poor and exploited should not be underestimated. As McCann notes, conscientization provides the theology of liberation with a new model of education, both in form (critical reflection) and with respect to proximate goals (individual and communal liberation and extrication from exploitation and ignorance) (McCann 1981:167). It provides a revolutionary theory of how change occurs, who is to enact the change, and what the result of such change will be. As a means of empowering this process of conscientization, liberation theology borrows from Marx the notion of a "hermeneutic of systematic suspicion" as a means to education and transformation (Ricoeur 1970:32–36).

Rather than approaching education as a process that encourages the appropriation of specific facts, knowledge, and intellectual skills, it is the task of the liberation theologian to encourage critical thinking, questioning, "negative analysis," and the "deconstruction" of aggressive physical and psychological structures (Friere 1982:57–74). It is only through a process of deconstruction, of tearing down, of destroying the patterns and structures that enslave, that humanity can hope to assume responsibility for its own development and the construction of a just society. Indeed for the liberation theologian, as for the classical Marxist-Leninist, the cardinal human "sin" is not avarice, hate, injustice—but sloth, the unwillingness to engage in an active process that overcomes the boundaries that enslave humanity. The true education of the Christian revolutionary will not be ensured by appropriating doctrinal truths, but only through the appropriation of a subversive method of social criticism, conscientization, interpretation, and praxis.

Liberation Theology's Criticism of Developmentalism

The political, economic, and social development of the continent is not a peripheral concern to liberation theologians but the most tangible and concrete goal of action. Authentic theological reflection must empower a practical and political posture that focuses on issues of human liberation, development, and the establishment of sustainable and participatory social and political structures. Liberation theology claims that its theological orientation, tools of social analysis, and partisan commitment provide the movement with a coherent and compelling vantage point from which to evaluate and criticize past development efforts that have failed. In addition, it claims to be able to offer a range of creative, dynamic, and efficacious models of development.

I have already identified the constructive Christian and Marxist elements that provide the fundamental justification for this political theology. With respect to immediate and concrete development issues, three other factors are of importance in establishing the movement's strategy.

First, traditional Catholic theology, since its earliest times but more systematically in this century, has spoken of the important role that the Church must have in addressing the social and economic needs of the least fortunate. Indeed, the systematic development of social justice concerns in modern Catholic social teaching (beginning with the encyclical *Rerum Novarun* under Pope Leo XIII in 1891; Hollenback 1977) and the grounding of these concerns in biblical injunctions, theories of natural law, and the Enlightenment conception of natural rights provided a coherent warrant and constructive framework from which liberation theology could advance its critical task. One should not lose sight of the fact, then, that liberation theology is developing its interest in social justice on a foundation laid much earlier. But one can appreciate, through even cursory readings of these earlier social teachings, the distinctive position being advanced by liberation theology.

Second, liberation theologians (in concert with other scholars and social scientists) have been intent on describing the oppressive and paternalistic relationship that has existed historically between their continent and those European nations that were originally in control of colonial Latin America. Such a task has demanded a complete revision and rethinking of the process and content of the history of the continent.

Liberation theology's revisionist historical analysis has been an essential precursor to the third and most critical and constructive element in support of its vision of development. The *dependency theory* attempts to understand Latin America's present relationship to the industrialized West, and the relationship's effect on the continent's present and future chances for meaningful development and progress. It advances four claims: (1) that Latin America's present relationship with the industrialized West (particularly the United States) follows in the pattern of earlier colonial relationships; (2) that this relationship is paternalistic and oppressive; (3) that it is defined in terms of Latin America's intellectual and cultural dependence on the West; and (4) that it ultimately leads to Latin America's economic and cultural underdevelopment (McCann 1981:133–136; Todaro 1985:86–87).

First, the dependency theory explains the precarious and destructive relationship that holds between Latin America and the West in terms of the "developing" nations' dependence on already developed nations (Gutierrez 1973:81–88; Todaro 1985:85–88). While "development" appears at first blush to be a value-neutral term that is appropriated by certain philosophers of history to suggest ways in which societies evolve and advance (Gutierrez 1973:23), it is given a pejorative connotation by liberation theologians and denotes the result of an unequal relationship that masks the true nature and process of economic and political progress. Theotonio Dos Santos (1973:109) elaborates the significance of this theory to the issue of economic development when he notes:

> By dependence we mean a situation in which the economy of certain countries is conditioned by the development and expansion of another economy to which the former is subjected. The relation of interdependence between two or more economies, and between these and world trade, assumes the form of dependence when some countries (the dominant ones) can expand and can be self-sustaining, while other countries (the dependent ones) can do this only as a reflection of that expansion, which can have either a positive or a negative effect on their immediate development.

Such a theory of dependent development implies exploitation. It is a mistake to assume that the social and economic problems of the Third World, which sits on "the oppressed periphery of the great economic empires," can be overcome by gradual and incremental improvement, since underdevelopment is an outgrowth of earlier actions taken under the guise of beneficent development (Segundo 1979:245). A causal relationship, expressed in zero-sum terms, exists between rich and poor nations: "Underdeveloped countries exist because developed countries exist" (Segundo 1970:28). As a given sector of the global economy develops and expands, the degree of poverty, suffering, and oppression increases proportionately for others. The dependency theory provides a casual explanation of Latin America's most tangible problems: the lack of reasonable commodity prices for their natural resources; problems with debt restructuring and retirement; weak capital generation capabilities and a lack of necessary hard currency reserves for international trade; and the inappropriate application of technologies and education systems to the needs of the population.

The very structure of global capitalist economics makes it impossible for the Third World to accomplish a program of economic growth and development. There are two reasons for this. First, past exploitation has destroyed the possibility of Third World nations' overcoming their situation under their own impulse. The path traversed by earlier nations on the way to development has rendered the path unpassable by those who follow (Segundo 1970:25). But second, even if Third World nations could begin a successful process of development with the aid of developed nations, it would be impossible for the former ever to achieve their goals. As long as a capitalist economic system exists, the pretext of aid to developing nations must be understood as a self-serving and exploitive process, a witness to self-interest, not a statement about the importance of either justice or charity (Segundo 1970:27, 1969:213). Development aid thus leads inevitably toward "increasing dependence, culture mimetism, and permanent underdevelopment" (Berryman 1973:360).

In opposition to the liberation theologians and other advocates of the dependency theory, the supporters of "developmentalism" (including representatives of the International Monetary Fund, the U.S. State Department, and a range of free-market economic theorists) claim that Latin America will be able to escape its underdeveloped status when it establishes a free-market and consumption-driven mechanism for economic development. For the developmentalists, two presuppositions hold. First, the development miracle of the United States and postwar Europe and Japan can be replicated in Latin America. Second, Latin America's best hope of economic, political, and social success is to follow the policies advocated by the industrialized nations. Of crucial importance to this argument is the claim that participatory political structures are a function of and logically follow the policies advocated by the industrialized nations. Of crucial importance to this argument is the claim that participatory political structures are a function of, and logically follow from, free-market economic development. Third, such economic and political development in Latin America will be, to a large degree, the result of the economic growth of the industrialized nations. The present structure of international trade in raw materials, labor, and finished products unequivocally links the economic fortunes of Latin America to those of the industrialized West. In addition, infusions of capital from the industrialized nations (in the form of both loans and grants) will stimulate a wave of self-perpetuating economic growth that will establish sustainable and productive economies, the just distribution of goods and services, and the ultimate triumph of democracy. Such claims have, since the first development programs to

Latin America in the 1950s and later under the Kennedy administration's Alliance for Progress in the 1960s, served as the justification for all aid development to Latin America (McCann 1981:136–137; Gutierrez 1973:82–85). Expressing the view of the developmentalists, McCann notes that "thanks to the Enlightenment perception of self-interest [by the] developed nations, whose prosperity depends on further economic growth, the underdeveloped nations receive the benefits of foreign aid and investment, strategically placed in order to promote development" (McCann 1981:146).

Liberation Theology's Advocacy of Liberation from Dependence

According to liberation theology, several steps must be taken in order to ensure viable economic and social development in Latin America. A theory of "development through liberation" free from the determinism of dependence must be advanced as a first response to the economic ideology and policies forced on Latin America by outsiders. It must go beyond a simple rejection of the present relationship and provide the mechanism for uncoupling Latin America's economic future from that of the industrialized West. This requires a theory of economic and social development that is coherent, plausible, and efficacious, and that advances in a constructive manner antidevelopmentalist positions.

While liberation theology rejects a developmentalist economic system and the correlative determinism of the dependency theory, the movement is not rejecting economic development. There is an attempt, rather, to provide a new framework for understanding the process and goal of development, a redefinition of the agents who are responsible for this development, and the way in which economic and social development are seen to relate.

First, liberation theology suggests that Latin America's development must be uncoupled from the development of the industrialized nations. This imperative, however, contains two provisos. First, liberation theology is not suggesting that aid from the West would be refused if offered. Indeed, some liberation theologians have suggested that the West might provide them a "gift of development" that would be understood in terms of charity or imperfect obligations (Segundo 1970:29, 1968:32). A second proviso introduced by some thinkers suggests that because the West's path to industrialization and development has rendered impossible such an option for other nations, it owes, as compensation, the goods necessry for "ultimate" development (Segundo 1970:25). Occasionally, liberation theologians claim that there exists, on the part of the industrialized nations, a perfect moral obligation to provide economic aid to the Third World. A correlative moral right to such aid, grounded in a principle of justice, is thus held by all developing nations. This "right to development" also engenders in developed nations a positive obligation actively to promote political and social progress on the continent by supporting democratic reform and recognizing the political sovereignty of existing governments.

Most consistently, however, the arguments advanced by liberation theology appear to be grounded on the principle of negative autonomy and the right to noninterference (though none of these positions are ever framed in terms of autonomous moral principles by the thinkers themselves). Fundamentally, liberation theology is claiming that Latin America has a right to be left alone to engage in the development of its own political and economic order (Christians for Socialism 1973:391).

Liberation theologians advocate the primacy of socialist over capitalist modes of economic development (Christians for Socialism 1973; Segundo 1979:249, 1968b:577). In part, the position is a result of their disdain for the industrialized and capitalistic West, which they feel is responsible for their problems. But additionally, there is a general belief, shared by all liberation theologians, that the best chance of achieving a just, sustainable, and participatory society will be realized in an environment which is "radically leftist," since only this political orientation permits a nation and people to be "permanently open to its future . . . this sensitivity to the left is an intrinsic element of any authentic theology" (Segundo 1979:257, 1968a:32). Such leftism will empower a socialist economy where the means of production is controlled not by corporate or market forces but by the people who are simultaneously able to integrate economic development with socialist political programs (Segundo 1979:249, 1968b:577). Capitalism and socialism are seen as the only two economic alternatives available to the world today (intermediary options are seen as impossible) (Fierro 1977:68), and socialism is the only economic option compatible with Christianity.

A Critique of Liberation Theology's Reflections on Issues of Third World Development, Suggestions for Further Research

I begin my comments with an observation. For all of its theological reflection, for all of the conferences that have been held in both the United States and abroad to discuss the direction of the theology of liberation, for all the talk of the importance of concrete and efficacious action, the practitioners and supporters of this movement have provided little guidance in ways of effecting concrete economic and political change. Liberation theology's greatest problem with respect to the issue of economic and social development is that it possesses a theology but no ethics, a vision but no norms for action, the foundation for a commitment to praxis but little idea of precisely what that praxis will require. These charges are not new (Sturm 1982:748–749), but the problems of oversimplification and inconsistency in theological doctrines take on profound importance when they fail to provide or even permit the construction of a normative ethic and hence a concrete framework for practical thinking. The language of praxis provides an attitude, aspiration, and goal, but liberation theology offers no adequate framework for putting into place the policies that it envisions. Indeed, the claim is made by some theologians of liberation that ethics and praxis are incommensurable, that to engage in the development or definition of a content-based ethic that would go beyond a general and absolute commitment to liberation through orthopraxis is to undercut the dynamic character of the vision being advanced. This lack of concrete specificity is ironic, since it was with respect to providing an understanding of an efficacious praxis that liberation theology made its most powerful claims.

This observation raises an interesting question. Is a distinctive liberation ethic or praxis possible? While not every doctrinal formulation in the theology is novel, I believe that the general theological vision and method of the movement are distinctive. Liberation theology provides a distinctive orientation, attitude, and disposition toward lived reality. However, distinctiveness at the level of theology and faith does not imply distinctiveness at the level of praxis, norms, and action. And if liberation theology fails to offer any distinctive contribution at the practical level, can it claim to offer anything tangible in the area of political and economic development?

My answer to this last question is both no and yes. I do not believe that given its present leftist orientation and its affirmation of economic and social plans that are borrowed from other sources (sources outside the movement), the theology shows any sign of either desiring or being able to offer a distinctive concrete ethic or position. However, as numerous thinkers on both sides of this debate have shown, theological justification for a position is itself an important contribution to bringing about change since it provides a warrant, an attitude, an orientation that many people require in order to justify their involvement in a movement. Thus, liberation theology, in providing believers with the reasons they require for empowerment to action, may be supporting a most effective tool that will indirectly advance revolutionary change on the continent. There is strong empirical evidence that this theological vision was instrumental in empowering the Sandinista revolution in Nicaragua and the forced moderate settlement in El Salvador.

While practical, normative, and policy contributions may not be areas where liberation theology will make distinctive and lasting contributions (though of course, individuals working in other capacities may provide major insights and constructive innovations), it would be in the best interests of the movement to "fine-tune" its position on ethics and praxis to provide followers with a clearer vision and more compelling arguments for engaging in such a process. Here, I introduce a range of areas for improvement, which also suggest some areas of further work and research.

First, liberation theology must specify the process and content of the development program it advocates. The theories of dependency and development linked to that of the industrialized nations provide important insights into what liberation theology is opposed to. But the movement has yet to provide a clear picture of what exactly it advocates in this vision of "autonomous development" and authentic praxis. Is development a process of economic growth, expansion, and improvement that is characterized by certain activities and efforts? Or is it a goal or result that is characterized by the attainment of specific objective criteria, such as predetermined infant mortality rates, per capita income, balance of trade, or level of employment? If authentic economic development is characterized at least in part by a lack of dependence on the industrialized West, the precise characteristics of this state must be specified as well. How does authentic development incorporate the necessity in the present global economy to engage in trade with industrialized nations? Is authentic development a function of total economic autonomy and self-sufficiency? In addition, what degree of dependence on loans and grants from the industrialized nations is legitimate, and what degree of interference in decisions about how to allocate that money will be tolerated? What role will banks and private investors play in the financing of development projects (both grass-roots and industrial) in developing nations? Such questions must be addressed now, for as the governments of Central and South America continue to move toward democratic social structures, well-formulated positions on these issues will be essential to the success of preferred political candidates. Clear positions will be essential to prevent the tragic flow of capital out of the country by those who fear economic depression and political anarchy (witness the crisis encountered by recent governments in Nicaragua, Mexico, and El Salvador). In short, what I am suggesting is that liberation theology needs to start doing its economic homework, to develop a stronger command of economics. Such formulations need not, perhaps cannot, be novel or distinctive. But in order to argue their position effectively, liberation theologians will have to school themselves in the fine points of economic options available to developing nations either to complement or undercut their theological vision. Presently, there is not a single recognized liberation theologian who possesses even a rudimentary knowledge of micro or global economics.

Second, liberation theologians and others who interpret events with the help of dependency theory must develop a coherent theory of economic causation for underdevelopment. On the one hand, as an outgrowth of the theory of dependency and developmentalism, arguments are advanced that Third World economic disenfranchisement is a result of exploitation by all individuals and governments in the industrialized West (interestingly, Soviet economic or political involvement in the affairs of other nations is never examined). This formulation fails to account adequately for the causative influences of situation-based harm. Liberation theologians consistently blame all individuals in the industrialized world, and their surrogates in Latin America, for oppressive acts and economic systems (Segundo 1970:30) when it is not clear that the defined casualty or capability holds between either (1) the actions of individuals and those of their governments or (2) the effects of all actions in the Third World and the policy decisions made by Western governments. Its interpretation of dependency and oppression may be too mechanistic, and at the very least contradicts our lived experience concerning the way we normally assign responsibility and capability.

Third, liberation theology needs to clarify how the language of "rights" is to be employed in discussions of political economy. What exactly is the nature of the "right to development"? Does it find its source in a conception of individual or communal justice or autonomy? Is it a right to a certain level of liberation, well-being, goods and services, and freedom, or a right to a specific process? Is there a right to a specific economy (socialism), and if so, does this imply a right to a specific policy?

I raise these questions with respect to the language of rights as a way of highlighting what I take to be a more serious and systemic problem with liberation theology's ethic (or lack of it). While the movement has done an impressive job of synthesizing theology and the social sciences into a revisionist theological method, and while it has a rough idea of the goals toward which it wishes to aim, its position lacks any concrete ethical norms or principles that bridge the gap between theory and practice. In this regard, middle axioms or concrete principles are necessary, for three reasons. First, they permit public validation of the continuity of theory to practice. With the help of concrete moral principles (such as respect for persons, autonomy, beneficence, utility, and justice as fairness) liberation theology could provide its critics—and supporters—with greater clarity concerning how it is able to move from a theological vision to a specific political or economic position. Second, such norms or principles would serve as important links in developing a theory of reasoning that would be essential to the continued growth and vitality of a practical theology. In justifying specific choices concerning economic, social, and political development, the liberation theologians will inevitably seek to justify their prescriptions with respect to their fundamental theological and moral positions. A body of norms would do much to assist in sorting out relative priorities to a range of commitments (peace, order, justice, well-being, an end to suffering, respect for individual aspirations for self-determination and community solidarity) that are presently conflated under unhelpful labels such as liberation, humanization, christification, development. It would also force the liberation theologians to recognize that the imperatives implicit in binding moral principles can often conflict with each other, engendering a tragic situation in which responsible persons must engage in hardheaded reasoning and choosing to resolve their dilemmas. Finally, the establishment of a well-defined set of norms would provide liberation theology with a publicly proclaimed normative position that could provide a lasting foundation for collaboration with nonliberation theologians, both Christian and non–Christian. Presently, there is a tendency among some segments of the movement to avoid dialogue with those who fail to advocate socialist revolution. My suggestion is that the establishment of a set of clear though somewhat general norms could do much to open dialogue between liberation theology and other Christian groups. For instance, while evangelical Protestants in both North and South America fail to support certain theoloical formulations and specific means to liberation advocated by the liberation theologians (e.g., the use of unrestrained force or the establishment of centralized socialist economies), they do support the demand for change and for more practical solutions to intractable economic problems. Emphasis on shared moral norms as the starting point for dialogue and discussion would permit the relegation of areas of disagreement (in theology and in economic models), at least for a time, to a position of secondary importance. The same principle would work with respect to dialogue and collaboration with non–Christians in both Latin America and the West. Presently, only socialists and Marxists appear to be aligned with liberation theology, and then only on specific issues and strategies (in much the same way that feminists and the Moral Majority in the United States are in agreement over their disdain for pornography). By establishing a body of moral norms that are logically distinct from religious norms (though perhaps informed by a religious perspective) and that do not absolutely require a single practical strategy for their implementation, liberation theology may find itself in a larger company of confederates and supporters.

Fourth, liberation theology must acquire at least a respect, and perhaps even a preference, for pragmatism and realism over economic and political ideology. It is not clear to me that liberation theology takes seriously enough the facts of human limitation of the tendency of human beings to subvert their aspirations and ideals. This is to say, in effect, that liberation theology has an inadequate doctrine of sin and little or no appreciation of the fact that reality may impose limits on what humanity is capable of. Liberation theology needs to incorporate into its theological, economic, and political visions an appreciation of the contingencies of human existence. Such an appreciation will, I suspect, render the commitment to specific economic ideologies and goals less stringent and perhaps force a reassessment of the necessity of procedural constraints and checks and balances in the process of praxis and the structuring of political communities. Such a move would, through the introduction of procedural law and the balancing of centers of competing power, render less plausible the possibilities of dictatorship of one kind or another. It may also inform economic choices, open versus closed models, centralized versus decentralized mechanisms, forms where a range of individuals and intermediate structures might hold at least some of the means of production. Ironically, it may be that with a greater respect for the doctrine of human nature—theological anthropology—liberation theology may be able to make the most tangible and lasting contribution to the process of development.

19

New Egypt: The Saving of American-born African Minds and Spirits

Mwatabu S. Okantah

> You hearers, seers, imaginers, thinkers, rememberers, you prophets called to communicate truths of the living way to a people fascinated unto death, you called to link memory with fore-listening, to join the uncountable seasons of our flowing to unknown tomorrows even more numerous, communicators doomed to pass on truths of our origins to a people rushing deathward, grown contemptuous in our ignorance of our source, prejudiced against our own survival, how shall your vocation's utterance be heard?
>
> —Ayi Kwei Armah

To be an American-born African poet crying out in the wilderness— how shall my vocation's utterance be heard? In America, American-born African people have forgotten how to listen, have forgotten, have been made over to forget who we are. Worse still, when we do choose to listen, rarely if ever is it to our poets, our seers, our rememberers. We have become a people grown insensitive to the sound of our own collective voice, to our own heartbeat singing. Yet the poets, the singers, continue to sing, even in this still-strange land, even in this pain-filled season of our discontent.

I

Two Thousand Seasons, Armah's remarkable novel, speaks directly to the world consciousness of all so-called Third World peoples. For Africans and peoples of African descent, this novel represents a journey deep inside the seemingly impenetrable rain forest of our racial memory. Armah forces us away from the utter chaos of this present into a search for causes inside our own ancient African past.

Armah, the artist, is the master storyteller-historian engaged in the ritual act of retelling the old story. The omniscient narrator introduces us to the multiple voices of the seeress Anoa:

> Turn from this generosity of fools. The giving that is split from receiving is no generosity but hatred of the giving self, a preparation for the self's destruction. Turn. Return to the way, the way of reciprocity. This headlong generosity too proud to think of returns, it will be your destruction. Turn. (Armah 1979:25)

Armah, the cultural worker, is the contemporary African writer recreating the African world present as prophecy voiced during our ancient of days. We are there. Prophet Anoa offers the warning vision:

> Two thousand seasons: a thousand you will spend descending into abysses that would stop your heart and break your mind merely to contemplate. The climb away from there will be just as heavy. For that alone can you be glad your doors have been so closed, your faculties are now so blunted. You will need them blunter still.... (Armah 1979:25)

The novel effectively reconnects the umbilical cord of our New World consciousness to the placenta of our own classical antiquity.

Armah, the artist–cultural worker, is a new image maker. The novel's impact is at once both visceral and visual. The narrative unfolding is almost too real, too cinematic. Anoa, the imaginer, with calm voice:

> One thousand seasons with the deepest of the destroyers' holes behind, beneath you calling.... Slavery—do you know what that is? Ah, you will know it. Two thousand seasons, a thousand going into it, a second thousand crawling maimed from it, will teach you everything about enslavement, the destruction of souls, the killing of bodies, the infusion of violence into every breath, every drop, every morsel of your sustaining air, your water, your food. Till you come again upon the way. (Armah 1979:26–27)

Until we come again upon the way. *Two Thousand Seasons* is a significant novel because in it, Armah frames the present condition of Africa and African peoples in a culturally specific context.

He moves us closer to answering this tormenting question: What kind of seeds did our ancient African ancestors sow so that we reaped our current state of oppression and universal underdevelopment? For this writer, Armah's work, including *The Beautiful Ones Are Not Yet Born* and *Fragments*, is important because it suggests that any understanding of, as well as the proper healing solutions to, our predicament is to be found in using our traditional African heritage as a basis for whatever it is we choose to be or to become.

Like Anoa before, Armah's voice is yet another African seer's voice crying out in today's wilderness. Some of us hear him, realizing we are now "crawling maimed" from under the yoke of white world subjugation. Given the scope of this discussion, Armah's novel is a vivid example of the kind of art that must be produced if meaningful development is to take place in the Third World. It will be the primary objective of this essay to participate in the process of redefining the role of traditional cultures and the attendant function of artists and cultural workers in developing societies.

As a practicing American-African poet-musician, my perspective on this issue has been shaped by the peculiarities of the North American experience. However, the common history of American-born African people is, fundamentally, a part of the general Third World predicament, and the American-African condition, vis-à-vis development, especially urban development, holds particular implications for any developing nation.

The chapter will therefore focus attention on three interrelated areas: (1) the impact the failure to develop a true Pan-African cultural worldview has had on the course of American-African development; (2) the creation-implementation of an indigenous cultural process that will properly nurture the course of American-African development; and (3) the role of artists and cultural workers in the aforementioned course of development as defined by the imperatives implicit in a true American-African philosophy of culture.

In America, the 1980s have proven, beyond question, that the dilemma of American-born African people is cultural in nature. In a time of severe group psychological crisis, the existence of a sustaining cultural field of reference holds the key to group recovery. Moreover, and in relation to the larger issue of Third World development, I propose to argue that Third World transformation cannot realistically proceed according to Eurocentric models of development that too often oppose indigenous cultural norms.

To a great degree, many of the problems being experienced in developing countries today—including a paralyzed American-African community in the United States—can be attributed to ill-conceived, Western-derived solutions to indigenous Third World conditions. Historical Western expansion into the so-called Third World *is* the problem. Any development scheme that does not seriously consider the central function of traditional Third World cultural imperatives will be doomed to failure.

The verdict is already self-evident here in the American-born African community, and if the novels of Armah, Achebe, Sembene, and Ngugi, to name only a few, are any indication, problem signs are already appearing throughout Africa—especially in the cities. Any program that acts to deny or subvert the traditional role of culture and/or the role of artists and cultural workers will impact negatively on the essential humanity and worldview of Third World people. Developing nations must begin to look inward to their own indigenous traditions to construct a foundation upon which to build any concept of a new society.

II

In *The Crisis of the Negro Intellectual* (1967) Harold Cruse has written a profound analysis of the historical American racial dilemma. Given the present state of crisis in the Third World, his observations have implications for all oppressed peoples of color far beyond the specifics of the American-African experience. The question of cultural self-definition is *the* crucial question in the development of all Third World peoples.

The current state of group psychological paralysis now gripping the American-born African community in the United States must be seen as a clear warning to development-minded Third World leadership. To the extent that Western-derived "high tech" images of popular "Afro-American" culture are presently having a negative impact in the Third World, it is important to note how the failure of American-African leadership to define an indigenous program of development for the black community is already contributing to the potential corruption of Third World development strategies. Put another way, Michael Jackson, Millie Jackson, Prince, and Tina Turner, not to mention *Ebony* and *Jet* magazines, are not necessarily the influence needed in today's developing world.

Cruse suggests to would-be black creative thinkers that they should (1) familiarize themselves with their own intellectual antecedents and with previous political and cultural movements; (2) analyze critically the basis for the pendulum swings between the two poles of integration and black nationalism, and try to synthesize them into a single and consistent analysis; (3) identify clearly the political, economic, and cultural requisites for black advancement in order to mold them into a single politics of progressive black culture; and (4) at all costs avoid slavish borrowings or uncritical importations of ideologies and strategies from other continents or cultures, from other times, or even from other ethnic groups in the United States. The Afro-American experience is unique, and the irrevocable imperative of cultural self-definition demands that it be treated as such (Cruse 1967). Third World would-be creative thinkers must come to realize his instructions are also applicable to them within the contexts of their respective cultural situations.

A walking tour through any of America's major urban centers—those areas where United States–born Africans and other Third World peoples predominate—will provide even the casual observer with ample evidence of the devastating legacy of the failure of mainstream African-American leadership to grasp its proper role and function. An understanding of the so-called Black American experience on this level is necessary among Third World people, generally, for at least two reasons: (1) Euro-American–derived images of popular Black American culture are being used to induce a false sense of security in the Third World vis-à-vis U.S. global intentions, and (2) communication between United States–born Africans and the Third World is distorted relative to the impact of Western cultural aggression in both communities.

Although I have not yet traveled to any African or Third World country, I am alarmed by the surreal spectacle of the growing number of Third World people who come to the United States and subsequently behave in a fashion that can best be described as "more American than the Americans." When I see Muslim Arabs handling pork and selling it to the African American community; when I encounter misnamed *jheri*-curled native Africans; when I encounter Hispanics who strive to disguise their accents; and when I am assaulted by American-African ignorance, a palpable ignorance distinguishable because of its brazen arrogance and self-hatred (Okantah 1987), I am forced to recognize the intimidating complexity of this issue of culture and cultural self-definition.

For our purposes, a slightly more detailed look into the question of the American-African leadership predicament is in order. Due to space limitations, a more comprehensive investigation will not be possible. I will, however, attempt to illustrate the more salient points that must clearly be understood if there is to be meaningful progress in Afro-America and if there is to be genuine development in Africa and elsewhere in the developing world. We have to explore below the surface of what we think we see when we consider the condition and nature of the African experience in America.

I agree with Cruse when he identifies the opposing positions of "integration" and "black nationalism" as the two major streams of African-American social thought. He writes,

> Historically, this "rejected strain" (nationalism) emerged simultaneously with its opposite—the racial integration strain—although the word "integration" was not then in the Negro vocabulary as a synonym for civil rights or freedom. The prototype leader of the latter strain was Frederick Douglass ... and there is almost a direct line of development from him to the NAACP and the modern civil rights movement. However, the rejected, or nationality strain that exists today can be traced back to certain Negro spokesmen who were Douglass' contemporaries but who are now barely remembered—Martin R. Delaney, Edward Blyden, Alexander Crummell, Henry M. Turner, and George Washington Williams. (Cruse 1967:4–5)

In Third World terms, this debate within the ranks of the American-

African intelligentsia can be likened to the necessary, and also historical, debate over the nature and degree of Western technological, as well as Western cultural influences, in culturally distinct non-Western societies. When the American-African version of this discourse emerged into the twentieth century, first during the 1920s New Negro Renaissance and then a second time during the 1950s–1960s civil rights–Black Liberation Movement and now for a third time during the post–civil rights 1980s, mainstream black leadership has repeatedly failed to comprehend the actual historical and cultural implications of the crucial issues being debated relative to a new vision for an American-African future.

As a result, the chaos and utter hopelessness that characterize the lives of countless United States–born Africans must be seen as the residual consequence of the watershed periods in American-African development that have transpired amid virtual torrents of creative activity, while at the same time, frontline participants either ignored, overlooked, obscured, subverted, or denied the very questions and issues their movements attempted to confront. In other words, as a group, American Africans must begin to see our present condition as a product of our own historical lack of cultural insight.

Writing about the seminal Harlem period, for example, Cruse observes,

> It goes without saying that the Negro intellectuals of the Harlem Renaissance could not see the implications of cultural revolution as a *political demand* growing out of the advent of mass communication media. Having no cultural philosophy of their own, they remained under the tutelage of irrelevant white radical ideas. Thus they failed to grasp the radical potential of their own movement. (Cruse 1967:69)

This frank criticism allows us to move closer to the core of our present crisis. We must, however, place Cruse's searing pronouncements in perspective.

The failure of the New Negro artists and cultural workers must be weighed, in the final analysis, against the enormity of their task and the legacy of their overall contribution, that they nurtured a movement aimed at gaining authority over the portrayal of African-American images (Kent 1972). We can turn to Sterling Brown's *Negro Poetry and Drama* (1972) for a fair appraisal of their contribution.

Brown points out that the New Negro movement operated according to five major concerns: (1) a discovery of Africa as a source for race pride, (2) a use of Negro heroes and heroic episodes from American history, (3) propaganda of protest, (4) a treatment of the Negro masses (frequently of the folk, less often of the workers) with more understanding and less apology, and (5) franker and deeper self-revelation. The irony here, again, is the fact that the correctness of their five pillar concerns is offset by our present condition of unrealized potential, a legacy set in motion by the New Negro intelligentsia's failure to understand the practical implications of their own collective artistic vision.

In 1987, the future is now. The bare essence of Cruse's analysis is intended to clearly focus our attention on the function of culture in any program of black development:

> Harlem is a victim of cynical and premeditated cultural devegetation. Harlem is an impoverished and superexploited economic dependency, tied to a real estate, banking, business-commerical combine of absentee whites who suck the community dry every payday. In short, Harlem exists for the benefit of others and has no cultural, political or economic autonomy. Hence, no social movement of a protest nature in Harlem can be successful or have any positive meaning unless it is at one and the same time a *political, economic and cultural* movement.... The unique problem facing a combined Harlem social movement is that if the cultural aspects and implications of Harlem are left out of the equation, the movement collapses. Hence, a political protest that is not economic and cultural as well, cannot get off the ground. (Cruse 1967:86)

What is true of Harlem, as a black community, is fundamentally true in all of America's urban centers. At best, one might hope to find variations on a group theme.

Cruse's analysis was published in 1967. Developments over the past twenty years, undeniably, have borne out the essential accuracy of his basic thesis. For Third World purposes, the implications are universal. The degree to which American-Africans, as a group, have not yet come to terms with the dynamics between culture and culture movements and the general issue of national development *is* a weakness that *must* be avoided in the Third World.

For black people in the United States, Cruse's observations provide us with a powerful beam of light to assist us as we move through the dark tunnel of our own ignorance. We have become victims of our own misguided intentions.

> Harlem, once the artistic and cultural mecca of the Negro world, has been almost completely deracinated culturally; this deracination happens to coincide with the Northern Negroes' highest gains in integration. Integration is thus leading to cultural negation. (Cruse 1967:85)

Herein lies the fundamental lesson American-African people *must* learn.

The New Negro Movement, then, must not be viewed solely on the basis of its obvious shortcomings. Rather, we must see it as a beginning.

No renaissance runs its course in a mere decade. Although a cogent cultural critique was not developed, the movement produced creative thinkers who were sowers of black cultural seeds, who were tillers of a fertile cultural soil. In the work of Langston Hughes, Zora Neale Hurston, Sterling Brown, Jesse Fauset, Aaron Douglass, Duke Ellington, and Bessie Smith, to name only a few, the hard work of defining the role and function of the American-African artist and cultural worker was begun.

In spite of the movement's inherent contradictions, the groundwork was laid for what is potentially a genuine renaissance in American-African culture. The New Negro intellectuals prepared the cultural landscape for artistic fruit that would be harvested by later generations. There would be no Toni Morrison, Larry Neal, Toni Cade Bambara, or Earnest Gaines without them. The New Negro artists were forerunners. To their credit, they broke a productive cultural soil, while at the same time they became distracted away from tending that same artistic garden because they were more concerned with, and actively courted, Euro-American acceptance and validation according to the dominant culture's criteria for success.

III

> The value system for whatever we will be must, if it is to be operational, spring from readily available sources. What we need to do, however, with African and other Third World references is to shape them into a cosmological and philosophical framework. We need to shape, on the basis of our own historical imperatives, a life-centered concept of human existence that goes beyond the Western worldview.
>
> —Larry Neal

New Egypt: to recreate ourselves into a psychologically and spiritually whole people. In the Third World in general and in the American-African community in particular, we are in need of solutions, in need of total recovery. Toward this end, Cruse's analysis is important because, today more than ever, we are in need of cultural revolution. Our survival into the twenty-first century is dependent upon the development of an indigenous, Afrocentric cultural process.

In both structural and substantive terms, we cannot offer a new vision to the American-born African community, or to the larger Third World, based simply on borrowing or appropriating from what is undoubtedly a spiritually bankrupt and morally decrepit Western society. For American-Africans, to the degree we do not recognize and separate ourselves from America's decadence, we are in no position to offer the black community anything of real and lasting value. To date, our mainstream leadership has been so committed to so-called liberal-based Eurocentric solutions for our condition, they have blinded themselves to the radioactive nature of the Euro-American lifestyle.

We cannot merely blacken essentially Western white supremacist behavioral pathologies and expect our people to respond in a positive manner. The call for group cultural self-definition, as such, moves us closer to an organic reordering of our development priorities. In the 1980s, we were collectively in need of a healing something, something integrating into white society cannot ever give. We have to recreate ourselves into something other than so-called Negroes or Black Americans. To accept the term *Negro* or the placing of *black* as a prefix before *American* is effectively, albeit unwittingly, to negate our actual history as an African-derived people living in the New World.

More significantly—and here I must add that our acceptance of the term *Third World* is also symptomatic of this—it is a tacit acceptance of our oppressor's definition of not only our reality as a people but of reality, period. We must constantly remind ourselves that we are First World peoples. We are decendents of the ancients of Africa, India, China, etc.— those ancients who used compasses and globes when Europeans believed the earth was flat. Indeed, we are descended from civilization builders. As First World peoples, therefore, *we* must realize that the very process of shaping reality is the primary function of group cultural self-definition.

If group recovery is to be successfully achieved, development must be cast in culturally specific terms. For so-called Black Americans, this means the idea of black programs must be placed in a clearly defined Pan-African context. This is to say the African continent as ancestral homeland, and African cultural heritage, and an organic sense of an inclusive African history are basic to an American-African cultural frame of reference. Culturally speaking, and, in commonsense terms, there is no other development approach able to accommodate the acknowledged uniqueness of the "Afro-American" experience.

It is possible, despite attitudes to the contrary, to develop the fundamentals of a truly American-African cultural critique. If we accept Cruse's premise that the "Afro-American" experience is unique, it follows that we must clearly recognize that this originality is rooted in our essential African-ness as a people. As American-Africans we must begin to internalize the realization and the awareness that the spirituals, work songs, field chants, storytelling tradition—body of folklore, blues, gospel, jazz, etc.—exist as the result of the evolution of African cultural imperatives in a Euro-American–dominated field of reference.

The scope of this essay will not permit a fully detailed discussion of the African origins of American-African culture. I do assert, however, that true American-African culture is the sum total of an historical process within which a traditional West African worldview-lifestyle was forced to adapt

itself to a Euro-American–dominated cultural field of reference. This asser-
tion must inform the center of any new cultural critique. The question of
origins is academic. To recognize that our group dilemma is essentially
cultural is to recognize the need to define and control the actual dynamic
of the American-African lifestyle.

There is such a thing as a definitive American-African lifestyle.
However, as a people, a major flaw in our collective character has been our
stubborn refusal to see our individual dark-skinned selves as a distinct people, a people who share a common language, a common heritage, and a
common history. In failing to accept the reality of our own group consciousness, we have failed to understand the pivotal role culture must play
if we are to be in control of the group's quality of life and destiny. Relative
to the first part of this discussion, the "rejected" black-nationalist strain,
vis-à-vis culture, must be taken more seriously. No longer can we tolerate
a leadership with limited perception and judgment.

The operative question, then, becomes: If an indigenous American-
African philosophy of culture is attainable, where do we begin? In his essay
The Africanization of Black Studies, Fela Sowande places us on the proper
course when he argues,

> I see the Africanization of Black Studies as requiring the restructuring
> of Black Studies—a total restructuring if need be—so that it rests on the
> traditional Thought-Patterns of Traditional Africa, which thereby
> become its reason for being, its life-essence, the actualization of these
> Thought-Patterns in the day to day lives of common folks being its
> specific objective, to achieve which nothing will be allowed to be an in-
> surmountable obstacle. (Sowande 1972:4)

The cultural implication should be obvious. A cultural process of
Africanization seems the logical course of action, given the issues Cruse
raises in his analysis. Again, a detailed discussion of traditional African
thought patterns will not be possible (see Bibliography for suggested
readings). Suffice it to say, however, the implementation of a genuine process of cultural Africanization will require certain fundamental changes in
our basic outlook as black people living in America.

Sowande (1972:6), in his wisdom, warns:

> This Africanization is not to be regarded as a political platform or a new
> ideology; it is not to be approached in the manner of the chef who adds a
> little more of this or that to the soup that is all but cooked on the stove; it is
> not to be confused with the adoption of African names or dress-styles,
> although these may have their place in it, but Africanization means the
> total adoption of the World-view of traditional Africa as the foundation on
> which to build. Such adoption will require substantial changes in our ways
> of thought and of action; it will require the jettisoning of many of our prej-
> udices and fond beliefs, and it is here that the real problems will arise.

It is on this level, also, that cultural workers and creative artists can no longer be brushed aside as frivolous, weird, or products of the latest fad.

In practical terms, the use of symbols, images, drama, languages, music, and creative thought must be taken more seriously by mainstream American-African leadership. It necessarily follows that if the position of culture is raised in the equation of black progress, the status and role of artists and cultural workers must also be elevated. We cannot offer a new vision to our people if we ourselves do not see one and if we ourselves are insensitive to our artists, who traditionally have been charged as the guardians of the group's psycho-spiritual horizons. Any course of development that focuses only on material progress will lead, invariably, to the kind of psychological and spiritual chaos that now racks the American-African community.

A process of cultural Africanization, then, is grounded in the primary assumption that, properly defined, culture is the antithesis of civilization. It is a way of life in which the spiritual-ethical forces of progress are just as much at work as the material forces of progress over which they have priority. A program of total Africanization for our people is by no means an easy undertaking. We will not impose this process. Instead, our present crisis demands a process, a means to healing and recovery. It is on this level that the artist–cultural worker role and function must be reconsidered.

It is the function of the artist–cultural worker to create the forms and means to express and maintain the vital spiritual forces of progress. They are the guardians of a people's *language* of symbols, images, music, etc. The artists are the keepers of the group lore. In American-African terms, the artists and cultural workers are the keepers of our collective racial mind, our collective racial language. The racial mind operates as a unit, and language is the expression of this racial mind. A language is not an invention, but an evolution, the infallible counterpart of the evolving psychology of the race.

In terms of cultural Africanization, we must develop day-to-day processes designed to promote black behavioral change. Day-to-day processes imply culture and lifestyle. Put another way, this means we must supply the life-giving content and put ritual, ceremony, pageantry, rites-of-passage initiation, etc. back in the community life of our people. There can be no change in our lives as American-Africans if we do not create the proper environment for it. Pan-African festivals, Kwanzaa, African-American History Month, manhood training programs like Simba, ceremonial dances like The Grand March, community-based theater groups and dance companies, American-African High Holy Days—King is not the only hero or saint worthy of annual tribute; these are some of the cultural elements required to redirect our people toward a realizable self-determination.

The solutions to our problems are not as complex as some of us, particularly some of the "experts," have been led, and continually lead us, to believe. Even now, we are in a position to implement aspects of a program of cultural Africanization. Hard choices will have to be made, as Sowande (1972:25) notes:

> African culture is a foreign culture to the Black American, as it is to the Black African, who, as individual, is unable or unwilling to accept the fact of his African origin. Being an American or an African does not begin to matter. The determining factor is whether or not the individual, in his mind, accepts and lives by the conditions imposed on him by the fact of his African origins. If he does, then African culture becomes for him a warmblooded loving mother who, even when she disciplines him, does so out of concern for his spiritual and moral growth, and on the basis of a profound love. . . . But if the individual cannot or will not consciously and interiorly identify himself with his African origin, then that culture is as foreign to him as it is to those born and bred in Alaska.

In the final analysis, independent cultural institutions will have to be established in our communities if we are both to sustain and perpetuate ourselves as a people. A program of Africanization cannot be implemented without a completely autonomous cultural base. It must be an American–African–derived cultural base. The Euro-American lifestyle is psychologically and spiritually alien to both our present and our future needs as a people. We do not have to reinvent the proverbial wheel. To move forward, we must return to "the way" of our ancestors, who gave humanity its original human civilization. We have the resources and the requisite skill.

New Egypt. The new vision is alive in our poets, our seers, our rememberers, our thinkers, our imaginers, our prophets. The bottom line remains: We will get what we are willing to pay for. To the extent we continue naively to ask our oppressors to fund and administer to the destiny of our people, I can only signal the warning alarm to alert us against what must now be seen as criminally obscene leadership judgment. With clear vision, we can be the hope of our people. It remains to be seen if we, as an American-African people, will muster the courage and the collective will necessary to make of the poet's vision a new reality for all of our people.

Part IV
Economic Issues
of Development

20

Human Resource Utilization: Increasing Food Demand

William M. Alexander

In 1861, Colonel Baird Smith remarked that famines in India were "rather famines of work than of food; for when work can be had and paid for, food is always forthcoming." (Swaminathan 1982:331)

Demand, in the title of this chapter, is used in its proper economic meaning. A hungry human does not have a demand for food; a hungry human must have a legitimate claim on food, an entitlement, usually market exchange. The *human resource* mentioned is work, in this case paid work, a common basis for entitlements through market exchange. There are, of course, food entitlements among family members, and food may be produced and consumed entirely within such family groups. However, the demand referred to here is effective market demand, a demand involved in the market exchange of valuable commodities, work, and food. Accordingly, this essay offers a simple thesis: The human resource, work, may be utilized to allow an increase in the demand for food by the hungry throughout the world.

First World studies of Third World development, such as this one, necessarily presume that there will be intrusions from the First World into the Third World. The nature and the desirability of such interventions are subjects of these studies. The particular purpose of this chapter is to show how First World governments, businesses, and financial institutions may intervene to motivate Third World managers to broaden and extend work opportunities to all humans. A specific object (and a measure of success) of such interventions is the reduction, in absolute numbers, of the incidence of malnutrition and starvation. The alleviation of hunger leading to population stabilization is a public policy objective most consistent with images of what Americans want to have happen in the Third World.

American Attitudes

Public attitudes of Americans about the Third World are reactive and somewhat contradictory. First, the Third World is perceived as a threat to

252

American status quo privileges. This threat is commonly seen as competition for well-paid work opportunities in America—competition by the movement of manufacturing processes overseas and by the movement of Third World workers into American neighborhoods. At the same time, there are genuine humanitarian urges to alleviate the most abject of poverty conditions in the Third World—hunger and starvation.

Americans strongly believe that we ought to take care of our own problems here at home before being helpful overseas, and simultaneously Americans overwhelmingly agree that we ought to do what we can to alleviate poverty and hunger in the Third World (Contee 1987). In short, Americans believe we should care for our own first, and then we ought to help hungry Africans and others. After both the security needs and the welfare needs of Americans have been satisfied, the food needs of Africans and Asians should be considered. If feeding the hungry can be made to serve the welfare needs of American food-production businesses, then by all means, feed the hungry, that is, send food aid.

For the more sophisticated Third World watchers, two complications immediately arise. First, Third World hunger cannot be satiated by American food aid. American food-producing resources do not have the capacity to deliver to the Third World the amounts of food needed for distribution as welfare. Second, rapid population growth in the Third World increases the human numbers competing for the privileged opportunities of Americans controlling scarce resources. This population growth is a measurable cause of the perceived threat to American privileges, usually described as "American jobs."

Population Threat

In accord with Americans' views of their relationships to the Third World, public policies must be seen to mitigate the threat of Third World population growth. Although logical enough, it is politically difficult (and when premature, a wasted effort) to inject family-planning programs into the Third World. These political difficulties occur both in the Third World and in America. We may hope that Third World nations may have the political fortitude of China to limit their numbers effectively, and we hope that American political ambivalence about a proper role for government in birth-control efforts may settle on the side of limitation.

Fortunately, there is a better response to the Third World population threat. This response does require a thoughtful appreciation of population dynamics and its relationship to food provisioning. Food security is an essential condition for population stabilization. That is to say, the set of conditions necessary for food security are the same conditions necessary to encourage the choices limiting family size. Professor William Murdoch clearly demonstrates that poverty and high fertility rates have the same causes (Murdoch 1980). Similarly, others have shown that "the process of modernization that lies behind the present increased growth rate both of population and per capita income is also operating to bring about fertility reduction" (Easterlin and Crimmins 1985:191). In his time, Malthus had no evidence to show this human capacity to control fertility behavior. Barry Commoner titled his cogent and much-quoted insights "Poverty Breeds Overpopulation (and not the other way around)" (Commoner 1975).

Population History

In order to reinforce the essential but poorly understood relationship that hunger is a cause of high fertility, we need an appreciation of our own population history. Referring to Figure 20.1, we can locate ourselves about halfway up the population curve at 5 billion humans in 1990.

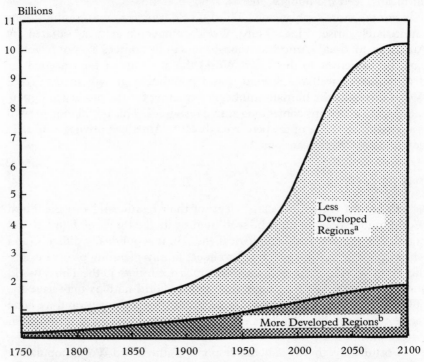

Figure 20.1: World populations: regional divisions. *Sources*: United Nations (1973), Vu (1985).

[a]Less developed regions=Africa, Asia (minus Japan), and Latin America.
[b]More developed regions=Europe, U.S.S.R., Japan, Oceania (including Australia and New Zealand, and North America).

Looking forward in time, we can see ourselves at a point halfway to a world population of 10.5 billion by the year 2100. In 1990, we are also at that point where the rate of increase has reached its maximum force and is beginning to decline.

Looking backward in time, we can think about our population history as a process in the elimination of hunger involving three steps. In the first step, we see those changes which occurred as we were transformed from peasants into commercial societies. Second, we apply our understanding of those changes to a future view of the less-developed regions of the world. Third, we explain the causes and cures of hunger applied in transitional societies, that is, societies changing from peasant to commercial social values and institutions. This thinking requires some large assumptions. Fundamental is the assumption that a transition from peasant society to a commercial society is a desirable change for all humans. Also necessary is the assumption that population events which have occurred in the histories of contemporary commercial societies are recurring in transitional societies.

North America, Europe, and Japan are current prototypes of commercial societies. These and other nations in a similar stage of development are often grouped together and called the more-developed regions of the world. Peasant societies predated current commercial societies and continue to exist today within some nations. Such nations and others not classified as more developed are categorized as less-developed regions.

Most inhabitants of the less-developed regions are currently in transition from peasant to commercial values and institutions. This change process within societies and nations is commonly referred to as development.

Europe and Africa

Figure 20.1 illustrates the phenomenon called the population explosion as now anticipated in the less-developed regions. In demographic terms, this explosion is caused by an enormous increase in life expectancy. The more-developed regions experienced a similar period of rapid growth, but relatively speaking an explosion was avoided. In order to show clearly the differences in the early growth patterns of Europe and Africa, Figure 20.2 was specially constructed.

The population of Africa was multiplied to give it the same starting point as Europe in 1750, and the populations are not added on top of each other as was done in Figure 20.1.

After 1850, Africa matched the growth rate started in Europe one hundred years earlier. Europe reached a maximum growth rate between 1950

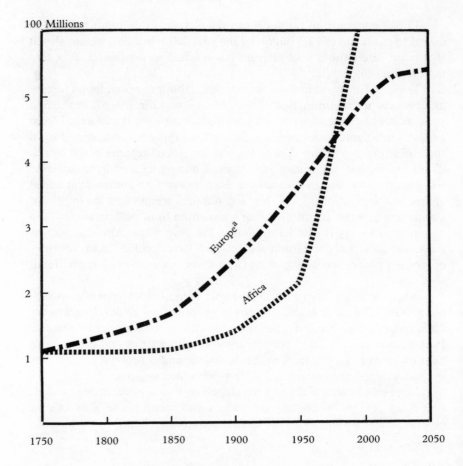

Figure 20.2: Population growth: Europe and Africa compared. *Sources*: United Nations (1973); Vu (1985).

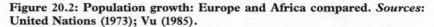

[a] The population figures for Europe have been reduced to 63 percent of actual in this time sequence to create comparable patterns and to start Europe and Africa at the same point in 1750.

and 2000. During the same period, African growth went up and right off the chart. During the history represented in this comparison, both Europe and Africa (one hundred years later) experienced an increase in life expectancy. Due to the time delay, it is reasonable to observe that European intrusions into Africa were a cause of both the initiation and the rapid acceleration of higher life expectancies in Africa. The impact of slavery is not factored into this assessment. Toward the end of this period, Europe experienced a fertility decline, but Africa did not. As shown in Figure 20.1,

African and other less-developed nations are also expected to experience fertility declines. That we are on the right track looking for explanations in the food production systems is evident in the difference in the proportions of agricultural producers on the two continents. Food and Agricultural Organization data show comparative figures of 64.3 percent agricultural producers in Africa as compared to 13.8 percent for Europe (United Nations 1983).

Food Connection

During most of the thousands of years since the last ice age, life expectancy was so low that high fertility rates were necessary for the survival of the human species. In recent times, humans have learned to increase their lifespans. Consulting the growth curves again, we see that such learning was first successful in regions now populated by commercial societies. As the availability and the quality of food increased the average lifespan, it was possible to sustain human numbers at lower fertility levels. However, the rate of fertility decline was slower than the life expectancy increase, and population grew rapidly (relative to the previous zero growth). It is now estimated that life expectancy will reach a maximum potential in commercial societies by about 2000 and birthrates will stabilize at replacement levels.

In early times, families and households hunted and gathered the food which they consumed. For millennia, these hunters and gatherers created a social and sedentary lifestyle characterized by land cultivation and village life. Such food producer–consumers eventually constituted a large portion of all humanity; we call them peasants. In commercial societies, we now find a small occupational group called farmers. Farmers produce food (and other products of the soil) which they sell to the multitude of consumers. The differences between the food-producing performance of peasants and farmers is revolutionary. The proportion of persons engaged in food-provisioning activities may exceed 90 percent in peasant societies. The proportion of farmers in commercial societies is often less than 5 percent.

Revolutionary Change

The revolutionary change transforming peasants into farmers is most fully explained in Ronald Seavoy's *Famine in Peasant Societies* (1986). Seavoy uses the concept of "subsistence compromise" to explain the low per capita food production in peasant societies. This compromise is a social balance among three values within subsistence cultures. These are not individual choices as assumed by the economic theory of commercial societies. The three social values governing food production in peasant societies are (1) equalized opportunities for all qualifying households to share cultivation rights on village land; (2) equalized sharing of harvests to ensure the subsistence food safety of all village households; (3) minimal labor expenditures in food production in normal crop years. Combined, these social values produce the subsistence compromise, the choice by peasants to grow food for their own consumption with the least expenditure of labor.

This peasant choice may be contrasted with the commercial rationality which governs behavior in developed economies. The social goal of commercial cultures is the production of the maximum amount of goods and services (including an assured surplus of food). Subsistence rationality, by placing a low social value on physical labor, seeks to minimize labor expenditure and to transfer labor to the weakest members of society. In order to emphasize this low-labor characteristic of peasant societies, Professor Seavoy uses the word *indolence*. Indolence has a high social value in peasant societies. In contrast, commercial rationality places high social value on physical labor, rewarding labor with a hierarchy of money incomes scaled according to skills demanded, skill levels, and hours worked.

Peasant motivation to produce food surpluses is limited by village equalizing customs, and at the same time peasants are motivated to have large families. In normal crop years, labor expenditures provide households with adequate nutrition. During poor crop years, harvest sharing allows each household to subsist with hunger on a minimum diet until the next harvest. After two consecutive poor crop years, there may be famine.

Peasant Famine

After each famine, peasant societies increased their populations beyond the normal crop-year carrying capacity of the land, repeating their minimum work and high fertility right up to the next famine, just as Malthus described. It was not lack of experience with periodic hunger and famine which allowed this behavior. Famine and famine conditions were well known within the memories of many persons in each village. Yet, after each famine, peasants did not create an assured surplus of food, and populations grew to equal or exceed previous levels.

The subsistence compromise explains why peasant societies have periodic famines regardless of population densities, soil fertility, and cultivation techniques. There is a revolutionary difference between the motivations in commercial societies for farmers, who produce food and other commodities for market sale, and peasants, who produce for subsistence consumption. Farmers maximize their own labor inputs to produce surpluses, and peasants minimize labor inputs.

Minimizing Work

Peasant societies minimize their labor in two ways. The first is the food-prodution method. For example, peasants emphasize grazing at the expense of cultivation and use shifting cultivation (slash and burn) in favor of continuous cultivation. In societies which have moved to continuous cultivation, communal control over land use distributes enough land to each qualifying household to grow subsistence quantities of food in normal crop years. A usual way of equalizing subsistence opportunities in land use is equally dividing a household's cultivation units among the sons or among all surviving households at the death of a household head. In non-rice-cultivating societies, the practice of allowing livestock to graze on the open fields after a certain date, whether or not the crops are fully harvested, forces all peasant households to plant and harvest at the same time, a method of averaging labor inputs and crop yields. Divided, scattered, and periodically redistributed cultivation units, combined with equalized labor expenditures, create a self-operating average limiting the amount of food any household will produce in a peasant village.

The second method of minimizing labor is to transfer agricultural work to low-status persons, particularly women and children. In most peasant societies, adult women perform disproportionately large amounts of agricultural labor. A high birthrate can mitigate some of the women's labor obligations. Where the good life is equated with minimal labor, having many children and transferring labor to them at the earliest possible age are expected peasant behavior. As long as customary law enforces the transfer of the fruits of child labor (for as long as the parents live and often regardless of the age of the children), a real benefit is conferred on parents. Parenthood is a universal means by which peasants avoid large amounts of agricultural labor.

Food Equalization

Feudal landlords, moneylenders, and storekeepers play a role in the peasant food-equalization processes. These landlords accumulate food surpluses in normal crop years by extracting as much grain from the peasantry as it will contribute without overt reaction. The distinction between an acceptable contribution and exploitation appears to be how much food remains in the hands of the peasants after levies have been collected rather than how much has been taken. Feudal lords will extract less in poor crop years by extracting as much grain from the peasantry as it will contribute without overt reaction. In the event of a famine, the landlords will distribute food from their granaries.

Storekeepers and moneylenders are usually strangers or outsiders in peasant villages. As outsiders, they are excluded from cultivation and are not usually subject to the fair-sharing obligations of the peasant community, thereby allowing them to become relatively rich. Nonetheless, they respect and help preserve subsistence social values. In poor crop years, the food they have accumulated for market sale becomes a food insurance distributed to households in the form of loans.

Neither the peasant, the storekeeper, nor the moneylender wants the loans paid off. Peasants allow a patron moneylender a claim on a part of a harvest; in poor crop years a hungry household will have a claim on its patron's grain store. The patron has an interest in allowing his client peasants enough food in poor crop years for subsistence and to replace seed grain that may have been eaten. Deaths of their clients would extinguish the storekeeper's or the moneylender's future opportunity to collect a share of the peasant's harvest.

In the event that food from a source external to the village (such as USAID) may be supplied to modern peasants, we should expect peasants to regard such assistance as similar to the aid due them from landlords, moneylenders, and storekeepers. That is, the aid will be used to maintain the subsistence compromise. Within the compromise the availability of outside food will allow an increase in peasant numbers without an increase in per capita food production. Such peasants may continue to enjoy their high social value, low work.

Commercial Revolution

Professor Seavoy's analysis of the subsistence compromise of peasant societies shows periodic famines to be both endemic and necessary; necessary because periodic famines limit human numbers to those maintained by the subsistence compromise. Looking at the long sweep of human history, suddenly, in the last few hundred years, a revolution occurred, a revolution in the social values defining the very existence of peasants. This revolution sent population numbers soaring and in time brought famine under control in commercial societies.

The commercial revolution was not an intellectual exercise from the peasants' point of view; it was a bitter struggle over control of the land and the peasants' right to their low-labor lifestyles. This revolution was initiated and led by early entrepreneurs—traders and bankers. The instruments of this social revolution were unfamiliar in peasant societies, inventions of the new commercial societies—markets, money, and laws enforced by governments. The revolution has involved much violence, peasant suppression, and peasant rebellion, peasants vainly trying to maintain their way of life against government forces acting on behalf of traders, bankers, and others.

Violent or not, these revolutions are always traumatic for peasants who are forced against their wishes to remake themselves into wage laborers and farmers. In the struggle, the peasants lose their important social value, low work, and they are forced to accept continuous work. The fruits of hard work, material comforts, replaced low work as the highest social value. A Nepali peasant educated in America, commented on his return home: "In Nepal, we work like princes and live like slaves while in America you live like princes and work like slaves."

Work Ethic

Seavoy's labor-avoiding explanation of peasant behavior, the subsistence compromise, may have been the longtime norm for human behavior. The labor-seeking behavior of farmers and others in commercial societies needs explaining. Today, it is not work but the lack of it which stigmatizes the individual and relegates him or her to the margins of "the good life." Sociological studies in commercial societies show that individuals who need work and are unable to find it experience high levels of alcoholism, drug abuse, divorce, and other forms of unhappiness. All this would have been incomprehensible to our peasant forebears. So why is the loss of work or the inability to find it so traumatic for those without work? What accounts for this strange addiction to work in commercial societies?

According to the renowned German sociologist Max Weber, the roots of this "work ethic" may be traced back to the Protestant Reformation some four hundred years ago. One of the prominent reformers, John Calvin, believed that our salvation or eternal damnation was predestined. However, people who succeeded in work and lived exemplary lives were the most likely candidates for salvation. It wasn't long before the predestination views of salvation were overtaken by a belief that one could actually earn one's way into heaven through diligent effort. What became firmly implanted was a general cultural belief that hard work of any kind was good and indolence, even leisure, was wicked. There were references to the "deserving poor," humans who were willing to work hard even under the most miserable and hopeless conditions. Those who sought hard work deserved a modicum of respect, maybe even a place in heaven.

Weber's work ethic was ideally suited to the system of industrial capitalism then emerging in Western Europe and North America, a system which required both a disciplined work force and entrepreneurs who would limit their consumption, saving to produce even greater wealth. The entrepreneurial formula for profit and savings was: increase the work of each worker, and reduce the number of jobs. The necessity of earning wages in the new commercial society uprooted peasants from their communal patterns and threw them into a dog-eat-dog competition for available paid work. Under these circumstances, the opportunity to work at any job became urgent.

In view of the fact that a similar exaltation of work has occurred in places unaffected by Christian teaching, it is possible that it was the competition of individuals for survival in commercial societies which fostered the high value of work rather than Weber's Protestant work ethic. On the other hand, a lack of religious emphasis on the virtue of hard work may account for the high resistance of some peasant societies to participate in the commercial revolution. In any case, a human without work in a developed region is a human without commercial social value.

Commercial Values

Within peasant societies there was an equalization of access to the land and an equalization of the opportunity to cultivate the land, both adjusted according to the food needs of each household. This was an equalization of power relationships among households within the village, a balancing and counterbalancing of power that may be analogous to the concept of pluralism in the modern study of politics.

The focus on the accumulation of material possessions as a high social value of the new commercial societies destroyed the equalizing relationships of peasant communities. It is worth noting that there was a lifetime limit on the indolence any peasant could enjoy, whereas there is no limit on the material possessions one individual can accumulate. In the beginning of the transition to commercial societies, the principal possession available for accumulation was land. With the development of central governments, concentration of land control became the important representation of power.

Land Reform

Conversely, equalization of land control is a method of sharing power, promoting pluralism in support of democracy. The American homestead law offering 160 acres of free land had this purpose and effect. In the Third World, Land to the People has been and continues to be a powerful slogan rallying the multitude of displaced peasants to the side of various political leaders seeking to establish and control governments.

Power symbolized in land guides much current thought among those sympathetic both to democratic principles and to the plight of displaced peasants. Power should be widely disbursed; therefore, distribute land ownership. This policy worked well in the vast American West. It also succeeded in Taiwan where sharecroppers were converted to owners at the end of World War II when their Japanese overlords left. These were both unusual cases where experienced cultivators could acquire land titles within a commercial context at little expense to governments.

Human Resources

Taking land out of the low-work communal control of peasants and putting land in the hands of commercially motivated farmers have been essential steps leading to enormous increases in food production. Nevertheless, the human resource, work, may be even more important. Theodore Schultz has noted "the decline of the economic importance of farm land and the rise in that of human capital. . . . While land per se is not a critical factor in being poor, the human agent is" (Schultz 1980:642–643).

The transition of peasants into farmers and laborers does end the periodic famines of peasant societies. The demise of peasant societies, however, does not end hunger. Hunger in commercial societies, individual hunger, remains. The cause of famine in peasant societies was identified as the subsistence compromise. In commercial societies, the cause of famine was the peasants' choice to avoid unnecessary labor, feeding themselves in normal crop years without producing an assured food surplus. The cause of hunger in commercial societies is an apparent opposite—the lack of opportunity to work. In peasant society, peasants minimize work accepting famine as a normal condition of their subsistence compromise. In commercial society, the worker may not be allowed to work.

The welfare model is easily dismissed as a temporary expedient; it does not empower the poor to control the most basic necessity of their own lives. Quite the contrary, welfare maintains the power of the powerful over the powerless. The ownership model may be criticized for its lack of relevance to an increasing number of humans in a world changing to a commercial society. Without access to new land, the poor no longer have this opportunity to feed themselves. These criticisms of the welfare and the ownership models direct our attention to the most viable method of acquiring food, the work model.

Work Model

Within the work model, the explanation of food-human relationships may be highlighted by an examination of five interconnected elements — resources, food, work, dignity, and management. Each deserves special attention. **Resources** encompass all natural and material things on earth, including many things humans have created — for example, houses, roads, factories, supplies, and accumulated credits. We are particularly interested in those **resources** owned and controlled by individuals, group enterprises, and nations.

Human **food**, treated as a unique element from the resource category in this analysis, includes all those materials ingested by humans which support growth and sustain the human body. All **food** in its multitude of varieties is included. Thinking of nutritiously valuable foods in their cheap and simple forms will help focus on the object of this explanation, understanding the human **food** which eliminates hunger.

Work has several meanings, with both good and bad connotations, depending on context. The definition necessary to the logic of modern markets for work, and the definition central to this essay, is the **work** economists call wage labor. As such, **work** is a commodity, another resource, but work has other special characteristics. **Work** is fixed in time quantity, nonrenewable, and impossible to save. Further, **work** is inseparable from human life.

This emphasis on the human significance of work is certainly not original. Saint Thomas Aquinas advised that work is a natural right and duty; work is the sole legitimate basis of society, the foundation of property and profit. Adam Smith told the readers of *Wealth of Nations* in the first sentence of his introduction that everything following is an analysis of labor: "The annual labor of every nation is the fund which originally supplies it with all the necessaries and conveniences of life which it annually consumes." Henry Kissinger tells us about current changes in the thinking of Chinese rulers and predicts that "the government will be confined to what the West would call fiscal policy: legislation, taxation and indirect controls. Markets will play an increasing role." According to Kissinger (1987:6), these changes are pragmatic.

> Experience everywhere, including the Soviet Union, has demonstrated that direct central planning cannot work, but only China has been prepared to face the full implications. In the absence of markets that balance, the planner will impose more or less arbitrary judgments. As a result, the goods that are wanted are not produced and the goods that are produced are not wanted.

There is, of course, one commodity which is always wanted — food.

This chapter argues that the commodity work must be treated differentially by market systems, distributing some paid work to all as a means to maintain full demand for food, eliminating hunger. Paid work is thus a necessary condition for ending hunger, but payment alone is not sufficient. The work must be seen as useful to the larger community. Make-work situations can be created that do distribute income, but the worker is made to look like a fool, doing work regarded by the community as useless. **Dignity** is a community affirmation of respect accorded those who observe group-serving norms. In commercial societies, valued and useful work is an essential norm. In the case of the poor, work is especially valued; it may be their only opportunity to gain community respect. Young children, untrained in group norms, may be unconcerned about **dignity**. For the very old, **dignity** is based on past work relationships serving family and community.

The paid work necessary to buy food is designed, organized, allocated, and motivated by leaders. In commercial societies, we call such persons and the necessary function they perform **management**. In relation to markets, a manager is a buyer of work. When groups act on the basis of democracy and pluralism, **management** responsibilities are shared by nearly everyone. However for some humans, half or more of their purposive activity is **management**. Even though management is a form of work, management is set apart for special consideration in this analysis. **Management** is the entry point into human food systems, an entry point for the First World into the Third World. Without doubt, it would be possible for managers everywhere to design and create sufficient work opportunities for all humans. It is equally clear that managers everywhere lack the necessary vision and motivation to carry out this critical step. Expanding that vision and providing that motivation are precisely the interventions which should occur.

Before describing means for encouraging managers in their necessary roles, let us summarize the essential relationships of the five elements of the work model for ending hunger. Humans combine their work with resources in a process to produce food and other commodities to exchange for food. Within commercial society, this work also provides that essential of humanity, human dignity. Management organizes the human resource, work, and all other resources into humanly useful productive processes. Work directly connects all five elements. Proper organization of work, allowing work opportunity for all, eliminates hunger and maintains human dignity.

Work Opportunity

As a matter of public policy, there are two ways of implementing work opportunity for all—more work and sharing work. Kathleen Newland has described a public vision utilizing surplus labor to enhance the natural environment and create productive resources. In rural areas of most poor countries, there are desperate needs for projects of reforestation, water conservation (including irrigation, drainage, and flood control), land reclamation, sanitation (linked to fertilizer and biogas production), and soil conservation. Labor-intensive projects in these areas have the effect of transforming surplus labor into valuable capital.

Some outstanding examples are found in rural China. Using very little but their own labor, workers built check dams to store irrigation water and to control floods, dug irrigation canals and drainage ditches, planted trees, leveled fields, constructed terraces, and erected dikes. Chronic unemployment has been eliminated, and the productivity of the land has been dramatically increased. The dry, degraded cropland would support only one crop a year, and farm laborers could work only 120 to 150 days. Today, such areas allow more than 300 days of productive work annually. Government finance of labor-intensive public works to create productive assets in the countryside represents a transfer of resources from the urban to the rural areas. Such transfer from the powerful to the powerless may require an extraordinary public vision, or perhaps a revolution as was the case in China. Resistance to such transfers will come not only from the urban elite but also from the urban working class, those with secure employment and relatively high wages.

Policies that can end the waste of human resources and the persistence of hunger caused by the lack of employment can be devised by governments that have a genuine commitment to economic justice. "Governments that lack this commitment may be prodded toward it by the real economic gains that progress toward equitable distribution does present in many cases." They may be bribed into it by aid agencies, and they may be frightened into it by the threat of political unrest of those unable to find work (Newland 1979:38–41).

An alternative to a gross increase in labor demand is the sharing of available work opportunity. In this case, market rules would limit the amount of work allocated to each job applicant, a fair share of work opportunity for each. In the context of human hunger, it is possible to show a minimum kind of "equality." Among humans, the amount and quality of food which is biologically necessary to maintain proper growth and good health throughout a long life posits an equality of food need. Accordingly, that amount of work needed to provide a fair exchange for the minimum amount and quality of food each human body requires is a fair share of work opportunity. In this equation, the price of the food must be high enough to cause producers to bring food to the market, and the price of work must be high enough to allow the workers to buy food. Not denied this minimum power, the power to survive, humans will act to secure for themselves other basic needs such as shelter, health, and education.

Management Incentives

There are differences of opinion concerning the extent and proper degree of government intervention and government rules affecting markets, differences based in part on political ideology. Without further analysis or speculation, however, it is fair to assert that government intervention and rule making in the markets of the Third World are extensive. For example, we can easily see taxation of imports and exports, prohibition and licensing of traders and brokers, banking and exchange rules. In respect to labor, the government may set minimum wages and allow or prohibit labor organization. A full list of actual and possible interventions may be endless.

The purpose of either policy, maximizing work or sharing work, would be to distribute work to all so that all can buy food. As such, both policies are related to a program for full employment, but neither has full employment as its specific object. A fair share of work is defined above in terms of human food need. Would it be possible for a Third World government to adjust, up or down, its interventions and rules in ways that will make the design, creation, and allocation of work opportunities the best management choice for each enterprise, public and private? Public and private policy decisions which cause managers to utilize the work of the hungry will increase the demand of the hungry for food.

Pluralistic Management

We have noted above how governments can encourage managers of public and private enterprises to design, create, and allocate work opportunity for all. Within the science of efficient management, there are trends consistent with the flexibility needed. In earlier times, property was symbolized by land, and land was not usually regarded as a market commodity, something that could be exchanged in markets. In modern times, new types of property have been invented, and the markets of the world now have the capacity to handle any and all property as commodities. In addition, a single property unit held by a join stock corporation may now have many owners.

This change in the character of ownership accentuates the manager's role, sorting out the proper mix of the properties of many owners and the work of many workers. Managers stand at the nexus between owners and workers in the market. Such managers can and do establish customs of the market and market behavior. Traditional and customary reasons for favoring owners over workers still exist, but as the differentiation between owners and managers increases, managers are treated more like workers by the owners.

TABLE 20.1: Development and Population Density

	Up to 1 billion / High Death Rate / High Birthrate / 1800	1 to 3 billion / Declining Death Rate / High Birthrate / 1960	3 to 8 billion / Low Death Rate / Declining Birthrate / 2020	Over 8 billion / Low Death Rate / Low Birthrate
Less developed	All of the World	Asia,[a] Latin America, and Africa		
Developing			Africa	Africa
More developed		Europe, USSR Japan, Oceania, No. America	Asia,[a] Latin America	Asia,[a] Latin America
Developed			Europe, USSR, Japan, Oceania, No. America	Europe, USSR, Japan, Oceania, No. America

[a] Minus Japan.

TABLE 20.2: Peasant Societies Changing to Commercial Societies

	Condition of the Population Growth			
	High Death Rate / High Birthrate	Declining Death Rate / High Birthrate	Low Death Rate / Declining Birthrate	Low Death Rate / Low Birthrate
Dominant Work Organization	Communal / Work & indolence	Hierarchical / Hard work	Managerial / Efficient work	Pluralistic / Work & leisure
Food Supply and Demand	Limited supply / Full demand	Surplus / Limited demand	Surplus / Increasing demand	Surplus / Full demand
Nutritional	Famine	Hunger	Hunger	No hunger

Earlier management thinking, which carefully separated the roles of managers and workers, is rapidly being replaced by a team concept, workers sharing in the process of planning their work with management. The earlier management thought held that workers are inherently lazy and incapable of understanding and appreciating the objectives of their work. The modern view holds that in addition to a normal desire to avoid the discomfort of toil, there exists in each worker motivation to determine, to discover, to achieve, and to add to his or her being. The art of management has become less a matter of directing resources for company profit and more a matter of empowering middle management and workers to use their creativity in setting and achieving their goals. The latitude of managers, up and down the hierarchy of corporations, to add work opportunity to their agendas may be much larger than generally thought.

Changes Summarized

Tables 20.1 and 20.2 display a sequence of steps in the transformation of peasant societies into commercial societies and the pluralistic modification of commercial societies needed to end hunger.

Table 20.1 matches four degrees of development with four stages of world population growth. Following Seavoy, we examined the transition of peasants to farmers first as it occurred in the European group, bringing the world population to 1 billion, and again as the transition is currently occurring in the Asian group as the population reaches 5 billion.

Table 20.2 follows the transition from peasant to commercial society in terms of work organization, food supply and demand, and nutritional status in the four conditions of population growth. Peasant society is characterized by work-equalizing and work-minimizing communal relationships which produce a limited food supply widely shared. When disasters such as drought occur famines cause high death rates. Continual high birthrates replace the lost population and reduce the work load of elders and heads of households.

In the second stage, peasants lose communal control of their traditional lands and are forced to labor under a hierarchical system of bosses and overlords. The hard work required in this system produces a surplus of food available to all who work. Paid work providing income to buy food may not be available to all humans, and hunger persists.

In the third stage, the skills of both the workers and the supervisors have increased. The rising market value of the skilled worker causes managers to utilize such workers more efficiently and to restrict the numbers employed. The number of paid jobs is restricted, and hunger continues. The more wealthy societies respond with welfare food entitlements,

increasing food demand. The final stage is the hunger-free future envisioned in this chapter. Full demand for food is restored by a pluralistic system
of work management, sharing work opportunity with all.

Attentive Public

This chapter began by showing that the alleviation of hunger leading
to population stabilization was a policy objective most consistent with
American desires for the Third World. Concurrent with the development
of American attitudes supporting the relief of hunger in the Third World,
an attentive public has been organized supporting these policies. First into
the field was Bread for the World (1973). Bread is a Christian citizen movement focusing solely on world hunger issues with a grass-roots membership
of more than 40,000 nationwide. Bread is an effective lobby with a full- and
part-time Washington staff of about forty and an annual budget of $2
million.

While Bread is explicitly political and religious in its citizen base, the
Hunger Project (1977) is nonpolitical and nonreligious. The Hunger
Project promotes public will and commitment to end hunger in this century. Specifically promoting governmental action on behalf of the hungry
are Interfaith Action for Economic Justice (1975) and RESULTS (1981).
Interfaith is a lobby coalition acting for the staffs of the many churches
which maintain offices in Washington. RESULTS parallels Bread but
specializes in building indirect support for the hungry through the editorial
pages of the daily newspapers across the nation (Alexander 1984).

All of these groups publish regular reports on current issues and their
work on behalf of the hungry. Directly to the point is Bread for the World's
Newsletter, detailing the day-to-day legislative strategy and progress, and
Hunger Project's *World Development Forum*, focusing on hunger news from
around the world. Other periodicals written specially for this attentive
public are *Seeds, Hunger Notes,* and *World Food Monitor*. A guide to more
than 250 organizations which work on and/or are attentive to the general
problem of world hunger is available from the World Hunger Education
Service (Kutzner and Lagoudkis 1985).

21

National Planning, Economic Growth, and Equity in Sudan: An Analysis of Regional and Sectorial Disparities, 1962–1983

Lako Tongun

> The injection of planning into a society living in the twilight between feudalism and capitalism cannot but result in additional corruption, larger and more artful evasions of the law, and more brazen abuses of authority.
>
> —Paul Baran

Since independence in 1956 and the introduction and institutionalization of comprehensive development planning in 1961, Sudan continues to face increasing and widening disparities between and among regions, classes, and ethnic groupings. The national output has failed to increase appreciably in order to keep pace with the country's needs. Consequently, regional, class, and ethnic inequities have deepened and widened considerably, in spite of the introduction of planning processes. Inequalities in income, investment allocations, economic and political power have clearly become sharper and glaring. The national hopes and aspirations for improved material conditions of the majority of Sudanese have been disappointed and frustrated. Sudanese economic planners and policymakers and their external advisers seem to have consistently failed to pay much attention to the relationships between planning and the deepening disparities.

One apparent reason is that in the neoclassical scheme of developmental policies, there is a disavowing and a camouflaged ideological attitude, as noted by Peppard (1976:1).

> Distributional issues are difficult ... to handle because the choice among different distributions of income or wealth is not one that can be made purely on economic criteria. To avoid the necessity of making

value judgements, these kinds of choices are typically relegated to the political process which most orthodox economists are usually anxious to ignore.

Increase the pie and divide it later has been the economists' view. The other explanation is the neoclassical notion of equity and planning, which assumes that the price-market system, reinforced by distributional impact of (government) fiscal and monetary policies and by reformist intervention in the economic and planning process, is quite compatible with the objectives of egalitarian distribution.

This chapter is an attempt to shift our focus and analysis of national maldistribution from the process of development to the location of conditions of underdevelopment within the planning process itself. In other words, the sharpening regional, ethnic, and class disparities in Sudan are not primarily an accident of history of the development process or of variations in natural endowments. Rather, they form the logical results of consciously designed processes of neocolonial development and governmental policies which are formulated and implemented by the Sudanese postcolonial state. The formulation and implementation of these accentuating factors of material inequities are accomplished through an agenda of local, national, and international institutions, and within a framework of the country's essentially capitalist development strategy. State planning in its present form, namely sectorial planning, constitutes the essence of the institutionalized "national" program to perpetuate the existing regional, ethnic, and class deprivation or exploitation in Sudan. In other words, the planning system and the state institutions interact with each another to reinforce each other and to produce increased regional inequalities in the country. The interaction also produces a set of laws of motion which operate to eternalize the existing social order in Sudan which benefits a few. This is illustrated quantitatively by investment allocations, location of industries, education and health programs. The relationships between Sudan's development strategy and planning on one hand, and regional ethnic and class contradictions on the other, are analyzed critically. The analysis poses the conclusion that regionalization of planning, in a national sense, and within a framework of a new development strategy, is essential for the minimization of the prevailing inequities and conditions of regional underdevelopment and class and ethnic contradictions.

Region, Ethnicity, and Class

Our first task here is briefly to discuss the concepts of region, ethnicity, and class—how they are related and what their relationships are to the question posed, namely, the effects of state planning on the prevailing inequities or material contradictions. To begin with, the concept of region is critical because it has a social content which reflects both ethnic and class relationships in Sudan, and for that matter in much of Africa. For instance, some regions have relatively developed, while others have lagged behind as a result of differential impact of colonial capitalism. In addition, regional development or underdevelopment coincides with ethnic welfare and consequently with class. In other words, colonial capitalist development in Sudan initially occurred in regions occupied by a particular ethnic group or groups from which the present ruling classes of postcolonial Sudan have emerged. This historical development has obviously created an intricate network of interrelationships between class, ethnicity, region and state planning in contemporary Sudan. Indeed, these interrelationships can be viewed as constituting a moving history of Sudanese society and its experiences in a concrete historical context. They also reflect the consequences of Sudan's incorporation into the world capitalist economy. In short, the analysis of region, ethnicity, and class is largely phrased in terms of these interrelationships.

Moreover, the concept of region also takes on some distinctive political and economic expressions which impinge on ethnic and class relations. For instance, colonial administration in Sudan utilized the notion of region as a basis for organization of the political administration of the country. That is, the construction of the administrative units was based on certain objective and subjective criteria, namely those considerations which reflected ethnic homogeneity within a given geographical area. These would include, for example, culture, language, religion, history, and customs. These are also elements which define ethnicity in both objective and subjective sense. However, not all the administrative units necessarily reflected most of these criteria.

Nevertheless, the term *region* has emerged as a self-identifying concept for most Sudanese. It still serves as a locus of cultural, linguistic, and historical identity. At the national level, it also functions as the context within which the postcolonial problems of resource allocation and distribution of political power are contested. Indeed, the colonial legacy of uneven regional development and exaggeration of the existing regional and ethnic differences, by policies of the postcolonial state made the region an object of collective identity. Ethnic groups which occupy a particular region make their demands to the national government on the basis of their region. The concept of region has been obviously concretized as a political category and a contiguously definable geographical space, with specific character and status in the minds of the inhabitants of each region. In other words, "regional consciousness" was and has been promoted and has consequently acquired a distinct political expression in Sudan.

The economic manifestation of the region on the other hand takes the form of spatial (productive) economic activities. For instance, regional economists sometimes refer to "homogeneous regions" in which similar economic activities occur. These activities are measurable by such indicators as industrial structure, employment and unemployment rates, income per capita, etc. They also talk of "polarized" or "nodal" regions, which are characterized by economic dualism between rural and urban sectors, reflecting what Jean Mayer (1977:79) calls a "network of complementary socioeconomic relations, organized around an urban centre, usually of the second order."

The "complementary socioeconomic relations," however, underscore nothing but unequal regional development and imbalances. They are a result of a geographically differentiated articulation of dependent capitalism within the largely precapitalist modes of production in Sudan. In this respect, we see the economic concept of region emerging historically in terms of its relation to the development of spatial divison of labor and the consequent regionalization of Sudan's social formations.

Here, spatial division of labor is associated closely with the dynamic behavior of how certain economic activities respond to geographic resource disparities in the process and conditions of accumulation in the country. For instance, it may be noted that investors often take advantage of the unequal distribution of resources by investing in those regions of the country which offer the most attractive returns. Such investments tend to create and accentuate spatial division of labor within the country. Consequently, spatial division of labor acquires a geographic character in terms of divisions between regions. At the same time, it becomes the basis of regional inequalities. The notion of spatial divison of labor is not, however, equivalent to the notion of regionalization of labor. The latter is not derived from or a consequence of the economic basis of a particular region.

For one thing, a noted characteristic influence of capitalism in Sudan, or capitalism in general, is the tendency to overcome regional barriers in its search for exploitation of labor power and resources, wherever they may reside. At the same time, it tends to conserve or destroy certain ethnic and cultural barriers. The degree to which this tendency occurs depends on what promotes its profitable expansion into and penetration of new or existing regions.

Charles Bettleheim (1972) has characterized this contradictory phenomenon of capitalist expansion and accumulation, particularly in the Third World or even developed capitalist countries, as the "conservation-dissolution" of the precapitalist modes. Indeed, Datoo and Gray (1979:261) explained why Bettleheim's observation fits the case in the Third World (and equally in Sudan):

This tendency towards the partial conservation and partial dissolution of pre-capitalist modes, together with the dominance of merchant or circulation capital, is a fundamental element in the *underdeveloped capitalism* typical of Third World countries. Underdeveloped capitalism refers to the "blocking" of development of the dependent economies' productive forces which arises out of a contradiction inherent in the dominance of merchant capital. On the one hand, it stimulates the generalization of commodity production, since the only way to achieve bigger profits is to increase turnover; on the other hand, it preserves the peasant producers, since profit can only be obtained by engaging in unequal exchange between what the peasant sells and what he buys. The development of the productive forces is therefore frozen within the limits set by precapitalist relations of production, and the surplus product appropriated is largely reinvested in trade rather than production.

The other point to note about spatial division of labor is that it is essentially specific to the socioeconomic formation of each of the country's regions and is therefore intrinsically influenced by the roles the regions play in both the national and the international political economy. In short, there is a substantial difference between regionalization of labor and "spatial division of labor."

However, the significance of our discussion here consists of the following points: (1) the regionalization of labor and spatial division of labor create simultaneously the process of class formation and politicization of ethnic or regional distinctions in Sudan; (2) ethnicity acquires an ideological function in the country's politics; (3) the politicization of ethnicity and class formation enter into the process of allocation of national product through the mechanism of state planning; in which case class and ethnicity enter into the determination of choices and priorities of the national plans; and (4) the process of internal politicization to ethnicity and formation of class is linked externally to international capitalism, so that the contradictions at the national-international level are reproduced at the national-regional level.

The ideological function of ethnicity in Sudanese politics deserves some attention because it constitutes an active variable of political expression. Moreover, ethnic and regional inequalities in Sudan tend to coincide considerably, giving rise to some of the most serious internal tensions and conflicts in the country. For example, the Civil War between the North and the South (1955–1972) and the continuing tensions between these are illustrative. We may also take note of the regional unrests and discontent in western Sudan. These regional dissatisfactions have been directed against the central government in Khartoum. Clearly, these conflicts are both regional and ethnic in nature. They also assume a class character, because the ruling elites in Khartoum are at the same time members of the most dominant ethnic groups in the North.

Furthermore, we may illustrate the ideological function of ethnicity by the following argument. If an individual (or group of individuals) perceives his regional or ethnic origin to be more important for the determination of his social mobility and material improvement than, say, class basis, then he is more inclined to be ethnically or regionally conscious than class. In this respect, interregional or interethnic consensus and coalescence of class interests may be more difficult to achieve and observe. The difficulty is exacerbated when the patterns of national allocation of development resources are skewed in favor of a region or a few regions, an ethnic group or a few ethnic groups. Under such circumstances, class interests are expressed within the ethnic or regional phenomenon rather than between ethnic groups or regions. In short, the ethnic phenomenon overshadows class consciousness in the domestic contest for development resources and material needs.

The important point here is not to suggest a denial of class interests and collaboration at the interethnic or interregional level in Sudan. On the contrary, urbanized sectors of the Sudanese society exhibit class collaboration within the ruling and working classes. For instance, the ruling elites at the present are not only made up of members of the dominant groups in the North along the Nile valley, i.e., the riverine ethnic groups, but include individuals from other ethnic groups or regions. These latter members of the ruling elites represent the interests of the dominant classes of their regions. Whether or not these individuals are used by the ruling classes of the riverine dominant groups to further the interests of the latter is a question that requires further research and analysis.

At the working class level, i.e., the urbanized workers, class interests are clearly represented by the development of collective bargaining or trade unionism. Trade union movements in Sudan have had a longer history than in most African countries. More importantly, the unions also become the most effective instruments of promoting working-class consciousness, among the unionized urban workers. In the words of Saad el-Din Fawzi (1957:34), the unions "gave impetus to the emergence of industrial labor as a self-conscious class and provided much needed centers for workers' activities." In 1972 there were 572 trade union organizations in Sudan, the most powerful umbrella organ being the Sudan Workers' Trade Union Federation (SWTUF), founded in 1950. Some of its important and powerful constituent members include the Sudan Railways Workers' Federation and Gezira-Tennants Union. The top leadership of the SWTUF have had close relations with the Sudanese Communist Party (SCP), once the largest and the most influential party within the working-class movement on the African continent. Indeed the leaders of the SWTUF have been noted to have effectively "campaigned for the welfare of Sudan's working classes while the major political parties continued to rely on sectarian or personalist loyalties" (Bechtold 1976:114–115).

The significant point to note is that the role of the Sudanese Communist Party in the trade union movements and the function of the latter played a crucial part in creating and promoting working-class consciousness. Indeed, some of the unionized urban workers in the major Sudanese industrial sectors did express their new class consciousness by, for example, voting for members of the SCP in past national elections. They replaced their traditional ethnic or regional loyalties and interests because the SCP represented distinct secular views on economic and political issues. On the other hand, the followers of the traditional ethnic and regional interests viewed politics as different from policies, so they voted more on the basis of ethnic or regional affiliation rather than on the ground of "economic" and class interests. They would vote for candidates who would more or less maximize ethnic or regional access to certain developmental resources and opportunities at the disposal of the postcolonial state. For instance, they may gain access to education, business, or appointments to critical national leadership positions. Here, ethnic or regional origin rather than merit becomes the basis of appointment.

Clearly, ethnic or regional consciousness cannot be regarded completely as "false consciousness," as Archie Mafeje (1971) and others would suggest. Rather, it is a genuine internal political expression which represents either a sense of social grievance and cultural solidarity or a desire for maintaining and strengthening one's privileged ethnic or regional position by accumulation of wealth and political power. In one respect, ethnic or regional consciousness in Sudan or other African countries can be characterized as a process of conservation or destruction and modification of the status quo. The former represents the tendency to exploit and dominate other ethnic groups or regions, while the latter reflects the resistance against that exploitation and domination. In another sense, ethnic or regional consciousness assumes the same basic conditions upon which class consciousness and struggles arise. Indeed, it is a manifestation of the latter in all their forms.

However, it should also be noted that ethnicity or regionalism (i.e., the ideological expression or feelings of belonging to a region as the basis of one's political status) does not necessarily assume ultimate primacy in the Sudanese political economy. For one thing, class and ethnicity or regionalism coincide extensively, so that it is difficult to assign primacy to one over the other, either statistically or by other methods of determining their relative weights. Secondly, interethnic collaboration at the national level also takes the form of class interests, rather than a purely ethnic or regional character.

The important point here is rather related to John Saul's suggestion that ethnicity must be taken seriously "as a *real* rather than ephemeral and/or vaguely illegitimate variable in Africa" (1979:39). In short, ethnicity plays such an important ideological function that it often becomes what Sklar (1967) calls "a mask for class privilege" for those in power. It is a political reality in Sudan, and it constitutes an important part of the regional problems in Sudanese development.

The State, Planning, and Regional Disparities

The role and functions of the Sudanese state constitute the most important factors in the regional, ethnic, and class contests, and in the planned development process. The state is a direct participant in the country's economy. Indeed, the public sector is the largest, and besides, the Sudanese state intervenes at every level of the society, namely, in economic, political, and ideological sectors (Oguda 1973). It is the state that can affect and determine the allocation of investment capital, location of development projects, structure of production, and changes in the ownership and control of capital. It also determines the distribution of income through a variety of mechanisms; for example, through its control of monetary and fiscal policies. Because of the large public sector, the Sudanese state can also influence income distribution through public employment and expenditures, and through control of prices and wages.

To accomplish its objectives, the Sudanese state adopts planning, in which case planning becomes an instrument for dealing with the problems of development and their solutions. However, these functions and the roles of the postcolonial state are largely determined by the dominant social forces and interests which control the state. The question of whose interests the postcolonial state serves is therefore critical to the effectiveness of planning as an instrument for development, one that benefits all sectors of Sudanese society. Hence, the relationship between the state and planning determines regional (ethnic) disparities in Sudan. Indeed, the present form of planning and the role of the postcolonial state have actually exacerbated regional inequalities.

Until very recently, development planning in Sudan has not specifically addressed or defined the nature and solutions of the country's regional problems as issues which deserve special attention. For instance, the *Ten Year Plan of Economic and Social Development, 1961/62–1970/71* tersely mentions regional development in an oblique manner and in the context of aggregate national objectives. The minister of finance and economics at the time simply expressed it in these general terms:

> Speaking about economic development means illustrating the policy
> and development projects which have been drawn up by the government

for the prosperity of our fellow-citizens in rural and urban areas, in the
south and in the north, in the east and the west; this also includes what
has been planned for the welfare of their sons, grandsons, and the coming
generations. (Sudan Government 1962:3)

No specific development programs or projects were instituted in a conscious
effort to address regional problems inherited from colonialism. Most
development projects and programs were located in or largely confined to
the various regions of the North, namely riverine sections of northern
Sudan. Few development schemes were allotted to the South and the West,
and none of them were effectively implemented under the plan. For instance, the planned development of agricultural projects and expansion of
the Nzara agricultural complex in the South were not implemented. In
general, the development projects, under the ten-year plan were conceived
within the confine of sectorial planning rather than in regional terms.

Similarly, the *Five Year Plan* (1970/71–1974/75) had no specific conception of regional development in a manner that addressed the prevailing
interregional inequities. The plan saw the regional questions in terms of
improving the general well-being of all the Sudanese people in the
aggregate, namely per capita increase, improved productivity, and realization of full employment as well as satisfaction of social needs of all
Sudanese. These are certainly correct goals of a plan, but they need to be
put into a specific distributional framework. The question of how the productive resources and benefits of economic growth and development are
allocated and distributed regionally or ethnically must be addressed in
specific terms.

The *Six Year Plan* (1977/78–1982/83), on the other hand, has explicitly
expressed concern over the need to address the question of regional
development. Indeed, the plan devotes a brief chapter in Volume One to
defining the nature and the role of regional development in the Sudanese
planning efforts. It stated, in part:

> Regional development is considered to be one of the main elements of
> comprehensive national planning. Its main purpose is the development
> of the rural and regional areas in order to cut down the economic and
> social disparities existing between these areas to the minimum and to
> realize maximum economic stability, economic integration and social
> justice. The need for regional planning is dictated by the economic and
> social differences which presently exist between the various provinces as
> regards income levels, level of economic development, the availability of
> infrastructure and social services such as education, housing and others.
> (1977:45)

The plan also recognized and warns against the consequences of regional
neglect to the country's development efforts. It declared:

> [The] gap would continue to widen year after year unless scientific measures are taken to mobilize the local resources and potentialities, provide employment opportunities, improve the standard of living for the rural and desert people, and achieve an optimum use of the available resources and potential to realize justice, equality and balanced regional growth. (1977:145)

Although the plan seems to express a strong sense of concern about the geography or regional context of national development, its intentions so far remain unfulfilled. For example, the plan promised £S150 million (about 42 percent) for the Southern Region, out of £S425 million appropriated for regional development. However, the South has not even received much of its portion of the allotment. Nor are there any development projects in the South that are being effectively implemented under the six-year plan.

Part of the problem is attributed to the fact that Sudanese plans rely heavily on the promises of foreign capital inflows. For example, the six-year plan expected £S3,000 million ($7.2 billion) from abroad, mainly from the Arab countries of the Middle East. But these high expectations have not materialized to the extent of the planned level. Regions which have been traditionally neglected often suffer most from cutbacks in development projects. The tendency has been a concentration of investments and development schemes in a few privileged regions. Rolf Gusten (1966: 49) has more or less noted the main reasons for the persistence of the tendency.

> The fact that only regions already enjoying a certain measure of development are capable of contributing towards the Development Budget justifies the policy of according priority to the focal centres of development. This policy, already followed in the past, of focusing the development effort on those areas possessing the greatest economic advantage, is doubtless being continued.... This policy (also known as 'spearhead development') is based on the view that, in the longer term, maximum growth will also be achieved over the whole economy, if development activities are concentrated in the first place on areas with an already developed infrastructure, natural advantages, and a population more alive to the rationale of economic thinking, from which the returns on additional investment are naturally higher than in the marginal areas and constitute therefore a surplus which may be skimmed off and reinvested. An investment policy founded on the 'watering can' method, which spreads investment evenly over the whole area, would result in a slower growth and lower tax receipts at the margin. And this would accentuate the tendency for the central budget surplus to shrink.

Gusten's observation points clearly to the prevailing thinking and explanation of regional inequities, derived from the neoclassical theories of economic development. This has been and remains the basis of Sudanese planning. In essence, the criteria of efficient use of resources and maximum returns on investments assume biased considerations against equity and social concerns of planning. Indeed, sectorial planning, which is basically "spearhead development," relegates the regions to the periphery of planned development in Sudanese planning experiences and practices. The result has been the peripheralization of the national economic space, in which the rural sectors and regions remain areas of underdevelopment and exploitation. In other words, regional inequalities are exacerbated by the sectorial nature of Sudanese planning.

Secondly, sectorial planning in Sudan has become, in essence, what might be explained as "regionalization of planning." The usual sense of regional planning implies spread of development activities to other regions of the country through conscious efforts by the state. The phenomenon of regionalization of planning in Sudan describes instead the concentration of development activities in one or few regions and through consciously planned government policies. It is a process that promotes regional disparities in Sudan. Most development efforts in Africa still promote this disparity pattern.

Finally, government development promoted, directly and indirectly, the concentration of the industrial enterprises in the three northern regions (Khartoum Kassala, Blue Nile, Darfur and Kordofar). Direct promotion involves industrial development through state agencies, participation in industrial ventures; either alone or jointly with private capital it controls government loans to private (and public) industrial schemes. It also decides on the feasibility and location of public industrial enterprises and counsels the private sector on the same proposals. Most criteria used involve profitability of or maximum returns to investments. Others may include social criteria; for example, employment creation and training of nationals. But many of these economic criteria have generally worked against regions which do not already possess infrastructural foundations. As a result, allocations of industrial investment loans are regionally biased. Khartoum leads with a yearly average of 44.3 percent. Kassala and Blue Nile follow with yearly averages of 18.2 and 15.5 percent, respectively. The Western and Southern regions remain at the bottom (Sudan Government 1977).

Other financial service sectors exhibit the same regional bias. For example, the State Bank of Sudan, a state-owned agency which handles loans and provides financial advice on urban housing construction, concentrates its loans in the Northern Region, where most of the modern economic activities are concentrated. Another important area of loan provisions is in the agricultural character (basis) of the Sudanese economy. The Agricultural Bank of Sudan, one of the state agencies, handles the disbursement of loans to agricultural enterprises, both private and public. Its lending policies are important in encouraging agricultural development in the country. It provides the incentives and loans for crop production and mortgages.

Turning to the social side of regional development or underdevelopment, data show strikingly similar regional disparities. Let us illustrate the social character of regional inequities by taking data from education and health services. The general role of modern education in development is well established in the literature on economic development (D'Arth 1974). The three national plans have all made emphatic recognition of the role of education. The ILO *Report*, which was commissioned by the Sudanese government in 1974, made a more elaborate description of the role of education in Sudanese development. The *Report* noted:

> The educational system has a major role to play—perhaps *the* major role—in ensuring that the linkages between modern and traditional sectors amount to more than "trickle down" effects. Schooling facilities are an important way in which the wealth created in the modern sector can be used to enrich the daily lives of those in the traditional sector. However, questions of redistribution are secondary; the heart of the matter is the transfer of new technology, attitudes and aspirations into the lives of the rural population as an essential complement to new material inputs. The proposals in support of a rapid spread of restructured mass education and training are not simply a gesture toward modernity; they are central to the hopes for raising productivity in the traditional sector of the economy, which is the surest way of giving the masses an equitable share in the fruits of economic development. (ILO 1976:137)

Clearly, raising the overall productivity of a nation's economy seems to be the major thrust of education. But for education to perform this role, it must be spread regionally and sectorially, as the ILO *Report* has noted. The fundamental question becomes one of how the educational opportunities are distributed regionally, i.e., their extensity. This is a critical issue because modern education has become an instrument of ethnic, class, and regional dominance, as well as the foundation of inequality in other areas of contemporary Sudanese society.

For instance, the urban sector, with 18 percent of the country's population (1973 census) dominates the educational system. In 1975, the distribution of enrollment ratios at the lower levels of education (primary) was 90 percent in urban areas and 30–35 percent in the rural sector, with 82 percent of the population—all of the South and most of the West. At the lower secondary levels, the ratios were 40 percent in urban and 3 percent in the rural sector. The South accounted for only 16 percent of the pupils enrolled in higher secondary (ILO 1976).

Educational disparities arise at every level of the educational system. Regional disparities in both facilities and student enrollments tend to increase or widen as one goes up the educational ladder. The privileged regions lead at the higher levels. For example, in 1974 Khartoum had 39 percent of higher secondary pupils, compared to 3 percent for the Southern Region (ILO 1976).

Clearly, the present regional educational policy does not address the relationship between the educational system and the process of rural and regional underdevelopment. The present development strategy and planning promote an educational system, which fosters and maintains the privileges and power of the elite class to dominate the country's political and economic life. It fails to realize that people are the main target of development planning and that they constitute the most important resource in the development process—their labor.

Regional distribution of health services exhibits similar disparities. For example, the ILO *Report* noted that the level of "population coverage," defined as the availability of at least one dressing station (for outpatient health care) per 4,000 people and not more than ten miles apart, is considerably uneven regionally. The most prosperous regions are better covered than the peripheralized areas, namely the Southern and Western regions. In 1969, over 50 percent of public hospitals, with 80 percent of the beds, were located in the major urban areas, mainly in the Khartoum complex. All the country's five specialized hospitals for tuberculosis, ophthalmology, mental health, maternity, and radiology were located in Khartoum. The distribution of medical personnel was and is similar to that in 1969, over 63 percent of doctors in Khartoum, nine times those in the South in both 1969 and 1975.

The concentration of medical personnel (mainly doctors) and health facilities (they reinforce each other) in the Khartoum area and other major urban centers in the North is a function of economics and elitist (class) tendencies which are the dialectical result of forces which operate both inside and outside the health sector. Those factors which originate from outside are much more powerful than those from the inside. This is because the former relate to the social policies of the postcolonial state as well as the capitalist development strategy (planning). Both promote an elitist model of the health sector and delivery of its services. The health sector, like education, is controlled and shaped by forces that are located in the very structure of the development strategy and planning. In other words, the prevailing social order and relations shape the context within which the distribution of health services is determined.

22

Marketing Policy Issues for Agricultural Development: A Case Study from Western Sudan

Mark Speece and Bakheit Adam Azrag

Introduction

This chapter will examine aspects of the agricultural marketing structure in one region of Sudan. The perspective adopted here is somewhat different from the common approach of economics, which usually analyzes problems of production and growth of production. This study will not look at these issues, except to the extent that production is affected by aspects of the marketing structure. Increased production is not by itself sufficient to bring increased prosperity to most agriculturally based economies. Surplus crops must also be moved from the farm to areas of demand. Otherwise, the farmer does not benefit from producing more than can be consumed on the farm. Nor can agriculture raise living standards for consumers unless their purchasing power can be increased by access to greater volumes and better assortments at lower prices. Furthermore, technical improvements which allow increased agricultural production usually require new agricultural inputs, which the market or some other mechanism must bring to the producers.

The nature and organization of the market mechanism itself can influence how much and what is produced by farmers. This, of course, translates into how much surplus and what kind of assortment will become available to consumers. If farmers do not receive a satisfactory return from the marketing channels for their surplus production of a particular crop, they will not continue producing that crop for market sale. Market structure, then, can stimulate or retard production, which should make marketing a central issue in any developing economy. The effectiveness and efficiency of the marketing system in moving goods and services are critical to the achievement of development goals, and marketing requires close evaluation.

The geographical context of this discussion is western Sudan (Kordofan and Darfur), which is a rain-fed agricultural area typical of semiarid areas in many developing countries. Rain-fed agriculture has long been a very important source of food and income for the inhabitants of most semiarid regions. Traditional rain-fed agriculture still employs substantial portions of the labor force in most countries, even though progress has been made in developing irrigation systems and in mechanization. Unfortunately, the traditional rain-fed sector usually receives very little attention by development planners, despite its considerable potential for greatly increased production. Efforts are focused on the irrigated sector or on large-scale mechanization schemes. Nevertheless, the traditional sector must usually operate under the policies which are developed for the sectors that do receive attention.

Living conditions for traditional farmers in such regions are harsh, even without poor policy influencing their lives. Agriculture throughout western Sudan is intimately tied to the environmental conditions under which the inhabitants must live. The northern parts of Kordofan and Darfur are largely desert, while further south, conditions improve enough that South Kordofan and South Darfur can be classified as merely semiarid. There is not enough water to serve as an irrigation source; crops depend on rainfall from the summer rainy season. Only one crop per season can be raised, and this one crop must provide food for the entire year until the new crop is harvested in the next season. In good years, the inhabitants call the several months before the new harvest the "hunger period." In years of drought, when many crops fail, the hunger period lengthens, and many inhabitants face starvation.

Western Sudan as a Representative Case Study

A brief review of the agricultural economy in Sudan will demonstrate that western Sudan provides an excellent case study for examining marketing issues in semiarid rain-fed agriculture. Sudan is a country with enormous agricultural potential by the standards of most countries of the semiarid zone. It is estimated to have 200 to 300 million *feddans* of land suitable for agricultural production (1 feddan=1.038 acres), less than 10 percent of which is currently cropped. Considerable irrigation resources are available from the Nile River, while the central and southern parts of the country normally receive sufficient rainfall to support rain-fed cropping. The agricultural sector contributed nearly 40 percent of the gross domestic product (GDP) in 1985.

Agriculture accounts for over half of government revenues, employs between 60 and 70 percent of the labor force, and contributes nearly 95 percent of all exports. Traditional rain-fed acreage has averaged around 9 million feddans over the last decade. The mechanized rain-fed sector expanded rapidly in the early 1980s to nearly 6 million feddans but contracted more recently due to the drought in the mid–1980s. Irrigated acreage does not fluctuate much, but has remained fairly constant at around 4 million feddans (Speece 1982; D'Silva 1985; and Zahlan and Magar 1986 review the agricultural economy of Sudan and contain more extensive references).

Agriculture is still largely subsistence-oriented for the majority of the population, although there are several major state-run and private commercial farming schemes. The main commercial crop is cotton, but groundnuts (peanuts), sesame, wheat, fruits and vegetables, sugarcane, and gum arabic are also important. Long staple cotton is usually grown in the government-irrigated schemes. Short and medium staple cotton is grown in rain-fed areas, both under mechanized schemes and by traditional methods, accounting for slightly less than one-third of all cotton production in Sudan. About three-quarters of all groundnuts, nearly all sesame, and all gum arabic are grown in the nonirrigated sector, and western Sudan accounts for the vast majority of rain-fed production of these important cash crops. Sorghum is the principal grain and the main subsistence crop, and millet is important in the drier rain-fed areas. Wheat is grown only in irrigated areas.

Less than two decades ago, there was widespread consensus that Sudan could become one of the most prosperous non-oil-producing countries in the Middle East or Africa. For example, the five-year plan beginning in 1970 projected eventual self-sufficiency in foodstuffs and a major export role on world agricultural markets (Sudan 1970). Sudan was to become the breadbasket of the Middle East, supplying surplus sorghum, millet, vegetable crops, and livestock to regional food markets (Sudan 1970). In addition, cash crop exports of cotton, gum arabic, and oilseeds would further contribute to development efforts (*Forbes* 1976; Oesterdiekhoff and Wohlmuth 1983b). Economic growth in other sectors was to be based on agriculture, which would supply raw material inputs and generate the needed funds for investment (Oesterdiekhoff 1983a, 1983b; el-Bushra 1985; UNIDO 1985).

Unfortunately, Sudan has not come close to achieving this potential. Agriculture has not prospered; in fact, for many crops, production has not even kept pace with population growth. FAO (1984) figures show that the indices of per capita food production and of per capita overall production have declined since the base years of 1974–1976. They stood at 92.42 and 90.18, respectively, in 1983. In some cases, aggregate production has even declined. In recent years, Sudan has had to import a substantial proportion of its own food needs; cereal grains imports stood at over U.S. $90 million in 1983, up from U.S. $25 million in 1978 (Oesterdiekhoff and Wohlmuth 1983a; D'Silva 1985; FAO 1985). As a result, investment funds from agriculture never materialized, and most sectors of the economy have posted somewhat less than outstanding performance.

Lack of attention to the traditional rain-fed sector and poor marketing policies have contributed substantially to agriculture's poor performance in Sudan. In recent years, some planners have realized that irrigated agriculture has largely failed to live up to its planned potential (Ebrahim 1983), and many have recognized that traditional rain-fed agriculture is quite important, if only by default (e.g., D'Silva 1985; World Bank 1985). Lack of interest also meant that little attention had been devoted to understanding marketing in the rain-fed sector. Planners knew almost nothing about key issues such as how the movement of agricultural products was organized or how public policy affected the marketing structure. The World Bank (1985) cited this lack of knowledge as an important impediment of better development planning in Sudan.

Recently, some efforts have begun to correct past ignorance about how traditional rainfed agriculture functions in western Sudan. Data from the Western Sudan Agricultural Research Corporation, Sudan (ARC), World Bank, and U.S. Agency for International Development (USAID) project, provide the basis for the rest of this chapter. Socioeconomic research on farming systems has been conducted since the project began in 1981. In particular, WSARP conducted an investigation of agricultural marketing structures in Kordofan in 1985 (Speece 1985).

Marketing Constraints to Agricultural Production

The long complex marketing channels in Kordofan and the wide variety of activities which the multitude of middlemen carry out are characteristic of economies where capital is scarce, transportation is poor, and storage facilities are inadequate. In any marketing channel, certain functions must be performed to move goods from producer to consumer. One important set of functions typically involves such things as buying/selling, which entails identifying, locating, and negotiating with parties interested in selling/buying products. A second main set has to do with the actual physical movement of product. Agricultural commodities must be assembled, transported, stored, graded/sorted, and broken down into lot sizes which customers/consumers are willing to buy. A third major set might be classified as facilitating functions. Financing/credit provisions must be made, risk must be assumed on transactions, and market information must be available.

Typical channels are made up of various levels of wholesalers and retailers, who assume responsibility for performance of the functions. Performance of any function entails a certain cost, and there must be an associated compensation if the function is to be performed at all. Capital scarcity and poor communications dictate that such operations are usually on a small scale, and the generally risky conditions dictate that there be many channel members as a mechanism for risk spreading. Still, agricultural marketing at most levels in Kordofan is actually quite effective, given the adverse conditions found there. Channel members provide real benefits to customers and suppliers through performing a wide variety of functions which are essential if product is to be moved from producers to consumers. Merchants are subject to intense competition, which does not allow them to realize excessive profits; indeed, profit margins are generally fairly low, certainly not above what one sees in other countries where free markets prevail.

Nevertheless, marketing is subject to many constraints which inhibit agricultural production. They can be categorized into three broad areas and concern limitations imposed upon commerce by the physical environment, inadequate infrastructure, or political intervention, rather than because of business practices by private merchants. Government intervention, which has taken many forms, is perhaps the most serious area. The government has attempted to maintain control over cash crop channels, but unfortunately, public channels do not operate very effectively or efficiently. Public monopsony has resulted in the near end of cotton production in Kordofan, and has led to drastic decreases in gum arabic production. Oilseed production had also consistently declined until public control over the market was ended in the early 1980s. In addition, government control constantly drains the public budget. In running cotton-marketing channels, for example, the Nuba Mountain Agricultural Corporation has posted large deficits every year since it was set up in 1970 and had accumulated losses of nearly £S15 million by 1985 (NMAC/GTZ 1985).

Public involvement in marketing of agricultural inputs has been no more successful. The government competes with the private sector in supplying some things, such as agricultural machinery (especially tractors). Farmers prefer the higher-priced, higher-quality tractor work by private merchants when they can afford it, and some feel that no tractor is better than the poor job done by state tractor services. For most inputs, the government does not compete but holds a monopoly. Private sector marketing of such items as fertilizer, seed dressing, and pesticides is largely restricted, and the government is usually the only organization with access to improved seed varieties. Policy gives the irrigated sector top priority in the use of such inputs. Very little is allocated to the rain-fed sector, and when they are made available, they are for use in mechanized agriculture. The result has been almost no access to most inputs by small farmers, even though many would like to buy them and technical research has clearly shown the economic benefits of increased use of such inputs.

Government manipulation of exchange rates has led to an overvalued currency, which reduces the domestic price that the producer receives for an exported product. Such policies are really disguised taxes on the agricultural sector, and they discourage production. Artificial rates contributed to the production declines just noted for cotton and oilseeds. A substantial portion of the prices needed to make cash crop production economically attractive to farmers could be met by simply allowing market exchange rates (Spece and Gillard-Byers 1986 present detailed calculations for the case of groundnuts). Additionally, imported goods have artificially low prices, which can lower the competitiveness of domestic agricultural products. Artificial exchange rates combined with bread subsidies have made imported wheat much more attractive to the consumer than the domestic sorghum which is produced throughout western Sudan (D'Silva 1985, 1986). The result is reduced incentive to produce and market sorghum.

Price controls discourage production of premium-quality agricultural products and discourage the development of a market for such products. Farmers will not produce and merchants will not trade products on which they must take a loss. Price controls in Kordofan have largely been applied to meat. They have had relatively little impact on production because they have been widely ignored. They have, however, reduced supply and restricted consumer choice in urban areas where the government maintains sufficient administrative structure to attempt enforcement of the controls. Kadulgi officials were among the most energetic in upholding the price regulations, and in that city many price-controlled goods simply became unavailable. They could still be purchased in the outlying villages where the regulators did not reach, but it was not profitable for livestock producers to move their stock to Kadulgi at the official prices (Louis Berger 1983).

Restrictive licensing policy inhibits entry of competitors into the market. In Kordofan, those merchants and traders who usually deal directly with producers do not require licenses, and this level of the marketing channel is therefore very competitive. Higher levels of wholesaling are sometimes less competitive because it is difficult for potential new channel members to get a license. The government has been particularly reluctant to grant licenses to exporters in the hide industry, for example. As a result, there are only a few firms licensed to export, and it is not difficult to keep producer prices low. Producer living standards in western Sudan, a major livestock region in the country, are held down to benefit large urban-based export firms. Policy also restricts entry of large grain wholesalers into the market.

The preceding discussion should not be taken as evidence that the government should not play any role in marketing. Some constraints do require government intervention because they concern system-wide deficiencies in infrastructure which individual firms cannot remedy. Physical infrastructure is very poor in Kordofan. Most merchants interviewed in WSARP's market analysis cited transportation as a serious impediment to the movement of goods, particularly during the rainy season. One wholesaler indicated that transport rates can increase up to 700 percent during the late summer and early fall. He tries to ship large quantities to his clients or partners in more remote areas before the rainy season starts so that they can stockpile to avoid excessive transport costs. (Storage constraints limit this strategy for perishable products). Similarly, transportation costs restrict the ability of village shopkeepers to operate profitably and competitively.

It is interesting to note that one grain wholesaler stated that poor transportation during the rainy season helped his business. This merchant operates on a regional scale and is not supplied from outside Kordofan. He felt that transportation problems limited the movement of grain (including free Relief Aid grain) into Kordofan. He was thus shielded from the competition of merchants from other market centers. Such examples make it clear that transportation deficiencies (mainly lack of all-weather roads) significantly raise costs to consumers. Sometimes this is because local merchants are able to take advantage of reduced competitive pressure. Merchants who import products into Kordofan, however, clearly prefer to avoid higher costs and the necessity of raising prices.

Storage constraints reduce the ability of channel participants to overcome predictable transportation problems. Storage does not seem to be a major problem to small traditional farmers whose capacity is generally adequate for their harvests and whose losses are quite low. Traditional storage methods are not adequate for large volumes, however, and mechanized farmers and merchants face considerable storage losses. Grain wholesalers face losses on the order of 20 percent when holding grain up to half a year and nearly 50 percent for crops they hold for the whole year. Louis Berger (1983) shows that if a merchant in Kordofan holds grain for six to nine months, prices must have risen at least 72 percent for him to break even. Coupled with high transportation costs, these storage problems contribute substantially to the very high prices faced by consumers in the preharvest months. Prices in such situations cannot be brought down through intensified regulation of merchants because they are high mainly due to infrastructure problems.

There are few merchants in Kordofan who specialize in storing grain, but most prefer to rent storage space, often from the government. Most merchants do not feel that they have the expertise to manage storage facilities, and they are therefore reluctant to invest in them. Government investment is probably essential in storage facilities as well as in transportation if these important physical infrastructure problems are to be eased. Of course, this is already widely recognized, and many foreign aid projects specifically stress building all-weather roads and modern storage facilities (Borsdorf and Haque 1984; USAID 1985).

The institutional infrastructure is also deficient in many cases. Credit is generally not available to small farmers in predominantly African areas, and is only available through the high-cost traditional *sheil* system in Arab areas. In this system, loans are made for repayment in kind at harvest time, and the loan is valued at the prevailing market prices. At harvesttime, the loan is repaid in agricultural produce, which is now valued at lower harvest-time prices. Sheil is not really exploitive in the sense that merchants earn exorbitant profits; indeed, if the default rate reaches about 20 percent, the merchant runs a deficit. (The Agricultural Bank can offer lower interest loans because it consistently operates at a deficit, and losses are covered by the government. Small shopkeepers do not, of course, have this option.) Nevertheless, the farmer is at a clear disadvantage when required to repay loans in a commodity which has declined substantially in value from the time the debt was incurred.

State institutions are usually unwilling or unable to deal with small farmers. Even when they do, terms may not be much better than those available through the sheil system. The Agricultural Bank and the Nuba Mountain Agricultural Corporation offer lower nominal interest rates, but they also usually require repayment at harvesttime when the farmers' assets (crops) have low values. When taking payment in kind, these institutions sometimes even set prices below the already low prevailing market prices. Farmers need mechanisms which will allow them to avoid selling immediately upon harvest to pay debts or to resupply the family's stocks. They would then be able to hold their crop until prices had risen. Selling later would also shift the sale to a time when more family labor was available. At harvesttime, labor demands are high, and the farmer must utilize channels within the village, which offer lower return because there is no free time to assume more marketing functions. With more time, farmers could move their own crops in many cases and sell in alternative higher return channels.

Market information about new products (innovations) is a greater problem than agricultural commodity price information. Price information is generally widely known, and the problem is not access to information but ability to act on the information. However, the flow of information about agricultural innovations is very poor. Extension services are nearly nonexistent in western Sudan, and information on improved agricultural techniques can take years to reach farmers. Many farmers do not understand the concept of hybrids, do not know planting instructions or growth characteristics of new varieties that they are asked to try, or do not know that fertilizer can be effective outside the irrigated sector. Farmers would have better access to knowledge of such innovations if agricultural inputs were available through private marketing channels, even in small quantities. Coughenour and Nazhat (1985) found that one of the most important sources of information about innovations was merchants and traders who carried the inputs.

Wide seasonal price differentials and extreme price volatility constitute the final major constraint that will be noted here (Speece, Gillard-Byers, and Azrag 1987). Analysis of South Kordofan price data indicated that fluctuations on the order of 100 percent within a few days were not at all uncommon for most agricultural commodities. Volatility increased as prices increased throughout the season. This has serious implications for the movement of product to market because it greatly increases risk on market transactions. Subsistence farmers are risk avoiders; they prefer enterprises with low yield and low risk to activities which may be more profitable but carry higher risk. Small shopkeepers and traders in western Sudan are very risk conscious as well. They regard themselves as farmers first, with only supplementary commercial activities, and they have the same mentality as other farmers. Even some slightly larger-scale merchants who regard trading as their primary occupation recognize the high price risk and sometimes choose not to move product.

Drought conditions can make the situation even worse. Kordofan data indicate that drought extends the length of the high-price/high-volatility period. It also changed the cost and compensation relationships of channel functions, with the result that functions were shifted to the lower ends of the channels. Large operators restricted their offering of credit/financing, and village shopkeepers had to extend more credit to keep customers, further increasing their risk exposure. They also became more responsible for functions associated with the physical handling of products, such as buying/selling, assembly, and storage. Farmers were less willing to take their crop to distant markets themselves and face price risk, so the shopkeepers had to purchase a relatively greater share of the marketed crop. (Of course, in absolute terms, there is less marketed crop in drought years). Responsibility for the transportation function shifted to them, because fewer merchants came to villages from the larger markets when the prospect of a good buy on crops was diminished.

Smaller operators are much less able to finance additional functions. Furthermore, the increased responsibility during the drought did not bring increased compensation to shopkeepers. Analysis of price series data showed average markups of 20 percent or less on sorghum sales by small merchants in Kadugli area villages in 1985 (Speece 1985). WSARP data from 1980 show a markup of 40 percent on sorghum by small merchants (Araujo 1981). Instead of taking advantage of the drought situation, a charge is often leveled at merchants, and such measures appear to cut their markups. With diminished markups but increased functional responsibility, one can safely conclude that profits suffered. The profit margins documented in 1985 were fairly low, in the order of a few percentage points. The fact that small operators do not receive increased compensation in return for shouldering additional costs makes them reluctant to take on these additional functions during drought. As a result, product flow is impeded.

Policy Recommendations

Marketing policy in Kordofan should be formulated to counter the constraints identified above. It will be no surprise that the first recommendation concerns the need for less public intervention in areas which are currently major concerns of the government. The public sector should not operate marketing channels. It should let the financial market determine exchange rates, it should let the commodities market determine prices of crops (cease price controls and subsidies), and it should stop licensing policies which restrict the entry of new channel members. Justification for lessened public intervention should be evident from the earlier discussion on the impact of intervention. It should be noted that a great many observers have pointed out to Sudanese government the need for reform in this area. The World Bank (1982), for example, specifically cited the need for shifting reliance to the private sector in rain-fed agriculture areas.

Dissolving public corporations in western Sudan would allow the government to shift resources to areas where public intervention is greatly needed. The Nuba Mountain Agricultural Corporation lost $2 million in 1984/1985 alone (NMAC/GTC 1985), which could have been allocated to production-enhancing programs instead of ones that provided disincentives. Many of the requirements in marketing are beyond the scope of the private sector to provide. Some government role is certainly necessary to solve physical infrastructure deficiencies, for example. Improved roads and storage facilities are greatly needed to allow lower-level channel members to stay in the market during bad years. Large operators can deal with the high cost over a large volume. When functions are shifted to small operators, they must either take losses or raise prices to maintain their margins.

A network of all-weather roads which are easily passable in the rainy season would contribute significantly to a more efficient, less costly market structure. Such projects must concentrate on feeder roads and a regional network rather than on trunk roads to connect major cities in western Sudan with Khartoum. Road development which only builds trunk roads has contributed to the decline of lower-level market centers in some countries. This may be occurring in North Kordofan; Coughenour and Nazhat (1985) report that some villages have suffered a decline in the number of shops and the level of economic activity within the village. Elimination of some of the marketing system's multiple channels leaves producers and small operators with fewer options if they are not satisfied with the performance of a particular channel and thereby increases the risk they must face. Local and regional trade usually offers producers and small traders better deals and less risky markets than does involvement in supplying distant national and/or international markets.

Public intervention is also needed to construct storage facilities. Provincial governments should be granted ownership of publicly financed facilities so that storage policy remains closely attuned to the needs of local markets. Management contracts should be worked out so that private business operates the facilities for the provincial government. Business expertise is readily available in the private sector but is in short supply in government. Facilities should be run on a profit-making basis, and management contracts should be granted and renewed based on acceptable profit performance. Over time, such a plan will increase private sector experience with storage management and will eventually lead to increased private sector investment in storage facilities.

Charges for use of the modern storage facilities should be similar to the current cost structure which grain merchants face. The facility must remain profitable because Sudan, especially provincial government, simply does not have the financial resources to operate yet another subsidy program. In addition, cumulative storage losses currently limit the ability of merchants to hold grain off the market during shortage periods, because losses may rise faster than prices. With better facilities, losses will be lower, and fees must be correspondingly higher to discourage hoarding. Modern facilities will also moderate the seasonal price differential because more of the stored grain will actually be available instead of lost.

Mechanisms which eliminate the need to sell immediately after harvest would reduce postharvest grain supplies and increase availability later, thereby reducing seasonal price differentials. Such programs would probably have to come through some sort of village-level credit cooperative since large institutions will not lend to small farmers. Such co-ops could grant short-term consumer loans to hold farmers until a few months after harvest when prices had stabilized at higher levels. They could also grant production investment loans which did not come due at harvest. Local loan decisions and community pressure on borrowers greatly decrease the default rate, and loan cost to such a co-op would be lower than for large institutions. As with storage, however, credit should not be subsidized but should reflect the cost of operating a credit co-op. (How this would work under Islamic law, which prevails in Sudan, will not be addressed here.) Loan cost would also be lower for the borrower since the portion of the crop allocated to repaying the loan would be less. Further, increased competition would likely force sheil lenders to improve their terms.

Such co-ops would need income-generating activities in order to raise loan capital. WSARP has had considerable success at introducing cooperatively owned oxcarts into several villages in South Kordofan. These oxcarts are owned by village cooperative corporations, managed by village leaders, and rented to villagers to haul crops and other goods. They are popular because the technology is easy to learn and is compatible with the local socioeconomic system. Oxcarts meet a critical need for transportation capable of carrying relatively large loads. They free labor during labor shortage periods, and they help small farmers bypass very expensive local hauling methods (up to several dollars per sack for relatively short distances). The village co-ops have generated considerable income for village projects through these oxcarts (Gillard-Byers, Bunderson, and Azrag 1985).

Information flow about agricultural innovations is very poor. Farmers learn about innovations primarily from three sources: institutions, markets/ merchants, and personal contacts in the community (Coughenour and Nazhat 1985). The institutional source in western Sudan is very deficient; the provincial and national governments simply do not have the resources to staff or supply an effective extension program. Because government policy rarely allows inputs into private channels, merchants do not know much about them. Therefore, agricultural product information must be disseminated by other means. Radio is quite popular but is not currently used much for agricultural education. Programs should be developed which provide understandable information about such things as fertilizer, insecticides, new seed varieties, and other inputs. Programs should also be developed which explain basic agricultural marketing principles, so that farmers will be able to evaluate various marketing options better.

A second way to improve information flow about agricultural input products is to allocate some of them to the private sector. If fertilizer was available on the private market, for example, most of it would be sold in rain-fed agricultural areas, including western Sudan, because merchants would not be able to compete with government suppliers in the irrigated sector. Merchants and the farmers who bought fertilizer would gain experience with it. Since merchants are a major source of information about innovations, and since the other major source of information about innovations, is community opinion leaders, information about input would be spread far beyond the circle of farmers who actually bought it initially. It is also likely that farmers who were able to buy fertilizer would allocate some of it to their own research programs. WSARP found that farmers who were given seed or fertilizer for on-farm trials often conducted their own trials also. The research design may not have been as tight as that of the station scientists, but the transferability of the results of local farming was infinitely better.

Finally, agricultural research projects themselves can be organized to incorporate local farmers and opinion leaders into the on-station research program. Increased involvement by projects in on-farm trials would also improve information flow about innovations. With these kinds of programs, the often-discussed problem of how to introduce the innovation would become moot. Farmers would not need to be convinced that an innovation worked because they would have gained the experience firsthand. Farmers themselves would lead the introduction of promising new technology by using it in their own cropping systems. They would have knowledge of how to use the new technology correctly from hands-on experience (Trail 1985).

Implementation of recommendations discussed above would address the problem of high price differentials and volatility, but further price moderation could be achieved through floor and ceiling prices set by the provincial government. The floor should not be an administered price imposed upon private traders, but rather a trigger price at which the government would step in to buy grain for a regional stockpile. It should be determined at harvesttime and set only slightly above the prevailing market price. Ceiling should not be fixed or imposed upon private merchants. It should be set only slightly below prevailing prices during the hunger period. Sales would be made out of the stockpile accumulated during the harvest. The objective is to moderate the seasonal price differential rather than to eliminate it, and to accumulate modest stockpiles for emergencies (drought years). Such recommendations for western Sudan are not new (Louis Berger 1983).

Such a program must be self-supporting. Realistic prices would ensure that a modest stockpile could be accumulated, but the government would not be forced to buy major portions of the harvest because the private market would continue to operate. Subsidized prices which drove private merchants out of business would suggest that the government program would be operating at a loss.

As noted above, provincial governments do not have sufficient resources to finance subsidized programs. Nor would consumers be very well served if the government held a virtual monopoly over channels for a particular crop. Prices must be set so that merchants who compete with government channels remain profitable, or no grain will be stored by the private marketing channels. However, competition from the government would force merchants to reduce costs to remain profitable. In particular, there would be a greater incentive to improve storage capabilities, which contribute the major cost involved in taking advantage of temporal price fluctuations.

23

Budget Priorities, National Security, and Third World Development

Stanley W. Moore

Introduction

Advances in knowledge during much of this century have often come from specialization and narrow concentration on the phenomena being examined. However, sometimes this has led to reductionism—a too narrow focus that obscures the broader interconnections between the disparate components that make up reality. Instead, we will attempt to look at several major components and interconnections that structure both the domestic and international policies of the United States, risking oversimplification in order to gain the broader perspective.

David Easton (1953) has defined *politics* as the allocation of values for society. Today it is imperative to recognize that politics is the allocation of *scarce resources*—both for our society and the entire world (Lasswell 1958). Politics, as Harold Lasswell succinctly stated, determines who gets what, when, where, and how. Today, to view it conversely, it determines who does *not* get—both here in America and around the planet. If there were unlimited resources, then all needs might be capable of being met. But there are not. When our society, via a research hospital in Utah, expends several hundreds of thousands of dollars to implant an artificial heart in a sixty-two-year-old man, that represents resources that are not available to meet the medical needs of the poor, minorities, and the elderly of our society. When the United States establishes as its priority the spending of $253 billion for military expenditures in fiscal year (FY) 1984 and $199 billion for weapons system, those dollars are not available to meet other pressing needs here and abroad (Wood and Irwin 1983). Because there is a scarcity of both capital and material resources, this is too often an *either-or* world. "Funding for new construction and substantial rehabilitation of low-income, elderly and handicapped persons' housing was $10.2 billion in the last Carter budget. It was down to $1.8 billion last year (1982)" (Kondracke 1983). The Reagan administration's decision to build an MX missile system for $40 billion (before cost overruns) means that some people's needs will go unmet—including hunger due to lack of agricultural research.

President Dwight D. Eisenhower forcefully asserted our dilemma in April 1953 to the American Society of Newspaper Editors:

> Every gun that is made, every warship launched, every rocket fired signifies, in the final sense, a theft from those who hunger and are not fed, those who are cold and are not clothed. This world in arms is not spending money alone. It is spending the seat of its laborers, the genius of its scientists, the hopes of its children. . . . This is not a way of life at all in any true sense. Under the cloud of war, it is humanity hanging on a cross of iron. (Greenstein 1983)

Politics is ultimately a matter of priorities, of values. It should be a rational attempt to adjust means and ends—to choose means appropriate to our desired ends. Choices confront us, individually and as a polity. The choices are not easy, not obvious, yet they cannot be avoided. Values, the allocation of scarce resources, have to be marginalized—weighed vis-à-vis one another. The issue confronting us is what balance should be striven for between guns and grain? What balance of expenditures will give us the most short-run and long-run security?

What is the definition of *security*? Is it primarily military? To what extent must nonmilitary considerations enter our national security equation? It is our thesis that "national security" must be broadened to include (1) national cultural survival in conjunction with future planetary resource scarcity and (2) the pressing need for a reduction in the antagonism and conflict between the developed countries and the less developed, primarily stemming from the increasing gap between the "North" and the "South." Security must be defined not only in terms of military security, for the world is not only dangerous because it is an increasingly armed world but also because it is a hungry world. In establishing our expenditure priorities we must at least move in the direction of greater fairness, humaneness, and justice—for these must be included in *security* in its broadest sense.

The Historical Search for Security

The search for peace and security has probably existed as long as humans have lived in social groupings, as long as an "us versus them" mentality has separated mankind, as long as individuals and groups have striven for dominance over others. Systematic strategies for international peace are not a recent phenomenon. Because modern technology is causing an acceleration in the destructive capability of weaponry, the search for peace and security is increasingly crucial for planetary survival. The latest studies on the possibility of a "nuclear winter" in *Science* and *Scientific American* heighten the critical importance of the search for security in its broadest dimensions (Turco, Ackerman, and Pollack 1984).

Historically, nations have tried unilateral armament, bilateral and multilateral treaty arrangements, and a European balance-of-power strategy in the nineteenth century—all unsuccessfully. Morton Kaplan (1967) has developed a systematic, logical, theoretical statement of the working principles underpinning a balance-of-power system. Such a system seems to have dominated much of the period between 1815 and 1914. This period was a time of relative peace as well as overabundance of ever-changing treaties and alliances. It was also a period when the best statesmen often misperceived reality and the expectations of allies and treaty partners were subject to delusion. A. J. P. Taylor (1954:527–528) summed up the failure of the system in his masterful study *The Struggle for Mastery in Europe 1848–1918*:

> None of the Powers acted according to the letter of their commitments, though no doubt they might have done so if they had not anticipated them. Germany was pledged to go to war if Russia attacked Austria-Hungary. Instead, she declared war before Russia took any action; and Austria-Hungary only broke with Russia, grudgingly enough, a week afterwards. France was pledged to attack Germany, if the latter attacked Russia. Instead she was faced with a German demand for unconditional neutrality and would have had to accept war even had there been no Franco-Russian alliance, unless she was prepared to abdicate as a Great Power. Great Britain had a moral obligation to stand by France and a rather stronger one to defend her Channel coast. But she went to war for the sake of Belgium. . . . As to the Balance of Power, it would be truer to say that the war was caused by its breakdown rather than by its existence.

In the end, the balance-of-power system did not guarantee peace or security. And because of the extreme complexity of the system, Taylor observes elsewhere, you could almost hear the sigh of relief when war erupted, as the known (the war) would resolve all of the uncertainties.

Unilateral efforts to achieve security are unworkable; ultimately, if every nation seeks security unilaterally, the probability of war increases rather than decreases. While a balance-of-power system operated with some success in the nineteenth century, intensified ideologies today make highly probable another failure—even if it were possible to transform the present loose bipolar system into a balance-of-power one. Instead, in this century, there have been two attempts to devise another strategy for security—"collective security." The League of Nations was to be a place where parties to a dispute might meet and resolve their differences. It provided for "cooling off" periods to allow human rationality to reassert itself and resolve all conflicts. The assumptions of human rationality and efficacy of discussion collapsed under the supranational designs of Italy and Germany. Nevertheless, as early as 1942, President Roosevelt initiated a group to study and plan for the postwar world and again discussion focused on the development of some kind of collective institutional arrangement that might achieve the elusive goal of security. The other alternatives — unilateral, bilateral or multilateral, and balance-of-power systems — were rejected; the search focused on redesigning and improving a collective arrangement for international security.

A thorough analysis of the United Nations San Francisco Conference's minutes and reports indicates that the delegates had a number of vague and sometimes ambiguous ideas concerning the prerequisite for a collective security system (Moore 1967). It is not surprising, then, that the UN Charter provides for both collective security arrangements as well as for unilateral and regional defensive systems. A "chain-of-logic" led to veto power for the "Big Five" over Security Council decisions, for if there were serious disagreement between permanent members of the council, war was probable if actions were taken that were unacceptable to one or more of the five.

Prerequisites for Collective Security

What are the prerequisites for a collective security system? Can we rely on collective arrangements backed up by regional ones? Can we rely on such systems enough not to build or position some weapons system — relying on the regional or collective system? If a collective security system is to be realizable and reliable, what criteria must be satisfied?

Table 23.1 presents nine objective and subjective criteria that must be met. Because of the focus of this study, we cannot explore these prerequisites in detail. It should be noted, however, that the United States has never been able to agree on (1) a definition of *aggression* or (2) that it is totally undesirable or (3) that member nations must subordinate individual goals to the ultimate goal of collective security. Furthermore, although membership has expanded to 157 nations, there are still nations that desire to belong that have been excluded for ideological reasons. Today, with competing economic and political ideologies, ancient historical enmities, and widespread rejection of the present status quo by both Marxists and many Third World nations (objective criterion 4), the attainability of these criteria seems ever more remote.

The keystone of a successful collective security system appears to be subjective criterion 9 — confidence in the system and its members. Given the history in internation behavior since the Treaty of Westphalia (1648),

TABLE 23.1: Criteria for a Viable Collective Security System

Objective Criteria	*Subjective Criteria*
1. Agreement on the definition of *aggression*.	1. Agreement on value judgment that war "ought" to be prevented.
2. Agreement that aggression is *totally* undesirable.	2. Agreement on the value judgment that force is low on the scale of response of international disputes.
3. All within the system are willing to subordinate national goals for the goal of collective security.	3. High level of commitment to and for peace.
4. All members have the *same* conception of security—the *status quo.* (a) Agreement on definition of status quo. (b) Agreement to permit peaceful change.	4. Isolationism is rejected.
5. *Open to all* nations desiring to join the system, in contrast to a closed system; e.g., regional alliances such as NATO.	5. Rejection of self-help and the individual use of force.
6. The system must *function impartially*; i.e., no other values or ideologies can be permitted to hamper the system.	6. Principle of *universal concern.*
7. *Automatic universal community reaction* to aggression, regardless of ideological considerations.	7. Agreement on the status quo allowing for peaceful change, and domestic revolutionary change.
8. Response is *predictable*—guaranteed.	8. Submerging of national core interests (an objective criterion also).
9. *Preponderance of power* is on the side of the collective status quo. (a) International power is diffused, in contrast to polarization or the monopolization of power. (b) Economic vulnerability of all nations to sanctions short of physical force.	9. *Confidence* in the system.

there is abundant evidence for legitimate distrust. Objective criterion 3—
that all within the system are willing to subordinate their individual nation-
state goals for the paramount goal of collective security—seems to be ruled
out by a long history of nation-state behavior combined with twentieth-
century ideological conflict (Taylor 1954).

The criteria for a collective security system have not been, and are not
likely to be, realized in the real political world. Thus since the early 1950s,
the United States has turned to nuclear weaponry and deterrence theory
for national security. A balance of terror, mutually assured destruction,
first and second strike capability, launch on warning, etc., are concepts that
have dominated strategic security theorizing for more that a quarter century. Is this the approach the United States should utilize in its search for
security? Obviously no way is without dangers. No way guarantees security.
While neither of the major nuclear powers is willing to meet the criteria of
a truly viable collective security system, evidence is mounting that any full-
scale resort to the use of nuclear weapons would also be fatal to the initiator
of such an action, as it would fall victim to the nuclear winter and the
destruction of the biosphere's web of life. Apparently the only security in
nuclear deterrence ultimately resides in its nonuse.

What, then, does security mean? What is the optimum marginalization
of military strength when compared with other key ingredients of national
power-security? President Eisenhower wrote in April 1956 to Richard L.
Simon, president of Simon and Schuster, the following:

> . . . I doubt that any columnist . . . is concerning himself with what is
> the true security problem of the day. That problem is not merely man
> against man or nation against nation. It is man against war.
>
> I have spent my life in the study of military strength as a deterrent to
> war and in the character of military armament necessary to win a war.
> The study of the first of these questions is still profitable, but we are
> rapidly getting to the point that no war can be won. War implies a con-
> test; when you get to the point that contest is no longer involved and the
> outlook comes close to destruction of the enemy and suicide for
> ourselves—an outlook that neither side can ignore—then arguments as
> to the exact amount of available strength as compared to somebody else's
> are no longer the vital issues.
>
> When we get to the point, as we one day will, that both sides know that
> in any outbreak of general hostilities, regardless of the element of sur-
> prise, destruction will be both reciprocal and complete, possibly we will
> have sense enough to meet at the conference table with the understand-
> ing that the era of armaments has ended and the human race must con-
> form its action to this truth or die.
>
> . . . I do not, by any means, decry the need for strength. That strength
> must be spiritual, economic and military. All three are important and
> they are not mutually exclusive.
>
> But already, we have come to the point where safety cannot be assumed
> by arms alone. . . . (Greenstein 1983)

Economics and Security

Given the history of internation behavior and the failure of the various approaches to national security (although deterrence has so far lasted for thirty years), any attempt to freeze or reduce the destrucitve capability (nuclear, gas, or germ) of the superpowers must follow or be concurrent with efforts to develop greater communication and confidence between the opposing sides. All proposals, of course, will need to be mutual and verifiable. But it is obvious that the definition of *security* must be broadened. True security requires more than the threat of mutually assured destruction or a nuclear winter. Military expenditures alone cannot purchase security. Might not greater security be purchased by trying to address some of the unjust social and economic problems of our planet? The root causes of war are political. National and international security will not be achieved until the causes of conflict and war are addressed and at least partially resolved. It is also overwhelmingly obvious that the United States does not have unlimited resources. Thus the issue of security, and the correlated questions, pose issues of values and priorities that must be examined within a context of resource scarcity.

The gross inequalities between North and South and the present socioeconomic injustices in the international trade and finance system must be rectified for there to be any serious hope for peace and security. The present status quo is unacceptable to the vast majority of the Third World peoples (see Table 23.1). Repeatedly during the past decade the Third World nations have demanded a new international economic order. That these demands have substance can be seen in that they have been echoed by individuals predisposed to be friendly to the Western democracies, such as Gunnar Myrdal, Raoul Prebisch, the Sprouts, and Willy Brandt. But it has been twenty-six years since the United Nations Conference on Trade and Development (UNCTAD) was established in 1964— despite the opposition of the Western developed nations—and its repeated calls for greater economic fairness have largely gone unanswered.

We are confronted by two questions in particular: To what extent is security obtained through primarily military expenditures? Could greater security be achieved by attempting to ameliorate the social and economic inequalities within the international system—thus increasing confidence between and within the members of the system while making the status quo more acceptable to all? These issues are not either-or; they represent continua. We are forced to weigh our *goals and resources* vis-à-vis one another. Hans Morganthau (1961:143) noted:

> Good government, then, must start by performing two different intellectual operations. First, it must choose the objectives and methods of

its foreign policy in view of the power available to support them with maximum chance of success.

We want to buy the maximum security possible within the constraints of *scarce resources and multiple national goals.* If we totally maximize one goal, our other goals may suffer. Have we maximized our military preparedness (a key component of national power) at the expense of other elements that jointly comprise national power, such as national morale and diplomacy? Are domestic cuts so deep as to hurt national morale—or the morale of the minority members within the military itself? Is our foreign aid so insufficient in comparison with needs that the quality of our diplomacy is undermined?

The relation between economic well-being and peace, between gross inequalities and conflict, has been recognized since Aristotle. He believed that the distribution of wealth within a community was important; the richest individuals in a polity should be only four times as wealthy as the poorest—otherwise enmity and class warfare would develop. Also after having examined more than one hundred political communities, he felt that either a too poor or too rich community would have an adverse impact on the moral substratum of its citizens and laws. President Roosevelt arrived at the same conclusion and assigned American planners in 1942 to consider methods, strategies, and institutions that could help remedy the social and economic problems of the postwar world. Permanent peace would be unattainable unless the basic needs of all humankind were met (Moore 1967).

Forty-eight years later, Third World social and economic needs have worsened rather than improved. The gross inequalities between North and South are steadily widening (Mesarovic and Pestel 1974). An international communications revolution will soon make this gap all too obvious to hundreds of millions of people. And as their resources become increasingly valuable with the exhaustion of the North's, their leverage will increase. Our failure to support massively their development attempts has reaped and will reap a harvest of antipathy and hatred toward us. This is *not* a good foundation upon which to seek security. The widening gap cannot be allowed to continue. If we fail to act and it does worsen, then insecurity for the world and the United States is probable. "The United States will not be truly secure unless the people of the world are reasonably secure also" (Vanderslice 1982).

President Reagan, sadly, all too well typified the values of many in the present administration when he counseled the twenty developing countries (and by implication all Third World countries) present at Mazatlan, Mexico, in May 1981 to go forth and raise themselves up by their own efforts— just as we did. His counsel was neither historical nor wise. The United

States was exceptionally endowed with massive unexploited resources (stolen from the aboriginal inhabitants), a temperate climate, some of the most productive soils on the planet, *and* much investment capital at low interest rates from Europe during the nineteenth century. Furthermore, we did not have to suffer the kind of colonial rule that most present developing countries experienced. Colonialism had severe deleterious effects on the societies and cultures of the oppressed nations. It bred dependency, lack of leadership, corruption, antiagricultural development attitudes, rejection of technical and applied education (Myrdal 1970). President Reagan's comments could not help but produce a negative response from informed Third World listeners. His advice was essentially to say to the cold and starving, "Go in peace, be warmed and filled." However, the apostle James asserts, "Without giving them the things needed for the body, what does it profit?" (James 2:16). Reagan's unempathetic, actionless words could only engender anger. Self-centered parochialism reaps only a harvest of hostility.

Third World Development Needs

Most Third World countries are severely handicapped in ways that the present developed countries (DCs) are not. Indeed, because of their desperate straits, the developing countries are forced to bid against one another to market their mineral wealth as well as their labor. If they attempt to get a higher price for their labor, they may be eliminated by mechanization—or by the departure of Western businesses to another poor country offering tax breaks and even lower wages. Out of their desperate poverty and the corruption of their leaders, often very poor economic agreements are made with the multinational corporations (MNCs) of the DCs. All in all, the obstacles to social and economic betterment for most Third World countries are almost overwhelming. The result is an ever-increasing gap between the DCs and the developing Third World and the nondeveloping "Fourth World."

The poverty of the world is staggering. The poorest 60 percent (2.4 billion people) in 1975 "had only 9 percent of the world's aggregate product" (World Bank 1981). Since then, the situation has actually *deteriorated* because of (1) the increases in the cost of oil, (2) the international recession, and (3) the decrease in loans and grants from the DCs. The World Bank's *World Development Report 1981* states that even with *the best scenario*, "average per capita incomes are expected to grow by only 1.8 percent a year in the low-income oil importers, compared to 3.4 percent in the middle-income oil importers and 3.1 percent a year in the industrial countries." Half the world population does not have clean water to drink; 12 million babies die annually because of malnutrition and malnutrition-related diseases; and while the richest 20 percent of the planet has 120 percent of daily caloric requirements, the poorest 20 percent has 86 percent of the daily requirement—and even this is dropping (Sivard 1982). Security Pacific's *Trends* projects that from 1975 to 2000, population growth will outrace agricultural production (even though this will grow approximately by 37 percent) and that calorie consumption per person will drop from about 2,140 to under 1,600 calories per person per day.

Can the United States reasonably expect to remain isolated from the probable turmoil that will result from worsening conditions among three-fifths of the world's people? We think not. Mesarovic and Pestel's model shows that the first region of the world to suffer "collapse" is Southeast Asia (Mesarovic and Pestel 1974). They do not believe that the United States will be unaffected by such a catastrophe; furthermore, additional regions will eventually suffer the same fate. Mesarovic, and the fifty-five other scholars that participated in this project, believe that massive transfers of funds are necessary from the DCs to the UDCs in order (1) to stave off this possibility and begin narrowing the gap, so that (2) the Third World will continue to allow the DCs access to their raw materials. The funds that could be transferred to the projects in UDC are staggering—ranging from $2 trillion in 1975 to over $10.7 trillion if we delay action until 2005 (Mesarovic and Pestel 1974). In the end they question whether there are enough raw materials on the planet to allow such massive development— for the DCs would still be growing even as the Third World economies begin to narrow the gap. They observe that "if a material is in a finite supply, it is more appropriate to consider it as a 'stock' that is being depleted" (Mesarovic and Pestel 1974:67).

Mesarovic and Pestel (1974:68–69) concluded:

> If every nation were to use oil at the same per-capita rate as the developed world, our computer simulation indicates that the entire world reserves would be used by 1982; if oil discoveries continued at that same rate as in the preceding decades, the reserves would be exhausted by 1985....
> *The industrialized world is thus granted the time to develop alternative energy sources only by using nearly the entire world oil reserves and by the action pre-empting the supply.*
> ...Whether there should be maximum limits on consumption of materials which have finite reserves ... industrialized regions put a stop to further overdevelopment by accepting limits on per-capita use of finite resources.... Unless this lesson is learned in time, there will be a thousand desperadoes terrorizing those who are now 'rich,' and eventually nuclear blackmail and terror will paralyze further orderly development. [emphasis theirs]

Because of their poverty, the governments of the poor nations are vulnerable to corruption, to capital flight, and to increasing military expenditures—to keep their own citizens in line. During the 1970s the military weaponry the United States exported to UDCs grew from less than $2 billion a year to over $12 billion (Sivard 1982). Where there has been some development, as in Brazil, too often a few at the top have received the benefit while the many have not. The poorest 60 percent in Brazil are worse off today than they were in 1964 when the United States encouraged the overthrow of the democratically elected Kubitschek government. Since then, the United States has consistently supported the military dictatorship there, in spite of its well-publicized repressive actions.

One strategy the United States can opt for is to support corruptible repressive regimes, gambling that they will be able to maintain themselves indefinitely in power, financially and militarily supporting their repression in anticipation that revolution will not succeed. If successful—i.e., if the repressed people are unable physically or psychologically to initiate and sustain revolutions—then this may be a less financially costly strategy (though damaging to our ideology and image of ourselves) than a long-term developmental alternative. If successful. . . . If not, then it could be *exceedingly costly*, including alienation of many if not most Third World nations and even the loss of access to some raw materials. This appears to be the strategy we have consciously pursued in Central America for much of this century. Now in Nicaragua and El Salvador we are paying the price. This "they're-our-bastards" strategy will encourage the spread of communism, terrorism, and instability. It is unlikely, but it may succeed. It is, of course, incompatible with our historical pretensions of fairness, justice, and democracy, and the tension between our exalted goals and our expedient behavior may be greater than can be bridged by any governmental propaganda.

A Developmentalist Alternative

There are some critical uses for the resourcces presently available to the United States government other than military expenditures. There are long-term domestic and planetary crises that need to be considered. In response to the above-sketched "megacrises," budget priorities need to be critically reexamined. Our global strategies for security must be reconsidered in the light of finite planetary resources. It is imperative that a better balance be struck between foreign economic aid for Third World development and military aid and sales. The stopgap spending bill passed November 12, 1983, included $11.5 billion in foreign aid appropriations—in contrast to the more than $12 billion in weaponry sales in 1979 (Wood and Irwin 1983).

Assuming that it is a poor long-term Pascalian wager to identify the United States with corrupt repressive regimes because the consequences of failure of such a strategy would be too great (as well as unacceptable to the morality and ideology of the United States), another strategy must be adopted. We believe that greater wisdom, as well as security, lies in a developmentalist strategy—a long-term program to ameliorate conditions conducive to the spread of hostile ideologies and socioeconomic instability in the Third World.

A *first* step toward such a strategy would be the *discouragement of corruption* in any relations between public and private U.S. institutions and Third World nations and institutions. Mydral has termed these countries "soft states," because rampant corruption undermines the ability of these nations to get citizen support for developmental programs and for the kinds of cultural changes that must occur if they are to make economic advances (Myrdal 1970; see Appendix B). Too often Western corporations encourage corruption. Under the Carter administration the United States took a strong stand against corporate bribes; under the Reagan administration it was legal to "grease" the wheels of business if this was part of the "normal customs" of a country. In the long run this will have very negative developmental consequences, and in all likelihood, disastrous political consequences.

Second, because Western governments and businesses align themselves with corrupt ruling elites—for example, the Marcos regime—counterelites have been driven away from the West. Mass activity is usually interpreted as threatening and communist-inspired rather than expected nationalistic reactions to repressive corrupt regimes. The United States must adopt a more realistic, broader long-term perspective. It must cease to support repressive regimes tacitly. It must stop permitting our business corporations to operate without restraint from our government. Most people of the Third World do not understand or accept the distinction between policies of the United States and policies of United States–based corporations. Our corporations are perceived as the United States. We may protest. We may claim that our "free enterprise" ideology means that U.S. corporations are completely independent and uncontrolled by our government. But such protestations fall on deaf ears. If our corporations extract obscene profits from their overseas enterprises, if they draft unfair contracts with the leaders of Third World nations, these actions are *attributed* to the United States. We *are* blamed for their actions. And in the end, when our corporations are expropriated because of such behavior, their calls for U.S. governmental intervention belie their earlier declarations of nongovernmental control. It is time for national policymakers to recognize that *we cannot have it both ways* (Mueller and Barnet 1974).

Third, United States military expenditures must be reexamined in light of the long-term planetary crises projected by the MIT team, the Mesarovic-Pestel group, Lester Brown and Worldwatch, and others. The Reagan administration proposed a $1.6 trillion military budget over five years. In contrast, there has been virtually no increase in real dollars for economic assistance. The $11-plus billion in aid for FY 1984 included military as well as economic aid—and over $4 billion was to go to two countries, Egypt and Israel. NATO expenditures have grown from $100 billion to over $400 billion between 1960 and 1980; in contrast, NATO's foreign economic aid grew during those decades from less than $10 to approximately $25 billion (Sivard 1982; the figure $25 billion is deceptive—it includes loans that must be repaid). Strong leadership is needed from the president if the Congress is to break out of its two-year election mentality and realistically address the long-term crises of our planet—including the absolute need to begin to reduce the gap between the DCs and UDCs. Security, true security, must weigh many factors other than short-term military hardware procurements. MX missiles must be weighed vis-à-vis financing much needed population control programs, against the need to reforest, against the need to stop the expansion of the planet's deserts, etc.

The problem of military expenditures has not only a domestic focus but a Third World focus as well, namely, the military expenditures by the UDCs themselves. We have already noted the increase in U.S. military sales, as well as the sales of all military suppliers. Ruth Sivard (1982) has detailed the growth in such sales, the increase in Third World military personnel (from 8.7 to 15.1 million in the past twenty years), and the increase in the number of military-dominated Third World governments. Many in the world suffer repression because of the actions (military sales, loans, outright grants, training in the conduct of "small wars," i.e., prevention of the reestablishment of civilian control) of Western nations that claim to be freedom-loving. The result is that *counterelites are driven to seek support from wherever it is forthcoming*—and the Communist regimes of the world are only too glad to comply.

In sum, military sales to developing countries should be drastically cut. The burden of proof must be *against* such sales. Our goal should be to reduce our sales to the $2 billion range of 1970 while pressuring other Western countries to do the same. In addition, the UDCs should be "bribed" not to spend their limited capital on military expenditures; for example, we might double or triple our economic aid to countries that reduce their military budgets. Regardless of the formula, we must seek to balance our trade deficit some other way.

Fourth, much greater economic aid needs to be channeled to the UDCs. Loans with low interest rates, such as the U.S. received during the nineteenth century, and especially outright grants are imperative. Presently our military expenditures are increasing while our foreign aid as a fraction of our GNP is dropping. In 1967, the United States supported the United Nation's adoption of the Pearson Report, which called upon the DCs to accept the goal of giving 1 percent of their GNPs to the UDCs. Since then, the United States' percentage has dropped from .37 to less than .15 of 1 percent. While in gross amounts the United States contributes the most money, in terms of percentages (based on GNP), the United States has dropped to last among seventeen Western aid-giving nations (Sider 1978).

Aid should be channeled through multinational institutions wherever possible to avoid the generation of negative reactions that receivers sometimes have to their donors, to reduce corruption, and to allow a third party, the World Bank for instance, to supervise the manner in which the recipient nations carry out their proposed projects. The use of private relief organizations and church-related organizations ought to be explored. Aid to Uganda, for instance, might use the Anglican Church of Uganda as a major conduit—thereby reducing wastage and corruption.

Fifth, agricultural research and aid should be emphasized. Evidence is mounting that development should first focus on increasing agricultural productivity (Myrdal 1970). At present, much UDC development results in little enclaves, like raisins inside a loaf of poverty and nondevelopment. A more rational strategy would be to encourage "appropriate technology," i.e., agricultural-centered manufacturing of steel plows, irrigation pipe, etc. In much of the world the steel plow would be a major advance—and the manufacture of the plows could stimulate a small steel industry as well. Agricultural research centers need to be established and maintained around the world—centers that will do research adapted to the soils and climates of the UDCs. Temperate zone agriculture does not necessarily transfer automatically to other areas of the world.

Sixth, the Third World desperately needs agricultural skills, while the United States has a surplus of such skills. Annually, thousands of U.S. farmers are forced to leave farming against their desires. The United States should establish an Agricultural Peace Corps consisting solely of farmers receiving attractive salaries whose task would be to assist in the transfer of agricultural skills and technology by living in the UDCs. Private efforts (such as those of the Heifer Project International, which sends superior breeding stock overseas to improve Third World heads, and Dr. Martin Price of ECHO [Education Concerns for Hunger Organization] who sends underutilized grains, fruit trees, etc., adaptable to the tropics and to marginal agricultural lands) must be supported with government funding.

The most basic freedom that humanity seeks is freedom from hunger. If the peoples of the world are not fed by their present socioeconomic arrangements, then they must seek other arrangements.

Seventh, population control must be encouraged, financed, and expanded. Many nations are so poor that they cannot develop birth-control programs by themselves. The U.S. budget should be *unlimited* in this sphere. If called upon to help, the United States should design, produce, and help distribute the necessary materials. It should fund the native workers of any and all nations desiring to control their population increases.

There are, of course, many other things that need to be done, from educational reforms to recycling of resources, and they all need to be done now. Nevertheless, a *systems approach to long-term development* must be adopted and given the *highest priority.* Long-term planetary security lies in this direction—not in the spending of another $100 billion for another weapons system. Military security is important, but long-term survival of civilization is more important. Military expenditures must be much more carefully weighed against other pressing needs in this world of scarcity than they have heretofore.

A Case Study: Brazil and Central America

This is not the place for a tedious recounting of the United States' numerous military incursions into Central America, the Caribbean basin, and elsewhere in Latin America. Too often the United States has made a Pavlovian response when entrenched elites have screamed "communism" at all attempts to bring any change to their systems. They see any proposal for change as Communist-inspired. And the United States has been only too ready to rush in and lend military assistance to the ruling oligarchs. We have consistently been identified with repressive terroristic regimes. In the short run this may have been somewhat successful, but in the long run it has forced all potential counterelites to look elsewhere for support for change—increasing the probability that future revolutionary movements will be Marxist.

How, in midstream, can the United States switch strategies—from support of right-wing reactionary regimes to a long-term development strategy? It will not be easy, and some failures will occur in the short run. Nicaragua has finally held a free election and a democratically elected president is in office. In order to assist the newly elected government to survive, we can assist in agriculture and industry. We can offer them exceptionally good trade terms, student exchanges, etc. We can *operate on a two-decade rather than two-year timetable,* fully expecting that the leaders of Nicaragua are not stupid and that they can see that the Soviet and Eastern European economic development strategy has been a failure. Confident in our own economic and democratic philosophy, we can proceed to help in such a way that twenty years from now there will exist a reciprocal respect between the leaders of our two nations and that the reduction of the poverty gap and the ongoing progress within Nicaragua will end any threat of Marxism. We can channel aid through the Christian community of Nicaragua. Our technicians will be displaced American farmers from the Midwest and South, not disguised CIA agents. Aid, consistency of purpose, mutual respect that permits disagreements over instrumental means and goals, and a long-term perspective would produce a Nicaragua that would not be hostile to the United States' broader world goals, while free to disagree with us as a sovereign nation.

In Guatemala, the United States should align itself with the revolutionary movement. Again, using the developmental strategy outlined earlier, the United States should encourage development where possible. Private and religious groups should again be channels for massive amounts of aid. Quietly the ruling oligarchy should be offered sizable bribes and U.S. citizenship to leave the country; $500 million to $1 billion to get the reactionary elite of Guatemala and El Salvador to emigrate could well be a bargain investment. We should tacitly convey to the elites and counter-elites of Guatemala that we will massively support progressive democratic change and will oppose the forces supporting the status quo.

Given the *historical baggage* that accompanies the United States in its relations with Central America, a past that we would like to forget but which Central America cannot, we should not be surprised if our motives are questioned and that successes are rare in the beginning. The developmental strategy is a long-term strategy. It requires the United States to stop throwing its military weight around and instead to act as a concerned assistant. It requires the United States to put some controls on its multinational corporations—forcing them to become socially responsible beyond their present behavior, even in this country. Failures will occur. A decade may pass before many Latinos can begin to trust the United States. But unless we begin to identify ourselves with the legitimate desires of the masses in Central America for an end to excruciating poverty, terror, and voicelessness, *we will find the economic cost of trying to stop change increasingly expensive and unlimited in duration.* And eventually we will reap a harvest of hostile anti–American regimes that will attempt to spread their hostility closer to home—in Mexico.

Brazil typifies the successes and failures of the "they're-our-bastards" strategy. Its GNP is the eighth largest in the world, and Brazilian executives are among the highest paid in the world (Meadows 1981). During the late 1960s the Brazilian economy grew at an incredible rate of 11.1 percent per year, yet the calorie intake of the peasants in the northeastern part of the country has fallen to a level that is about one-half the United Nation's prescribed minimum level of nutrition. Two-thirds of the salaried workers in Rio de Janeiro earn less than $100 a week, and Brazil's minimum salary of $25 a week is the second lowest in Latin America (Weil 1982). In the agricultural sector, 1 percent of the country's farmers own 43 percent of the land, whereas 52 percent of the country's farmers occupy only 3 percent of the land (Fishlow 1980).

In 1964, the military overthrew the Goulart administration and imposed a military dictatorship. To what extent the United States was involved in this coup is not clear; however, "after the 1964 coup the greater availability of exchange for investors was an incentive and aid did signal Washington's approval of the new situation" (Kaplan and Bonsor 1973). Peasant unions, worker political parties, and nonagricultural unions were either dismantled or put under "firm" control (Brook 1981). Numerous political leaders, including three former presidents, lost their political rights. The poor and a large part of the working class have neither political nor economic power. It is presently illegal for illiterates to vote in Brazil, which includes over 30 percent of the adult population (Fishlow 1980).

Today, Brazil faces severe internal political and socioeconomic problems. Strict IMF loan requirements have triggered food riots and demonstrations for the direct election of the president. Kaplan and Bonsor (1973:46) noted:

> It is already reasonable to consider the existence of two Brazils: one in which the larger portion of the populace lives and which has remained relatively stagnant and attached to primary agriculture; the other, in which there is a slowly growing middle class . . . aligning itself with advanced Western economies.

Today, 60 percent of the Brazilian people are worse off than twenty years ago. The nation is internally divided. Too many governmental decisions benefit only the minority. How long can this minority, supported by an oppressive military using terror and torture, maintain control? Should the United States identify itself with that minority? A "they're-our-bastards" strategy may be the best in the short run, but only in the short run.

We believe that in the long run, the developmentalist strategy will provide the United States with greater security in the twenty-first century from war, threats of terrorism, and the spread of hostile economic and political ideologies. Gross inequalities in a society are inherently destabilizing. We believe that inequality in a society can be justified only if it works to the advantage of the least-well-off member of that society when compared to what any other alternative might provide. If differences in incomes are necessary to induce people to increase the national output, and if as a result of the output the incomes of the poorest groups of the community are raised, then the policy is justified. But when two nations develop within one, then the probability of, and justification for, revolutionary change have been created. All of the Brazilian society should be getting some economic improvements; economic sacrifices should not be borne by only one segment of a healthy society. When one part of society has the second highest salaries in the world and another part, the majority, is worse off, then the perfect prescription for revolution has been written.

The developmentalist strategy is concerned about the "health," the viability, of the entire society—its culture, politics, values, etc. A redistribution of wealth with continued economic growth through tax reform and land reform is required. In a democratic society such reforms can be accomplished only under the following conditions: 1. That the wealthier minority see that its long-term interests are served by some reduction in their present wealth to diminish social inequalities that cannot be sustained in the long run; and 2. That the political power also be dispersed and redistributed so that public policy is a compromise in which benefits and sacrifices are borne in a more equitable fashion, rather than a zero-sum manner.

If the United States desires peace and security in the future, then it will assess its international relations so the long-term outweighs the short-term considerations. It will aid Brazil economically but not militarily (Black 1977). It will encourage population control, literacy, agrarian reform, etc. It will encourage a reciprocity between itself and Brazil based upon common concerns. And it will expect disagreement in policy to occur without panicking.

Appendix A

The Differences Between Conditions When the Developed World Developed, 1700–1940, and Those Confronting the Third World Today*

A. Today's developed countries (DCs) were independent consolidated states with generally similar cultures, broad rationalistic and pro-change traditions. Most underdeveloped countries (UDCs) are *recently independent not consolidated states administratively* capable of pursing national politics effectively.

B. Because of the Renaissance, Reformation, Enlightenment, and exploratory expositions of the European world, the DCs had *changes in attitude and institutions,* with widened intellectual and emotional horizons, *slowly over time.* Most UDCs' educated classes adopted modernization ideals, but these are not indigenous and are often resisted by the masses, who are *tradition-bound.* Yet change must be rapid.

C. The UDCs are often less well endowed with natural resources than the DCs were when they began modernization.

D. All successful industrialization has taken place in temperate zones; most UDCs are in tropical and subtropical zones. Extremes of heat and humidity contribute to a decrease in human productivity and help deteriorate material goods and soils. Climate can slow development.

E. The UDCs confront much *higher man-land ratios* than the DCs confronted. Most are *overpopulated* in terms of their natural resources.

F. Most UDCs have much *higher population growth rates* than the DCs, with their populations doubling in twenty to thirty years—*straining social infrastructures* with a large dependent population under fifteen years of age.

G. Latecomers are at a *trade disadvantage.* Since World War I most UDCs trading positions have *deteriorated.* International trade was an engine of growth in the DCs.

1. Rapid technological development in the DCs has slowed down the rise

*See Gunnar Myrdal, *The Challenge of World Poverty* (1970), for a discussion of most of these factors.

315

of demand for primary products other than oil—reducing raw material imports. 2. *Protectionism* has increased in most DCs. 3. Industrial substitutions have been developed. 4. Many DCs have *discriminatory tariffs*. 5. The entrenched industries in the DCs operate under markedly superior conditions; e.g., advance skills in producing and selling products, heavy national investment in research, and even more rapid advances in technology, etc. 6. The most important needs of UDCs are rising—from food to development goods. 7. Most UDCs have *balance of trade deficits*, with increasing burdens of interest payments (e.g., Mexico and Brazil's debts are $85 to $95 billion). 8. Many UDCs *lack political stability* since independence. 9. *Decreasing* amounts of *grants* and interest-free/low-interest loans; interest rates more than double historical rates available to the DCs when they developed. 10. The UDCs bid against one another, offering multinational corporations (MNCs) low wages, low taxes, and stability through suppression of their citizenry. 11. Many MNCs are larger and more economically powerful than their host UDCs. MNCs can often deal with corrupt leaderships to their mutual benefit, while the masses suffer. 12. Poverty-stricken, demoralized, and suppressed masses are often less productive; badly needed capital is diverted for military expenditures to keep the masses intimidated. 13. Widespread governmental and nongovernmental corruption is a cancer in most UDCs—and it is often encouraged by the business community of the DCs.

Appendix B
Inequality, Corruption, and Third World Development*

A. Many Western economists, according to Myrdal, assume a conflict between economic growth and egalitarian reforms; a price has to be paid for reforms, and it is often prohibitive for poor nations. 1. Western economists' preconceptions that social justice would have to be sacrificed for economic growth have been used to support the status quo of highly inegalitarian-authoritarian Third World countries. 2. However, large-scale egalitarian reform policies have been initiated in all of the developed countries (DCs)—first supported in terms of greater social justice, but were later found to be the basis for more steady and rapid economic growth.

B. Myrdal believes that greater equality in underdeveloped countries (UDCs) is a condition for more rapid growth. 1. In UDCs it is common for landlords and the rich to squander their incomes in conspicuous consumption and investment, or in capital flight. 2. In UDCs large masses of people suffer from undernutrition and malnutrition. This impairs their willingness and ability to work productively. 3. Social inequality is tied to economic inequality, affects the entire society, education and illiteracy efforts, and impedes development. 4. Greater equality should positively affect national integration—help the nation-state to consolidate, and permit the development of rational planning for societal needs. 5. Greater equality should improve nutrition and raise productivity. 6. Inequality acts as a powerful disincentive to public participation in development. 7. At very low economic levels, there will be little room for human generosity, with a stronger need for maintaining social distinctions. "When the trough is empty, the horses will bite each other." This reinforces inequality, leads to military suppression of the many by the few, more social injustice, and almost creates of necessity a revolutionary situation that can be exploited by movements such as communism. 8. The masses are mostly passive and

---

* These comments are based on many sources, but perhaps most heavily on Gunnar Myrdal, *The Challenge of World Poverty* (1970).

inarticulate, but they can be brought to riots and mob violence by religious fanaticism, ethnic prejudices and economic cleaveges.

C. Western governments and business usually align themselves with the ruling few; thus mass activity easily becomes allied with communism. Economic exploitation, often by U.S. business, drives people to communism.

D. Because new nationalisms are resentful, they tend to be anti-Western and anti-white. They are easily spread among the masses.

E. Colonialism and neocolonialism almost always are allied with the economic and social status quo, hindering development and modernization.

F. Inequality is associated with low agricultural yields and consequently causes serious nutritional deficiences, and thus low productivity, i.e., low yields — circular causation.

G. Everywhere in the UDCs, there is need for the type of additional labor input that is really investment in future productivity, i.e., building roads, irrigation systems, etc. But these presuppose collective action and organization — which are often absent in highly inegalitarian, faction-ridden villages, or peasants working for absentee landlords.

H. What is needed is an overall improvement in farming methods, accompanied by *many* induced *changes applied simultaneously*. But these will not be achieved without *land reform* to create a situation where the peasantry feels the incentive and opportunity to exert itself very much. But the land is owned by the few, who also control the government and the military. Thus the probability is that a greedy, irrational (in the sense of short-term) elite will not make the changes necessary to avert societal disruption, violence, and revolution.

I. The DCs' main responsibility is not to strengthen the powerful vested interests that have been delaying or stopping the necessary reforms in the UDCs. The United States, for example, must recognize that revolutionary movements in countries like El Salvador are not necessarily communist and that if they are supported, they might reform the system and be long-term pro-Western in their orientation.

J. The DCs can also assist in technological and management skills transfers, and on agricultural-related research adapted to the tropic and subtropic zones. Emergency aid, infrastructural aid such as the planting of forests, and economic trade restructuring should be emphasized, while military aid should be virtually eliminated.

Bibliography

Abbott, W. S. J. 1966. *The Documents of Vatican II.* New York: Guild Press.

Abdussalam, M. 1983. "The Practical Application of Food Safety Criteria in Developing Countries." *Food and Nutrition Bulletin,* 9(2):24.

Aboyade, O. 1987. "Growth Strategy and the Agricultural Sector." In Christopher L. Delgado, John W. Mellor, and Malcolm J. Blackie (eds.), *Accelerating Food Production in Sub-Saharan Africa.* Baltimore: John Hopkins University Press.

Adamu, Mahdi. 1968. "A Hausa Government in Decline. Yauri in the Nineteenth Century." Zaria: Ahmadu Bello University. M.A. dissertation (history), mimeo.

Adedeji, Adebayo, and Timothy M. Shaw. 1985. *Economic Crisis in Africa.* Boulder: Lynne Rienner Publisher, Inc.

Adepoju, J. A. 1974. "Rural-Urban Socio-Economic Links Between Urban Migrants and Their Home Communities in Nigeria." *Africa,* 44:383–395.

Adler, N. J. 1986. *International Dimensions of Organizational Behavior.* Boston: Kent Publishing Co.

African Business. 1987a. Zambian Bus Firms Queue for Forex." July: 5.

_____. 1987b. "Agro-Industries Are Feeling the Pinch." August: 20–21.

_____. 1987c. "Import Substitution Hits Nigerian Breweries." July: 66.

_____. 1987d. "Urban Somalis Prefer Easy Grains." August: 45.

Ahearne, John F. 1986. "Three Mile Island and Bhopal: Lessons Learned and Not Learned." In *National Academy of Engineering, Hazards: Technology and Fairness,* Washington, D.C.: National Academy Press.

Aird, J.S. 1985. "Coercion in Family Planning: Causes, Methods and Consequences." *Congressional Record.* U.S. Senate, June 7, S 7776–7778.

Ake, C. 1967. "Political Integration and Political Stability: A Hypothesis." *World Politics,* 19:486–499.

_____. 1985. *Political Economy of Nigeria.* London: Longman Press.

Alexander, William M. 1984. "American Church Politics in Behalf of the Hungry in the Late-Developing Countries." Sacramento: Paper Presented to the Annual Meeting of the Western Political Science Association.

Amin, Nazem. 1985. "Presentation: Meeting of the Executive Leaders from the PDP Governorates Between 15–17 September, 1984." *Population Studies,* 12:63–67.

Amin, S. 1967. *Le Capitalisme en Côte d'Ivoire.* Paris: Minuit.

_____. 1974. *Modern Migrations in Western Africa.* Oxford: Oxford University Press.

_____. 1980. *Class and Nation Historically and in the Present Crisis.* New York: Monthly Review Press.

Anderson, J. 1979. *Public Policy Making.* New York: Holt, Reinhart and Winston.

Andrae, Gunilla, and Bjorn Beckman. 1985. *The Wheat Trap: Bread and Underdevelopment in Nigeria.* London: Zed.

Anon. 1985. "Confidential Indian Report Blames Both US Firm and Subsidiary for Bhopal Disaster." *Mizingira*, 8(6):30.

Apter, D. 1955. "Political Democracy in the Gold Coast." In Calvin, W. (ed.), *Africa in the Modern World*. Chicago: University of Chicago Press.

Araujo, F. P. 1981. *Social Perspectives on Agricultural Research and Development in the Southern Kordofan, Sudan: Systems of Agricultural Production Among the Nuba* (WSARP Publication No. 11). Pullman: Washington State University.

Armah, Ayi Kwei. 1979. *Two Thousand Seasons*. Chicago: Third World Press.

Askin, Steve. 1986. "Zimbabwe Pays Dearly for Agricultural Success." *African Business*.

Aubertin, C. 1983a. "Histoire et Création d'une Région Sous-Developée: Le Nord Ivoirien," Cah. O.R.S.T.O.M., Ser Sci., Hum., 19:1.

————. 1983b. *Le Programme Sucrier Ivorien—Une Industrialisation Regionale Volontariste*. Travaux et Documents de L'O.R.S.T.O.M.

Bakary, T. 1984. "Elite Transformation and Political Succession." In W. I. Zartman and C. Delgado (eds.), *The Political Economy of the Ivory Coast*. New York: Praeger.

Banaji, R. 1985. "A Workers Perspective." *Econ. and Polit. Weekly*, 21 (50):2197–2199.

Bangura, Yusuf. 1987. "The Recession and Workers' Struggles in Vehicle Assembly Plants: Steyr-Nigeria." *Review of African Political Economy*.

Banton, M. 1957. *West African City: A Study of Tribal Life in Freetown*. London: Oxford University Press.

Baran, Paul. 1973. "On the Political Economy of Backwardness." In Charles K. Wilber (ed.), *The Political Economy of Development and Underdevelopment*. New York: Random House, Inc.

Bates, Robert H. 1984. "Some Conventional Orthodoxies in the Study of Agrarian Change." *World Politics*, 36 (2).

Bechtold, Peter K. 1976. *Politics in the Sudan*. New York: Praeger.

Bennett, J. M., and R. E. Kalman. *Computers in Developing Nations*. Amsterdam: North-Holland Publishing.

Berelson, B. 1969. "Beyond Family Planning." *Science*, 163:533–543.

Berg, Robert, and J. Whitaker. 1986. *Strategies for African Development*. Berkeley: University of California Press.

Berger, P. L. 1974. *Pyramids of Sacrifice: Political Ethics and Social Change*. New York: Basic Books.

Berghe, van den. 1975. *Race and Ethnicity in Africa*. Nairobi: Best African Publishing House.

Bergman, E. 1974. "American Population Policymaking: A Shift to the States." In E. Bergman, *Population Policymaking in the United States*. Lexington, Mass.: Lexington Books.

Bernard, G. M. 1985. *Food, Population and Development*. New Jersey: Rowan and Allanheld.

Bernet, Richard J., and Ronald E. Mueller. 1974. *Global Research: The Power of the Multinational Corporations*. New York: Simon and Schuster.

Berryman, P. 1973. "Latin American Liberation Theology." *Theological Studies*, 34: 357–395.

Bessis, S. 1980. "Côte d'Ivoire: Victime de ses Amis." *Jeune Afrique*, 13/3, 4, Juin.

Bettleheim, Charles. 1972. "Theoretical Comments." Appendix 1, in Arrighiri Emmanuel (ed.), *Unequal Exchange*. New York: Monthy Review Press.

Black, Knippers. 1977. *United States Penetration of Brazil*. Philadelphia: University of Pennsylvania.

Blackburn, Peter. 1987. "Growing Sahara Imperils Nomads." *Chicago Tribune*, June 8:17.

_____. 1987. "Ivory Coast Runs Out of Patience with IMF Austerity." *Financial Times* 25 June: 5.

Bongaarts, J., and S. Greenhalgh. 1985. "An Alternative to the One-Child Policy in China." *Population and Development Review*, 11(4).

Borgstrom, C. 1973. *Harvesting the Earth*. New York: Abelard-Schuman.

Borsdorf, R., and E. Haque. 1984. Project Design, Storage and Inventory Loan Component, Kordofan Rainfed Agriculture Project (650–0054), Sudan. (Improvement of Postharvest Grain Systems, AID/DSAN-CA-0256.) Manhattan: Food and Feed Grain Institute, Kansas State University.

Bortnick, J. 1985. "National and International Information Policy." *Journal of the American Society for Information Science*, 36 (3):164–168.

Botelho, A. J. 1987. "Brazil's Independent Computer Strategy." *Technology Review*, May–June:36–45.

Bourne, M. C. 1977. "Post Harvest Food Losses—The Neglected Dimension." In *Increasing the World Food Supply*. Monogram No. 56. Ithaca: Cornell University.

Bowonder, B., J. X. Kasperson, and R. E. Kasperson. 1985. "Avoiding Future Bhopals." *Environment*, 27(7); 6–13, 31–37.

Bragg, Wayne G. 1987. "Appropriate Technology for Development: Student Research in the Third World." In *Development and the High Tech Syndrome: Technology, Society and Communications*. Chicago: Third World Conf. Foundation.

Bragg, Wayne G., Debra L. Duke, and Eugene B. Shultz, Jr. 1987. "Rootfuel: Annual Roots as Cookstove Fuel in the Arid Third World." 28th Ann. Meeting, Society for Economic Botany, Chicago, IL, USA, June 22–25.

Bragg, Wayne G., and Eugene B. Shultz, Jr. 1987. "A Potential Solution to the Fuelwood Crisis in Third World Drylands: Annual Roots Instead of Wood as Cooking Fuel." *Forum of the Association of Arid Lands Studies*, Vol. 3, Int'l Ctr. for Arid and Semi-arid Land Studies. Lubbock: Texas Tech University.

Brandt, Willy, et al. 1980. *North-South: A Program of Survival*. Report of the Independent Commission on International Development Issues under the Chairmanship of Willy Brandt. Cambridge: The MIT Press.

Breese, G. 1969. *The City in Newly Developed Countries: Readings on Urbanization and Urbanism*. Princeton: Princeton University Press.

Brook, T. 1981. "Brazil's Inflation Is Rekindling." *Business Weekly*, 47.

Brown, Lester R. 1981. *Building a Sustainable Society*. New York: W. W. Norton.

_____. 1982. *U.S. and Soviet Agriculture: Shifting Balance of Power*. Washington, D.C.: Worldwatch Institute.

_____. 1987. "Analyzing the Demographic Trap." In L. Brown et al., *State of the World*. New York: W. W. Norton.

Brown, Lester, and Edward Wolf. 1985. *Reversing Africa's Decline*. Washington, D.C.: Worldwatch Institute.

Brown, Sterling. 1972. *Negro Poetry and Drama and the Negro in American Fiction*. New York: Atheneum.

Browne, Robert, and Robert Cummins. 1985. *The Lagos Plan of Action vs. The Berg Report*. Lawrenceville: Brunswick Publishing Company.

Bryce, M. D. 1960. *Industrial Development*. New York: McGraw-Hill Book Co.

Burgess, E. N. 1925. "The Growth of the City: An Introduction to a Research

322   Bibliography

Report." In *The City*, eds. Robert Park, Burgess, and Mekensic. Chicago: University of Chicago Press.

Calburn, Forrest D. 1982. "Current Studies of Peasants and Rural Development: Application of the Political Economy Approach" *World Politics*, 34:(2).

Caldwell, John, and Pat Caldwell. 1985. "Cultural Forces Tending to Sustain High Fertility in Tropical Africa." World Bank, PHN Technical Note, October, p. 1.

Callahan, D. 1971. "Ethics and Population Limitation." Occasional paper of the Population Council. New York.

Carr-Saunders, A. M. 1936: *The World Population*. New York: OUP.

Cassidy, R. 1978. *Jesus, Politics, and Society: A Study of Luke's Gospel*. New York: Orbis Books.

Chaudhuri, A. M. 1967. *The Wealth of Nations*. Calcutta: The World Press Private Ltd.

Chavez, A. L. Jose, and Fernandez G. Alfredo. 1985. *Le Calabacilla loca (cucurbita foetidissima GBK) Especie Con Potencial*. Saltillo, Coahuila, Mexico: Universidad Autonoma Agraria "Antonio Narro."

Chess, Caron. 1986. "Looking Behind the Factory Gates." *Technology Review*, 89 (6):42–53.

Christians for Socialism. 1973. "First Latin American Encounter of Christians for Socialism." In Charles Wilber (ed.), *The Political Economy of Development and Underdevelopment*. New York: Random House.

Christopher, G. 1970. "Les Causes de la Migration de la Champagne à la Ville: Le Cas de la Côte d'Ivoire." *CIRES*. no. 10, (Univ. d'Abidjan).

Clark, Robert P., Jr. 1974. *Development and Instability: Political Change in the Non-Western World*. Hinsdale: The Dryden Press.

Claude, Inis L., Jr. 1956. *Swords into Plowshares: The Problems and Progress of International Organization*. New York: Random House.

Clifford, W. 1963. "The Evaluation of Methods Used for the Prevention and Treatment of Juvenile Delinquency in Africa South of Sahara." *International Review of Criminal Policy*, 21:17–32.

Coale, A. J. 1973. "The Demographic Transition Re-Considered." Talk at the International Population Conference, Liege.

Coates, James. 1987. "Environmentalists Want Third World to Turn Over a New Leaf." *Chicago Tribune*, 31 May: sec. 1, p. 6.

Cohen, M. 1973. "The Myth of the Expanding Enter Politics in the Ivory Coast." *Journal of Modern African Studies*, 11(2):227–246.

_____. 1975. *Urban Policy and Political Conflict in Africa: The Case of the Ivory Coast*. Chicago: University of Chicago Press.

_____. 1984. "Urban Policy and Development Strategy." In I. William Zartman and Christopher Delgado (eds.), *The Political Economy of Ivory Coast*. New York: Praeger Special Studies.

Coleman, J. 1964. *Political Parties and National Integration in Tropical Africa*. Berkeley: University of California Press.

Commoner, B. 1974. "Population Problems." *Hospital Practice*, September.

_____. 1975. "How Poverty Breeds Overpopulation (and not the other way around)." *Ramparts*, 13 (10):21–25.

Contee, Christine E. 1987. *What Americans Think: Views on Development and U.S.-Third World Relations*. New York: InterAction and Overseas Development Council.

Costas, O. 1974. *The Church and Its Mission: A Shattering Critique from the Third World*. Wheaton: Tyndale Press.

Coughenour, C. M., and S. M. Nazhat. 1985. "Recent Change in Village and

Rainfed Agriculture in North Central Kordofan: Communication Process and Constraints." (INTSORMIL Report No. 4; Contract No. AID/DSAN-G-0149.) Lexington: University of Kentucky.

Coulton, O. 1980. "Person, Environment, Fit as the Focus in Health Care." *Social Work*, 80.

Coursey, D. G. 1983. "Post-harvest Losses in Perishable Foods of the Developing World." National Advance Study Institute Series A, 46:485.

Crockett, Andrew D. 1981. "Stabilization Policies in Developing Countries: Some Policy Consideration." *IMF Staff Papers*, 28:(1).

Crowder, Michael. 1970. Introduction. In M. Crowder and O. Ikime (eds.), *West African Chiefs*. New York: African Publishing Corporation.

————. 1973. *Revolt in Bussa*. Evanston: Northwestern University.

————. 1974. "Ethnography and Administration: A Study of Anglo-Tiv Working Misunderstanding." *Journal of African History*, 15:457–477.

Cruse, Harold. 1967. *The Crisis of the Negro Intellectual*. New York: William Morrow.

Cummins, Stephen K., Michael F. Lafchie, and Rhys Payje. 1986. *Africa's Agrarian Crisis: The Roots of Famine*. Boulder: Lynne Rienner Publisher, Inc.

Cushman, J. H., and J. W. Ranney. 1982. "Short Rotation Growth of Hardwoods for Energy Applications Across the United States—Field Results and Economics." *Proc. of IGT Symposium on Energy from Biomass and Wastes VI*, Institute on Gas Technology, Chicago.

Daddich, Cyril Kafrie. 1985. "Recovering Africa's Self-Sufficiency in Food and Agriculture." In Adebayo Adedeji, and Timothy M. Shaw (eds.), *Economic Crisis in Africa*. Boulder: Lynne Rienner Publisher, Inc.

D'Arth, Richard. 1974. *Education and Development in the Third World*. Lexington: Lexington Books.

Das, S. K. 1985a. "Mockery of Relief and Rehabilitation." *Econ. and Polit. Weekly*, 20(40):1679–80.

————. 1985b. "The Worse Aftermath." *Econ. and Polit. Weekly*, 21 (50):2192–2196.

Datoo, B. A., and A. J. B. Gray. 1979. "Underdevelopment and Regional Planning in the Third World." *Canadian Journal of African Studies*, 13:1–2.

Davies, W. J. 1975. "Politics, Perception and Development Strategy in Tropical Africa." *Journal of Modern African Studies*, 1(3):35–53.

Davis, K. 1971. "The Nature and Purpose of Population Policy." In K. Davis and G. Styles (eds.), *California's Twenty Million*, California: University of California Institute for International Studies.

Deihl, L. W. 1981. "The Environmental Constraint on Certain Management Practices." *Proceedings of the Academy of International Business*:123–129.

De Janvry, Alain. 1973. "A Socio-economic Model of Induced Innovations for Argentine Agricultural Development." *Quarterly Journal of Agricultural Economics*, August.

————. 1975. "The Political Economy of Rural Development in Latin America: An Interpretation." *American Journal of Agricultural Economics*, August.

————. 1981. *The Agrarian Question and Reformism in Latin America*. Baltimore: Johns Hopkins University Press.

De Lancey, Virginia. 1986. "Agricultural Productivity in Cameroon." In I. Williams Zartman and Michael G. Schatzberg (eds.), *The Political Economy of Cameroon*. New York: Praeger Special Studies.

de Lima Vaz, H. C. 1968. "The Church and Conscientizacao." *America*, 118(17): 578–581.

DeVeaux, Jennie S., and Eugene B. Shultz, Jr. 1985. "Development of Buffalo Gourd (*Cucurbita foetidissima*) as a Semi-aridland Starch and Oil Crop." *Econ. Botany*, 39(4):454–472.

Diamond, Marcelo. 1978. "Towards a Change in the Economic Paradigm Through the Experience of Developing Countries." *Journal of Development Economics* 5.

Diawara, M. T. 1970. *PDCI's Party Congress*. Abidjan: Franernite-Matin Editions.

Dizard, W. P., Jr. 1982. *The Coming Information Age*. New York: Longman, Inc.

Dobrzynski, J. H., W. B. Glaberson, R. W. King, W. J. Powell, Jr., and Leslie Helm. 1984. "Union Carbide Fights for Its Life." *Business Week*, 2984:53–56.

Dornbusch, Rudger. 1982. "Stabilization Policies in Developing Countries: What Have We Learned?" *World Development*, 10(9).

Dorward, D. C. 1974. "Ethnography and Administration: A Study of Anglo-Tiv Working Misunderstanding." *Journal of African History*, 15:457–477.

Dosa, M. L. 1985. "Information Transfer as Technical Assistance for Development." *Journal of the American Society for Information Science*, 36(3):146–152.

Dos Santos, T. 1973. "The Structure of Dependency." In Charles K. Wilber (ed.), *The Political Economy of Development and Underdevelopment*. New York: Random House.

Driver, E. 1972. *Essays on Population Policy*. London: Lexington Books.

D'Silva, B. C. 1985. "Sudan: Policy Reforms and Prospects for Agricultural Recovery After the Drought." (ERS Staff Report No. AGES 850909.) Washington, D.C.: International Economics Division, Economic Research Service, U.S. Dept. of Agriculture.

————. 1986. "Sudan: Agricultural and Economic Recovery After the Drought." *Sudan Studies Association Newsletter*, 6(3):11–13.

Dubresson, A. 1980. "Derrière le Contradiction, l'Etat Discours et Pratique de l'Aménagement du Territoire en Côte d'Ivoire." *Politique Africain*, no. 24.

Durand, J. D. 1967. "The Modern Expansion of World Population." *Proceedings of American Philosophical Society*, 111.

Easterlin, R. 1973. "Does Money Buy Happiness?" *The Public Interest*, 30:3–10.

Easterlin, Richard A., and Eleen M. Crimmins. 1985. *The Fertility Revolution: A Supply-Demand Analysis*. Chicago: University of Chicago Press.

Easton, David. 1953. *The Political System*. New York: Knopf.

Ebrahim, M. H. S. 1983. "Irrigation Projects in Sudan: The Promise and the Reality." *Journal of African Studies*, 10(1):1–13.

ECA. 1985. "Recommendations of the ECA Conference of Ministers of the Twenty-First Ordinary Session of the Assembly of Heads of State and Government of the Organization of African Unity." *Report of the Sixtieth Meeting of the Preparatory Committee of the Whole*. Addis Ababa, April 24.

Economic and Social Statistics Bulletin, January 1985.

Edfelt, R. 1986. "Telematics, Public Policy, and Economic Development with Special Reference to Brazilian Protectionism." *The Information Society*, 4/(3): 187–203.

Eicher, Carl. 1986. *Transforming African Agriculture*. San Francisco: The Hunger Project Papers.

Eisenhower, Dwight D. 1953. Speech to the American Society of Newspaper Editors. In Fred I. Greenstein (ed.). 1983. *The Hidden Hand Presidency*. New Haven: Yale University Press.

el-Bushra, S. 1985. "Development Planning in the Sudan." *ErdKunde*, 39(1):53–59.

Elkan, W. 1960. *Migrants and Proletarians*. London: Oxford University Press.

El-Meheiry, Theresa. 1984. "Attitudes of a Group of Egyptian Medical Students Towards Family Planning." *Social Science Medical*, 19(2):131–134.

Elridge, H. 1968. "Population Policies." *International Encyclopedia of Social Sciences*, 12th ed. New York: Crosswell, Collier and MacMillan.

Ember, L. R. 1985. "Technology in India: An Uneasy Balance of Progress and Tradition." *Chemical and Engineering News*, 63(6):61–65.

England, Robert. 1986. "The Union Carbide Version of Bhopal: A Deliberate Act." *Insight*, Dec. 22:42–44.

Engleberger, J. 1980. *Robotics in Practice*. New York: Amacom.

Evans-Pritchard, E. E. 1951. *Social Anthropology*. London: Cohen and West.

Family Planning Perspectives. 1987. 19(4).

FAO. 1969. "Bigger Crops—and Better Storage: The Role of Storage." In *World Food Supplies*, Rome: UN.

_____. 1977a. *An Analysis of a FAO Survey of Post-Harvest Food Losses in Developing Countries*. Rome: UN.

_____. 1977b. *Land, Food and People*. Rome: UN.

_____. 1980. *Regional Food for Africa*. Rome: UN.

_____. 1981. *FAO Production Yearbook*. Rome: FAO.

_____. 1983. *Road Production and Trade Yearbook*. Rome: UN.

_____. 1984. *FAO Production Yearbook*. Rome: FAO.

_____. 1984. *Potential Population Supporting Capacities of Lands in the Developing World*. Rome: UN.

_____. 1985. *FAO Production Yearbook*. Rome: FAO.

FAO/UNEP. 1981. *Food Loss Prevention in Perishable Crops*. Report of FAO/UNEP. Rome: FAO.

Farques, P. 1981. *Les Migrations en Côte d'Ivoire*, CIRES, No. 31–32. Abidjan: Univ. Nationale de Côte d'Ivoire, No. 42.

Fathy, Hassan. 1973. *Architecture for the Poor*. Chicago: The University of Chicago Press.

Fawzi, Saad el-Din. 1957. *The Laborer Movement in the Sudan, 1946–1955*. London: Oxford University Press.

Fierro, A. 1977. *The Militant Gospel*. Maryknoll: Orbis Books.

Fishlow, Albert. 1980. "Brazilian Development in the Long-Term Perspective." *American Economic Review*, 102.

Forbes. 1976. "Breadbasket?" August 1:56.

Foster, George. 1967. *Tzintsuntzn: Mexican Peasants in a Changing World*. Boston: Little, Brown & Co.

Frelastre, G. 1980. "Les Nouvelles Orientations du Développment Rurale de la Côte d'Ivoire." *Revue d'Etudes Politiques et Economiques Africaines*, 176(177):37–50.

Friedman, M. 1975. *There's No Such Thing as a Free Lunch*. LaSalle: Open Court Publishing Co.

Friedmann, S., and C. Weaver. 1979. *Territory and Function: The Evolution of Regional Planning*. Los Angeles: UCLA Press.

Friere, P. 1973. *Education for Critical Consciousness*. New York: Seabury.

_____. 1982. *Pedagogy of the Oppressed*. New York: Continums.

Gadalla, Saad M. 1978. *Is There Hope*. Cairo: The American University in Cairo Press.

Galenter, E. 1984. "Computers Will Unravel the Fabric of Our Social and Working Lives." *Words*, June-July:18–21.

Garland, J., and R. N. Farmer. 1986. *International Dimensions of Business Policy and Strategy*. Boston: Kent Publishing Co.

Gastellau, J. M., and S. F. Yapi. 1982. "Une Mythe a Décomposer: La Bourgeosie de Planteurs." In Y. A. Faure and J. F. Medard (eds.), *Etat et Bourgeoisie en Cote d'Ivoire*. Paris: Karthala.

Gbetibouo, Malthurin, and Christopher Delgado. 1984. "Lessons and Constraints of Export Crop Led Growth: Cocoa in the Ivory Coast." In I. William Zartman and Christopher Delgado (eds.), *The Political Economy of Ivory Coast*. New York: Praeger Special Studies.

Genovese, R. G. 1984. *Families and Change: Social Needs and Public Policies*. New York: Praeger Publishers.

Ghymn, K., and G. S. Evans. 1979. "Cross-Cultural Transfer of Management Practices." *Proceedings of the Academy of International Business*, 123–129.

Gilbert, N., and H. Sprecht. 1974. *Social Policy: Dimension of Choice*. Englewood Cliffs: Prentice-Hall.

Gillard-Byers, T. E., W. T. Bunderson, and B. A. Azrag. 1985. "Introduction of Animal Transportation Technology in the Nuba Mountain Area of Sudan." In *Sedentary Production System: 1984–1985 Research Results, Kadugli Research Station* (WSARP Publication No. 42). Pullman: Washington State University: 117–142.

Globerson, A. 1978. "Interaction Between Foreign Assistance Personnel and Local Counterparts." *Kyklos*, 31(2):48–62.

Gluckman, M. 1966. "Tribalism in Modern British Central Africa." In Wallersten (ed.), *Social Change: The Colonial Situation*. New York.

Goliber, Thomas J. 1985. "Sub-Saharan Africa: Population Pressures on Development." *Population Bulletin*, February. (Washington, D.C.: Population Reference Bureau.)

Graham, S. F. 1966. *Government and Mission Education in Northern Nigeria, 1900–1919*. Ibadan: Ibadan University Press.

Greenhalgh, S. 1986. "Shifts in China's Population Policy 1984–1986: Views from the Central, Provincial and Local Levels." *Population and Development Review*, 12(3).

Greestein, Fred I. 1983. *The Hidden Hand Presidency*. New Haven: Yale University Press.

Guardian. January 30, 1984.

Gunn, D., and F. P. Conant. 1960. *Peoples of the Middle Niger Region, Northern Nigeria*. London: International African Institute.

Gusten, Rolf. 1966. *Problem of Economic Growth and Planning: The Sudan Example*. New York: Springer-Verlag.

Gutierrez, G. 1970. "Notes for a Theology of Liberation." *Theological Studies*, 31: 243–261.

————. 1973. *A Theology of Liberation: History, Politics and Salvation*. New York: Orbis Books.

Haas, E. B., and J. G. Ruggie. 1982. "What Message in the Medium of Information Systems." *International Studies Quarterly*, 26(2):190–219.

Hall, J. 1960. *General Principles of Criminal Law*. Indianapolis: Bobbs-Merrill.

Hardiman, M., and J. Midgely. 1978. "Foreign Consultant and Development Projects: The Need for an Alternative Approach." *Journal of Administrative Overseas*, 17(4):32–41.

Hardin, G. 1968. "Tragedy of the Commons." *Science*, 162:1243–1248.

————. 1974. "Living on a Lifeboat." *Bio-Science*, 24(10): 561–568.

————. 1975. "Gregg's Law." *Bio-Science*, 25(7):415.

Harris, P. 1970. *Tribalism in African Urban Areas*. New York.

Harrison, P. 1987. *The Greening of Africa: Breaking Through in the Battle for Land and Food*. New York: Penguin Books.

Hart, Keith. 1982. *The Political Economy of West African Agriculture*. London: Cambridge University Press.

Hebblethwaite, P. 1977. *The Christian-Marxist Dialogue: Beginnings, Present Status, and Beyond.* New York: Paulist Press.

Heeger, Gerald A. 1974. *The Politics of Underdevelopment.* New York: St. Martin's Press.

Hellwig, M. 1977. "Liberation Theology: An Emerging School." *Scottish Journal of Theology,* 30:137–151.

Hernandez, D. J. 1985. "Fertility Reduction Policies and Poverty in Third World Countries." *Studies in Family Planning,* 16(2).

Herskovits, Melville. 1945. "The Process of Culture Change." In R. Linton (ed.), *The Science of Man in the World Crisis.* New York: Columbia University Press.

Hess, B. 1984. "Protecting the American Family: Public Policy and the New Right." In Genovese, *Families and Change: Social Needs and Public Policies.* New York: Praeger Publishers.

Hinderink, J., and J. J. Sterkenburg. 1983. "Agricultural Policy and Production in Africa: The Aims, the Methods and the Means." *The Journal of Modern African Studies,* 21(1):1–23.

Hirschman, A. 1958. *The Strategy of Economic Development.* New Haven: Yale Press.

Hollenbach, D. 1977. "Modern Catholic Teachings Concerning Justice." In J. C. Haughey, S. J. (ed.), *The Faith That Does Justice.* New York: Paulist Press.

Houphouët-Boigny, F. 1965. Discours du Chef de l'Etat Fratnité-Matin (May).

Hoyt, H. 1939. *The Structure of Residential Neighborhoods in American Cities.* Washington, D.C.: Federal Housing Administration.

Hwa, Erh-Cheng. 1983. "The Contribution of Agriculture to Economic Growth: Some Empirical Evidence." *World Bank Staff Working Paper,* No. 619.

Hyden, G. 1980. *Beyond Ujamaa in Tanzania.* Berkeley: University of California Press.

_____. 1983. *No Shortcut to Progress.* Berkeley: University of California Press.

_____. 1985. "Suburban Growth and Rural Development." In Patrick O'Meara and Gwendolen Carter (eds.), *Africa: Twenty-Five Years of Independence.* Bloomington: Indiana University Press.

ILO. 1976. *Growth, Equity and Employment: A Comprehensive Strategy for the Sudan.* Geneva: ILO.

INADES. 1986. *Etude des Conséquences Sociales de la Politique de Développement en Côte d'Ivoire.* INADES-Documentation.

India National Government. 1961. *Third Five Year Plan.* New Delhi.

Irvine, C. 1975. *Report on a Survey of African Independent (Separatist) Congressions in Nairobi.* Unpublished manuscript.

ISG. 1985. "Whom Will Union Carbide Blame Now?" *Econ. and Polit. Weekly,* 20(34):1417.

Jagdish and Vijay. 1985. "Carbide Workers: Farce of Rehabilitation." *Econ. and Polit. Weekly,* 21(50):2199–2200.

Jedlicka, A. 1982. "Technology Transfer in Latin America: The Managerial Imperative." *Proceedings of the Rocky Mountain Council on Latin American Studies,* 11–15.

Johnson, B. F., and J. W. Mellor. 1961. "The Role of Agriculture in Economic Development." *Proceedings of the Rocky Mountain Council on Latin American Studies,* 11–15.

Kahn, A., and S. Kamerman. 1977. *Not for the Poor Alone.* New York: Harper Colophon Books.

Kanbur, Ravi, S. M. 1987. "Measurement and Alleviation of Poverty with an Application to the Effects of Macroeconomic Adjustment." *IMF Staff Papers,* 1.

Kanon, D. Bra. 1978. "Pour une Nouvelles Problematiques du Développement Agricole Ivorien." *Revue Française des Etudes Politiques et Economiques Africains,* no. 130.

Kaplan, Morton A. 1967. *System and Process in International Politics*. New York: John Wiley and Sons, Inc.

Kaplan, Stephen S., and Norman C. Bonsor. 1973. "Did United States Aid Really Help Brazilian Development? The Perspective of a Quarter-Century." *Inter-American Economic Affairs*, 27:32.

Kasfir, Nelson. 1986. "Are African Peasants Self-Sufficient?" *Development and Change*, 17.

Kelly, A., A. Khalifa, and N. El-Khorazati. 1982. *Population and Development in Rural Egypt*. Durham: Duke Press Policy Studies.

Kent, George. 1972. *Blackness and the Adventure of Western Culture*. Chicago: Third World Press.

Kenya. 1983. *Growth and Structural Change*, vol. 2. Washington, D.C.: World Bank.

Kerr, March. 1981. "Family Planning in Egypt." *Planned Parenthood Review*, 1:18.

Khalifa, Atef M. 1976. "The Influence of Wife's Education on Fertility in Rural Egypt." *Journal of Biosocial Science*, 8:53–60.

Khalifa, Atef M., H. Sayed, N. El-Khorazati, and A. Way. 1982. *Family Planning in Rural Egypt 1980*. Columbia, Westinghouse Health Systems.

Kihl, Young Wan, and Dung Suh Bark. 1981. "Food Policies in the Rapidly Developing Country: The Case of South Korea, 1960–1978." *Journal of Developing Areas*, 16.

Kirk, J. A. 1979. *Liberation Theology: An Evangelical View from the Third World*. Atlanta: John Knox Press.

Kissinger, Henry A. 1987. "China Now Changing Rules and Ruling Party." *Los Angeles Times*, October 25, Part V:1, 6.

Kondracke, Morton. 1983. "Reagan-Style 'Progress' on Housing." *Los Angeles Times*: editorial page.

Korn, R., and L. McCorkle. 1957. *Criminology and Penology*. New York: Holt.

Krieberg, M. 1970. *The Marketing Challenge: Distributing Increased Production in Developing Nations*. Washington, D.C.: USDA.

Krivan, S. P. 1986. "Avoiding Catastrophic Loss: Technical Safety Audit and Process Safety Review." *Professional Safety*, 31(2):21–26.

Kutzner, Patricia L., and Nicholas Lagoudkis. 1985. *Who's Involved in Hunger: Guide to Urbanizations*. Washington, D.C.: World Hunger Education Service.

Lappé, Frances Moore, and Joseph Collins. 1986. *World Hunger: Twelve Myths*. New York: Grove Press.

Laquer, W., and B. Rubin. 1979. *The Human Rights Reader*. New York: Meridian Books.

Lasswell, Harold. 1958. *Politics: Who Gets What, When, How*. Cleveland: World Publishing.

Lee, T. H. 1971. *Inter-sectorial Study of Taiwan: Inter-sectorial Capital Flows in the Economic Development of Taiwan, 1895–1960*. Ithaca: Cornell University Press.

Lepkowski, Wil. 1985a. "Indians Criticize Handling of Bhopal Tragedy." *Chem. and Eng. News*, 63(4):24.

———. 1985b. "People of India Struggle Towards Appropriate Response to the Tragedy." *Chem. and Eng. News*, 63(6):16–26.

———. 1985c. "Chemical Safety in Developing Countries: The Lessons of Bhopal." *Chem. and Eng. News*, 63(14):9–14.

———. 1985d. "Questions Persist About Cyanide Poisoning in Bhopal Disaster." *Chem. and Eng. News*, 63(41):42–43.

_____. 1985e. "Bhopal: Indian City Begins to Heal but Conflict Remains." *Chem. and Eng. News*, 63(48):18–32.

Less, Francis A., and Hugh C. Brooks. 1977. *The Economic and Political Development of the Sudan*. London: Macmillan Press.

Lewis, W. A. 1967. "Random Reflection on Local Development in Africa." In Foreign Services Institute Pub., Washington, D.C.

Liebenow, J. Gus. 1986. *African Politics: Crisis and Challenges*. Bloomington: Indiana University Press.

Lippman, W. 1955. *The Public Philosophy*. Boston: Little, Brown and Co.

Lipton, M. 1977. *Why Poor People Stay Poor: Urban Bias in World Development*. London: Temple Smith Press.

Litwak, E., and I. Szelenyi. 1969. "Primary Group Structures and Their Functions." *American Sociological Review*, 34:465–481.

Lofchie, Michael. 1986. "Kenya's Agricultural Success." *Current History*, May.

Lofchie, Michael, and S. Cummins. 1982. "Food Deficits and Agricultural Policies in Tropical Africa." *The Journal of Modern African Studies*, 20(1): 1–25.

Louis Berger International, Inc. 1983. Sudan: Kordofan Region Agricultural Marketing and Transport Study (Contract No. 650-AID). East Orange: Louis Berger International.

Lugard, Lord F. 1922. *The Dual Mandate in British Tropical Africa*. Edinburgh-London: Blackwood.

Lunin, F. F., and B. K. Eres. 1985. "Perspectives on International Information Issues: Introduction and Overview." *Journal of the American Society for Information Science*, May: 143–145.

McCann, D. 1981. *Christian Realism and Liberation Theology. Practical Theologies in Creative Conflict*. New York: Orbis Books.

McCurdy, Patrick P. 1985a. "The Bhopal Ponies." *Chem. Week*, 136(6):3.

_____. 1985b. "Bridging the Bhopal Gap." *Chem. Week*, 136(18):3.

MacKinnon, Barbara. 1986. "Pricing Human Life." *Science, Technology, and Human Values*, 11(2):32–36.

Mafeje, Archie. 1971. "The Ideology of Tribalism." *The Journal of Modern African Studies*, 9:2.

Makris, J., and R. Wilkerson. 1986. "The Chemical Emergency Preparedness Program." *Pub. Management*, 68(3):9–10.

Mamalakis, Markos J. 1985. "Primary Sector: Composition and Functions." In Mats Lundahl (ed.), *The Primary Sector in Economic Development*. London: Croom Helm.

Markovitz, Irving L. (ed.). 1977. *Power and Class in Africa*. New York: Free Press.

Mayer, Jean. 1977. "Space, Employment and Development: Some Thoughts on the Regional Dimensions of Employment Policy." *International Labor Review*, 115(1).

Mbosowo, D. E. 1984. "Labor Migration and Criminal Behavior." In *Proceedings of NASA Annual Conference*.

_____. 1984. "Crime in Plateau State—Nigeria." *Indian Journal of Criminology and Criminalistics*, 5:77–84.

Meadows, Edward. 1981. "Brazil Spreads Its Wings." *Fortune* 113.

Medani, A. I. 1985. "Food Stabilization in Developing Africa." *World Development*, 6.

Meenaghan, T., and M. Mascari. 1971. "Consumer Choice, Consumer Control in Service Delivery." *Social Work*, 10:50–57.

Meenaghan, T., and R. Washington. 1980. *Social Policy*. New York: Free Press.

_____, and _____. 1982. *Macro Practice*. New York: Free Press.

Mellor, John W. 1973. "Accelerated Growth in Agricultural Production and

Intersectorial Transfer of Resources." *Economic Development and Cultural Change*, 22.

Mellor, John W., and Bruce F. Johnson. 1984. "The World Food Equation: Inter-Relations Among Development, Employment and Food Consumption." *Journal of Economic Literature*, 22(6).

Mellor, John W., Christopher Delgado, and Malcolm J. Blackie. 1987. *Accelerating Food Production in Sub-Saharan Africa*. Baltimore: Johns Hopkins University Press.

Mencher, S. 1970. *Poor Law to Poverty Program*. Pittsburgh: University of Pittsburgh Press.

Menou, M. J. 1984. "Challenges for the Information Future of the Third World." In *Proceedings of the 47th ASIS Annual Meeting*. White Plains, N.Y.: Knowledge Industry Publications, Inc.

————. 1985. "An Overview of Social Measures of Information." *Journal of the American Society for Information Science*, 36(3):169–177.

Merrick, Thomas W. 1986. "World Population in Transition." *Population Bulletin*, 41(2).

Mesarovic, Mihajlo, and Edward Pestel. 1974. *Mankind at the Turning Point*. New York: E. P. Dutton and Co.

Michael, J., and M. Alder. 1933. *Crime, Law and Social Sciences*. New York: Harcourt, Brace.

Miguez Bonino, J. 1975. *Doing Theology in a Revolutionary Situation*. Philadelphia: Fortress Press.

Miller, Matt. 1986. *The Wall Street Journal*, 24 September: 34.

Miller, Michael W. 1986. *The Wall Street Journal*, 6 November: 8.

Ministry of Planning and Economy. 1971. *The Five Year Plan of Economic and Social Development, 1970/71–1974/75*. Khartoum: Ministry of National Planning.

————. 1977. *The Six Year Plan of Economic and Social Development, 1977/78–1982/83*. Khartoum: Ministry of National Planning.

Miranda, J. 1974. *Marx and the Bible*. New York: Orbis Books.

Mitchell, Mark. 1985. *Agriculture and Policy: Methodology for the Analysis of Developing Country Agricultural Sectors*. London: Ithaca Press.

Mitchell, S. 1976. *Politics in West Africa*. London: Macmillan Publishing Co.

Mokhiber, R. 1987. "Union Carbide and the Devastation of Bhopal." *Multinational Monitor*, (April 6):6–8.

Mollett, J. A. 1984. *Planning for Agricultural Development*. New York: St. Martin's Press.

Moore, Stanley W. 1967. *The San Francisco Conference's Concept of Collective Security*. Unpublished master's thesis, Claremont Graduate School.

Morganthau, Hans. 1961. *Politics Among Nations: The Struggle for Power and Peace*, 3rd ed. New York: Alfred A. Knopf.

Moroney, R. 1976. *The Family and the State: Considerations for Social Policy*. New York: Longman's.

Morrison, D. 1975. "Cultural Pluralism, Modernization and Conflict: An Empirical Analysis of Sources of Political Instability in African Nations." *Journal of Political Science*, 15(1):90.

Morrison, Toni. 1984. "Rootedness: The Ancestor as Foundation." In *Black Woman Writers (1950–1980)*, ed. Mari Evans. Garden City: Anchor Books.

Mueller, Ronald E., and Richard J. Barnet. 1974. *Global Research: The Power of the Multinational Corporation*. New York: Simon and Schuster.

Murdoch, William W. 1980. *Poverty of Nations: The Political Economy of Hunger and Population*. Baltimore: Johns Hopkins University Press.

Murray, C. 1984. *Losing Ground*. New York: Basic Books.

Myrdal, Gunnar. 1970. *The Challenge of World Poverty: A World Anti-Poverty Program in Outline*. New York: Vintage Books.

Mytelka, L. 1984. "Foreign Business and Economic Development." In I. W. Zartman and C. Delgado, *The Political Economy of the Ivory Coast*. New York: Praeger Studies.

National Academy of Sciences. 1978. *Post-harvest Food Losses in Developing Countries*. Washington, D.C.: NAS.

Natkin, A. M. 1985. "Once Is Too Often—Corporate Responsibility in the Aftermath of Bhopal." *Journal '85 World Resources Institute*: 62–67.

Neale, R. S. 1976. *The Wealth of Nations: The Expenses of the Sovereign of Private Vices, Public Benefits*. Armidale: University of New England.

Neelameghan, A., and J. Tocatlian. 1985. "International Cooperation in Information Systems and Services." *Journal of the American Society for Information Science*, 36/(3):153–163.

Nelson, J. M., J. C. Scheerens, J. W. Berry, and W. P. Bemis. 1983. "Effect of Plant Population and Planting Date on Root and Starch Production of Buffalo Gourd Grown as an Annual." *J. Amer. Soc. Hort. Sci.*, 108(2):198–201.

Newland, Kathleen. 1979. *Global Employment and Economic Justice*. Washington: Worldwatch Institute.

Newsweek. 1983. 24 October: 18.

New York Times. 1985. 21 March: 22:1.

Noor, A. 1984. "A Framework for the Creation and Management of National Computing Strategies in Developing Countries." *The Computer Journal*, 27(3): 193–199.

Nortmann, D. 1975. "A Longitudinal Analysis of Population Policy in Developing Countries." In K. R. Godwin (ed.), *Comparative Policy Analysis*. Mass.: D. C. Heath and Co.

Nuba Mountain Agricultural Corporation (NMAC) and Deutsche Gesellschaft für Technische Zusammernarbeit (GTZ). 1985. *Cropping Alternatives for Smallholder Mechanized Farming in the Nuba Mountains* (Summary of Five Years of Pilot Work on Vertisols). Eschborn: GTZ.

Nyah, Okon. 1988. Personal consultation.

Nyerere, Julius. 1984. Interview, *Third World Quarterly*, 6(4):815–838.

O. A. U. 1981. *Lagos Plan of Action for the Economic Development of Africa*. Geneva: International Institute for Labor Studies.

O'Connor, D. C. 1985. "The Computer Industry in the Third World: Policy Options and Constraints." *World Development*, March: 311–332.

Oesterdiekhoff, P. 1983a. "New International Economic Order and Small Peasants' Export Production in Least Developed Countries—Case Study Sudan." In *The Development Perspectives of the Democratic Republic of Sudan*. P. Oesterdiekhoff and K. Wohlmuth, eds., IFO Institute für Wirtschaftsforschung, Afrika-Studien Nr. 109. München: Weltforum Verlag: 137–162.

_____. 1983b. "Industrial Development: Structural Deficiencies, Agroindustrial Prospects and Alternatives." In *The Development Perspectives of the Democratic Republic of Sudan*, ed. P. Oesterdiekhoff & K. Wohlmuth. IFO Institute für Wirtschaftsforschung, Afrika-Studien Nr. 109. Munchen: Weltforum Verlag: 164–194.

Oesterdiekhoff, P., and K. Wohlmuth. 1983a. "The 'Breadbasket' Is Empty: The Options of Sudanese Development Policy." *Canadian Journal of African Studies*, 17(1):35–67.

_____, and _____. 1983c. "The 'Breadbasket' Strategy of the Sudan: A New Option of Development?" In *The Development Perspectives of the Democratic Republic of Sudan*, ed. P. Oesterdiekhoff & K. Wohlmuth. IFO Institute fur Wirtschaftsforschung, Afrika-Studien Nr. 109. Munchen: Weltforum Verlag: 164–194.

Oguda, Oluwadare. 1973. "The State and the Economy in the Sudan: From a Political Scientist's Point of View." *Journal of Developing Areas*, April.

Okantah, Mwatabu S. 1987. "The Portrayal of the Images of African Culture in the West and Its Impact on People's Attitudes." Presented at the 13th Annual Third World Conference, Chicago.

O'Keefe, Phil, Peter Phillips, and Barry Munslow. 1986. "Marginal People in Marginal Places: Poverty Is Dangerous." In *Third World Affairs 1986*. Boulder: Westview Press.

Okowa, Willie. 1985. "Public Policy and Rural-Urban Distribution of Income in Nigeria." In Claude Ake (ed.), *Political Economy in Nigeria*. London: Longman Press.

Okoye, A. 1977. *The Growth of a Nation*. Enugu: Fourth Dimension Publishers.

Oluwandare, Oguda. 1973. "The State of the Economy in the Sudan." *Journal of Developing Areas*.

Oostuizen, G. C. 1987. "Africa's Social and Cultural Heritage." *Africa Insight*, 17(2).

Ophusa, William. 1977. *Building a Sustainable Society*. San Francisco: W. H. Freeman and Co.

Palen, J. 1986. "Fertility and Eugenics: Singapore's Population Policies." *Population Research and Policy Review*, 5:3–14.

Parsons, T. 1967. *Societies*. Englewood Cliffs: Prentice-Hall.

Pearson, C. S. 1985. "What Has to be Done to Prevent More Bhopals." *Journal World Resources Institute*, 85:58–61.

Peil, M. 1977. *Consensus and Conflict in African Societies: An Introduction to Sociology*. London: Longman.

"People." 1985. *International Planned Parenthood Journal*, 12(4).

Peppard, Donald M., Jr. 1976. "Toward a Radical Theory of Fiscal Incidence." *Review of Radical Political Economics*, 8(1).

Perrow, Charles. 1984. *Normal Accidents: Living with High-Risk Technologies*. New York: Basic Books.

Person, Y. 1981. "Colonialisation et Decolonialisation en Côte d'Ivoire." *Le Mois en Afrique*, 88–189 (Août/Sept.): 15–30.

Peterson, W. 1958. "A General Typology of Migration." *American Sociological Review*, 23:256–266.

Phatak, A. V. 1963. *International Dimension of Mangement*. Boston: Kent Publishing Co.

Pimenthal, D. 1978. *World Food, Pest Losses, and Environment*. Boulder: Westview Press.

Pine, A. 1986. *The Wall Street Journal*, 22 September:27.

Pirages, Dennis. 1978. *The New Context for International Relations: Global Ecopolitics*. North Scituate: Duxbury Press.

Pisani, Edgard. 1986. "The Habit of Courting Disaster." *The Nation*, 11 Oct.

_____. 1987. "Africa in Development: Seeds of Change Village through Global Order." *Journal of the Society for International Development*, 2(3).

Planning Document. 1975–1980. *Five Year Economic, Cultural and Social Plan of the Republic of the Ivory Coast*, Vols. I, II, III. Abidjan: Ministry of Planning.

Popline. 1984. Newsletter of the Population Institute. Washington, D.C., 6(1).

Population Division UN. 1983."Urbanization and City Growth." *Populi*, 10(2).

Power, Kevin. 1983. *The Wall Street Journal*, 9 June: 30.

Prakash, P. 1985. "Neglect of Women's Health Issues." *Econ. and Polit. Weekly*, 21(50):2196–2197.

Pratten, C. F. 1971. *Economies of Scale in Manufacturing Industry*. New York: Columbia University Press.

Rae, J. 1934. *New Principles of Political Economy*. Boston: Hilliard, Gray and Co.

Rameseshan, R. 1984. "Government Responsibility for Bhopal Gas Tragedy." *Econ. and Polit. Weekly*, 19(50):2109–2110.

Rateau, O. 1981. "Informatics: Evolution and Use in the 1980's with Particular Reference to Developing Countries." 3–9. In J. M. Bennett and R. E. Kalman (eds.), *Computers in Developing Countries*. Amsterdam: North-Holland Publishing.

Reckless, W. C. 1950. *The Crime Problem*. New York: Appleton-Century-Crofts.

Rein, M. 1970. *Social Policy: Issues of Choice and Changes*. New York: Random House.

Ricoeur, P. 1970. *Freud and Philosophy*. New Haven: Yale University Press.

Riggs, F. W. 1964. *Administration in Developing Countries: The Theory of Prismatic Societies*. Boston: Houghton Mifflin.

Robb, C. 1978. *Integration of Marxist Constructs into the Theory of Liberation from Latin America*. Ann Arbor: University Microfilms International.

Roberts, G. 1977. "Population Policy and Population Education." Doctoral Dissertation, Rutgers, The State University, New Jersey.

Robinson, R. D. 1984. *Internationalization of Business*. Chicago: Dryden Press.

Rondinelli, Dennis A. 1979. "Administration of Integrated Rural Development Policy: The Politics of Agrarian Reform in Developing Countries." *World Politics*, 31(3).

_____. 1986. "The Urban Transition and Agricultural Development: Implications for International Assistance Policy." *Development and Change*, 17.

Ronen, S. 1986. *Comparative and Multinational Management*. New York: John Wiley and Sons.

Rothchild, D. 1984. "Middle Africa: Hegemonical Exchange and Resource Allocation." In A. J. Groth and L. L. Wade (eds.), *Comparative Resource Allocation: Politics, Performance and Policy Priorities*. Beverly Hills: Sage Publishers.

Sacred Congregation for the Doctrine of the Faith. 1984. "Instruction on Certain Aspects of the 'Theology of Liberation.'" *Origins*, 14(13):193–204.

Salamone, Frank A. 1974a. *Gods and Goods in Africa*. New Haven: Hraflex.

_____. 1974b. "The Role of the Social Welfare Worker." *Africanus*, 6:33–51.

_____. 1975. "Becoming Hausa." *Africa*, 45:410–425.

_____. 1980. "Indirect Rule and the Reinterpretation of Tradition." *African Studies Review*, 23:1–14.

Sandbrook, R. 1982. *The Politics of Basic Needs: Urban Aspects of Assaulting Poverty in Africa*. Toronto: Toronto University Press.

Sanyal, Biswapriya. 1986. "Rural Development and Economic Stabilization: Can They Be Attained Simultaneously?" In Stephen K. Cummins, Michael F. Lafchie, and Rhys Payne (eds.), *Africa's Agrarian Crisis: The Roots of Famine*. Boulder: Rienner Publisher, Inc.

Saracevic, T., G. M. Braga, and M. A. Afolayan. 1984. "Issues in Information Science Education in Developing Countries." *Journal of the American Society for Information Science*, 36(3):192–199.

Sarrault, A. 1923. *La Mise en Valeur des Colonies Françaises*. Paris: P.U.F.

Saul, John. 1979. "The Dialectics of Class and Tribe." *Race and Class*, 20(4):371.

Sawadogo, A. 1977. *L'Agriculture en Côte d'Ivoire*. Paris: P.U.F.

Schnitzer, M. C., M. L. Liebrenz, and K. W. Kubi. 1985. *International Business*. Cincinnati: Southwestern Publishing Co.

Schultz, Theodore W. 1980. "Nobel Lecture: The Economics of Being Poor." *Journal of Political Economy*, 88(4):639–651.

Seavoy, Ronald E. 1986. *Famine in Peasant Societies*. New York: Greenwood Press.

Second General Conference of Latin American Bishops (CELAM). 1979. *The Church in the Present-Day Transformation of Latin America in Light of the Council*. Washington, D.C.: National Conference of Catholic Bishops.

Segundo, J. L., S. J. 1968a. "Christianity and Violence in Latin America." *Christianity and Crisis*, 28(3):31–34.

_____. 1968b. "Social Justice and Revolution." *America*, 118(17):574–577.

_____. 1969. "Has Latin America a Choice?" *America*, 120(8):213.

_____. 1970. "Wealth and Poverty as Obstacles to Development." In L. Colonnese (ed.), *Human Rights and the Liberation of Man*. South Bend: University of Notre Dame Press.

_____. 1973. *The Community Called Church*. Vol. 1 in *Theology for Artisans of a New Humanity*. Maryknoll: Orbis Books.

_____. 1976. *The Liberation of Theology*. Maryknoll: Orbis Books.

_____. 1978. "Theological Response to Talk on Evangelization and Development." *Studies in the International Apostolate of Jesuits*, November: 79–82.

_____. 1979. "Capitalism versus Socialism: Crux Theologica." In Gibellini (ed.), *Frontiers of Theology in Latin America*. Maryknoll: Orbis Books.

Sequeira, W. J. 1979. "The Transfer of Management Technology to Less Developed Countries." Unpublished Manuscript.

Shivji, I. 1973. *Silent Class Struggle in Tanzania*. Dar es salaam: Maji Maji.

Shultz, Eugene B., Jr., and Ianto Evans. 1986. "Dried Roots as Cookstove Fuel: An Innovation for Drylands Where Trees Grow with Difficulty." *Proc. 12th Annual Third World Conference*, Third World Conference Foundation, Chicago.

Sider, Ron. 1978. *Rich Christians in an Age of Hunger*.

Siffin, W. J. 1976. "Two Decades of Public Administration in Developing Countries." *Public Administration Review*, 36(1):27–42.

Silverman, M. 1979. "Dependency, Meditation and Class Formation in Rural Guyana." *American Ethnologist*, 6:466–490.

Simon, J. 1984. "Bright Global Future." *Bulletin of the Atomic Scientists*, November: 14–17.

Sivard, Leger Ruth. 1982. *World Military and Social Expenditures*. Leesburg: World Priorities.

Skinner, G. 1966. "The Nature of Loyalties in Rural Indonesia." In Wallersten, *Social Change: The Colonial Situation*. New York: Wiley and Sons.

Sklar, Richard. 1967. "Political Science and National Integration—A Radical Approach." *Journal of Modern African Studies*, 5(1).

Skywritings. 1985. "Jamaica's Data Entry Taking Off." November: 40.

Slameka, V. 1985. "Information Technology and the Third World." *Journal of the American Society for Information Science*, 36(3):178–183.

Smith, J. 1970. "The Relation of the British Political Officer to His Chief in Northern Nigeria." In M. Crowder and O. Ikine (eds.), *West African Chiefs*. New York: African Publishing Corporation.

Sobrino, J., S. J. 1978. *Christology at the Crossroads*. Maryknoll: Orbis Books.

South Special Report. 1986. "Information Technology." December: 51–53.

Sowande, Chief Fela. 1972. *The Africanization of Black Studies*. Kent: KSU Department of Pan-African Studies, African-American Affairs Monograph Series.

Speece, M. 1982. *Environmental Profile of the Democratic Republic of Sudan*. Tucson: Office of Arid Lands Studies, University of Arizona; for U.S. Man and the Biosphere, Dept of State. (AID RSSA SA/TAO 77–81).

_____. 1985. *Agricultural Marketing Structures and Marketing Constraints in Kordofan, Sudan: Recommendations for WSARP Research and Implementation*. (WSARP Publication No. 49). Pullman: Washington State University.

Speece, M., and T. E. Gillard-Byers. 1986. "Government Market Intervention in Kordofan, Sudan." *Northeast African Studies*, 8(2–3):111–119.

Speece, M., T. E. Gillard-Byers, and B. A. Azrag. 1987. "Public Policy Implications of Agricultural Market Performance Under Drought Conditions." Second International Conference on Desert Development, Cairo.

Sprout, Harold, and Margaret Sprout. 1971. *Toward a Politics of Planet Earth*. New York: Van Nostrand Reinhold Co.

Stewart, T. F. 1979. "International Technology Transfer: Issues and Policy Options." *World Bank Staff Working Paper*.

Stifel, L. D., J. S. Coleman, and J. E. Black. 1977. *Education and Training for Public Sector Management in Developing Countries*. New York: Rockefeller Foundation.

Stillman, D. 1971. "A Framework for the Analysis of Population Policy." Lecture, International Union for the Scientific Study of Population.

Stryker, R. E. 1970. "Center-Locality: Linkage and Political Change in the Ivory Coast." Ph. D. Dissertation, UCLA.

_____. 1971. "A Local Perspective on Development in the Ivory Coast." In M. F. Lotchie (ed.), *The State of Nations: Constraints on Development in Independent Africa*. Los Angeles: UCLA Press.

Sturm, D. 1982. "Praxis and Promise: On the Ethics of Political Theology." *Ethics*, 92(4):733–750.

Sudan Government. 1962. *The Ten Year Plan of Economic and Social Development, 1961/62–1970/71*. Khartoum: Government Printing Press.

Sudan Government. 1977. *Economic Survey*. Khartoum: Ministry of National Economy.

Sudan, Ministry of Planning. 1970. *The Five Year Plan of Economic and Social Development of the Democratic Republic of the Sudan for the Period 1970/71–1974/75*. Vol. 1: *Major Trends of Development*. Khartoum: Ministry of Planning.

Sunkel, Osvaldo. 1981. "Development Styles and the Environment: An Interpretation of the Latin American Case." In Heraldo Munoz (ed.), *From Dependency to Development: Strategies to Overcome Underdevelopment and Inequality*. Boulder: Westview Press.

Suret-Canale, J. 1971. *French Colonialism in Tropical Africa, 1900–1945*.

Swaminathan, M. S. 1982. *Science and Integrated Rural Development*. New Delhi: Concept Publishing.

Tandon, Yas. 1986. "Policy Issues and Management in the African Food Crisis: An Overview." *Zimbabwe Journal of Economics*, 1(3).

Taylor, A. J. P. 1954. *The Struggle for Mastery in Europe : 1848–1914*. Oxford: Clarendon Press.

Thurber, C. E., and L. S. Graham. 1973. *Development Administration in Latin America*. Durham: Duke University Press.

Tisdale, H. 1970. "The Process of Urbanization." In Consuis and Nagpaul (eds.), *Urban Man and Society*. New York: Knopf.

Todaro, M. 1985. "Ethics, Values, and Economic Development." In K. W.

Thompson (ed.), *Ethics and International Relations: Ethics in Foreign Policy,* Vol. 2. New Brunswick: Transaction Books.

Tongue, Steve. 1987. "The Adoption of a Fuel Efficient Stove by the Luo of Kenya: A Study of Motivation." In *Development and the High Tech Syndrome: Technology, Society and Communications.* Chicago: Third World Conference Foundation.

Torres, C. 1979. *Christianismo y revolucion.* Mexico: Ediciones Maldonado, Olivieri, Zabala.

Trail, Thomas F. 1985. *Recommendations for Strengthening Research—Extension Farmer Linkages in Kordofan and Darfur Regions* (WSARP Publication No. 150). Pullman: Washington State University.

Tuinder, B. A. Den., 1978. *Ivory Coast: The Challenge of Success.* Baltimore: Johns Hopkins University Press.

Turco, R. P., T. P. Ackerman, and J. B. Pollack. 1984. "Nuclear: Global Consequences of Multiple Nuclear Explosions." *Science,* 222(4630):1283–1293.

United Nations. December 1948. "Universal Declaration of Human Rights." In *Human Rights: A Compilation of International Instruments of the United Nations.* New York: United Nations.

―――――. 1973. *The Determinants and Consequences of Population Trends.* New York: United Nations.

―――――. 1974. *Action Taken at Bucharest.* World Population Conference. New York: United Nations.

―――――. 1975. *International Women's Year Plan of Action.* New York: United Nations.

―――――. 1980. *Directory of United Nations Information Systems.* Geneva: Interorganizational Board for Information Systems.

―――――. 1982. *Statistical Yearbook.* New York: United Nations.

―――――. 1983. *Demographic Yearbook.* New York: United Nations.

―――――. 1983. *FAO Production Yearbook,* vol. 37. Rome: Food and Agricultural Organization.

―――――. 1984. *Mexico City Declaration on Population and Development.* New York: United Nations.

United Nations Department of Economic and Social Affairs. 1982. *Demographic Indicators Countries: Estimates and Projections.* New York: United Nations.

United Nations/ECA. 1980. *Prospects for a Program of Action for Development of Food and Agriculture in Africa, 1980–85.* Rome: United Nations.

United Nations Fund for Population Activities. 1984. *Population.* April 10 (4).

―――――. 1986. *Population.* August 12 (8).

United Nations Industrial Development Organization (UNIDO). 1979. *Appropriate Industrial Technology for Food Storage and Processing.* New York: United Nations.

―――――. 1985. *Industrial Development Review Series: The Democratic Republic of Sudan.* UNIDO/IS. 541.

United Nations Social and Economic Commission. 1985. *Development Forum.* January 13 (1).

United Nations Social and Economic Commission for Asia and Pacific. 1987. *Population Headliners.* September.

U.S. Agency for International Development (USAID). 1985. *Kordofan Rainfed Agriculture* (Project No. 650–0054). Washington, D.C.: USAID.

USDA. 1970. *Improving Marketing Systems in Developing Countries.* Washington, D.C.: USDA.

―――――. 1984. "Estimate of Africans Fed with Imported Grain in 1984." Foreign

Agriculture Service, Foreign Agriculture Circular F.G. 8-84, Washington, D.C., May.

Vaidyanathan, A. 1985. "Bhopal: Accountability Is Bad for Business." *Science for the People*, 29:9–11.

Vanderslice, Lane. 1982. "Military Aid, the World's Poor, and U.S. Security." *Bread for the World Background Paper* #60(2). Washington, D.C.

Varma, V. S. 1986. "Bhopal: The Unfolding of a Tragedy." *Alternatives*, 11(1):133–145.

Verhey, A. 1978. "The Use of Scripture of Ethics." *Religious Studies Review*, 4(1): 28–39.

Vermeer, Donald. 1983. "Food Sufficiency and Farming in the Future of West Africa: Resurgence of Traditional Agriculture?" *Journal of African Studies*, 10(3).

Visvanathan, S. 1986. "Bhopal: The Imagination of a Disaster." *Alternatives*, 11(1): 147–165.

Vogel, G. N. 1978. "Feeding the World: A Challenge for All Mankind." In *Cereals 79: Better Nutrition for the World's Millions*. St. Paul: American Association of Cereal Chemists.

Vu, My T. 1985. *World Population Projections 1985*. Baltimore: Johns Hopkins University Press.

Wagley, C. 1975. *Minorities in the Second World*. New York: Columbia University Press.

Wa Mutharika, Bingu. 1987. "Special Assistance Needs for Africa, with Special Reference to Sub-Saharan Africa in Development: Seeds of Change." *Journal of the Society for International Development*, 2(3).

Weber, M. 1958. *The Protestant Ethic and the Spirit of Capitalism*. New York: Columbia University Press.

Weidner, E. W. 1964. *Technical Assistance in Public Administration Overseas: The Case for Development Administration*. Chicago: Public Administration Service.

Weil, Thomas E. 1982. *Area Handbook for Brazil*. Washington, D.C.: U.S. Dept. of State, 53.

Weisel, W. K. 1981. "Comparative Costs of Automation in Die Casting Using Robots." In *Industrial Robots*. Michigan: Robotics International of SME.

West Africa. 1988. "Technology Transfer." January 25.

Wilcox, W. F. 1940. *Studies in American Demography*. Ithaca: Cornell University Press.

Wilensky, H. L. 1975. *The Welfare State and Equality: Structural and Ideological Roots of Public Expenditures*. Berkeley: University of California Press.

Williams, F. 1980. *Urban Dynamics in Black Africa*. New York.

Wirth, L. 1933. "Urbanism as a Way of Life." *American Journal of Sociology*, 44:3–24.

Wolf, Edward C. 1987. "Growing a Forest from Scratch." *The Futurist*, July-August: 14.

Wolterstorff, N. 1983. *Until Justice and Peace Embrace*. Grand Rapids: Wm. B. Eerdmans.

Wood, David, and Don Irwin. 1983. "Senate OKs $253 Billion in '84 Defense Spending." *Los Angeles Times*, 9 November: 1, 16.

World Bank. 1978. *World Development Report, 1978*. Washington, D.C.: World Bank.

_____. 1980. *World Development Report, 1980*. Washington, D.C.: World Bank.

_____. 1980. *World Tables, Second Edition*. Baltimore: Johns Hopkins University Press.

_____. 1981. *Accelerated Development in Sub-Saharan Africa: An Agenda for Action.* Washington, D.C.: World Bank.

_____. 1981. *World Development Report.* Washington, D.C.: World Bank.

_____. 1982. *Sudan: Investing for Economic Stabilization and Structural Change* (Report No. 3551a-Su). Washington, D.C.: World Bank.

_____. 1984. *Sub-Saharan Africa: Progress Report on Development Prospects and Programs.* Washington, D.C.: World Bank.

_____. 1985. *Sudan: Pricing Policies and Structural Balances.* Washington, D.C.: World Bank.

_____. 1986a. *Financing Adjustment with Growth in Sub-Saharan Africa 1986–1990.* Washington, D.C.: World Bank.

_____. 1986b. *Population Growth and Policies in Sub-Saharan Africa.* Washington, D.C.: World Bank.

_____. 1986c. *Recovery in the Developing World: The London Symposium on the World Bank's Role.* Washington, D.C.: World Bank.

World Development Forum. 1985a. 3(19):2.

_____. 1985b. 3(2):2.

_____. 1985c. 3(2):3.

World Development Report. 1984. *International Bank for Reconstruction and Development.* Washington, D.C.: World Bank.

Worldwatch Institute. 1987. *State of the World.* New York: W. W. Norton and Company.

Wos, A. 1983. "Interaction Between Pre-Harvest and Post-Harvest Systems and Their Implications for Socio-Economic Development." *Food and Nutrition Bulletin,* 7(2):8.

Zahlan, A. B., and W. Y. Magar. 1986. *The Agricultural Sector of Sudan: Policy & Systems Studies.* London: Ithaca Press.

Zolberg, A. 1964. *One Party Government in the Ivory Coast.* Princeton: Princeton University Press.

Index

ABOUT THE CONTRIBUTORS

Dr. William M. Alexander is a Professor in the Political Science Department at California Polytechnic State University.

Bakheit Adam Azrag is a former Research Assistant in the Department of Business Administration, School of Business and Economics, at Central Washington University.

Dr. Wayne G. Bragg is an Affiliate Professor of Technology and International Development in the School of Engineering and Applied Science at Washington University in St. Louis.

L. T. Fansler (M.A.) is a Research Assistant in the Department of Food Science and Nutrition at California State University, Long Beach.

Mamdouh Fayek is an Associate Professor of Interior Design in the Department of Home Economics at California State University, Long Beach.

Dr. Valentine U. James is an Assistant Professor in the Department of Urban and Environmental Planning at the University of Virginia.

Dr. Hassan Omari Kaya is a Research Fellow in the Institute of Development Studies at the University of Dar es Salaam.

M. T. Knipe (M.A.) is a Research Assistant in the Department of Food Science and Nutrition at California State University, Long Beach.

Dr. Donald E. Mbosowo is an Assistant Professor in the Department of Sociology at the University of Jos, Nigeria.

Dr. Thomas M. Meenaghan is a Professor in the School of Social Work at Loyola University of Chicago.

Dr. Shah M. Mehrabi is an Associate Professor in the Department of Economics at Mary Washington College.

Dr. Stanley W. Moore is a Professor in the Department of Political Science at Pepperdine University.

Dr. Jonathan N. Nwomonoh is an Assistant Professor in the Pan African Studies Department at California State University, Los Angeles.

Mwatabu S. Okantah is a Director in the Afro-American Cultural Center at Cleveland State University.

Dr. Janet J. Palmer is an Associate Professor of Education in the Department of Secondary, Adult and Business Education at Lehman College, City University of New York.

Dr. Godfrey Roberts is an Assistant Dean for Instruction and College Liaison in the Faculty of Arts and Sciences at Rutgers, State University of New Jersey.

Dr. Frank A. Salamone is an Associate Professor and Chair of the Department of Anthropology at Elizabeth Seton College.

Dr. Eugene B. Shultz, Jr., is a Professor in the Department of Engineering and Policy, School of Engineering and Applied Science at Washington University in St. Louis.

Jean L. Shultz (M.A.) is in International Affairs at Washington University in St. Louis.

Dr. Bamijoko Smith is an Assistant Professor of Economics in the Department of Political Science at Howard University.

Dr. Mark Speece is an Assistant Professor of Marketing in the School of Business at the University of Alaska, Anchorage.

Dr. Ramses B. Toma, MPH, R.D., is a Professor of Food Science and Nutrition in the Department of Food Science and Nutrition at California State University, Long Beach.

Dr. Lako Tongun is an Assistant Professor of Political Science in the Department of Political Science at Pitzer College, Claremont, California.

Dr. Dwayne Woods is in the Department of Political Science at the University of California, Santa Barbara.

Dr. Joel Zimbelman is an Assistant Professor in the Department of Religious Studies at California State University, Chico.